Modern Roots

Studies of national identity

ALAIN DIECKHOFF
Centre d'Etudes et de Recherches Internationales, Paris
Centre National de la Recherche Scientifique

NATIVIDAD GUTIÉRREZ
Instituto de Investigaciones Sociales
Universidad Nacional Autónoma de México

Ashgate

Aldershot • Burlington USA • Singapore • Sydney

Published by
Ashgate Publishing Limited
Gower House
Croft Road
Aldershot
Hampshire GU11 3HR
England

Ashgate Publishing Company
131 Main Street
Burlington, VT 05401-5600 USA

Ashgate website: http://www.ashgate.com

British Library Cataloguing in Publication Data
Modern roots : studies of national identity. -
    (Contemporary trends in European social sciences)
    1. Nationalism
    I. Dieckhoff, Alain II. Gutiérrez, Natividad
    III. Interdisciplinary Centre for Comparative Research in
    the Social Sciences
    320.5'4

Library of Congress Control Number: 00-109869

ISBN 0 7546 1152 3

Printed in Great Britain by
Antony Rowe Ltd, Chippenham, Wiltshire

Contents

List of Contributors

Catherine Bertho-Lavenir
Catherine Bertho-Lavenir holds a doctorate in History, Professor in Modern and Contemporary History at the Clermont-Ferrand University and she specializes in History of Engineering and Media. She is the author of *Histoire des Médias, de Diderot à Internet* (Armand Colin, 1996), (with Frédéric Barbier), 'Le Voyage, une Expérience d'Écriture. La Revue du Touring-Club de France' in Daniel Fabre (coord.) *Par Ecrit-Ethnologie des Écritures Quotidiennes* (Editions de la Maison des Sciences de l'Homme, 1997) and *La Roue et le Stylo* (Odile Jacob, 1999).

Philippe Claret
Philippe Claret holds a PhD in Political Sciences and he is *Maître de Conférences* at the Montesquieu Bordeaux IV University where he teaches Public Law and History of Political Ideas. His principal areas of teaching and research are constitutional systems, western politics, the French political culture and psychological analysis of national cultures. Claret recently published *La Personnalité Collective des Nations. Théories Anglo-Saxonnes et Conceptions Françaises du Caractère National,* (Bruylant, Brussels, 1998).

Yolaine Cultiaux
Yolaine Cultiaux is Doctor in Political Sciences and lecturer at the Institute of Political Studies (Aix-en Provence). Cultiaux is the author of a thesis entitled *Le Nationalisme comme Différentialisme Integrateur: le Catalanisme face à l'Etat Espagnol et à la Construction Européenne* (IEP d'Aix, January 1999). She recently published *La Diversité Culturelle Vue de Catalogne* (Hermès, Spring 1999).

Corinne Delmas
Corinne Delmas is a Doctor of Political Science, whose works include a thesis on *Les Rapports du Savoir et du* Pouvoir: *l'Académie des Sciences Morales et Politiques de 1832 à 1914* (Université Paris IX, January 2000, 2 vols.), and articles on 'L'Affaire Proudhon. Lectures Croisées de *Qu'est-*

ce-que la Propriété?', in *Politix*, no. 29, 1995, 'La Place de l'Enseignement Historique dans la Formation des Élites Politiques Françaises à la Fin du XIXe Siècle', in *Politix*, no. 35, 1996, 'D'une Autonomisation à l'Académie des Sciences Morales et Politiques', in Eric Fauquet (dir.), *Victor Cousin Homo-Theologico-Politicus* (Kimé, 1997).

Alain Dieckhoff

Alain Dieckhoff is senior researcher at the *Centre Nationale de la Recherche Scientifique* and works at the *Centre d'Etudes et de Recherche Internationales* in Paris. He also teaches at the *Institut d'Etudes Politiques* (Paris). His main field of research is politics and society in Israel. He has also undertaken a global research on 'politics and contemporary nationalism', which will soon be published in French. He is the author of several books *Les Espaces d'Israël. Essai sur la Stratégie Territoriales d'Israël* (Presses de Sciences-Po, 1989), *L'Invention d'une Nation. Israël et la Modernité Politique* (Gallimard, 1993 - to be published in English by Hurst in 2000) and *Israéliens et Palestiniens. L'Épreuve de la Paix* (1996).

Julian Dierkes

Julian Dierkes is a doctoral candidate in Sociology at Princeton University. His dissertation, 'Teaching National Identity - Portrayals of the Nation in History Education in Post-war Germany and Japan', analyses post-war textbooks and curricula for middle-school history instruction in the Germanys and Japan as to their portrayals of the German and Japanese nation, respectively. His other research interests include economic sociology and organizational behaviour.

Catherine Durandin

Catherine Durandin was a former student of the *École Normale Supérieure* and she received her PhD from the Sorbonne. She is presently Professor at the *Institut National des Langues et Civilisations Orientales* in Paris where she chairs the Romanian section. She is also an analyst for Balkan Affairs at the French Ministry of Defence and the editor of a monographic series dealing with contemporary Europe. She has published nine books, among them *Histoire de la Nation Roumaine* (Brussels, Complexe, 1994) and *Histoire des Roumains* (Paris, Fayard, 1995).

Gérard Groc

Gérard Groc is a specialist of Turkey, Doctor in International Relations and former fellow at the French Institute in Istanbul (1983-1986). At present Groc is an associated researcher at the *Institut de Recherches et d'Études sur le Monde Arabe et Musulman* (Aix-en Provence) and lecturer at the Institute of Political Sciences also in Aix. In numerous articles Groc has studied diverse aspects of modern Turkey, such as press and communication, the religious revival of the 80s, the democratization and the emergence of civil society.

Montserrat Guibernau

Montserrat Guibernau, MPhil, PhD, University of Cambridge. She is the author of *Nations without States* (Polity Press, 1999) and *Nationalism* (1996). Together with John Rex, she has edited *The Ethnicity Reader: Nationalism, Multiculturalism and Migration* (Polity Press, 1997). She has taught at the universities of Barcelona, Warwick and Cambridge. At present she is lecturer in Government and Politics at the Open University, London.

Natividad Gutiérrez

Natividad Gutiérrez holds a Master and a PhD from London School of Economics, University of London. She is a full-time senior researcher and lecturer at the *Instituto de Investigaciones Sociales, Universidad Nacional Autónoma de México*. Gutierrez's most recent book is *Nationalist Myths and Ethnic Identities: Indigenous Intellectuals and the Mexican State* (University of Nebraska Press, 1999).

Christophe Jaffrelot

Christophe Jaffrelot is a research fellow at the *Centre Nationale de la Recherche Scientifique* and teaches South Asian Politics at the *Institut d'Etudes Politiques* of Paris and at the University of Paris 1, Sorbonne. He has recently published *The Hindu Nationalist Movement and Indian Politics, 1925 to 1990s* (New York, Columbia University Press; London, Hurst and Co; New Delhi, Penguin India, 1996). He has also edited *L'Inde Contemporaine - De 1950 à Nos Jours* (Fayard, 1996).

Anthony D. Smith
Anthony D. Smith is Professor of Nationalism and Ethnicity at the European Institute, London School of Economics. His main interests are in ethnic identity and nationalism. Recent publications in this field are *Nationalism and Modernity* (Routledge, 1998), *Myths and Memories of the Nation* (Oxford, 1999) and *The Nation in History* (New England University Press, 2000).

Anne-Marie Thiesse
Anne-Marie Thiesse holds a PhD in Arts and she is director of research at the *Centre Nationale de la Recherche Scientifique* and specialist in Cultural History. She is the author of *Ecrire la France, le Mouvement Régionaliste de la Belle Epoque à la Libération* (PUF, 1991), *Ils Apprenaient la France, l'Exaltation des Régions dans le Discours Patriotiqu*e (Editions de la Maison des Sciences de l'Homme, 1997) and *La Création des Identités Nationales, Europe, XVIIIº-XXº Siècle* (Editions du Seuil, 1999).

Sallie Westwood
Sallie Westwood is Professor of Sociology at the University of Leicester and has conducted research in Ghana, India, UK and more recently in Ecuador and Colombia on ethnicities, racisms and nationalisms. Her work has been widely published in book chapters and journals and she is the author of a number of books including *Viva: Women and Protest in Latin America* (1993) with Sarah Radcliffe, *Racism, Modernity and Identity* (1994) with Ali Rattansi, *Remaking the Nation: Place, Identity and Politics in Latin America* (1996) with Sarah Radcliffe, and *Imaging Cities: Scripts, Signs and Memories* (1997). Most recent books are *Power and the Social* (2000) and with A. Phizacklea, *Trans-Nationalism and the Politics of Belonging* (2000).

Oliver Zimmer
Oliver Zimmer, lecturer in Modern European History at the University of Durham, has published articles on Swiss nationalism in such journals as *Comparative Studies in Society and History* (1998), *Nations and Nationalism* (jointly with Eric Kaufmann) (1998) and *Past and Present* (2000). He is currently preparing a book manuscript for publication.

Preface

In the last fifteen years 'identity' has become a concept of growing significance in the media, the political world and academia. Popularity, however, does not make for clarity. Not only is the term understood in a variety of sometimes incompatible ways: the very connotations of the word seem at variance with what it purports to describe. 'Identity' implies 'sameness', i.e. that the subject, whether individual or collective, has a timeless permanence; yet even a cursory historical view shows that identity is contextual: it changes with the passage of time. Nevertheless, the evolutionary nature of identity does not mean that it is always changing. Take, as an indication both of continuity and of change, our own position as editors of this book. Our homelands - France and Mexico - have different histories and geographies. Obviously we may feel attached to what we are and represent, the languages we speak, the values we subscribe to, yet we can not claim that we have remained isolated from change, nor that our perceptions of what it means to be French or Mexican are shared by others -still less by all. We are not essentially French or Mexican, nor should we accept definitive conceptions of 'Frenchness' or 'Mexicanness'. But what we are, and the way we think and speak, has a degree of stability and commonality without which ordinary human existence would be unimaginable. Our capacities for both continuity and change are ultimately inseparable. And this dialectic of change and continuity is as true of national as of personal identity.

We approach the nation here as a mode of social organization and a category of political analysis that is fundamentally modern. Its emergence is an aspect of the development of the state as a new form of political order based on a hitherto unknown principle: the sovereignty of the people. In its revolutionary manifestations, this principle could present itself, at least in theory, as establishing an entirely new polity. However, a degree of continuity and historical legitimacy is invariably expressed in practice, and is arguably a theoretical requirement. In order to function as a political sovereign, any people needs to regard itself as a nation with roots through which it demonstrates, and thereby constructs, its peculiar history. Such historical roots offer, at best, a collective, affective, emotional framework for people's modern sense of continuity and change. The nations studied in this volume offer examples of 'modern roots', which while undoubtedly the product of deliberate strategies of invention and fabrication, in particular on the part of the state, are nonetheless neither fictitious nor unrelated to historical reality. 'The invention of tradition' builds on three major innovations designed to influence the masses by frequent repetition: a standardized school system, public ceremonies and mass production of public monuments. While fabrication may resort to 'artificiality' we show, through the different cases in this volume, how intellectual creativity influenced teachers, nationalists and intellectuals in building a convincing continuum between past and present, between nature and geographical boundaries, between history and teaching, to mention just some of the modes through which identity may be expressed.

Our conception of invention reflects the excitement of discovery in the passionate search for a common ground of shared identification through the countless possibilities implicit in nature, peoples, heroism, art, language, and religion. In certain cases, genuinely new discoveries - ceremonies, parades, cultural institutions - expressed creative energies applied to the organization of collective life. More often, perhaps, exploration meant digging up, literally or metaphorically, previous social artefacts, architectures, tales, or stories, which had been taken for granted, neglected, or forgotten. The identity of nations, in other words, is often rooted in the revival and recombination of proto-national elements such as ethnic ties, language or religion. Revival and recombination demand scholarly study and sensibility, and thus become the working field of antiquarians, experts, intellectuals and artists. The purpose, however, is rarely purely academic: nationalist leaders and state-makers have a pragmatic interest in such enterprises because they offer the people a language of historical and social coherence. For this reason, intellectual coherence is not always a major consideration. Nationalist leaders draw a line between the people they want to mobilize and their (imagined) 'forebears', ensuring detachment while highlighting ancestral prestige (Hellenes and Greeks, Hebrews and Jews, Daces and Romanians, Aztecs and Mexicans). In some cases, nationalists will even make use of epics and narratives forged by talented men of letters to portray the national self. An example is the 'Fragments of Ancient Poetry Collected in the Highlands of Scotland' ascribed to a third century bard named Ossian but in fact written by the eighteenth century poet James Macpherson. In other cases, national symbols use icons of indisputable originality which are capable of inducing shared cultural identification despite the diversity of peoples and of topography. A case in point is the Mexican national emblem which depicts typical flora (*Cactaceae*) and fauna (eagle and serpent). The historicity of the emblem parallels the age of *Mesoamerica* (since 800-400 B.C.) and still holds currency since it was first used by nationalists to epitomize the sovereignty of Mexico from 1821 onwards. No matter how much fiction or imagination is at stake, national identities can make sense only if traditions, myths, history and symbols grow out of the existing living memories and beliefs of the people who are to compose the nation. In this sense, Zionism invented the identity of the modern Jewish nation when it placed the people centre stage and established a historical continuity between contemporary Jewry and biblical times, but it could do so only by taking account of the real past, however selectively. Not surprisingly, the creation of a Jewish state in Uganda or Argentina, as was occasionally suggested, never had much appeal.

National identities are thus only marginally based on pure forgeries and falsehoods. It is more rewarding to stress their openness to discovery, recombination and adaptation of peoples' endless capacity to create and reproduce culture and history. In order to illustrate this view of traditions as both 'invented' and 'real', this volume covers a wide range of experiences of, or experiments in, the making of national identity. Starting with Europe -the prototypical case of identity formation in the context of the state -, we consider Switzerland, France, Catalonia and a comparative study of the two Germanys and Japan. Turkey, India, Romania and Ecuador will further illustrate how the search for identity can involve engaging combinations of imagination and rationality. The essays, however, do not presuppose a principle of geographical or continental specificity. What is distinctive for Switzerland may have no appeal for Germany despite the fact that the two countries are neighbours within Europe. The study of national identities is not the application of uniform abstract rules to diverse cases. For this reason, the volume is organized around certain themes emphasising the route taken by each nation and showing, accordingly, how national identity is forged, disseminated, represented and, until recently, contested.

The book is divided into six sections. The first section begins with a chapter by Natividad Gutiérrez, which seeks to update the major theoretical trends in the study of national identity. The author argues for the distinctiveness of national identity by focusing on two universal principles of the organization of the nation-state: the construction of homogeneity and common culture. In doing so, she brings into discussion the widespread use of markers of identity and citizenship, the archetypes and stereotypes through which we are able to identify two roles of national identity: the construction of self-images and the ability to express and recognize differences held by others.

The second section, entitled 'Dimensions of National Identity', includes three contributions that discuss the peculiarity of national identity as distinct from other types of collective identity. The second chapter, by Anthony D. Smith, shows how identity can be the subject of multiple interpretations. By establishing distinctions among the current trends of post-modernity, ethno-symbology, and modernism, he draws a typology of national identities, resulting in three main types: the plural, the ethnic and the civic. Such a typology is useful in identifying the different routes that nation-formation may take. However, Smith demonstrates that the durability of ethnic ties shapes the types of nations that compose the modern world.

Philippe Claret, in the third chapter, looks in depth at the analysis of 'national personalities' which, having enjoyed wide and long-lasting popularity, is now decisively out of fashion. Claret reviews the major sociological schools within the national personality perspective, the common feature of which is to assert that each nation is culturally and/or psychologically distinct. Such a view conflicts with the currently dominant modernist and post-modernist perspectives, which ascribe to nationhood a fundamentally artificial quality, derived either from deliberate nationalist strategies (modernism) or from artefactual webs of discourse (post-modernism).

National identity is central to our understanding of modern societies. Montserrat Guibernau, in the fourth chapter, discusses the dual importance of identity – symbolic and political – in creating culture and citizenship. The terms 'nation' and 'nation-state' tend to be used interchangeably. However, while both depend on shared culture, Guibernau argues that the distinctive feature of the nation-state project is to aim at the creation of common culture at the expense of pluriculturalism. As a consequence, she argues that Gellner's modern theory of nationalism overlooks the impact and assertiveness of stateless nations or immigrants by making the homogenization of culture constitutive of modernity.

The third section, 'Symbolizing the Nation', deals with the various ways of using and selecting symbols to represent the identity of the nation. There is a close link between national identity and the symbols that enable it to be taken for granted on the basis of routine, continual representation. The content and meaning of the symbols, however, make sense only for those who have forged them or to the people socially organized around them. The symbols of nationhood, which are the bearers of such notions as originality, authenticity and continuity, therefore usually have an institutional, or at least standardized, character. Breathtaking natural scenarios are potent and useful symbols of commonality in a context of ethnic and linguistic diversity. Oliver Zimmer demonstrates how the Alpine landscape has represented, since the late eighteenth century, the organic principle of Swiss national identity. The transformation of landscape as an 'assumed given' into a widespread symbol of identity leads Zimmer to distinguish between two suggestive concepts, the 'nationalization of nature' and the 'naturalization of nationhood'.

Catherine Bertho-Lavenir and Anne-Marie Thiesse, in their joint contribution, stress the paradox of folk culture taken as a symbol of national identity. European intellectuals, imbued with the spirit of romanticism, were convinced that true authenticity lay in the people. They thus sought to collect popular values and traditions. However, because there was in fact no such a thing as a pure and unspoilt popular culture, it had to be created in a systematic way – thereby ceasing to be 'authentic' and 'popular'. To follow this argument, the authors distinguish three stages: (1) the identification, collation and standardization of popular culture; (2) its dissemination through new means of communication (lithography, photography and recordings) and new sites (ethnographic museums, international exhibitions and so on); and (3) its transmission to the people as part of the process of nationalization.

In the consolidation of national identity, historiography has played a crucial role, connecting generations and rooting the nation in an immemorial past. Yolaine Cultiaux studies, in chapter seven, two phases in Catalan historiography: first, the development of Catalan historiography during the nineteenth century at a time when Catalan nationalism was on the rise and the writing of history was highly politicized; and later, after the re-establishment of democracy in Spain in 1977, the promotion of nation-building by the reinstated *Generalitat*. In the contemporary context, the author concentrates particularly on two instruments that serve to mould a sense of continuity: the commemorative celebrations of patriotic historians and the establishment of the Museum of the History of Catalonia.

National identity is not something spontaneously felt, it has to be taught. The fourth section of the book 'Teaching National Identity' focuses on the many ways in which national identity can be transmitted. It opens with Corinne Delmas's discussion of the recreation of the French nation in the last quarter of the nineteenth century. The national regeneration of France, after the defeat of the Second Empire, was thought to require reform of its higher education system in order to train political elites and civil servants capable of serving the Republic efficiently. The establishment of the *École Libre des Sciences Politiques* as a training ground for a new elite was the French answer to counteract Germany. The École was, therefore, premised on a firm belief in the psychological unity of peoples and in national institutions as an expression of national character (see also Claret's contribution in this volume), subscribing to a 'civic' and political nationhood, contrasting the German 'ethnic' conception.

National identity has also been challenged faced by the task of reconstruction after war and defeat, and teachers have not remained indifferent to this crisis. Chapter nine, by Julian Dierkes, is a comparative analysis of identity reconstruction in Japan and the two Germanys after the Second World War. Dierkes strategically compares teacher's trade unions to explain how those nations reworked their identities in a political ambience seeking internal unification and external recognition. This methodology allows him to identify three patterns. The Japanese teacher's union was forward-looking, politically oriented and internationalist. The West German Union looked to the achievements of the past and to culture, while East Germany articulated an identity akin to the emerging Communist block combining internationalism and localism, political progressivism and rootedness in traditional culture.

Christophe Jaffrelot, in the final chapter of the fourth section, focuses on the value assigned to Hindu culture, as the essence of Indian identity, by the Hindu nationalists of the BJP (Party of the Indian People). Contrary to Nehru's inclusive spirit of unification on the basis of a form of nationalism addressed to all Indians, the BJP defines Indian national identity in terms of 'Hinduness'. In order to promote this idea, activists have invested heavily in what Jaffrelot calls a 'social welfare strategy', based on the provision of health, social and educational services to the underprivileged. While the services are free, they demand ideological commitment, and thus serve to disseminate the idea of 'Hinduness'. We see here how, even when nationalism presents itself as the manifestation of an immemorial identity, the sense of belonging is in practice actively promoted by nationalist leaders.

Republican France is often presented as the archetype of the civic nation, embodying a national community of standard French culture made uniform by the national school system. While some states have long invested in such a model, political instability, cultural contestation or open rebellion are some of the factors accounting for the difficulties in defining and transmitting an encompassing identity in ethnically divided societies. The fifth section of the book, 'Disrupted National Identities', illustrates three cases of political struggle and contestation as a result of attempts to impose national identity. Sallie Westwood initiates the discussion with a critical assessment of nation-state formation in Latin America. She then looks at Ecuador and unveils multiple areas which have traditionally remained uncontested in the typical Latin American state. Behind the 'grand official' narrative which equates nationhood and citizenship, such factors as indigenousness, race, gender, region and class have achieved some degree of political visibility of their own, and have thus contributed to substantiating the notion of distinct peoples within the state and to questioning the viability of a unique national identity.

The case of Turkey, analysed by Gérard Groc, emphasizes the difficulties in the consolidation of Turkish national identity. Kurds, Muslim fundamentalists and Alevis have persistently questioned the official view that Turkey is a unitary and homogeneous nation-state. The building of a Turkish nation-state out of fragments of the Ottoman Empire was, for Groc, an enterprise of monumental proportions since neither the territory (Anatolia) nor the language were immediate attributes of Turkish nationhood. In addition, the new Turkish nationalism was ambivalent towards Islam, which was seen both negatively, as opposed to modernity, and positively, as a feature distinguishing Turkey from the West. As a result, Turkish nationalism is powerfully state-centred: the state is seen as both the expression and the protector of the nation. This explains why attempts to downplay nationalism are seen as a challenge to the authority of the state, the defence of which by most political elites and the army stands in the way of any real pluralization of civil society.

In the final chapter of this section, Catherine Durandin explores the vicissitudes of Romanian nationalism. Here we see the importance of imitation in the making of nationalism: the torchbearers of Romanian nationalism were Westernized elites imbued with French romanticism. Romania also illustrates the construction of national identity by demarcation from the 'Other', whether external (Russia and Hungary) or internal (the Magyars of Transylvania and the Jews). Hostility towards these 'others' was all the stronger that there was a terrible uncertainty about what it meant to be a Romanian. It is striking that this 'excessive nationalism' spanned the ages, from the young kingdom of Romania in 1878 to the authoritarian monarchy in the 1930s and to the national communist regime of Ceaucescu. Only with the departure of the neo-communist president Ion Iliescu in 1996 has Romania moved towards a more settled national identity and attempted to build bridges, at least with Hungary and the West, rather than antagonising them.

In the conclusion, Alain Dieckhoff returns to the discussion between culture and national identity, the linking thread of all chapters in this volume. His main point is that it is debatable to oppose two radically different conceptions of the nation, the first political and civic, the second cultural and ethnic. While often taken for granted in the literature, this dichotomy obscures the real dynamics of nation-building. The promotion of a national culture was vital not just for nationalist movements in the supposedly 'ethnic' East (Eastern Europe, Asia) but also in the supposedly 'civic' West (France, Great Britain, United States). Of course, culture was not used the same way in the various historical contexts but 'civic culture' is, precisely, cultural. National identities are always a combination of associative and communal relationships, and thus of politics and culture.

What we have offered in this volume is a view of national identity as a cultural system of information which bestows historical meaning and social cohesion on modern political communities. Although the different contributions reveal how diverse and vast the themes, practices and symbols used to encourage national identification may be, the essays also stress that the making of national identity corresponds to globally shared expectations: the longing for authenticity, the search for historical continuity and rootedness in a common territory. National identities are diverse and respond to change, but the ways in which nation-building seeks to inculcate in the masses a sense of belonging are strikingly similar all over the world.

Alain Dieckhoff   Natividad Gutiérrez
CERI, CNRS, Paris   *IIS, UNAM, Mexico City*

Acknowledgements

The present volume is partly the outcome of an ICCR (Interdisciplinary Centre for Comparative Research in the Social Sciences, Vienna) euro-conference on 'Nationalism and National Identity', held at the *Fondation Nationale des Sciences Politiques* in Paris in collaboration with the *Centre d'Etudes et de Recherches Internationales* (CERI), 3-6 July, 1996. About half the essays here included were presented during that conference, the others were expressly commissioned for their inclusion in the book.

We are grateful to John Crowley of CERI and Liana Giorgi of the ICCR in Vienna for their help in bringing this publication about. A special word of thanks to Nadia Auriat and UNESCO, for providing the English translation of those papers originally written in French. We are also very grateful to the European Commission and the British Council for their financial support to the conference. Finally, we acknowledge Siri Elisabeth Espeland (PAPIIT-UNAM) for the major task of putting together all contributions with remarkable efficiency and skill.

PART I
INTRODUCTION

1 The Study of National Identity

NATIVIDAD GUTIÉRREZ

The decade of the 1990s witnessed a renewed academic interest in identities. National identity is included in this revival and its study encompasses two broad perspectives. In the discussion *per se* the nation-state holds centre stage.

A first approach refers to the emergence in the political scenarios of social actors and movements previously marginalized and excluded from integrationist politics of nation building. The popularization of the so-called 'right to difference' is one of the key factors supporting the construction, negotiation and reinterpretation of identities presumably repressed or excluded. As mobilizations and demands seek an increase in political participation, it is becoming an accepted fact that no political claim for recognition within the nation-state can be substantiated and successful if it lacks a historical memory accounting for specificity of some sort (gender, racial and ethnic identities, and so on). Identities in this perspective allow disparity and fragmentation and a new wave of recognition.

A second approach visualizes identity as the arena for the unity and solidarity of peoples and for the realization of common goals. National identities reinforce social cohesion but can also activate political response from other groups who are capable of constructing their own limits of representation. In the study of national identity what fascinates is precisely this: on the one hand, the process in which absolute uniqueness is the goal inasmuch as no identity is ever the same, and, on the other, the recognition of the universal need of mankind for differentiation and the ability to handle increasingly greater degrees of distinctiveness.

Our interest in this chapter is to discuss what separates the study of national identity from other forms of collective identity. We argue that the peculiarity and ritualistic uses evident in national identity are inextricably linked to three imperatives of the nation-state: the standardization of practices, the construction of homogeneity and the delimitation of common culture for all citizens in a given territorial sovereignty.

Theories

Theories of nationalism continue influencing the study of national identity, it being practically impossible to disassociate identity from the typical polarization of views expressed in the methodology of nationalism. Is this type of identity a cultural continuum or an indoctrination sponsored by the modern state? To answer this question we first need to briefly clarify that nationalism, despite its many definitions, has one unmistakable attribute: the 'ideal of independence' (Smith, 1984). Nationalism is also closely linked to the policies of the state aimed at building a unified nation in a pluriethnic society, since most existing nation-states have not emerged as a result of political claims from one single ethnic group.

Modernists and historical culturalists dispute theoretical influence. While the former argue the instrumental role of the state in making the nation (Gellner, 1983), the latter looks at the cultural artefacts, rituals and memories (myths, symbols and legends) (Smith, 1991) which fulfil peoples's ethnocentrism. Identity and ethnocentrism run parallel although ethnocentric views in our approach are not limited to the act of conventional stereotyping or 'narrowmindness' used as parameters of belonging. Identity nurtures itself from strong beliefs, inherited perceptions or repetitive information, helping thus to conform 'the power of self' (Smith, 1991; 1994). For this author, 'the power of self' is of a clear subjective nature but very much required in times of crisis, wars, mobilizations; it gives people willingness and reasons to act and react.

A well known example showing the influential links between identity and ethnocentrism is provided by an ancient inquiry into the origins of a collectivity, that is: where do we come from? Interest in finding out what may be the beginnings of a social group establishing or seeking differentiation has provided a creative host of ideas of origin codified, according to Smith, in mythological accounts. The exaltation of beginning and origin is certainly a powerful and attractive cultural construct for the making of national identity. But this implies the unfolding of various problems, some of them dangerous. In the multicultural world of today, no nation is able to venture an open veneration of single origin when many other ethnic components coexist in the same sovereign territory. This is particularly true after the Second World War and the genocidal atrocities committed in the name of racial purity. The modern democracies of nation-states, their projects and policies for tolerance and multiculturalism, are inclined to neutralize any possible attempts to institutionalize rights and privileges unilaterally. So, would it be of relevance for modern citizens of nation-states to know their origins? Or, as Gellner has put it, *do nations have navels?*, in reference to mankind's impossibility to know what the past was really about. A few days before his sudden death in 1995 Gellner said, at the Warwick Debates, that 'my own view is that some nations possess genuine ancient navels, some have navels invented for them by their own nationalist propaganda and some are altogether navel-less. My belief is also that the middle category is by far the largest, but I stand open to correction by genuine research' (Gellner, 1997, pp. 90-6).

National identity recurs to fabrication and idealization if one follows the category of nations bearing 'invented navels'. The myth of origin of the Mexican nation is a case in point. There are no sociological or demographic arguments to support the claim that the majority of Mexican people are the result of interbreeding, between Spanish and Indian communities, from the early sixteenth century onwards. However, the myth of the *mestizo* people (people of mixed culture and race) has two important functions in the making of the modern Mexican nation. On the one hand, it produces (a) the idea of common origin for antagonistic groups and (b) the *mestizo* population itself - the result of an imposed myth of origin - became the yardstick of national integration for indigenous peoples in terms of adoption of language (Spanish), religion (Christianity) and way of life (urbanization). The result has been, so far, an elastic formula, or common identity, that has contributed significantly to the foundations of a diversified nation: social cohesion, political unity and cultural originality (Gutiérrez, 1998).

There are several routes to studying national identity. The possibilities are not surprising as the identity of any nation seeks to fulfil three aspirations, authenticity, originality and continuity. Hence, we identify two logical stages of national identity regarding the fulfilment of the above aspirations and the relevance of including the state of disciplines and science. On the one hand, we refer to the identification of sources in order to identify uniqueness, *essence* or personality. On the other, we include the inculcation of such *essence* into the population. Uniqueness may be found in the collective personality, thus psychoanalytical approaches have permeated most research on identity (see Claret in this volume) but also geography and art are two other well known sources. The study of collective behaviour was a useful instrument in the organization of the masses into new ways of seeking to respond to the challenges of nation building such as the introduction of a political culture, spread of mass literacy, communications and cultural homogenization. Official agencies were created to involve the masses in national goals, creating at the same time scientific interest in identifying people's character. A neat picture of people's character may reveal intimate, subjective or emotional tracts such as temperament, attitude, acceptance or reluctance to change and continuity. If the collective behaviour appeared to be far from satisfying ideals or plans, corrective measures could be applied. Thus, education became the tool for forging, redeeming or civilizing the masses. Space geography encompasses a wide arena for the search and recreation of national identity because it provides informed accounts of people's sensibility towards landscape, 'geo-political visions' (Dijkink, 1996) and natural environment. Amazement and pride of natural beauty create a suitable framework for elaborating symbols, narratives and tourist attractions of a given land, for instance, the Alps (see Zimmer in this volume). There is nothing one can do to improve or correct nature; thus, it is better appreciated as an intense inspiration for numberless possibilities of national pride or defense against cultural attack. An illustrative case was the pre-independentist claims of Peruvian intellectuals who rejected French eighteenth century environmental determinism, regarding the New World as naturally underdeveloped (De Paw and Leclerc called America, the *girlish continent in puberty*). But Peruvians retorted, arguing that a mild climate is not only a healthy phenomenon but also a priceless and exclusive possession for some, not for all (Gutierrez, 1990). Nature and landscape cannot be separated from the organization of social life. Evidence of this is the fact that they have frequently become an issue of political dispute in defining territorial frontiers and cultural boundaries and drawing the pertinent maps to reflect the changes. G. Dijknik, referred to above, provides the notion of 'geo-political vision' to give an account of peoples' construction of order and threat regarding the balance of power and security policies of states on the basis of geographical position and/or natural resources, transnational economies and minorities within nation-states (pp. 6-7).

Nations cannot survive without cultural history. One of the most deeply rooted collective emotions is a people's defense of self-determination. Creativity, artistic and literary movements, as well as people's sensibility to achieve (and preserve) independence, reflect a capacity to discover, reconstruct, depict or invent a distinctive collective self. A complex interrelation of cultural movements starting with Romanticism, the production of intellectuals and writers and the development of disciplines like archaeology, anthropology and philology, to mention but a few, have contributed to the search for and research of a cultural patrimony which gives an important substance to our understanding of national identity.

There is of course an impressive wealth of cultural patrimony. The challenge of understanding national identity from the perspective of the social sciences and humanities is not only to survey museum collections or debate cultural policies but to look critically at the way in which citizens relate to, defend and feel their patrimony, rituals or commemorations. Thus, no single approach is enough to study national identity and its various interconnections. Instead, and given the richness of sources inspiring identity, a combination of theoretical trends and a creative design of methodologies are concerns of modern research. Moreover, it is forever tempting to identify the construction of identity as a momentum of celebration and dignified remembrance, but identity is also nurtured by the collective experience in tragedy, suffering, humiliation and hostility. National identity cannot be reduced to the cultural expression of an ancient art, a literary piece, a monument or a sports competition, it constitutes a valid type and system of information ritually socialized. Thus, we now turn to a consideration of the specific nature of national identity.

The Peculiarity of National Identity

A useful point of departure is to bear in mind that national identity is, first and foremost, the self-identification of the peoples of nation-states. Therefore, its full expression can only be appreciated within a modern context, although its evolution and construction reveals discernible links with an accumulation of various historical pasts. This premise helps to clarify unmistakable attributes of national identity with respect to other types of collective identity, these being class, gender and race. Consequently, nation-states distinguish themselves from previous forms of polity or grouping due to the following facts and operations: they rule *citizens* either by liberal or authoritarian means and principles, that is, they establish a system of duties, rights and obligations regardless of race or ethnicity; at other times, they apply criteria of ethnic and racial differentiation.

Nation-states exist because of their belief, capacity and potentiality in exercizing self-rule and in defending their sovereign rights. A nation-state administers one clearly defined territory and seeks self-sufficiency through its own economy and commercial transactions. It believes in linguistic and cultural homogeneity as a condition for implementing equality and achieving common goals. It develops institutions and codes of practice which help it to standardize a wide range of factors such as the division of labour, the unification of loyalties and the activities and customs affecting everyday life, namely the educational system and mass media. Lastly, but no less important, a nation-state displays pride in its various pasts, its traditions and historicity, through which it claims and legitimizes modern nationhood.

At this point it would be useful to draw a line separating national identity from other types of collective identity which have provided a fresh reappraisal of civil society. These collective identities correspond to the first approach in studying identity, as mentioned at the beginning of this chapter. Normally, these groups seeking identity through mobilization focus their action on opposition to the state. Such groups, which are indeed numerous, include urban squatters and ecologists, socialist feminist groups, human rights campaigners, gay and lesbian coalitions, fundamentalists, workers co-operatives and peasant activists, defenders of the rain forest, antinuclear protesters and Afro-Caribbean musicians. These collective identities, also referred to as 'new' identities, have mainly emerged due to the events and influences of 'daily life'. The result: a rejection of existing institutional channels. The aim (one at least): to construct or negotiate more democratic spaces in which to act with greater autonomy (Alvarez and Escobar, 1992).

These groups embody a critique of institutionalization and centralization of power and resources. Their discourse enhances the restricted confines of their action in that they are obliged to work in partial, local and limited areas. In other words, small groups seek to find their own limited or domestic space and construct, recombine or invent an identity accordingly. Since the scope of the collectivity is reduced it does not require support for dissemination, although the interest of the media, together with assistance from other collectivities, are regularly provided.

In contrast, national identity has not emerged spontaneously or locally, it is learned and acquired and thus requires massive institutional support (e.g., schools, educational campaigns, mass media) as it aims at influencing the overall population of a national territory. Not all groups - ethnic, racial, gender - inhabiting a territory, identify with or are loyal to the dominant ethnic group representing the nation. Hence, the relevance of *national* identity is to achieve sustainable levels of assimilation and socialization among the population - no matter how diverse - by displaying and inculcating those socio-political facts (dates, sagas, episodes, heroes, nature) that celebrate the formation of nation-states - as all encompassing vertical and horizontal unities. Citizens are united by common culture and in this way express *identity*; in this way they learn what to do and how to perform (Renan's daily plebiscite - see Guibernau in this volume) in order to make possible the functioning and reproduction of the national collectivity; by the same token they also acquire a common set of beliefs, training and loyalties. People are made to believe that they have the same beginning (ancestry and origin) (Smith, 1984) and share a similar destiny (Bauer, 1979). Moreover, such communal self-identification creates powerful emotional sentiments and attitudes because *national identity makes people aware of themselves as a unique collectivity conscious and protective of their historical possessions such as territory and culture.*

The Uses of National Identity

Nation-states are committed to fulfilling three basic goals: the standardization of practices, the construction of homogeneity and the delimitation of cultural originality. It has been sufficiently demonstrated that institutions such as the educational system in the Gellnerian tradition, the printing press and, today, the electronic mass media, textbooks and civic rituals, play a decisive role in inculcating and transmitting through the practice of repetition, the *modern culture of nationalism* (Hobsbawm and Ranger, 1983; Anderson, 1992). However, modern nationhood, despite its alleged 'break with the past' (which means conditions for introducing and allowing standardization to cope with the high demands of modernity), also confronts the need of rescuing or rediscovering cultural originality.

To possess an authentic culture is an imperative of nation-states and it may take the form of a systematic search resulting in revivalism, reconstruction, and reconstitution of past cultural traditions, ethnicity or popular culture. In this context the arguments advanced by ethno-symbolists or historic-culturalists such as A.D. Smith (1994), J. Hutchinson (1987) and W. Connor (1972) effectively persuade that the nation cannot afford to get rid of its past and neglect its origins. Another kind of cultural search responding to purposes of national identity making, is the appropriation of cultural sources located in nature or people. This is exemplified in the contemporary situation of some indigenous and aboriginal peoples struggling to recover their inheritance seized by policy makers and intellectual elites servicing the nation-state (Urban and Sherzer, 1992; Keeffe, 1988). If on the one hand the nation (and its dominant cultural group) is a subject of ritualistic veneration, on the other, and from the ethnicist viewpoint, its construction has discouraged and invalidated the multifarious expressions of ethnicity (and perhaps of potential nationalisms).

Archetypes and Stereotypes

National identity is often described as a set of habits, attitudes, beliefs, sentiments and emotions reflecting the standardization of practices to meet the demands of modern labour, as well as the representation of cultural originality to which citizens with shared identity recreate their sense of belonging in the ever increasing interdependent world.

Notwithstanding the several purposes and meanings attributed to national identity, this is not an empty category. School children, factory workers and teachers (to mention a few) learn and acquire the social memory of national identity through the repetition of an often eclectic mix of codes of practice, ceremonials, narratives, heroes and histories (Connerton, 1992).

To recognize the various components of national identity is a basic task. These components interact in continuous contradiction and conflict expressed by the conjunction of reality and historical fact, of traditional values and modern practices, of ethnic regionalism and cosmopolitanism. One way of making sense of this labyrinth is by locating precise empirical guidelines which in our analysis are represented by the identification of archetypes and stereotypes to be found in a very vast field of cultural constructs. For example, universal ways of testing how the nation is conceptualized and portrayed have been carried out through the study of the various trends of both pictorial art and literary creations (Baddeley and Fraser, 1989). Analysis of school textbooks continues to be the most well known supplier of studies of identity (Citron, 1987). Adding to the role of schooling is the case of teacher's trade unions, discussed comparatively by J. Dierkes in this collection. Furthermore, a recent interest in exploring perceived changes of popular identification caused by the demise of Communist politics in Eastern Europe has stimulated new studies of collective identity using the medium of cinema as the main provider of symbols and images of collectivities from the 1980s. Another attractive field awaiting exploration is the study of a nation's sense of humour; similarly, certain historians provide us with new data helpful in compiling the history of national identity through the study of national cuisines.

By looking at such sources one can identify the permanent form assumed by events, characters, values, tastes or places. Archetypes and stereotypes help with the routine of standardization because of their permanent forms, and mark the difference between authenticity and foreignness; they foster internal solidarity and create deep rivalries and enemies (See Gutiérrez, 1998, 1998a).

Archetypes condense in someone or something those important characteristics which epitomize models of perfection, accomplishment and beauty and thus worthy of admiration and emulation. For instance, suffering heroes and martyrs (Admiral Nelson, Saint Ignatius of Loyola) (Colley, 1992), protectors and defenders of independence and civil rights (The 'fathers' and 'founders' of the American civic nations: S. Bolívar, B. Franklin and B. Juárez), as well as virtues, values and deeds. As components of the national imagery one can also include 'archetypical' places, a typical town (Stratford), landscape (the Alps) and monumental architecture (Petra, Teotihuacán and Fuzhou).

Stereotyping, on the other hand, implies reference to a state of fixation or staticism imposed arbitrarily on others. It gives us an account of the extent of preconceived ideas or assumptions held by one social group with respect to another. An interesting quality of stereotyping is the forging of fixed ideas about someone or something as well as the assumption that these ideas are predictable, that is, the belief in static patterns of behaviour. While archetypes reinforce a sense of cultural pride by encouraging emulation and admiration, stereotypes convey prejudices and derogatory meanings towards other social groups by assuming their staticism and repetitive behaviour (e.g., all indigenous peoples are passive political actors).[1]

Obviously, we are entering the domain of plain generalizations and, as such, they should be treated with care, but consideration has to be given to such guidelines helping us to delimit the two modern imperatives of national identity. The construction of the ideal type of homogeneity - a core convention of nation-states - and the system of information through which we manage to know our own identity and, at the same time, to distinguish the identities of others.

The Construction of Homogeneity

There are no culturally and linguistically homogeneous nation-states in today's world. A truism despite considerable official investment in educational systems, policies of integration, control of mass media and other forms of political coercion. One well known practice of national states has been to neutralize or disappear unwanted ethnicity - either immigrant or indigenous - by moulding ethnic members into national citizens. The cultural orientation of citizens-to-be is the imposed belief in the existence of a single macro-ethnic community with shared history, language and culture. *In the search of homogeneity the role of national identity is to instigate how to learn to form part of the artificial construction of unity by socializing the individual into unified styles of life, meanings and language.* Citizens with shared national identity presumably have a precise idea of their geography, history, culture, and resources, thus allowing them to value and defend sovereignty and self-rule.

Is it adequate to apply this argument to the expectations of multiple ethnic minorities who already form part of the life of a nation-state? Is national identity a yardstick of inclusion and exclusion? Stereotypes and archetypes as parameters of national identity also permeate ethnic groups through ritual and repetition via the standardized school. This type of explicit learning and indoctrination, plus a willingness to become assimilated on behalf of the ethnic individual might result in the acquisition of citizenship, but not of historicity.

In a research conducted in 1993, we were interested in ascertaining the degree of cultural integration held by indigenous peoples and the extent to which they had adopted two central narratives of the modern Mexican nation: the myth of foundation and the myth of common ancestry. The results of a sample of sixty indigenous students positively declared recognition of the nationalist mythology and ritual, but more importantly, they expressed lack of identification, emotionality, and a clear unwillingness to sacrifice or die for the idea of a single *patria*. Statements declaring preference and interest in knowing their own local and regional histories and mythologies were common. The above example shows a typical case of ethnic people's reluctance to conform to the patterns of the dominant tradition imbued with national culture and identity; and such an unresolved fragmentation represents a major challenge to the homogenizing projects of nation-states (See Gutiérrez, 1998a, 1999).

What is the Purpose of National Identity?

It is not possible to perceive other national identities (as different from ours) without first looking and experiencing pre-established assumptions and fixed images of given peoples and places (e.g. any traveller to Scotland expects to see kilts and tartan cloth). What is considered genuinely characteristic of 'us' by others, becomes for 'us' a matter of routine and triviality (Billig, 1995). National identity embodies artistic sensibility and heroic epics but is also saturated with and nurtured by details from every day life. Its intrinsic mundane environment is often rejected and ridiculed by artists and intellectuals,[2] who seek to replace this with a less conventional and more exotic way of life. Despite the official imprint of national identity, recent studies have documented the creative participation of popular imagination enriching the many sources of identity. Thus for the inhabitant of Latin America it makes sense to express an impassioned interest in soap operas or to reveal great fervour in football tournaments (Radcliffe and Westwood, 1996).

Archetypes and stereotypes are also relevant because of their widespread popularization; people believe in them and adopt them even when they carry a mixture of fact, fiction, distortion and exaggeration. 'People throughout the world believe that all Scotsmen are frugal and thrifty, all Germans hopelessly belligerent, all Frenchmen amorous, all Swedes cold, and all Americans naive and aggressive' (Snyder, 1990, p. 236). People identify themselves, and others, through precise symbols taking the form of countless imagery found in iconography, popular songs and sayings, to mention but a few. National identity is useful in constructing ideal type homogeneity as discussed earlier. Thus, homogeneity creates its own cultural limits in order to establish what is different with respect to others and how to recognize such differences. The cultural strength of identity allows for the practice of stereotyping and its corollary attitude of ridiculing and exaggerating characters and attributes of a given homeland and peoples. But the capacity of so-called *stereotyped* people to counteract stereotyping has been refashioned by cultural or social movements of earlier decades, taking unforeseen identity as a negotiating flag. Such peoples' capacity (or awareness) is a result of their gradual access to modernity e.g., the welfare state system and information technology. Mexican Americans have subverted their attributed passivity or inability to transform or react by exaggerating archetypes or stereotypes of the Mexican homeland, thus expressing a degree of cultural confidence that, on the other side of the frontier, cultural prejudices would no longer allow for exclusion or discrimination.

More dramatic aspects of national identity are those which have been used by some to deny others the right to 'roots' or 'homeland'. Ethnic conflict and war are, to a large extent, responsible for eroding cultural identity, as C. Cockburn (1998) demonstrates with the story of a Serb woman called Rada. Rada, who is over forty, was educated in Tito's Communist state and learnt to be a Yugoslavian citizen. However, she began to grasp the meaning of being a Serb when war broke out and ethnic cleansing and its stringent claims for 'our land' were propagated with untold violence. The extent of the atrocities committed by the Serbs has now made her reluctant to manifest openly any form of ethnic or national pride (pp. 211-31). Diaspora, forced immigration or deportation, are other important reasons that have encouraged people to become aware of what they have once represented in another time or another place. A pervasive need to express identity occurs when people are misunderstood and misrepresented, forcing them to rethink what they are. Homi Bhabha, a so-called 'black intellectual in Britain' experiencing displacement, argues that all cultures are in a process of 'hybridity' in replacing essentialism as a condition for 'originality'.

> ...the importance of hybridity is not to be able to trace two original moments from which the third emerges, rather hybridity to me is the 'third space' which enables other positions to emerge. This third space displaces the histories that constitute it, and sets up new structures of authority, new political initiatives, which are inadequately understood through received wisdom (Rutherford,

1990rp, p. 210).

At the outset, we asked whether national identity was a cultural continuum or an indoctrination sponsored by the modern state. To sum up, national identity is a system of knowledge and information necessary to cope with the demanding needs of the nation-state: standardization, homogenization and cultural originality. Satisfaction of these demands make the intervention of the state paramount, for example, the labour market and social mobility can only work if a given unification of codes and practices (including language) exists in society. People's awareness of culture, history and territory are concerns of national identity, and these have gradually evolved along with respect for 'others'. While national identity eulogizes the golden past or heroism, it is also nurtured by surrounding common places, hostilities and prejudices. National identity is indeed flexible and no longer essentialist, and cannot be reduced, therefore, to pure culturalism.

Conclusion

National identity is not a phenomenon which can be constructed and experienced differently by every individual. The search for cultural originality and the construction of homogeneity cannot be sustained and reproduced by confusing and conflicting information. Thus, institutions undertake the unification and dissemination of the typical artefacts of the nation (rituals, narratives or histories). In order to make sense of the nation's deep and complex cultural meanings we need explicit, permanent and pre-conceived 'markers' of identity and nationality which allow us to conceptualize and practice diverse forms of socialization such as acceptance, astonishment or tolerance towards our own group and members of other nationalities. National identity is shaped by the conflictive interplay between emotional attachments to traditionalism and the rational forces of modernism, as well as by popular mobilizations at times of negotiation or during cultural contacts resulting from rivalries, competitions or cooperations fostered by the interdependent world of nation-states. These practices and attitudes draw the contours of a limited, self-sufficient and introspective collectivity - the nation-state. In doing this we are manifesting two qualities of national identity: a) the capacity for self-recognition, and b) the ability to detect, recognize and acknowledge who the *others* are.

Notes

1   'The glorification of the archetypal peasant was a mainstay of the movement for Irish revival, and was as absurd and pathetic to Joyce as the boosting of the Russian peasant had been to Chekov' (Benstock, 1970, p. 71).

2   'The soul is born, he said vaguely, first in those moments I told you of. It has a slow and dark birth, more mysterious than the birth of the body. When the soul of a man is born in this country there are nets flung at it to hold it back from flight. You talk to me of nationality, language, religion, I shall try to fly by those nets. David knocked the ashes from his pipe. - Too deep for me, Stevie, he said. But a man's country comes first. Ireland first, Stevie. You can be a poet or mystic after. Do you know what Ireland is? Asked Stephen with cold violence. Ireland is the old sow that eats her farrow' (Joyce, 1977, pp. 184-5).

References

Alvarez, S. and Escobar, A. (1992), *The Making of Social Movements in Latin America: Strategy and Democracy*, Boulder Westview, San Francisco, Oxford.

Anderson, B. (1992), 'El Efecto Tranquilizador del Fraticidio: O de Cómo las Naciones Imaginan sus Genealogías', *El Nacionalismo en México*, in C. Noriega Elio (ed.), El Colegio de Michoacán, Michoacán, pp. 83-103.

Baddeley O. and Fraser V. (1989), *Drawing the Line: Art and Cultural Identity in Contemporary Latin America*, Verso, London.

Bauer, O. (1979), *La Cuestión de las Nacionalidades y la Socialdemocracia*, Siglo XXI, Madrid.

Benstock, B. (1970), *James:Joyce: The Unidiscover'd Country*, Gill and Macmillan, Dublin.

Billig, M. (1995), *Banal Nationalism*, Sage, London.

Citron, S. (1987), *Le Mythe National: L'Histoire de France en Question*, Les Editions Ouvrières, Paris.

Cockburn, C. (1998), *The Space between US: Negotiating Gender and National Identities in Conflict*, Zed Books, London, New York.

Colley, L. (1992), *Britons Forging the Nation 1707-1837*, Pimlico, London.

Connerton, P. (1992), *How Societies Remember,* Cambridge University Press, Cambridge.

Connor, W. (1972), 'Nation-building or Nation-destroying?', *World Politics*, (24), pp. 319-55.

Dijkink, G. (1996), *National Identity and Geopolitical Visions*, Routledge, London, New York.

Gellner, E. (1983), *Nations and Nationalism,* Cornell University Press.

Gellner, E. (1997), *Nationalism*, Orion Books, London.

Gutiérrez, N. (1990), 'Memoria Indígena en el Nacionalismo Precursor de México y Perú', *Estudios Interdisciplinarios de América Latina y el Caribe*, vol. 1 (2), pp. 99-113.

Gutiérrez, N. (1998a), 'What the Indians Say of the *Mestizos*: A Critical View of a Cultural Archetype of Mexican Nationalism', *Bulletin of Latin American Research*, vol. 17 (3), September, pp. 284-301.

Gutiérrez, N. (1998b), 'Arquetipos y Estereotipos en la Construcción de la Identidad Nacional de México', *Revista Mexicana de Sociología*, vol. 60 (1), January-February, pp. 81-90.

Gutiérrez, N. (1999), *Nationalist Myths and Ethnic Identities: Indigenous Intellectuals and the Mexican State*, Nebraska University Press, Lincoln, London.

Hobsbawm, E. and Ranger, T. (1983) (eds.), *The Invention of Tradition*, Cambridge University Press, Cambridge.

Hutchinson, J. (1987), *The Dynamics of Cultural Nationalism: The Gaelic Revival and the Creation of the Irish Nation State*, Allen and Unwin, London.

Joyce, J. (1977), *A Portrait of the Artist as a Young Man*, Triad and Panther Books, Herts.

Keeffe, K. (1988), 'Aboriginality: Resistance and Persistance', *Australian Aboriginal Studies*, (1), pp. 67-81.

Radcliffe, S. and Westwood, S. (1996), *Remaking the Nation, Place, Politics and Identity in Latin America*, Routledge, London.

Rutherford, J. (1990rp), 'Interview with Homi Bhabha' in J. Rutherford (ed.), *Identity. Community. Culture. Difference*, Lawrence and Wishart, London.

Smith, A.D. (1984), 'National Identity and Myths of Ethnic Descent', *Research in Social Movements, Conflict and Change*, (7), pp. 95-130.

Smith, A.D. (1991), *National Identity*, Penguin, Harmonsdsworth.

Smith, A.D. (1994), 'The Problem of National Identity: Ancient, Medieval and Modern', *Ethnic and Racial Studies*, vol.17, (3), pp. 375-99.

Snyder, L. (1990), *Encyclopedia of Nationalism*, St James Press, Chicago, London.

Urban, G. and Sherzer, J. (1992) (eds), *Nation States and Indians in Latin America*, University of Texas Press, Texas.

PART II
DIMENSIONS OF NATIONAL IDENTITY

2 Interpretations of National Identity

ANTHONY D. SMITH

If it is true that terms and concepts become fashionable when the phenomena to which they refer become problematic, then we have a clue to the popularity of the concept of 'national identity' today. For there is no doubt that, at least in the advanced industrial societies of the West, identity in general and national identity in particular is a topic of widespread interest and concern, both among scholars and among the wider public. This was not the case in earlier times. From the later seventeenth through the eighteenth century, its place was taken by the ideas of 'national genius' or 'character'. From Lord Shaftesbury to Rousseau and Herder these concepts served to delineate both cultural difference and authentic collective experience, with important consequences for the organization of states and societies (Kemilainen, 1964; Macmillan, 1986, ch. 3; Berlin, 1976). In the nineteenth century, we hear less of national character and more of 'national consciousness', as groups and populations that had been politically silent and/or disunited began to make their voices heard and their demands known, on the grounds that they constituted self-aware communities animated by national sentiments (Kohn, 1967, ch. 1; Seton-Watson, 1977, chs. 1-4). It is really only in our century, and especially since 1945, that 'national identity' has become the preferred term for referring to the cultural and social psychological aspects of the nation and especially to a presumed stability in the relations between the members of a culturally defined population (See Harris, 1995, ch. 6).

Of these concepts, national identity is the most contested. This is because identity of any kind is regarded as a social construct, one that is fluid and malleable, the outcome and product of particular situations. Collective cultural identities are multiple, porous and often overlapping; ethnic, regional, religious, gender and class identities slide into each other in given situations and are easily penetrated. More recently, social observers have emphasized the gulf between traditional, received narratives of national identity and the actual cultural identifications of individuals today, which are multiple and situational, the result of relationships and practices of individuals in a multicultural society.[1]

In the first part of this chapter, I examine the assumptions behind some recent work in the field of nationalism and national identity, starting with the so-called 'post-modernist' approaches of Homi Bhabha and Benedict Anderson, followed by the recent works of Eric Hobsbawm in the Marxist tradition, and finally the revised version of Ernest Gellner's modernist theory. The second part briefly advances an alternative approach based on the idea of reconstruction of a distinctive ethno-heritage, and applies this to ethnic, civic and especially plural nations.

Hybridized National Identity

The multiple and situational nature of modern identities is the point of departure for so-called 'post-modernist' theories of national identity, notably those of Homi Bhabha and Benedict Anderson.

For Homi Bhabha, the national self is constructed in relation to the Other, i.e. significant outsider, who thereby defines the self. Though the project of the Enlightenment attempts to incorporate the totality of being and hence the Other, no nation can claim that totalizing homogeneity that nationalist narratives purport to demonstrate. Cultural difference is irreducible, and it reveals the ambivalence and hybrid nature of national modernity in every state. In concrete terms, the great influx of immigrants, ex-colonials, asylum-seekers and *Gastarbeiter* has eroded homogeneous national identities, or rather the traditional, received pedagogical images and narratives of national homogeneity, and has thereby revealed the hybrid nature of national identity today.

Modern national identities which are composed of narratives of 'the people' are found to operate under a 'doubled' and 'split' signifier - between past and present, self and the other, pedagogical and performative - with the received versions of the nation taught by nationalists always being challenged and broken down into their component parts by alternative narratives of the actions and performances of members of the community. In Simmelian manner, Bhabha directs our attention to the role of the outsider and stranger in defining group identity. Only he goes much further, suggesting that today all collective identity is hybridized and fragmented. Housed in anxious states, every national identity turns out on inspection to be ambivalent and precarious, being composed of fragments from the ex-colonial periphery that cannot, and refuse to, be integrated and assimilated (Bhabha, 1990).

Anderson's claim is very different, but his emphasis on text and narrative reveals a parallel understanding of national identification. For Anderson, nations and national identities are self - rather than other - defined, and they are far from being the hybridized and split narratives of Bhabha. On the contrary: nations and nationalism are akin to culture and religion rather than ideology in their depth and extent. The nation is best seen as an imagined political community, at once sovereign and spatially finite-imagined, because most of its members will never see or know each other. But once created, this imagined communion of the nation represents a powerful sociological reality as a community imagined to move in linear fashion through 'empty, homogeneous time'. Yet, for Anderson, the sociological reality of national identities can best be apprehended through the analysis of the narratives and images of those who represent the imagined community to others. It is in the literary devices and tropes of the narrators of national identity - novelists, playwrights, journalists - that we can grasp both the nature of the national community and its hold over its members. For its members are also its consumers: the novels, plays and journals of the writers are avidly consumed by a public that has become able and accustomed to read standardized print languages.

This reading public was created over two to three hundred years by the dissemination of mass-produced books, and later newspapers, in standardized administrative and vernacular languages, once Latin's dominance had been overthrown. Aided by and aiding the rapid progress of Protestantism and the rise of administrative languages of state, the new technology of printing and the market economy of mass-commodity capitalism revolutionized social communications from the late fifteenth century in Europe and helped to forge a new kind of community around standardized print-languages. Popular identification with such 'print-communities' gradually displaced the former loyalties to sacred realms and their monarchs and to large-scale liturgical communities. Perhaps most fundamental of all was the revolution in our conceptions of time, from the pre-modern cosmological and messianic conceptions to the modern linear mode of measuring time by clock and calendar. Together with the inherent linguistic diversity of our world and the deep-seated human desire to overcome the oblivion of death through individual and/or collective immortality in this world or the next, these developments created the conditions for the rise of encompassing national identities and destinies based on print-languages and their reading publics, which give finite human beings a meaning beyond their short life-spans (Anderson, 1983).

Anderson's and Bhabha's interpretations of national identity rightly highlight its problematic status as a concept, and the difficulty of defining present-day nations as homogeneous entities. Immigration on a vast scale, widespread intermarriage and cultural mingling, have made it increasingly difficult to find homogeneous nations today. We can no longer 'imagine' the nation as a unitary whole; it is inevitably plural and frayed at the edges.[2] And yet, we may ask, when was the nation ever homogeneous, or perceived to be so? Some 'organic' nationalists ardently desired such homogeneity, even purity; but the fact that they had to fight so hard to realize their dreams suggests that even they acknowledged that the reverse was normally the case. For civic nationalists, ethnic homogeneity was never part of their agenda. For many others like Daniel Defoe the ethnic plurality of the nation constituted no problem, indeed, some nations like the Swiss and the Belgian welcomed their ethnic diversity.

Besides, have not immigration and refugees been hallmarks of the modern world for at least two centuries? Is not it a bit myopic to find a theory of national identity on the fact that a few cossetted western democracies have experienced an upsurge of immigration since 1945? As William McNeill has reminded us, ethnic mixing and polyethnic hierarchy have been features of all civilized societies throughout the ages, and the modern era is no exception. The ideal of national unity as a territorial and political community is quite compatible with ethnic and cultural diversity within that unity, and was practised also by a number of pre-modern kingdoms and empires such as Rome, China and Persia (McNeill, 1986).

A second problem concerns the notion that national identity can be read as a narrative, a set of texts to be deconstructed, to reveal the imagined community. This is a suggestive idea, one that directs us to an important and relatively untapped area for research, linking national identity to artistic and literary creativity and symbolism. At the same time it deprives the nation of its social and political anchorage in pre-modern structures and modern processes. The emphasis on the imagined, and perhaps imaginary and re-presented nature of national identity - rather than its felt, known and acted dimensions - allows for little independent verification of the nature and components of national identity, and privileges literary analysis and cultural studies at the expense of causal investigation and political and historical sociology.[3]

Third, the emphasis in Anderson's work on the printed word and literary products is unduly restrictive for an understanding of national identity. It tends to relegate other artistic modes of communication which may have greater mass appeal such as music, painting, film, TV, and radio, and omits the role of popular sentiments and ties in defining national identities, focusing mainly on the role of elites, especially the intelligentsia. The intelligentsia is undoubtedly important in any explanation of nationalism, and hence national identity, but their significance lies in their relationship with other strata and they tend to be more prominent in the early stages of nationalist self-discovery and self-assertion. Most people who struggled and died for their countries, did so out of a strong and immediate familial sense of belonging and loyalty, not because they had internalized newspaper images, let alone the fictions of novels and plays, even when they could read them (See Hroch, 1985; Connor, 1993).

Finally, we should be wary of Anderson's idea that, historically, nations and national identities grew up around different 'print-communities'. More often, such communities helped to weld together pre-existing *ethnies* and states. Print-capitalism and the books and newspapers it spawned helped to forge nations out of reading publics most of whose members were already united by an accumulated heritage of symbols, memories, codes and myths of ethnic community and by the processes of bureaucratic incorporation by strong states, often led by able monarchs and clerics.

These objections should put us on our guard against the more extreme positions which would see 'national identity' as little more than a situational construct, a *bricolage*, formed by selecting bits of the past to suit the present and its needs and preoccupations. Such a 'blocking presentism' obscures the two-way relationship between past and present, and runs up against the continuing importance for so many people of 'national identities' as the vessel and medium of that collective past. The 'gastronomic' theory of national identity evades the problem of explaining continuities as well as discontinuities, and fails to account for the often explosive character of nations and their nationalisms (Peel, 1989; Tonkin, McDonald and Chapman, 1989, Introduction; cf. A.D.Smith, 1995b).

The Marxist Invention of Tradition

A more conventional but sociologically rooted view would see in 'national identity' a construct of the bourgeoisie, which answered to the political needs of ruling classes in a capitalist epoch.

Eric Hobsbawm is a recent representative of this view. He argues that capitalism is destabilizing and universalizing: mass commodity production and monetization are global and impersonal and destructive of use values. At the same time, capitalism also increases social misery and alienation for the workers, who become class conscious, form unions, agitate for economic reforms and join revolutionary movements. To stave off revolution, the ruling classes make concessions, including the franchize and welfare measures. But the twin processes of industrialization and democratization still threaten the social order and hence the position of the ruling classes. They find they must channel the revolutionary energies of the masses into constructive and stable organizations. To this end, they invent traditions of community, status and order - sports associations, scouts, annual celebrations, choral societies, etc. - which will control the masses. The most effective set of these 'invented traditions' is that of the nation and national identity. The rulers and intelligentsia set about endowing the masses with a national consciousness and identity, which they never before possessed, in order to control and mobilize them better in times of danger; the classic example being that of France during the Third Republic, where the education system, public festivals and monumental art all drove home the message of French republican grandeur and liberty and sought to create French citizens out of the mass of regional peasants that made up most of 'France' in that period. But Hobsbawm is able to back his theory with a wide array of evidence drawn from other countries in Europe and North America in the period 1870 to 1914 (Hobsbawm and Ranger, 1983, chs. 1, 7; Weber, 1979).

Here 'national identity' is regarded as a diversionary invention of the ruling classes, substituting the status hierarchy of the nation for the horizontal comradeship of class. More dangerous still because divisive is the 'ethno-linguistic' nationalism, which first flourished in Europe in the

1870-1914 period and has reappeared today. For Hobsbawm, this kind of nationalism is a product of the aspirations of the petty bourgeoisie, the 'lower examination passing classes', in contrast to the more progressive and unifying mass political nationalism of Western Europe in the earlier nineteenth century (Hobsbawm, 1990, chs. 1, 4).

This comes dangerously close to accusing the masses of labouring under false 'consciousness', of being politically inert and an easy prey to fear of radical change. The resulting focus upon the concerns and aims of ruling elites contradicts Hobsbawm's own desire to get away from the exclusively 'top-down' approach for which he criticizes Gellner and others and which he seeks to remedy by examining popular 'proto-national' communities. What remains unclear is why the nation and national identity continue to mean so much to so many people of all classes and why they so often accord it priority over other loyalties.

Nor does Hobsbawm indicate the components of national community and identity. He resolutely refuses (except in the Russian case) to link popular 'proto-national' communities and sentiments with modern mass political nationalism, on the ground that the former do not aim to create a sovereign state, whereas that is the whole purpose of modern nationalisms. This is all the more curious, because 'invented traditions' which can only form part of any national identity or community, presuppose other, older and more durable traditions, memories, symbols, myths and values. If they did not, if they were indeed just 'invented' *ex nihilo* in the nineteenth or twentieth centuries, they would find little response or following. Thus, in Britain, the institution of the British Legion and Remembrance Sunday in 1920 was clearly a new tradition, and intended and accepted as such; but it took its meaning and significance from other earlier commemorations and from the long history of unity and solidarity and self-sacrifice of British peoples and their national sentiments. Without that history and solidarity, Remembrance Sunday would not have been able to retain its hold on popular emotions and imaginations. New traditions that do strike a deep chord in the hearts and minds of many people are those that seek to build on the ethnic myths and national memories of a community of history and destiny (See A.D.Smith, 1991b).[4] At the heart of the Marxist account is a theory of bourgeois manipulation. But the idea that national identities and nationalism can be simply manipulated by rulers and elites is a half-truth. Examples of nationalist manipulation certainly occur, as Kedourie documents. But in these and other cases, nationalist leaders succeed only where the soil is prepared, where social and political conditions make a larger constituency receptive to their ideas and programme. Democratization took place in the context of an assertion of national will and national pride among the newly enfranchised; you could not 'make Italians' unless many of them also aspired to be Italians and to participate in the Italian political process (See Kedourie, 1971; Brass, 1991, chs. 1-2).

Identity and Modernity

A third approach regards nations and national identity as products of modernity. In fact, identity is a product of a particular kind of modern culture and education, a 'high culture' and exo-socialization.

For Ernest Gellner, there can be neither nations nor nationalism before the modern era because the culture of the elites was utterly unlike those of the many small communities of peasants. There was in such societies neither need nor possibility of national identity. The contrary is the case in modern societies. Here a mobile, growth-oriented industrial society requires national identity as the cement and inspiration for citizens.

The reason is that the tide of modernization has destroyed the role structures of traditional societies, uprooting many people who flock to the anonymous city, and forcing them to relate to each other through a new linguistic culture. Their adoption of a new urban and literate or 'high' culture turns the newcomers into loyal citizens - 'acceptable specimens of humanity' - and gives them a new national identity.

In the city, however, the newcomers must also compete for scarce resources with the old-timers, and this leads to class conflict. Where the newcomers to the city can be distinguished from the old-timers on cultural grounds - in terms of pigmentation, religion or language - and where the educated members of the newcomer category, the intelligentsia, join forces with the mass of uprooted peasant newcomers, ethnic conflict ensues and with it, the chance of national secession arises (Gellner, 1964, ch. 7).

In general, for Gellner, what turns peasants into citizens is a new kind of mass, public, standardized and academy-supervised education or exo-socialization - as opposed to education in the family or village school. This is what turns spontaneous, wild, 'low' cultures into sophisticated, literate, 'high' or garden cultures serviced by specialists. Industrial society requires such high cultures to ensure mobility, substitutability, literacy and competence in semantic and technical labour. But a society with a high culture is a nation, and national identity is the high culture, which they share and which inspires their loyalty as citizens (Gellner, 1983).[5]

This is a much more sophisticated and comprehensive account. It stems from a few theoretical premises such as 'culture replaces structure' in modern societies, and derives national identity and nationalism from them. Nevertheless, it contains some serious flaws.

To begin with, the theory operates at a high level of abstraction using ideal-types, which are often not easily applicable to specific situations. For example, the distinction between family education and exo-socialization, while conceptually clear, is in most societies impossible to draw, especially where religion is a dominant force. Moreover, we cannot equate 'low' with pre-modern, and 'high' with modern, cultures, or language adoption with cultural assimilation: there are too many counter-examples and other possibilities.

There is also a very clear materialist and functionalist bias in regarding national identity and nationalism as explicable in terms of the needs of industrial society. While Gellner pays much attention to the role of culture, ultimately it is secondary in theoretical terms to the need which the nation satisfies of furnishing a fully educated, literate, mobile workforce and cadres without which no industrial society can function or survive. Nationalism and industrialism have become symbiotic. But a moment's glance at the historical record is enough to remind us of the way in which nationalism and national identities can emerge well before industrialism - in Greece and Serbia, Norway and Poland, India and West Africa, but also in early modern England and France - and how they can revive and be maintained in every kind of economic situation (See Connor, 1984; Greenfeld, 1992, chs. 1-2).

Then there is the problem of determinism. History is seen as a sequence of plateaux - pre-Neolithic, agrarian, industrial - with giant leaps upwards between each. The nation is a product of the irreversible leap to 'industria' and nationalism is its cultural-political expression. On this reading, national identity is the collective cultural and psychological counterpart of the industrial plateau. It is the specific expression of an industrial 'high culture', not the product of the experiences and actions of successive generations and competing sections of the members of cultural communities.[6]

Finally, little place is accorded in this account to pre-modern cultural legacies and their continuing influence on modern structures. The origin of many of the modern 'high cultures' in those of the dominant ethnic communities of pre-modern epochs is obscured. The continuities with the ethnic past in so many 'provinces' and 'regions' are dismissed, and there is no attempt to relate modern nations to their different ethnic bases and historical trajectories. The importance of folk heroes, customs, traditions and myths in so many areas for so many people, and the ways in which nationalists, often quite sincerely, utilize them for ideological ends while at the same time resurrecting and universalizing them, is underestimated (See A.D.Smith, 1989).

Reconstructing the Nation

This brief review of some leading theories of nationalism reveals how most of them tend to disregard the concept of 'national identity' in favour of those of 'nationalism' and the 'nation'. At the same time, they ignore or relegate the historical roots of these national identities. In contrast, ethno-symbolists such as John Armstrong and Anthony Smith have argued that 'national identity' is a separate concept from that of 'nationalism', and that it emerges as the subjective component of collective identification within the context of the formation of nations. The concept of 'national identity' may be defined as the *maintenance and continuous reproduction of the pattern of values, symbols, memories, myths and traditions that compose the distinctive heritage of nations, and the identifications of individuals with that particular heritage and those values, symbols, memories, myths and traditions.*

They see national identities as being continually reconstituted through processes of selection of symbolic elements from that ethno-heritage and re-identifications with the reconstituted ethno-heritage. Processes of reconstruction, reinterpretation and re-identification of ethno-symbolic components are central to the durability and flexibility of so many national identities, especially in the modern epoch (Armstrong, 1982; A.D.Smith, 1986 and 1991a).[7]

These processes do not operate in a vacuum. Internally, various groups within the population of the nation are involved in the processes of selection, reconstruction and re-identification, notably intellectuals and professionals, but also bureaucrats, clergy and rulers. But the choices and activities of these elites are constrained by their need to appeal to wider strata, including the working class, traders and clerks, and at times, the peasants and tribesmen (See Breuilly, 1982, ch. 15).

Moreover, external events such as wars, immigration, economic transformations and religious movements, continually induce changes, gradually or within a single generation, in the current components of national identities, in their interrelations, in their images as relayed in official or widely recognized texts, artefacts, traditions and customs, and therefore in the national identifications of individuals.

Nevertheless, these changes always remain within the parameters of an ethno-heritage, or of a historic confluence of such heritages (as in Britain or Switzerland), which are determined by the patterning of historical sequences, territorial associations, traditions and values of a particular ethnic community. Elites will therefore operate within the limits of the popular resonance of traditional identifications, current historical knowledge and shared historical traditions, if they wish their cultural innovations and reinterpretations to have lasting social and political consequences (Robinson, 1979).

Finally, to be 'national', such identities must pertain to all the members of that community in such a way as to satisfy the minimum requirements of the ideology of nationalism, namely, that their components be 'authentic' and distinctive, that they unite all the members in a single social and territorial body of theoretical equals, and that they be autonomous, i.e. free of external or internal constraints.[8]

This view of *national identity* is based on a perspective that roots nations and national identities in cultural traditions and continuities, and hence requires an analysis of the *longue duree*. The main assumptions of this perspective are:

1. The components of national identities derive from those of the dominant ethnic communities or *ethnies* within the state, and nations and their identities are formed on the basis of one or other (or perhaps an amalgam) of these ethno-histories and ethno-heritages.
2. Many of these ethno-histories and heritages are *pre*-modern, and some of them are ancient. As a result, the radical break in cultural and social continuity with pre-modern agrarian eras postulated by modernist and post-modernist theories of nationalism is often

exaggerated.

3. On the other hand, the ethnic heritage has often, and continues to be, transformed in the modern epoch by the processes of rediscovery, selection, reconstruction and re-identification of 'authentic' ethnic components, so that none of these elements should be regarded as perennial, let alone primordial.

4. Symbols are the medium and means, through which whole peoples may be mobilized, and their identifications reattached, on the basis of pre-existing vernacular histories and cultures, and this is why symbolic issues are so important today and for ethno-nationalist struggles.

Patterns of National Identity

Ethno-symbolic reconstruction can be found everywhere. It is the basic process through which national identities are reconstituted out of ethnic ties and characteristics, and then reproduced or modified. It occurs in every generation, more or less thoroughly, altering but never destroying the basic patterning of the dominant ethno-heritage which underpins any popular and recognized national identity.

So far I have been arguing as if there were only a single model of national identity. As one might expect of such an elusive and protean concept, this is a gross simplification. In fact, we can distinguish several kinds of national identity, according to the *trajectory* of their historical formation. Three of these types have been particularly important, historically: the ethnic, civic and plural.

If the trajectory of national formation was one of vernacular mobilization, that is, the mobilization of the mass of the designated population through vernacular history and modes of expression, then the ensuing national identity will tend to be more ethnic and genealogical in character. It will be based more directly on mobilization through the politicization of the ethno-heritage of the dominant (or sole) *ethnie*, which will have been of the 'vertical' or demotic kind, where most of the community shares in the vernacular culture in opposition to cultural outsiders (See A.D. Smith, 1986, ch. 4).

Greece furnishes a good example of an ethnic national identity. The modern Greek nation emerged as a result of the mobilization of Orthodox and Greek-speaking populations by Greek intellectuals and others, on the basis of a pre-existing shared history and culture. Of course, that culture and history was subject to selection and interpretation in the process of reconstructing a modern Greek nation, to make it consonant with the ideals of autonomy, unity and distinctiveness preached by Greek nationalism. Nevertheless, the idea of a Greek nation was formed on the basis of pre-existing traditions of a Greek vertical community, Hellenic and Byzantine, which, despite many cleavages, possessed a measure of cultural, religious and historical unity based on successive visions of the ethnic past (Campbell and Sherrard, 1968, ch. 1; but cf. Kitromilides, 1989).

If, on the other hand, the trajectory of national formation was one of bureaucratic incorporation by a strong state formed by the ruling class of a dominant *ethnie*, then the ensuing national identity will tend to be more civic and territorial in character. It will be based more directly on the territory and political institutions of the bureaucratic state created by a 'lateral' or aristocratic *ethnie*, a high status ethnic community with ragged and extensive boundaries but little social depth, since the ruling elites generally have no desire to share their culture with those they rule and whose labour they exploit. Only in a few cases has the strong bureaucratic state built up by aristocratic and clerical *ethnies* sought to spread its culture to outlying areas and subject classes, inducing a middle class territorial and civic patriotism which is then generalized to other classes as they are incorporated into the political arena (A.D. Smith, 1991, chs. 3, 5).

The classic instance of a civic and territorial nationalism is that of France. Here the key to French national identity is the interplay between a strong, centralizing bureaucratic state and the standardization of French culture around the territorial hexagon of the French kingdoms. Once again, statesmen, intellectuals and professionals proposed rival versions of French identity (Frankish or Gallic) and interpreted the long history of the Frankish and French kingdoms in a selective manner, to accord with the ideals of autonomy, unity and distinctiveness preached by French republican nationalism. The role of the French language in the decisive moment of late eighteenth century revolutionary nationalism was critical for the crystallization of a secular cultural standardization, which formed the bedrock of a rigorous civic and territorial French identity. But the ethnic component of French nationalism was never absent: it stemmed from later interpretations of the 'lateral' aristocratic *regnum* of the Franks, and of the French kings, as a chosen realm with a special mission as the defender of Catholicism, and later as the source of a grandiose literary and artistic civilization (Poliakov, 1974, ch. 1; Lartichaux, 1977; Armstrong, 1982, ch. 6; Citron, 1988).

Finally, if the trajectory of national formation was one of pioneering settlement, then the ensuing national identity will tend to be more 'plural' and multicultural in character. It will be based more directly on the providential mission of immigrant colonist fragments of *ethnies*, intent on building a new life in vast open spaces.

The United States is the standard example of a plural national identity, based on the providential mission of immigrant White Anglo-Saxon colonists and their pioneering settlements, and on the selective reconstruction of that ethno-history to accord both with the ideals of autonomy, unity and distinctiveness preached by American nationalists and with the circumstances of successive waves of immigrant colonists of different cultures. Here the basis of national formation was furnished by the many varied pioneering settlements of Protestant colonists, whose diversity and autonomy became the model for the freedoms granted by a federal Constitution to both the individual states and later to ethnic cultures of varying origins. This in turn gave rise to the characteristic liberal balance between a basic all-American pattern of national identity through the assimilating power of the English language, law and political institutions, on the one hand, and, on the other, the successive diverse ethnic cultures which have reached into the public realm and have modified that pattern over the last hundred years and given it increasing openness and flexibility (Tuveson, 1968; Glazer and Moynihan, 1975, Introduction; Gans, 1979).

It is this last or '*plural*' pattern that comes closest to the post-modernist understanding, and it is possible that the plural pattern may become the model of future national identities in 'post-modern' societies. But, as of now, they form a distinct minority of national identities and identity types, found mainly in immigrant societies; we should guard against extrapolating from them to the whole field, or defining our understanding of the concept of national identity by reference solely to one of its sub-varieties. Certainly, ethnic and civic patterns of national identity have been the dominant and formative modes of collective identification in the last two centuries.

Of course, these are ideal types. Individual cases of national identities are often composed of elements from two or more sub-types. In the course of their formation and development, we can find one type giving way to another; and back...from, say, an ethnic to a civic or plural identity and back again. This overlapping and oscillation of elements from different sub-types can be found in a number of instances of national identity; a well-known example is the clash of ethnic and civic patterns of national identity in France at the time of the Dreyfus Affair, with Dreyfusards embracing the revolutionary republican tradition of secular, civic and territorial French identity, and their opponents campaigning vociferously for an ethnic, religious and genealogical vision of France (See Kedward, 1965).

Similar clashes can be found in contemporary India. Here the early stages of Indian nationalism sought to create a secular Indian state and define Indianness in terms of civic belonging and territory. In this way, minorities - religious, regional and linguistic - could become equal citizens and participate fully in an Indian political identity and community. Yet, even at the beginning of this century, voices were raised in favour of a more vivid but narrower vision of Indian identity, one based on Hindu religion and an 'Aryan Vedic' interpretation of Indian history and culture. From Tilak to the BJP, a growing number of Indians have reacted against Western values and espoused a more sharply defined and indigenously based Hindu Indian identity, to the detriment of minorities and inter-communal relations. Thus it becomes difficult to characterize Indian national identity in terms of any one of these ideal-typical patterns (See McCulley, 1966; Juergensmeyer, 1993, Part II).

As an example of the transition to a more 'plural' type of national identity, Switzerland's mosaic of cantonal, ethnic, linguistic and religious units and ties has often been held up as the exemplar. The Old Confederation certainly had from the first both a cantonal and an ethnic character. The Oath of the Rutli, the document regarded as the foundation charter of the Swiss *Eidgenossenschaft*, was essentially a treaty between three Alemmannic and German-speaking forest cantons against the failure of the Habsburg emperor to renew their existing privileges. But with the accession of other cantons and free cities, and the defeats of Habsburg forces at Morgarten, Nafels and Sempach, myths, memories and symbols of the sturdy virtues of Stauffacher and William Tell gradually helped to forge a wider demotic *ethnie* which received canonical expression by the late fifteenth and early sixteenth centuries after the victories of Grandson and Morat over the Dukes of Burgundy, in such texts as the *White Book of*

Sarnen and Aegidius Tschudi's *Chronicon Helveticum* (See Thurer, 1970, ch. 1; Im Hof, 1991, ch. 1).

With the religious divisions of the Reformation and the accession of French-speaking and Protestant cantons, a new wider definition of the Confederation became necessary, although its possibilities were not realized until the French-inspired Helvetic Republic of 1798 had put into practice some of the ideals of the Swiss enlightenment in Zurich, Bern and Geneva. Only then could a new civic and territorial patriotism become widely diffused; and only after the religious war of 1847 and the promulgation of the new Constitution of the Federal Republic, could its full civic character be realized. What helped to tilt the movement of national identity even further towards the 'plural' mode was the strong desire to retain cantonal rights and linguistic and religious differences within a federal arrangement. Today, despite the recent 700th anniversary celebrations of the foundation myths and the William Tell saga, modern Swiss perceptions of ancient ethnic legends and symbols have become increasingly civic in character, and the plural nature of Swiss democracy is highly prized (See Kohn, 1957; Steinberg, 1976, ch. 2; Fahrni, 1983; Kreis, 1991).

Post-Modern Plural Nations?

It may be conceded from these and other examples that ethnic and civic types of national identity still predominate today; and that, given the illiberal and unpredictable character of so many ethnic nationalisms around the world, from the Serbs to the Sinhalese, the humanization of nationalism requires a greater stabilization of national identity around civic and territorial symbols, memories, myths and values (Porter, 1975; Ignatieff, 1993).

Alternatively, we may hope to sit out the present proliferation of angry, unsatisfied ethnic nationalisms, and wait until the full effects of 'globalization' are felt and the 'plural' model of national identity, now mainly to be found (with perhaps the Swiss exception) in immigrant societies, becomes the norm for all advanced industrial and 'post-modern' societies. This is the argument behind Hobsbawm's denigration of the present spate of divisive ethno-linguistic nationalisms; but it also informs McNeill's much more conservative scepticism (See Hobsbawm, 1990, ch.

6; McNeill, 1986, ch. 3).[9]

Neither of these perspectives, for all their good intentions, is likely to hold up in the face of present long-term trends. For one thing, there are still too many unsatisfied *ethnies* aspiring to political recognition, still too many unresolved ethnic conflicts over land and status, to allow much hope of any diminution of ethnic nationalisms in the near to medium term (though we may expect peaks and troughs in their incidence and frequency). More fundamentally, the structure of the state system, regional and global, and the economic inequalities associated with regions and states, continually create the conditions for new rivalries and conflicts, whose popular expression is likely to be ethnic (and religious). Similarly, the structure of global and regional ethno-symbolic systems is equally unlikely to permit a steady progression from ethnic to civic to plural modes of national identification. That structure is deeply uneven; some regions and communities are well endowed with ethno-symbolic resources, while others are less so, some have well documented and visible ethno-heritages, others less so, some have vivid ethnic myths of election, whereas others are muted or absent. Given these differences, the widespread quests for collective dignity, continuity and destiny which characterize populations all over the world, can only fuel and sustain popular aspirations for political recognition in terms of ethnic and cultural criteria, and therefore underpin, if not crystallize, ethno-nations (A.D. Smith, 1990).

Besides, the civic and even more the plural modes of national identification face serious internal problems of social and political solidarity. Without a widely accepted myth of ethnic descent, without shared ethno-historical memories, including those of one or more 'golden ages', without a sense of ethnic election and mission, only a revolutionary civic nationalism with exemplars drawn from widely accepted canons of virtue and grandeur (such as ancient Greece and Rome provided), could provide that criterion of political solidarity and social cohesion that can sustain political community and stabilize the sense of national identity. In this respect, ethnic nationalism possesses advantages denied to other modes of national identification: a definite standard of authenticity, a clear criterion of communal belonging and a powerful basis for a sense of collective destiny. These are important considerations if and when, like Rousseau, we are desirous of endowing a population with a 'national character' and a common purpose and will, as the basis for democratic government and civic rights (See Cobban, 1964).

In other words, the stabilization of national identities - and their ethno-symbolic components - through the reinterpretation and reconstruction of collective history and culture, which is what in fact takes place from generation to generation, is more likely to be achieved through the interweaving of ethnic and civic (and where circumstances permit, plural) modes of national identification, than by rejecting ethnic identification and pursuing the chimeras of a wholly civic or plural nation. This means that our focus must be on the exploration of each nation's ethnic heritage, the maintenance and reproduction of the peculiar historical pattern of values, memories, symbols, myths and traditions of that ethno-heritage, and the identifications of individuals with that pattern and its ethno-symbolic components. Rather than filtering out the vital ethnic components, we can see how they interact with, or even sometimes transmute into, civic and plural elements in particular historical contexts. Above all, we must guard against the all too pervasive tendency to overlook the historical pattern of national formation over the *longue duree* and the critical importance of the ethnic past or pasts in the formation and reconstruction of modern national identities. Without this long-term perspective, there can be no understanding of the problems and complexities of national identity in the modern world.

Notes

1   The idea of multiple and overlapping identities is especially associated with the debate between 'instrumentalists' and 'primordialists' and the former's preference for seeing ethnic ties as 'situational' rather than pervasive. See for example, Okamura (1981) and Eriksen (1993, chs. 2-3).

2   This is the main *sociological* message of Bhabha's critique of received concepts of national identity. There are also more specifically literary and cultural messages concerning the nature of discourse and narratives about collectivities, but insofar as they are susceptible to sociological translation, they are couched in too general a context to yield much insight into the dynamics of national identity. Migration is far less important in Anderson's perspective: *or it does not seem to have eroded the bases of imagined communion that transcends mortality by harnessing linear time to the judgement of posterity.* See A.D. Smith (1991b).

3   For an analysis that emphasizes these other dimensions, see Fishman (1980). There is, of course, a vital difference between Bhabha and Anderson: the former only adumbrates a sociological background (immigration, colonialism, etc.) whereas the latter attempts to situate his analysis of narrative and text within a historical and sociological framework (print-capitalism, administrative languages, Protestantism,

reading publics, linear time). Nevertheless, the popularity of the concept of 'imagined community' has severed it from its Andersonian moorings: the nation is reduced to the narrative dimension and causal analysis is treated as supplementary or redundant.

4   This is also what for Renan qualifies the voluntarism and presentism of the nation. The nation may be a continuous plebiscite of its members, but it is one based on shared memories: of joys and sorrows, victories and defeats, and of heroic sacrifices, for the community *in the past*. It is not simply about state-creation, and nationalism presupposes the community (*ethnie*, nation) which it aspires to liberate or strengthen (Renan, 1882).

5   Gellner's later (1983) account is generally more materialist and determinist. It also transfers the integrative emphasis from language as such to state-supervised, standardized, mass, public education. It is, if anything, more abstract, in that the drama is largely confined to the globally inexorable transition from wild 'low' to garden 'high' cultures - or nations.

6   In fact, there is little interest in 'national identity' *per se* in modernist accounts, except Anderson - and Karl Deutsch (1953). Deutsch did advance an analysis of national identities or 'nationalities' as the product of social communications and ethnic complementarity. In this he was foreshadowed by Florian Znaniecki (1952) who regarded nationalities as sociological culture communities. In all these analyses, language ties are crucial. The problem arises where the nation and its collective identity is not, and cannot be, defined by language (See Edwards 1985, ch. 2).

7   Of course, there are considerable differences in approach between Armstrong and A.D. Smith, notably over the historical periodization of nations and the types and transformations of *ethnies*. But what is important here is the commonality of their approach in terms of the constituents of ethnic and national identity: the emphasis on the ethno-symbolic components of collective cultural identities, and the need to explore these over the *longue duree* (See Armstrong, 1992).

8   For a formal definition of the concept of 'nationalism' as an *ideological movement to attain and maintain autonomy, unity and identity on behalf of a human population deemed by some of its members to constitute an actual or potential 'nation'*, see A.D. Smith (1973, section I) and (1991a, ch. 4). The basic concept here is that of 'nation', conceived as a *named human population occupying an historic homeland and sharing myths and memories, a common public culture, a single economy and equal legal rights and duties for members*. On it depend, logically, both the concept of nationalism and that of 'national identity' as defined here. See Connor (1978) for the terminological issues.

9   The move from sociological to normative modes of analysis is very prevalent in the study of nationalism and national identity. The subject is still not studied as a set of neutral social phenomena possessing an intrinsic social and political interest, like social mobility or state formation. Hence, it is necessary to engage with this normative interest, which undoubtedly colours the main thrust of the sociological analysis. Given the current public and media interest in ethnic conflict and nationalism, there is considerable pressure on scholars to make this transition in their discourse. For critiques of ethnic, civic and plural modes of national identification, see Breton (1988); A.D. Smith (1995a, ch. 4).

References

Anderson, B. (1983), *Imagined Communities: Reflections on the Origins and Spread of Nationalism*, Verso Books, London.

Armstrong, J. (1982), *Nations before Nationalism*, University of North Carolina Press, Chapel Hill.

Armstrong, J. (1992), 'The Autonomy of Ethnic Identity: Historic Cleavages and Nationality Relations in the USSR', in A. Motyl (ed.), *Thinking Theoretically about Soviet Nationalities: History and Comparison in the Study of the USSR*, Columbia University Press, New York.

Berlin, I. (1976), *Vico and Herder*, Hogarth Press, London.

Bhabha, H. (1990) (ed.), *Nation and Narration*, Routledge, London, New York.

Brass, P. (1991), *Ethnicity and Nationalism*, Sage, London.

Breton, R. (1988), 'From Ethnic to Civic Nationalism: English Canada and Quebec', *Ethnic and Racial Studies*, vol. II, no. 1.

Breuilly, J. (1982), *Nationalism and the State*, Manchester University Press, Manchester.

Campbell, J. and Sherrard, P. (1968), *Modern Greece*, Benn, London.

Citron, S. (1988), *Le Mythe National*, Presses Ouvriers, Paris.

Cobban, A. (1964), *Rousseau and the Modern State*, Allen and Unwin, London.

Connor, W. (1978), 'A Nation is a Nation, is a State, is an Ethnic group, is a...', *Ethnic and Racial Studies*, vol. 1, no. 4.

Connor, W. (1984), 'Eco- or Ethno-Nationalism?', *Ethnic and Racial Studies*, vol. 7, no. 3.

Connor, W. (1993), 'Beyond Reason: The Nature of the Ethnonational Bond', *Ethnic and Racial Studies*, vol. 16, no. 3.

Deutsch, K. (1966), *Nationalism and Social Communications*, MIT Press, New York.

Edwards, J. (1985), *Language, Society and Identity*, Basil Blackwell, Oxford.

Eriksen, T. (1993), *Ethnicity and Nationalism*, Pluto Press, London.

Fahrni, D. (1983), *An Outline History of Switzerland*, Pro Helvetia. Arts Council of Switzerland, Zurich.

Fishman, J. (1980), 'Social Theory and Ethnography: Neglected Perspectives on Language and Ethnicity in Eastern Europe', in P. Sugar, (ed.), *Ethnic Diversity and Conflict in Eastern Europe*, ABC-Clio, Santa Barbara.

Gans, H. (1979), 'Symbolic ethnicity', *Ethnic and Racial Studies*, vol. 2, no. 1.

Gellner, E. (1964), *Thought and Change*, Weidenfeld and Nicolson, London.

Gellner, E. (1983), *Nations and Nationalism*, Basil Blackwell, Oxford.

Glazer, N. and Moynihan, D. (1975) (eds.), *Ethnicity: Theory and Experience*, Harvard University Press, Cambridge, Massachusetts.

Greenfeld, L. (1992), *Nationalism: Five Roads to Modernity*, Harvard University Press, Cambridge, Massachusetts.

Harris, H. (1995) (ed.), *Identity*, Oxford University Press, London.

Hobsbawm, E. and Ranger, T. (1983) (eds.), *The Invention of Tradition*, Cambridge University Press, Cambridge, Massachusetts.

Hroch, M. (1985), *Social Preconditions of National Revival in Europe*, Cambridge University Press, Cambridge, Massachusetts.

Ignatieff, M. (1993), *Blood and Belonging: Journeys into the New Nationalisms*, Chatto and Windus, London.

Im Hof, U. (1991), *Mythos Schweiz*, Verlag Neue Zurcher Zeitung, Zurich.

Juergensmeyer, M. (1993), *The New Cold War? Religious Nationalism Confronts the Secular State*, The University of California Press, Berkeley.

Kedourie, E. (1971) (ed.), *Nationalism in Asia and Africa*, Weidenfeld and Nicolson, London.

Kedward, R. (1965) (ed.), *The Dreyfus Affair*, Longman, London.

Kemilainen, A. (1964), *Nationalism, Problems Concerning the Word, Concept and Classification*, Kustantajat Publishers, Yvaskyla.

Kitromilides, P. (1989), 'Imagined Communities and the Origins of the National Question in the Balkans', *European History Quarterly*, vol. 19, no. 2.

Kohn, H. (n.d.), *Nationalism and Liberty: The Swiss Example*, Macmillan, London.

Kohn, H. (1967), *The Idea of Nationalism*, Macmillan, New York.

Kreis, J. (1991), *Der Mythos von 1291: Zur Enstehung des Schweizerischen Nationalfeiertags*, Friedrich Reinhardt Verlag, Basel.

Lartichaux, J.Y. (1977), 'Linguistic Politics during the French Revolution', *Diogenes* 97.

Macmillan, D. (1986), *Painting in Scotland: The Golden Age*, Phaidon Press, Oxford.

McCulley, B.T. (1966), *English Education and the Origins of Indian Nationalism*, Smith, Gloucester, Massachusetts.

McNeill, W. (1986), *Polyethnicity and National Unity in World History*, University of Toronto Press, Toronto.

Okamura, J. (1981), 'Situational Ethnicity', *Ethnic and Racial Studies*, vol. 4, no. 4.

Peel, J. (1989), 'The Cultural Work of Yoruba Ethnogenesis', in E. Tonkin, M. McDonald and M. Chapman (eds), *History and Ethnicity*, ASA Monograph 27, Routledge, London.

Poliakov, L. (1974), *The Aryan Myth*, Basic Books, New York.

Porter, J. (1975), 'Ethnic Pluralism in Canadian Perspective', in N. Glazer and D. Moynihan (eds), *Ethnicity: Theory and Experience*, Harvard University Press, Cambridge, Massachusetts.

Renan, E. (1882), *Qu'est-ce qu'une Nation?*, Calmann-Levy, Paris.

Robinson, F. (1979), 'Islam and Muslim Separatism' in D. Taylor and M. Yapp (eds) *Political Identity in South Asia*, SOAS, Curzon Press, London.

Seton-Watson, H. (1977), *Nations and States*, Methuen, London.

Smith, A.D. (1973), *Nationalism, A Trend Report and Annotated Bibliography*, *Current Sociology*, vol. 21, no. 3, Mouton, The Hague.

Smith, A.D. (1986), *The Ethnic Origins of Nations*, Basil Blackwell, Oxford.

Smith, A.D. (1989), 'The Origins of Nations', *Ethnic and Racial Studies*, vol. 12, no. 3.

Smith, A.D. (1990), 'The Supersession of Nationalism?', *International Journal of Comparative Sociology*, vol. XXXI, no. 1-2.

Smith, A.D. (1991a), *National Identity*, Penguin, London.

Smith, A.D. (1991b), 'The Nation: Invented, Imagined, Reconstructed?', *Millennium, Journal of International Studies*, vol. 20, no. 3.

Smith, A.D. (1995a), *Nations and Nationalism in a Global Era*, Polity Press, Cambridge.

Smith, A.D. (1995b), 'Gastronomy or Geology? The Role of Nationalism in the Formation of Nations', *Nations and Nationalism*, vol. I, no. 1.

Steinberg, J. (1976), *Why Switzerland?*, Cambridge University Press, Cambridge.

Thurer, G. (1970), *Free and Swiss*, Oswald Wolff, London.

Tonkin, E., McDonald, M. and Chapman, M. (1989) (eds), *History and Ethnicity*, ASA Monograph 27, Routledge, London.

Tuveson, E.L. (1968), *Redeemer Nation: The Idea of America's Millennial Role,* University of Chicago Press, Chicago, London.

Weber, E. (1979), *Peasants into Frenchmen: The Modernisation of Rural France, 1870-1914*, Chatto and Windus, London.

Znaniecki, F. (1952), *Modern Nationalities*, University of Illinois Press, Urbana, Illinos.

3 Theories of National Personality Revisited: Anglo-American Models and French Conceptions

PHILIPPE CLARET

In France since the late nineteenth century and in the Anglo-Saxon world, especially in the United States since the Second World War, there have been substantial theoretical developments in the concept of national personality, which is a legacy of the old idea of the character of peoples. These developments involve cultural anthropology as well as social psychology, political psychology, the psychology of peoples and ethnopsychology, political sociology and the history and sociology of international relations. The studies in question are neither literary, nor journalistic, nor ideological (nationalist or racist). They are based on the hypothesis that there is a general psychological and/or cultural configuration within each national society that might explain similarities in individual behaviour during a given period, and the persistence, over long periods of time, of some collective behaviours.

This is not a new hypothesis. It corresponds to an old idea whereby the properties of a personality or individual are transposed to human communities, i.e. the time-honoured idea of the psychological and cultural specificity of peoples. Applied to modern national societies considered as general psycho-social units, this idea is no longer restricted to cataloguing the distinctive traits specific to each national grouping, but attempts to identify a general configuration or structure whereby this set of traits is coherently organized and aggregated. In other words, this hypothesis postulates the existence within national groups of distinctive psychological and/or cultural characteristics and their organization in theoretical models with the power to influence both individual and collective behaviour and institutional structures, and even to modify their development. It is a reflection of the effort made by the modern social sciences to give a scientific basis to the old question of 'national character'.[1]

The idea of national personality implies the existence of distinctive characteristics - whose type needs to be specified - which pertain not to an individual but to an entire human group, in this case a national group within the framework of a State. It also implies the existence of a kind of common matrix that is inherent in all the group's attitudes and cultural productions and ensures consistency of behaviour and the persistence of distinctive national features. The concept of national personality thus rests on the basic premise of an invariant (or relatively so) structure of national distinctiveness and subsumes the idea of an existential singularity specific to the form of general society found in modern nations. The underlying implications of this concept must thus be distinguished from those subtending more recent psycho-sociological studies on the theme of national identity.

Studies of national personality endeavour to deduce, from the cultural manifestations of a national group, a specific cultural and/or psychological stock. Consequently, the theories developed in this field propose, in line with their different conceptions, a substantialist definition of the national personality concept: national characteristics are here seen as the product of factors that are distinctive and singular. From this standpoint, national personality is basically considered as an objectifiable reality. In theoretical studies it is thus presented as a model constructed objectively, mainly via investigation of the national group's cultural products, but also via its collective representations.

Work on the theme of national identity, stemming from psycho-sociological research into the concept of social identity, proceeds from a different approach. Research focuses on perception by individuals of their social - in this case national - allegiance, and then on their methods of structuring their nation-oriented psycho-social references. National identity is perceived as a subjective reality or, more exactly, as a process of identification with a complex social reality. It is considered as a specific form of collective identity experienced by individuals within the framework of a nation-state.

This fundamental distinction between the concepts of national personality and national identity originated in a theoretical contrast strongly emphasized by psycho-sociologists between the concepts of 'ethnic personality' and 'ethnic identity'. The former, as Edmond Marc-Lipiansky explains, may be defined as 'a conceptual pattern constructed via inductive generalizations based on specific data' (G. Devereux) or as directly or indirectly observable behaviours. The latter stems from 'a premise of existence, an impulse of allegiance, an awareness of a sense of belonging: it has taxonomic value.'[2] These two analytical approaches are in fact complementary insofar as collective personality and identity overlap in practice: a group's objective personality is given unconscious expression in the observable behaviour of its members and is experienced subjectively by each of them; conversely, subjective identity takes its bearings from the group's behavioural and attitudinal norms. There is thus a 'dynamic complementarity' (E. Marc-Lipiansky) between the concepts of subjective identity and objective personality. But the distinction between the two concepts remains fundamental.

As a matter of fact, the concept of national personality has no theoretical substance in itself: it is a general research hypothesis which lends itself to many theoretical formulations and methodological approaches. Its content is entirely determined by researchers' conceptions about the nature of collective personality and, more specifically, by two dominant conceptions of culture-society relations: firstly, the culturalist paradigm developed by the Anglo-American school via the 'national character' and 'political culture' models; secondly, the psychological orientation current in the French school using concepts like 'national temperament' (psycho-geographical approach), national 'ethnotype' (characterological and ethnopsychological approaches), 'national mentality' (psycho-historical approach) and studies on 'national images' (imagological approach).

I. Modern Research into National Personality: Formation and Development

The Anglo-American theory of 'national character' is regarded in the modern social sciences as the first comprehensive scientific theory about the collective personality hypothesis applied to national societies. It derives from an attempt to make a systematic analysis of the formative processes of characteristic national traits, integrating all the constituent factors of national personality. It reflects the determination of a generation of anthropologists, the American culturalists, to apply psycho-cultural research hypotheses to modern national societies in order to isolate the personality traits characteristic of the cultures of the great nation-states, especially those involved in military operations in the Second World War. A change in study subject in the culturalist area of work thus led to the implementation in the United States in the early 1940s of a collective scientific endeavour, in close collaboration with specialists in social psychology, by a truly interdisciplinary school, the modern school of national character, of which Margaret Mead was the instigator and subsequently the leader.

The influence of the cultural anthropologists was decisive in the emergence and formation of the modern theory of national character. The American culturalists rose to the challenge, turning their investigations to complex rather than primitive societies and moving into a field of study hitherto occupied by sociologists, whose concern for the specific and whose taste for empirical observation they shared. This research field also owed its range and success to the large-scale mobilization of Anglo-American researchers, the scope of study programmes, excellent organization of research, and the determination of authors to promote a 'science of national character' (O. Klineberg, 1944) designed to encourage psychological action at both individual and collective level, this being harnessed, after the war, to serve ideals of peace and development.

In 1960s and 1970s America, new scientific developments in research into national personality in complex societies took place via sociologically and psychologically oriented studies on national political cultures. The determination of some American political scientists to introduce into their field a new approach with a strong culturalist flavour is the reason for the existence during this period of a research school focusing on the concept of national political culture. Culturalist analysis in political science was introduced and developed by the political culture school headed by Gabriel Almond, Lucien Pye and Sidney Verba, which emerged from post-1930s developments in culturalist research in the social sciences in the Anglo-American world, especially research on national character in modern societies. The orientation and research methods of the culturalist school in political science revitalized scientific study of the national personality hypothesis, developing a theoretical 'political culture' model and giving rise to a series of research studies into national political cultures.

In twentieth century France, there have been a number of scientific developments of the national personality hypothesis, mainly during the post-war period. This is not, however, a research movement comparable to that which developed during the same period in the United States. France has not seen the development of a research dynamic bringing social scientists together around a common set of problems and giving rise to an interdisciplinary scientific school, but scattered pockets of research. The relative degree of compartmentalization between the different approaches and the lack of co-operation between researchers are particularly noticeable. This situation is fully consonant with the endemic state of the French social sciences, which show the imprint of a centralizing, mandatory model of teaching and research, and longstanding habits of compartmentalization between disciplines. In France, the constitution of a research school is widely regarded as the official embodiment of an established scientific position or sometimes even as the crowning point of a personal body of scientific work rather than as the formal embodiment of an intellectual dynamic centring on an original project backed up by substantial practical resources (public or private). In France personal commitment and intellectual enthusiasm on the part of researchers seem less important, reflecting the smaller and far less frequent demands made on scientific producers by society as a whole and its leaders.

In France, the first significant developments in the scientific study of the collective personality of nations date from the beginning of the century, with work on political psychology, notably by André Siegfried, which, though still somewhat literary in flavour, was a far cry from the many purely literary studies produced at that time. This line of study really developed after the Second World War, in a more or less synchronized way and from somewhat different viewpoints, mainly under the aegis of the *'Institut Havrais de Psychologie des Peuples'*, headed from 1938 to 1970 by Abel Miroglio (A. Miroglio, 1978). Quantitatively speaking, the Institute produced the largest research output in France on the psychology of national societies and the concept of national character and, from a scientific point of view, was clearly in the forefront in this field; other contributions came from work on social psychology by Jean Stoetzel, who introduced into France the American statistical approach to national character (Klineberg, 1981), and from work on the history of contemporary international relations directed by Pierre Renouvin and by Jean-Baptiste Duroselle, on the theme of national mentalities.

So in France, unlike the United States, no fully fledged scientific schools existed bringing together researchers from different backgrounds in a pluridisciplinary setting; instead, several approaches developed more or less autonomously, in most cases without any attempt to construct a model for theoretical analysis. These approaches developed within a variety of disciplines and each had an original research slant on the national personality hypothesis, with some distinctive socio-historical developments. Approaches in this field of research all share an essentially psychological orientation.

II. Theories of National Personality: Schools and Research Orientations

All research in the social sciences bears the imprint of a dominant theoretical thrust, a unity of thought which governs the selection, re-examination and re-interpretation of conceptual inputs from different theoretical traditions. So it is appropriate to outline at this point the guiding principles which may, taken as a whole, give an account of modern research into national personality carried out in parallel by the 'Anglo-American School' and the 'French School' (these expressions are used here to designate, in a general way, all the schools and currents of thought developed in the United States and in France respectively).

The Anglo-American School clearly differs from the French School in being entirely oriented by a conceptual system, amounting to a research paradigm, which forms the theoretical core of the studies it has carried out on national personality. The roots of this theoretical core of Anglo-American research into national character and political culture are to be found in the intellectual context of American cultural anthropology. Anglo-American analysis of the personality of modern nation-states is based on the psycho-cultural hypothesis of the collective personality, developed by American culturalist thinkers. The culturalist account of personality is central to modern theories of national character and national political culture. In line with this, the Anglo-American school of national personality gives weight to the study of psycho-cultural processes in national cultures.

By placing the concept of personality at the centre of anthropological analysis, the culturalists - the 'Culture-and-Personality' school - made a decisive shift from the study of culture to the study of cultural personality and developed an original theory of the relationship between personality and culture. The culturalist paradigm is an original synthesis of the two basic methods of studying personality (the anthropological approach to collective personality and the psychoanalytical approach to individual personality) and establishes the idea that, through the psycho-cultural personality, society produces culture and the social becomes cultural.

The cultural personality phenomenon is thus at the heart of culturalist theory. The main problem the culturalists look at is the individual's identification with the community to which he/she belongs. The central process they study is how a society's members internalize the society's specific cultural models. They thus look for a scientific explanation of relations between individuals and culture, between individuals and society. By making the concept of personality the nub of anthropological explanation, culturalist theory adopts a dual approach: an anthropological approach to culture and a psycho-cultural approach to personality. Culturalist thought is essentially an attempt to arrive at a holistic interpretation of the collective personality of human groups by focusing on a study of the cultural differences between societies, and mechanisms of individual socialization.

The scientific roots of the Anglo-American School of national personality lie in the psycho-cultural theory of personality developed by American anthropologists during the 1930s. The concept of 'national' character emerged directly from this, and its formulators (Ruth Benedict, Margaret Mead, Abram Kardiner, and Ralph Linton) were also responsible for the culturalist theory of personality. The intellectual and bibliographical references of the initiators of the concept of national political culture (G.A. Almond, S. Verba, and L. Pye) provide clear and abundant evidence of the same roots. The Anglo-American schools of national character and political culture thus took their cue from the same research paradigm, the culturalist paradigm.

The French school was less concerned to develop theoretical models and less conceptually united than the Anglo-American school. It developed without reference to a real system of thought and encountered important theoretical obstacles in winning recognition for its research hypothesis and in finding its place in the French social sciences. Most research carried out in France during the twentieth century on the concept of national personality has been based on a psychological approach to national cultures. This approach is rooted in a tradition of study found in the great eighteenth century political works (Montesqiueu and Tocqueville) which emphasizes analysis of psychological factors in collective phenomena. Though it was returned to and developed during the last third of the nineteenth century by E. Boutmy, A. Fouillée, G. Le Bon and others, this line of study never formed a structured, homogeneous current of thought in the social sciences in France; it was definitely more in the nature of a theoretical trend than a true research paradigm.

Collective psychology studies the mental processes at work in different kinds of human groups: its goal is to study the mental life specific to each of these groups. The fundamental idea, which subsequently became commonplace, is that the social group is distinct in character from the individuals of which it is composed and that consequently its psychology should be studied *sui generis*. This brings us to the premise underlying all studies of collective psychology: the belief that in all social groups there is a collective psychological being, a 'collective soul' which can explain all the group's collective reactions and behaviours. This assertion of the individuality of human groups is, basically, merely the application to society of the idea that the whole is more than the sum of its parts.

French specialists in ethnopsychology, and all the authors associated with this field of research, study the character of peoples, especially of national populations. They are all concerned with the study of human communities, not of their cultures. This is a fundamental aspect of this research, differentiating it from Anglo-American culturalist research into primitive societies and complex societies. The French conception of ethnopsychology is concerned with the study of peoples not of cultures, analysing underlying collective personality rather than a population's general cultural configuration. Unlike cultural anthropology, which focuses exclusively on a people's culture, French ethnopsychology gives priority to the study of the people who vehicle a culture (or even several cultures).

There is therefore a clear-cut distinction between the Anglo-American and French schools in their conception of the hypothesis of the collective personality of peoples and in the attitudes of researchers in this field. American culturalists regard national personality as, ultimately, the product of society's 'primary institutions' (family, custom, education, etc.). French specialists in collective psychology regard it as basically the product of 'ethnic character' or the 'collective mentality'. The American culturalist conception of the relationship between individuals and society makes for a dynamic vision of social progress. Acting upon processes of human socialization is regarded as the key factor in the change and transformation of societies, especially national societies. For this reason, Anglo-American specialists in the study of cultures became involved in public activities, being commissioned by their governments and by various international institutions to respond to world problems and issues. French thinking, on the other hand, is imbued to various degrees by a somewhat determinist picture of social processes. Though its authors readily admit that the culture and civilization of a human group largely ensue from the 'ethnopsychological stock' or from the 'core of collective personality' (A. Miroglio, 1971). It is regarded as something almost impossible that effective action might be taken to transform or modify national behaviour.

III. Anglo-American Psycho-Cultural Models: From General Culture to National Culture

Anglo-American theories of national personality are organized around two basic theoretical models: national character and political culture. Though they are outgrowths of the same research paradigm, they are linked to two different fields of study, one centring on analysis of the general social culture, the other on analysis of the general political culture. The central national character model closely correlates with a hypothetical general psycho-cultural structure specific to a national population. The model derived from national political culture, which largely proceeds from the same theoretical orientation, modifies the field of application of the psycho-cultural hypothesis, restricting it to the political aspects of the general culture. The transition from the general social culture to the political sub-culture, i.e. from the general social system to a particular sub-system, indubitably reflects a narrowing of vision when compared with early American culturalist research into complex modern societies. Furthermore, this transition goes hand in hand with a significant change in methods of investigating and analysing national cultures.

A. National Character and General Culture

The central national character model is the product of work in two lines of study with different theoretical contexts: on the one hand the anthropological or psycho-anthropological approach practised by specialists in cultural anthropology and culturalist psychoanalysis (mainly G. Bateson, R. Benedict, E. Fromm, G. Gorer, A. Kardiner, R. Linton and M. Mead); on the other, the psychological or psycho-sociological approach of specialists in social psychology and psycho-sociology (in particular M.L. Farber, A. Inkeles, O. Klineberg, D. Levinson and D. Riesman).

1. The Psycho-Anthropological Approach

The central idea of the psycho-anthropological approach practised by cultural anthropologists and culturalist psychoanalysts of the Margaret Mead school is that each national culture is linked to an original collective personality or a 'typical personality' (M. Singer, 1961), whose different strands to some extent mould the personality of each of its members. The two main premises of this analytical approach are the integration of national culture and the coherence of the different strands of the national personality. The psycho-anthropological approach to national character is thus a comprehensive, 'organic' approach (J. D. Singer, 1968).

From this standpoint, the concept of national character is basically defined as a structured body of collective personality traits, a basic personality, a kind of common matrix which governs the national group's attitudes, opinions, behaviour and cultural values by moulding the individual personality of each of its members. However, this general definition of the concept of national character encompasses two different conceptions and theoretical models - anthropological and psychoanalytical - produced by the two analytical processes current in the psycho-anthropological wing of the Anglo-American school.

The Anthropological Model: Cultural Character. The cultural anthropologists (Ruth Benedict, Margaret Mead, Gregory Bateson, Geoffrey Gorer) define national character as 'cultural character', by which they mean a cultural configuration, the dominant personality in the national group. The concept of cultural character came out of work by cultural anthropologists on personality in primitive societies and was used as a theoretical model in anthropological research into national character in complex modern societies. It is to some extent a synthesis of the two most important culturalist theories, Ruth Benedict's configuration theory and Abram Kardiner and Ralph Linton's basic personality theory. According to the former, all societies consist of an aggregate configuration, a whole dominated by a general pattern. The latter theory maintains that all societies are characterized by an enduring constellation of psychological traits reflecting the way in which adaptation to the natural surroundings has taken place and the type of education received.

For Margaret Mead, the concept of cultural character refers to a set of personality traits regularly observed in the behaviour of members of the same social unit (the modern nation in studies of national character) which together form a 'cultural character structure'. As a matter of fact, this is an abstraction, a conceptual tool used to designate the intrapsychic personality specific to a set of individuals sharing the same general culture: the national culture.

Geoffrey Gorer situates modern research into national personality in an analysis of the psycho-cultural habits and motivations shared by members of a culturally homogeneous social group. He postulates the existence of 'motivations' shared by all group members, causing each individual to react in a characteristic way. These motivations are not directly observable so they are analysed by studying observable acts of individual behaviour and types of learning and education current in the group, especially through childhood experiences. According to Geoffrey Gorer, cultural character is a structured whole rather than a sum total: it is the characteristic cultural structure specific to a national population. His analysis is therefore more an analysis of structures than of quantities, techniques of general rather than of statistical understanding.

The American anthropologist Gregory Bateson's work on the concept of national character reflects an even more original standpoint. Instead of looking for a national group's cultural character in personality traits supposedly characteristic of the group and shared by all its members, Bateson looked more closely at relations between individuals and between groups within the national group: he then deduced the cultural character specific to the group from an analysis of the forms of these relationships. Here again, the concept of national character is defined as designating a 'common character structure', but in terms of interpersonal relations rather than of personality traits. Bateson believed that the specificity of a national group's cultural character is to be sought in the proportion and combination of relational themes within it. He was the first to formulate the hypothesis of twinned roles whose distribution is specific to each social group. Differences between national characters lie in the different proportions of these relational themes and their different modes of combination.

The Psychoanalytical Model: Social Character. Moving beyond anthropological and psychological analyses of personality which reduce society to its cultural dimension or define the whole of social organization in psychological terms, the culturalist psychoanalysts of the Anglo-American national character school (Abram Kardiner, Erich Fromm) stress the importance of socio-historical factors and the role of socio-economic factors in the formation of the collective personality of societies, pointing to the links between the psycho-cultural personality and social institutions, and define national character as 'social character'. With this concept of social character, Erich Fromm's most important contribution to the culturalist theory of personality was to establish a bridge between studies of a population's character structure and studies of its social structure. This noted psychoanalyst developed the idea that the organization of each economical-social system is conducive to a certain character among the individuals within it corresponding to the behaviour, attitudes and values which the system requires for its operation and reproduction.

This line of study was taken further by culturalist sociologists, notably David Riesman, using a socio-historical approach to national character to account for processes of social change in the analysis of the collective personality of modern societies. In *The Lonely Crowd* (1950), David Riesman developed a historical theory of national personality, postulating a link between demographic structures and psycho-social structures in national populations, a correspondence between a certain form of social personality, hence of national character, and a phase of demographic development.

2. The Psycho-Sociological Approach

The research orientations of the psycho-sociological wing of the Anglo-American national character school are very different from those developed by the psycho-anthropological wing, though they too are grounded in the basic culturalist premise about personality. They centre on a different conception of personality from that developed by the psycho-anthropologists. In contrast to the holistic conception of the anthropologists and culturalist psychoanalysts, based on the hypothesis of a personality common to all the members of a national group and specific to that group, the psycho-sociologists have a statistical conception of personality based on the hypothesis of a plurality of personality traits (and cultural models) within each national group. They propose an 'aggregated-personality concept' (N. J. Smelser, 1968) which stresses the idea of a number of associated personality traits.

In point of fact, psycho-sociological analysis of national character is based on a two-fronted approach. In psycho-sociological terms, the personality of a social group can be observed from two standpoints, as object and as subject, as a social fact and as a social representation. On the one hand the objective aspect, perceived as a factor in a sure and relatively stable existence; on the other, the subjective aspect, the reflection of a social reality. The psycho-sociologist can thus locate personality both in a set of attitudes and behaviours specific to the group being studied, and as a subjective reality, in the awareness of individuals belonging to the group, expressing themselves via images and social stereotypes. This dual psycho-sociological viewpoint leads authors to construct two models for the statistical analysis of national character: an objective model, the 'modal personality' and a subjective model, 'national stereotypes'.

The Objective Model: Modal Personality. The concept of modal personality defined by Alex Inkeles and Daniel J. Levinson is the basis for the psycho-sociological definition of the objective concept of national personality. Here the study of national character mainly involves studying the regularity of appearance of certain personality traits in individual behaviour within a national group; this requires the use of techniques for studying broad samples of individuals, especially polls and surveys. The psycho-sociological conception of national character thus seeks to grasp the personality of the national group directly and objectively via analysis of individual behaviour, unlike the psycho-anthropological approach which analyses collective behaviour and cultural models, and usually concedes primary importance to observation and analysis of collective data (collective documents, cultural and social products). In contrast, the psycho-sociological approach to objective manifestations of national character (the objective national personality) relies essentially on observation and analysis of individual data taken from opinion polls and surveys usually covering broad representative samples of individuals. Psycho-sociological analysis of national personality thus situates differences in national character between one complex society and another not in the presence or absence of personality traits deemed to be specific to one or another national group, but in the different breakdowns of basic personality traits between national groups. Each national group is distinguished by a specific breakdown of these basic traits.

The Subjective Model: National Stereotypes. Analysis of national personality as a social representation involves studying national images and stereotypes. Initially based on a solid set of theoretical and methodological studies, this field of research made considerable headway in the early 1940s and during the 1950s and 1960s, partly because of the emergence and development of new methods of psycho-sociological investigation, but mainly because of the attention it attracted during the Second World War from the military and civilian authorities on the grounds of its potential practical applications and, after 1945, from the large international organizations, in particular UNESCO.

National stereotypes and images are collective mental representations relating to national groups, expressed in the form of verbal clichés and stereotyped judgements. They are the widely accepted and shared beliefs and opinions that each national group has about itself (inner-stereotypes) and about other national groups (outer-stereotypes). These mental representations are a vitally important psychological reality which exercises a decisive influence on relations between peoples and on the behaviour of each national group. Otto Klineberg believed that these stereotypes should be 'processed' and efficient ways found to combat the tendency to think in stereotypes, in particular via the education of young people. The instigators of the scientific study of national stereotypes believed that it could be used therapeutically in international conflicts, improving awareness and understanding between peoples. Numerous methods have been used in this field, drawing on the full spectrum of social psychology's experimental techniques: statistical analyses made on the basis of opinion polls, personality tests and interviews, content analyses of cultural products (literature, journalism, films, etc.). The methods used are tailored to the kind of stereotype being studied. Researchers use content analysis techniques to study collective stereotypes diffused by the media. To study individual stereotypes as vehicled and expressed by group members, three main methods are available: lists of qualifiers, correlations and semantic fields.

B. The Politological Model: National Political Culture

The model derived from national political culture was constructed through the determination of a generation of sociologists and political scientists, especially Gabriel Almond, Lucien Pye and Sidney Verba, who wished to reformulate hypotheses of psycho-cultural research into national personality on a more rigorous basis and within a more restricted field of study, under the influence of developmentalist and functionalist theories that were current in American political science in the 1950s and 1960s. The basic premise of the Anglo-American political culture school is that there is a national political personality which is capable of furnishing an ongoing, determining explanation for each national community, the singularity of its structure, attitudes and political behaviour.

In 1956 Gabriel Almond introduced the concept of political culture in the context of a functional analysis of the national political system. Its starting point was that the political system is made up of a political structure and a political culture. The basic idea is that political structure alone cannot explain how a political system functions; it is the political culture that gives meaning to the system. Almond therefore put forward the hypothesis of a political culture distinct from the general social culture (though linked to it), which he defined as a set of attitudes and orientations towards the political system. Gabriel Almond and the American school see the national political culture as fulfilling the vital function of ensuring the durability, regulation and reproduction of the national political system. In line with the dominant theoretical orientations of the period, whereby a study of the political system's maintenance mechanisms establishes a close link between culture and socialization, political socialization is regarded as a mechanism for the inculcation and transmission of political culture. Individuals internalize values, attitudes and orientations towards the political system via socialization processes.

The political culture theory fulfils the need felt by political science in the United States to establish a bridge between two levels of analysis: the micro-political level based on a psychological interpretation of the political behaviour of individuals, and the macro-political level based on a sociological interpretation of collective behaviour. In the Anglo-American school's founding texts, the political culture concept is presented as the link between micro and macro politics, i.e. as an approach to the same research objective combining study of the behaviour and dynamics of the political system itself and of the individuals living within the system. The political culture theory may therefore be regarded as both a micro-political theory based on observation and analysis of individual attitudes and as a macro-political theory involving study of the collective characteristics of very large social units.

The concept of political culture thus serves to designate the way in which a political system is internalized by a population via its beliefs, feelings and perceptions. It corresponds to a set of dominant opinions and attitudes that are relatively stable and empirically observable within a nation. In this context, a society's political culture is seen as a set of psychological orientations whose function is to ensure the integration of its members into the political system. By adopting, after Almond and Verba, this essentially psychological conception of culture, the Anglo-American school of political culture definitely moved away from the culturalist approach to this concept. More specifically, it used reductively the concept of culture as formulated and developed by the American culturalist school, for whom culture, generally speaking, means ways of living in a society, learnt and transmitted via social processes. The culturalist analysis made by political scientists thus tends to focus on the political attitudes of individuals observed within the framework of national political systems and to explain these attitudes in terms of cultural models.

Gabriel A. Almond and Sidney Verba, the authors of *The Civic Culture* (1963), distinguished three main types of political culture: parochial political culture, subject political culture and participant political culture, which each correspond to a particular type of political attitudes, i.e. a set of reactions or dispositions toward political objects. Each type of political culture is characterized by a dominant type of relationship between citizens and their political system. Almond and Verba saw these three types of political culture as ideal types (in the Weberian sense of the term). They are analytical models designed to permit a statistical and comparative approach to the political aspects of national cultures. Nevertheless, according to these authors, there is a general correspondence between types of political culture and the political structures observed by constitutionalists. Each type of political culture is associated with a type of political structure: parochial culture with a traditional decentralized structure, subject culture with an authoritarian, centralized structure, and participant culture with a pluralist democratic structure.

According to Almond and Verba, the national political cultures observable in reality do not coincide with one or another of the three types of political culture portrayed, i.e. parochial, subject and participant. Analysis reveals them to be composite cultures combining elements from each of the three models, to different degrees. Each national political culture is defined as a 'mixed' political culture incorporating a specific proportion of elements from the three models. Each national political system thus relates to the political culture models in a specific way. For the researcher, all observable national societies consist of different possible combinations of types of political culture, which must be deciphered and explained.

Here, the difference between the analytical model of political culture and certain other theoretical models of national personality, especially psycho-anthropological models of national character, is clearly apparent. The latter are based on the premise of cultural homogeneity within societies, whilst the former reflect the heterogeneity and cultural diversity of such societies. Almond and Verba believe that the cultural 'mix' characteristic of the general political culture is observable at individual as well as at collective level. In complex modern societies each member's political culture is considered as an original 'constellation' of parochial, subject and participant-type attitudes. Similarly, general or national political culture is perceived as a distinctive assemblage of parochial, subject and participant 'political sub-cultures'. What we have here, in the restricted field of the study of political phenomena, is a return to a hypothesis formulated in 1954 by Alex Inkeles and Daniel Levinson: the concept of modal personality, i.e. a definition of national personality based on a specific incidence of breakdown of general cultural traits.

IV. French Psychological Conceptions: The Ethnic Personality and the Cultural Personality of Nations

French psychological conceptions of national personality do not, on the whole, show the same coherence and theoretical substance as Anglo-American culturalist models. The proliferation of concepts in this field merely reflects the multiplicity or, more exactly, the juxtaposition of approaches. These approaches, unlike the Anglo-American theories, focus much more on the study of populations (especially national populations) than on the analysis of cultures (especially general national cultures). Their roots lie in the same analytical orientation, collective psychology, and they share an idea of a relatively enduring collective psychological structure, a 'stable irreducible psychological residue' (G. Bouthoul, 1981) specific to each society. Though there are differences and nuances between them, these conceptions share a 'basic psychological preoccupation' (A. Miroglio, 1971). They can be divided into two categories - fundamental approaches and complementary approaches - on the basis of the type of data they use, their theoretical premises and their respective importance in the development of research on this topic in France since the beginning of the century. Fundamental approaches focus on analysis of ethnic data and study the ethnic infrastructure of human groups, especially national groups. Complementary approaches focus on analysis of cultural data and examine the mental structures of peoples.

A. Fundamental Approaches

Fundamental approaches, developed around the core concept of ethnic personality, look for an explanation of the collective personality of peoples in an analysis of their ethnic infrastructure. They share the idea that a people can be seen as equivalent to an irreducible collective individuality, the study of which requires the specific use of concepts and methods of varying degrees of complexity. The concept of national personality designates the ethnic psychological infrastructure which pre-forms individual conduct and orientates group behaviour. Three approaches were developed successively in order to study this psychological substratum. What distinguishes them is the type of data they use about human groups in a geographical location and, most importantly, the increasing complexity of the type of analysis they practise.

1. The Psycho-Geographical Approach: National Temperament
In France, the modern psycho-geographical approach to national personality is part of a long-standing tradition of geographical interpretation of the personality of populations which emphasizes the importance of place and geographical location in the formation of the collective behaviours, mentalities and characters of human groups. Two

authors - André Siegfried and, to a lesser degree, Georges Hardy - sought to give this field of study a more scientific basis by seeking to identify correspondences rather than unilateral influences in this field, latent trends rather than clear-cut determinants. Their psycho-geographical analyses of collective personality emphasize the power of geographical influences in conditioning the formation of national, and even regional, needs, opinions and behaviours, especially regarding political matters. This approach does not, however, establish an exclusively geographical determinism, as a critical re-reading today of André Siegfried's works clearly shows.

André Siegfried's lifelong preoccupation with the political personality of nations can be seen throughout his work, from beginning to end. As early as 1913, in his *Tableau Politique de la France de l'Ouest*, he clearly expressed his intention to look beyond diversity of political temperament and isolate 'the complex personality of the nation'. In his later research into national personality, he turned his attention to other countries, mainly those of the English-speaking world. His main thesis was the enduring nature of the political temperaments of peoples. To put it to the test, he examined populations of different sizes: countries and regions, nations and vast demographic units like the Latin countries and the English-speaking peoples. He identified political temperaments of different types - regional, national and continental - the enduring nature of which he explained in terms of the effect of the geographical, historical and sociological conditions characteristic of the populations studied. 'Ethnic characterography' as developed by Siegfried consists of drawing a psychological portrait of peoples using vocabulary borrowed from the science of characterology. His most typical work is indubitably *L'âme des Peuples* (1950). But great though Siegfried's concern for objectivity and methodological rigour may have been, this approach to national personality betrays a research on psychology that is more literary than scientific.

2. The Characterological Approach: Ethnic Character

The characterological approach to national personality arose from the development in post-1945 France of scientific characterology which built on research started at the beginning of the century by Gerard Heymans and E.O.Wiersma of the Netherlands (the Groningen School). The goal of scientific characterology is to identify the 'constituent properties of human beings' via a series of relevant observations and surveys and to determine characterological types on the basis of different possible combinations of these 'properties'. Two French psychologists, René Le Senne and Paul Griéger, have devoted particular attention to the development of collective characterology, i.e., characterology applied to the study of human groups, especially nations. The hypothesis of the characterologists is that a nation's distinctive features reflect its population's character traits in line with specific modalities. As a general rule, the characterological approach to national personality consists of adjusting methods for the analysis of individual characterology to collective psychological data.

René Le Senne transposes into collective characterology the basic distinction made in individual characterology between character, which is made up of congenital dispositions, and personality, which results from a confrontation between character and historical factors. Character is analysed at the individual and collective levels as a set of predispositions to confront situations in one way or another, though the individual or group retains a degree of freedom. The characterological make-up of a people at a given moment in its history and for a longer or shorter period of time constitutes a kind of matrix determining its actions, conduct and behaviour. The percentage of different characters in the population as a whole conditions its type of behaviour. A nation's characterological formula, provided it remains constant, explains similarities in its members' conduct and reactions and also the differences between these and the conduct and reactions of other nations with different characterological make-ups.

La Caractérologie Ethnique (1961) by Paul Griéger is today unquestionably regarded as the fullest account, in France, of collective characterology. Building on the ideas of René Le Senne, Griéger endeavours to draw up a typology of the traits of characterological organization in different human populations by examining national or regional geographical areas at different periods. Griéger's basic aim was to write a theoretical work. Using an inductive approach based on the broadest possible sample of characterological traits in different populations (national and regional), he attempts to identify general types of ethnic character, i.e. regularly recurring characterological 'types of organization' which are presented as 'veritable structural laws' in the ongoing evolution of ethnic phenomena. The subject of Griéger's work is not so much the ethnic character of the different populations observed (national and regional) as the constitution of a general typology of ethnic characters, whose essential traits can be found among different peoples living in different historical periods.

The method described by Griéger in *La Caractérologie Ethnique* is more subtle and complex than that expounded by Le Senne in his *Traité de Caractérologie*. Essentially, it consists of identifying the character of peoples, i.e. genuine ethnotypes, not on the basis of the proportion of individual character types observed within them (the characterological recruitment method applied by René Le Senne) but on the basis of the frequency or rarity of certain characterological traits directly perceptible within each people viewed as a whole. In this perspective, the concept of the character of peoples (national or regional character) is not perceived as a kind of average character, i.e. a mean of individual character traits, but as a set of conformities within the group's institutionalized behaviours. The dominant behaviours identified by analysis are characteristic not of an individual subject but of a person as a member of a social unit, the term 'institutional French person' being then used. This conception emphasizes the socialization function of the group's 'institutional behaviour', through which individuals are put in contact with one another and with society as a whole. Paul Griéger's ethnocharacterological approach here coincides with Anglo-American theories of 'basic personality' (Abram Kardiner and Ralph Linton) and 'modal personality' (Alex Inkeles and Daniel J. Levinson).

3. The Ethnopsychological Approach: The Ethnotype

The ethnopsychological approach to collective personality is indubitably in the tradition of earlier research carried out in France into ethnic temperament and character, but goes much further in terms of methodology and the originality of its theoretical perspectives. It forms part of work placing ethnopsychological science on a formal footing which began in the early 1970s and went on for ten or more years under the direction of Guy Michaud, in the wake of Abel Miroglio's efforts to relaunch the study of the psychology of peoples in France after 1945 with the backing of a research Institute and an international scientific review - *'Revue de Psychologie des Peuples-Ethnopsychologie'* (Claret, 1996). Michaud's ethnopsychological research into the concept of collective personality (ethnic or national) fits into a far-reaching scientific project, whose theoretical building blocks he gradually put in place. The aim is to build a comprehensive model for the study of cultures and societies with a view to a 'science of civilizations', which the author attempted to present in a work written with Edmond Marc and published in 1981.

Guy Michaud makes a sharp distinction between ethnopsychology and cultural anthropology, the latter of which, in his opinion, reasons in terms of production, with primary institutions as producer and culture as product. Ethnopsychology, on the other hand, reasons in terms of creation, culture or civilization being the object created, the ethnic group or nation being the creating subject. G. Michaud thus believes that it is wrong to try to reduce a subject (ethnic group) to an object (culture) or even to try to define the former by the latter. His approach is based on structural isomorphism: on the one hand, between the author regarded as an individual subject and an ethnic group regarded as a collective subject; on the other, between a work regarded as a message-object (literary or artistic) and a civilization, i.e., a set of substantial or non-substantial manifestations, perceived as observable objects. In the systemic chart G. Michaud devised for the analysis of a society as a whole, he locates the community (ethnic group or nation) as the creating collective subject at the centre of the societal system. Similarly, in his 'model for the study of civilizations', he places collective personality (the ethnotype) at the centre of the schematic representation of the social body.

The ethnopsychological approach to national personality has given rise to a genuine theoretical model for the analysis of collective personality phenomena. It is a comprehensive, complex model which fits into genuinely interdisciplinary approaches to study, drawing directly upon the principles and procedures of systems analysis. The starting point of analysis is consideration of the ethnotype as an element in the cultural sub-system, an essential element which acts as a filter. According to G. Michaud, the ethnotype filters information in order to ensure the cultural sub-system's self-preservation in the same way as parties and pressure groups operate in the political sub-system. Following David Easton's model, G. Michaud makes a distinction between information produced by the cultural sub-system and circulating within it (withinputs) and information originating from other sub-systems or even from the extra-societal environment (inputs). As a result, the ethnotype's specific function of filtering information takes place at three levels: 1) at the primary level, within the cultural sub-system, via non-stop interplay of action and retroaction; 2) at the secondary level, in relation to other sub-systems of the general social system (the intra-societal system), from which it receives and selects information; 3) at the wider level, in relation to the extra-societal environment, i.e. other ethnic or national communities.

In the general ethnopsychological model, the ethnotype engages in two-way communication with these three levels: it reacts, but more important, it acts on each of them (outputs). Firstly, within the cultural sub-system (withoutputs) whose different components - education, information, arts and letters, sciences, philosophy and religion - it registers. Secondly, directly or indirectly, on the other sub-systems (political, economic and social). Thirdly, and more diffusely, on the other ethnic communities, and therefore on the other ethnotypes, especially via the interplay of national images. The ethnotype is thus considered as a 'filter' or 'matrix' able to generate specific kinds of conduct and behaviour. The ethnotype's internal structure is seen as the equivalent of a code, i.e. a set of rules defining real behaviour. These rules have a normative character since they guide, to a greater or lesser degree, the conduct and behaviour of group members.

B. Complementary Approaches

The complementary approaches to national personality developed in the modern French social sciences focus on analysis of the national community's mental structures rather than its ethnic substratum. Though the basic theoretical orientation remains the same, i.e. psychological analysis of collective behaviours, the subject of study changes: not the national group's constituent ethnopsychological basis but its mentality and collective representations; not directly observable and measurable attitudes but phenomena of mental representation, which are equally difficult to define and locate. The goal of these approaches also seems different: they do not propose an explanation for the hypothesis of collective personality at national level, but only seek to measure objectively observable manifestations of national personality in terms of phenomena of public opinion (in the broad sense of the term). They are much more concerned with the structures of cultural personality than with those of the national group's ethnic personality. Objective manifestations of the national cultural personality are analysed in two ways: firstly, as products of a mental structure specific to the national group (national mentalities hypothesis); secondly, as instances of mental representation (national images hypothesis).

1. The Psycho-Historical Approach: National Mentalities

The psycho-historical approach to the concept of national personality has emerged from recent French historical studies analysing the relationships between mentalities and international relations. This vast field of research opened up to historians of contemporary international relations after a decisive intellectual change which affected the whole French historical school. This change took place between the 1950s and the 1960s and had a far-reaching effect on the direction of research conducted by the French school of the history of international relations headed by Pierre Renouvin and Jean-Baptiste Duroselle. Traditional diplomatic history gave way to the history of mentalities applied to the study of international relations. The history of socio-cultural factors in international relations now took precedence over the narrative history of inter-State relations. For historians of international relations and historians of political ideas alike, the study of collective mentalities paves the way for an understanding of diplomatic activity and the international situation, insofar as traits of collective psychology partly determine the relationships between nations.

The basic preoccupation of the French historical school of international relations is an analysis of the relationship between politics and 'deep-rooted forces'. In this context, Pierre Renouvin and Jean-Baptiste Duroselle's seminal work *Introduction à l'Histoire des Relations Internationales* (1964) presents a framework for analysis of the deep-rooted forces influencing the foreign policy of nation-states and attempts to evaluate their respective importance. For the first time in the study of international relations, mentality became the subject of systematic study; Renouvin and Duroselle's thinking on the national personality hypothesis took place within this framework.

Through its interest in the 'deep-rooted forces' - especially collective mentalities - governing foreign policy options, the French historical school of international relations encountered, in its research into national mentalities, the hypothesis of the national collective personality. Though it has not developed a theoretical model in this field comparable to the ethnotype model that emerged from work on collective characterology and ethnopsychology, Pierre Renouvin and Jean-Baptiste Duroselle's school has sought to dovetail this hypothesis into its own lines of study, i.e. 'the deep-rooted forces/decision-making dialectic in the history of international relations' (J. Thobie, 1985), and to evaluate the influence of collective psychology on the conduct of foreign policy and the development of relations between nations. In this vein, three major theoretical contributions (R. Rémond, 1969; J.B. Duroselle, 1974 b; and P. Milza, 1980) present a general approach to phenomena of opinion and mentality in inter-State relations and attempt to construct a theoretical model of the linkage between collective mentality/general opinion and decision-making strategy. They cover the whole analytical field of concepts of national temperament and character, but do not make any really new theoretical contributions to these concepts.

2. The Imagological Approach: National Images

In post-1945 France there has been substantial development in the approach to national personality based on images, i.e. collective representations of peoples, partly due to work by specialists in comparative literature, to work on the history of mentalities and international relations, and to ethnopsychological research. The latter gave rise to imagological studies closely linked to the national personality theoretical hypothesis which have shown that one possible line of approach to the study of the personality of peoples is an analysis of their collective representations.

As a general rule, the imagological approach studies the collective representations which take root in the collective mentality and consciousness, deep in the collective personality of groups. In the field of national images, i.e. peoples' collective representations of themselves (inner-images) and of other peoples (outer-images), the gap between these images and reality seems *a priori* so wide that many people consider this field of study to be a 'science of appearances' (R. Bastide, 1966). And yet the imagological approach to national personality is based on the idea that a people's representation of itself or of another people is an objective reality different in nature from the objective reality of either of the two peoples since it springs from phenomena of collective mentality. This approach analyses national images in two ways, as a reflection of and as a pointer to a supposedly established reality, national personality: as a reflection of the personality of the people-object, the object of a collective representation, and as a pointer to the personality of the people-subject, i.e. the people issuing this representation. In this sense, national images - especially outer-images - are considered as 'providers of hypotheses about what is real' (S. Marandon, 1971).

The hypothesis of specialists in ethnic imagology is that national hetero-images (images of other peoples) always contain a 'kernel of truth'.

The character or national personality of a people (people-object) cannot, in their opinion, be reduced to the collective representations other peoples have of them (hetero-images of peoples-subjects); nevertheless this approach should be used to complement other basic approaches, in order to analyse the national psychology of peoples. The underlying idea is that national images are acceptable because they are true up to a certain point, but only relatively so.

In fact, and this is the second aspect of national hetero-images, these images may be more instructive about the personality of the people issuing them (people-subject) than about the personality of the people concerned (people-object). According to specialists in imagology, there is a causal relationship, the extent of which has yet to be determined, between the personality of a national group and the images it has of foreign peoples. S. Marandon puts forward the hypothesis of a close correlation between a specific type of national character or personality and a given category of hetero-images. This correlation, which should be understood in terms of trends, is thought to be located between two positions: on the one hand full conditioning, on the other a highly flexible link. In the former case, the author believes it would be possible to chart existing links between the personality of peoples and the group images these peoples have of other peoples: a people with a certain type of personality, a certain national ethnotype, would tend to develop a certain category of hetero-images, on the basis of the relationship existing between people-subject and peoples-objects (closeness, inferiority, hostility, etc.).

Modern theories of national personality thus divide into two broad homogeneous categories, independent of each other: on the one hand culturalist theories, on the other hand psychological theories. The former emphasizes the decisive influence of cultural learning and modes of socialization in the life of individuals in society. They give credence to the idea of a psycho-cultural configuration specific to each nation, a kind of matrix able to register individual and collective behaviours in an identical, continuous way. The latter believe they can discern a kind of collective individuality at work in each national group which can explain, in accordance with specific processes defined by each theoretical approach, a certain similarity of behaviour in all group members. However divergent the viewpoints between Anglo-American theories and French conceptions of collective national personality, they have all, certainly contributed to the introduction of the cultural factor into modern political analysis.

Notes

1 For a detailed critical and comparative analysis of developments on this theme in the French and Anglo-American social sciences in the twentieth century, we refer the reader to our study: Claret, P. (1998), *La Personnalité Collective des Nations. Théories Anglo-Saxonnes et Conceptions Françaises du Caractère National*, Organisation Internationale et Relations Internationales Series, no. 40, Bruylant, Brussels.

2 Marc-Lipiansky, E. (1978), 'Groupe et Identité' in G. Michaud (ed.), *Identités Collectives et Relations Inter-Culturelles*, Editions Complexe, Brussels, p. 60.

References

Abel, M. (1978), 'Souvenirs et Hommages', *Ethnopychologie*, 34, no. 3.

Almond, G.A. (1956), 'Comparative Political Systems', *Journal of Politics*, vol. 18, no. 3, pp. 391-409.

Almond, G.A. and Powel, G.B. (1966), 'Political Structure and Culture', *Comparative Politics. A Developmental Approach*, Little Brown, Boston, Chap. 3, pp. 42-72.

Almond, G.A. and Verba, S. (1963), *The Civic Culture. Political Attitudes and Democracy in Five Nations*, Princeton.

Almond, G.A. and Verba, S. (1980) (eds), *The Civic Culture Revisited*, Little Brown, Boston.

André, S. (1989), 'La Politique et la Géographie', Actes du Colloque (Paris, Sorbonne, December 1988), *Etudes Normandes*, vol. 38, no. 2.

Bastide, R. (1966), 'Y a-t-il une Crise de la Psychologie des Peuples?', *Revue de Psychologie des Peuples*, vol. 21, no. 1, pp. 8-20.

Bateson, G. (1942), 'Morale and National Character', in G. Watson (ed.), *Civilian Morale*, S.P.S.S.I., Boston, pp. 71-91.

Benedict, R. (1934), *Patterns of Culture*, Boston.

Bouthoul, G. (1981), *Les Mentalités*, coll. Q.S.J. no. 545, P.U.F., Paris, 6th ed.

Claret, P. (1996), 'Regards sur l'Histoire d'une Entreprise Intellectuelle', L'Institut Havrais et la Revue de Psychologie des Peuples - Ethnopsychologie (1946-1982)', *Cahiers de Sociologie Économique et Culturelle*, no. 26, pp. 17-36.

Duijker, H.C.J. and Fridja, N.H. (1960), *National Character and National Stereotypes*, A Trend Report Prepared for the International Union of Scientific Psychology, Confluence I, North-Holland Publishing Co., Amsterdam.

Duroselle, J.B. (1974), 'La Décision de Politique Étrangère. Esquisse d'un Modèle Type', *Relations Internationales*, no. 1, pp. 1-26.

Duroselle, J.B. (1974), 'Opinion, Attitude, Mentalité, Mythe, Idéologie: Essai de Clarifcation', *Relations Internationales*, no. 2 ('Mentalités Collectives et Relations Internationales'), pp. 3-23.

Farber, M.L. (1950), 'The Problem of National Character: A Methodological Analysis', *The Journal of Psychology*, vol. 30, pp. 307-16; reprinted 'The Analysis of National Character' in N.J. Smelser and W.T. Smelser (1963) (eds), *Personality and the Social System*, New-York, pp. 80-7.

Farber, M.L. (1955), 'The Study of National Character: 1955', *The Journal of Social Issues*, vol. 11, no. 2, pp. 52-6.

Fromm, E. (1941), *Escape from Freedom*, New York.

Gorer, G. (1950), 'The Concept of National Character', *Science News*, no. 18, London; reprinted in C. Kluckhohn and H.A. Murray (1956) (eds), *Personality in Nature, Society and Culture*, Knopf, New York, pp. 246-59.

Gorer, G. (1953), 'National Character:Theory and Practice', in M. Mead and R. Metraux, (1966) (eds), *The Study of Culture at a Distance*, Chicago, 4th ed., pp. 57-82.

Grieger, P. (1959), 'De la Caractérologie Individuelle à la Caractérologie Ethnique', *La Caractérologie. Revue Internationale de Caractérologie*, vol.1, pp. 89-101.

Grieger, P. (1961), *La Caractérologie Ethnique. Approche et Compréhension des Peuples*, coll. 'Caractères', no. 16, P.U.F., Paris.

Hardy, G. (1939), *La Géographie Psychologique*, coll. 'Géographie Humaine', Gallimard, Paris.

Inkeles, A. (1959), 'Personality and Social Structure', in R. Merton (ed.), *Sociology Today. Problems and Prospects*, Basic Books, New York, pp. 249-76.

Inkeles, A. (1961), 'National Character and Modern Political Systems', in HSU F.L.K., (ed.), *Psychological Anthropology*, The Dorsey Press, Homewood, pp. 172-208.

Inkeles, A. (1990), 'National Character Revisited', *The Tocqueville Review*, vol. 12 (1990-1991), pp. 83-117.

Inkeles, A. and Levinson, D.J. (1954) , (1969) , 'National Character : The Study of Modal Personality and Sociocultural Systems', in G. Lindzey (ed.), *The Handbook of Social Psychology*, Cambridge, 1st ed. (1954), vol. 2, pp. 977-1020 ; 2nd ed. rev. (1969), vol. 4, pp. 418-506.

Kardiner, A. and Linton, R. (1939), *The Individual and His Society, The Psychodynamic of the Social Organisation*, New York.

Kardiner, A. and Linton, R. (1945), *The Psychological Frontiers of Society*, New York.

Klineberg, O. (1944), 'A Science of National Character', *Journal of Social Psychology*, S.P.S.S.I. Bulletin, no. 19, pp. 147-62.

Klineberg, O. (1950), *Tensions Affecting International Understanding. A Survey of Research*, Social Science Research Council Bulletin, 62, New York.

Klineberg, O. (1981), 'Jean Stoetzel et l'Etude Scientifique du Caractère National', in *Science et Théorie de l'Opinion Publique. Hommage à Jean Stoetzel*, Retz, Paris, pp. 42-8.

LeSenne, R. (1946a), 'Caractérologie Politique', *Traité de Caractérologie*, 'Logos. Introduction aux Etudes Philosophiques', P.U.F., Paris, pp. 571-9.

LeSenne, R. (1946b), 'La Caractérologie et la Psychologie des Peuples', *Revue de Psychologie des Peuples*, vol. 1, no. 3, pp. 193-210.

Linton, R. (1945), *The Cultural Background of Personality*, Appleton Century, New York.

Linton, R. (1951), 'The Concept of National Character', in A.H. Stanton and S.E. Perry (eds), *Personality and Political Crisis*, The Free Press, Glencoe, pp. 133-50.

L'Oeuvre Scientifique d'André Siegfried (1977), *Colloque du Centenaire d'André Siegfried* (Collège de France, 1975), Presses de la Fondation Nationale des Sciences Politiques, Paris.

Marandon, S. (1964), 'Les Images des Peuples. Bilan pour Servir d'Introduction aux Recherches à Venir', *Revue de Psychologie des Peuples*, vol. 19, no. 1, pp. 8-21.

Marandon, S. (1971), 'Caractère et Images des Peuples', *Ethnopsychologie*, vol. 26, no. 2/3, pp. 245-55.

Marc-Lipiansky, E. (1994), 'Identité Nationale et Psychologie: Alfred Fouillée', in J. Chevallier (dir.), *L'Identité Politique*, Publications de l'Université d'Amiens, P.U.F., Paris, pp. 32-41.

Mead, M. (1951), 'The Study of National Character', in D. Lerner and H.D. Lasswell, (eds), *The Policy Sciences: Recent Developments in Scope and Method*, Stanford, pp. 70-85.

Mead, M. (1953), 'National Character', in A.L. Kroeber (ed.), *Anthropology Today: An Encyclopedic Inventory*, Chicago, pp. 642-67.

Mead, M. (1961), 'National Character and the Science of Anthropology', in S.M. Lipset and L. Lowenthall (eds), *Culture and Social Character: The Work of David Riesman Reviewed*, The Free Press, New York, pp. 15-26.

Mead, M. and Metraux, R. (1953) (eds), *The Study of Culture at a Distance*, Chicago, (4th ed., 1966).

Michaud, G. (1971), 'Un Concept à Définir: l'Ethnie' and 'Architectures', *Ethnopsychologie*, vol. 26, no. 2/3, pp. 193-204 and pp. 311-33.

Michaud, G. (1978), 'L'Ethnotype comme Système de Significations' and 'Mises au Point', in G. Michaud (dir.), *Identités Collectives et Relations Inter-Culturelle*s, coll. 'L'Autre et l'Ailleurs', Ed. Complexe, Bruxelles, pp. 19-34 and pp. 109-25.

Michaud, G. (1996), 'Partage de Midi. L'Heure de l'Ethnopsychologie', *Cahiers de Sociologie Economique et Culturelle*, no. 26, pp. 45-60.

Michaud, G. and Marc, E. (1981), *Vers une Science des Civilisations?*, Ed. Complexe, Brussels.

Milza, P. (1980), 'Culture et Relations Internationales', *Relations Internationales*, no. 24, pp. 361-79.

Milza, P. (1985), 'Mentalités Collectives et Relations Internationales', *Relations Internationales*, no. 41, pp. 93-109.

Miroglio, A. (1971), *La Psychologie des Peuples*, coll.Q.S.J, no. 798, P.U.F., Paris, (4th ed.).

Miroglio, A. and Miroglio, Y.D. (1978) (eds), *L'Europe et ses Populations*, Martinus Nijhoff, The Hague.

Pye, L.W. (1965), 'Introduction: Political Culture and Political Development', in L.W. Pye and S. Verba, *Political Culture and Political Development*, Princeton, pp. 3-26.

Pye, L.W. (1968), 'Political Culture', *International Encyclopedia of the Social Sciences*, Macmillan, London, vol. 12, pp. 218-25.

Pye, L.W. (1972), 'Culture and Political Science: Problems in the Evaluation of the Concept of Political Culture', *Social Science Quarterly*, vol. 53, no. 2, pp. 285-96.

Pye, L.W. (1997), 'Introduction - The Elusive Concept of Culture and the Vivid Reality of Personality', *Political Psychology*, vol. 18, no. 2, pp. 241-54.

Remond, (1969), 'Options Idéologiques et Inclinations Affectives en Politique Étrangère', in L. Hamon (dir.), *L'Élaboration de la Politique Étrangère*, Entretiens de Dijon (avec le concours de l'A.F.S.P.), P.U.F., Paris, pp. 85-93.

Renouvin, P. (1954), 'L'Histoire Contemporaine des Relations Internationales. Orientations de Recherches', *Revue Historique*, vol. CCXI, pp. 233-55.

Renouvin, P. and Duroselle, J.B. (1964), *Introduction à l'Histoire des Relations Internationales*, coll. 'Sciences Politiques', A. Colin, Paris; 4th ed. (1997), Agora, Pocket, Paris.

Riesman, D. (1950), *The Lonely Crowd: A Study of the Changing American Character*, New Haven.

Riesman, D. (1953), 'Psychological Types and National Character: An Informal Commentary ', *American Quarterly*, vol. 5, pp. 325-43.

Siegfried, A. (1913), *Tableau de la France de l'Ouest sous la IIIe République*, A. Colin, Paris ; reed. (1964).

Siegfried, A. (1950), *L'Âme des Peuples*, Hachette, Paris.

Singer, J.D. (1968), 'Man and World Politics: The Psycho-Cultural Interface', *Journal of Social Issues*, vol. 24, no. 3, pp. 127-55.

Singer, M. (1961), 'A Survey of Culture and Personality Theory and Research', in B. Kaplan (ed.), *Studying Personality Cross-Culturally*, Harper and Row, New York, pp. 9-90.

Smelser, N.J. (1968), 'Personality and the Explanation of Political Phenomena at the Social System Level: A Methodological Statement', *Journal of Social Issues*, vol. 24, no. 3, pp. 111-20.

Stoetzel, J. (1954), *Jeunesse sans Chrysanthème ni Sabre. Etude sur les Attitudes de la Jeunesse Japonaise d'Après-Guerre*, coll. 'Recherches en Sciences Humaines', no. 3, Plon-Unesco Paris.

Stoetzel, J. (1959), 'Contribution des Sondages à l'Étude du Caractère National', Actes du 15e Congrès International de Psychologie (Brussels, 1957), *Acta Psychologica, European Journal of Social Psychology*, vol. 15, pp. 533-4.

Stoetzel, J. (1963), *La Psychologie Sociale*, 'Nouvelle Bibliothèque Scientifique', Flammarion, Paris.

Thobie, J. (1985), 'La Dialectique Forces Profondes - Décision dans l'Histoire des Relations Internationales', *Relations Internationales*, no. 41, pp. 29-38.

Verba, S. and Almond, G.A. (1963), *The Civic Culture. Political Attitudes and Democracy in Five Nations*, Princeton.

Verba, S. and Pye, L.W. (1965), *Political Culture and Political Development*, Princeton.

4 National Identity and Modernity

MONTSERRAT GUIBERNAU

Introduction

The concept of national identity has become prominent at a time when we are witnessing the withering away of many traditional sources of identity (such as class). To study national identity, we need to examine the changes which have affected the meaning of identity from an historical perspective, and focus upon the renewed strength which this concept is currently enjoying by analysing its close ties with nationalism.

Nationalism can only be successfully understood if two major dimensions of it are taken on board: these are its political character and its role in creating identity. The political character of nationalism stems from its quality as a doctrine closely linked to the territoriality of the nation-state. This reconceptualization of legitimacy is a product of the expansion of ideas of popular sovereignty and democracy that emerged following the French and American revolutions. It fostered a slow and contested process by means of which individuals were recognized to possess rights to influence the ways in which the future of their communities should develop. Citizenship and its outcome, the right to decide upon one's nation political destiny, had to be struggled for. In this context, nationalism proved successful in moving people's loyalties away from the monarch and fostering the nation as a new kind of attachment. The political dimension of nationalism brought into a (conflictual) relation the Enlightenment doctrines and the emphasis of the Romantics upon the underlying importance of cultural and linguistic diversity. Nationalism not only reinforced the nation-state building process, at the same time it contained the seeds of new tensions affecting national minorities included within the boundaries of already established nation-states.

The Nation-State, The Nation and Nationalism

The nation-state, the nation and nationalism form a triad in which each element is related to the other two in such a way that changes affecting one of them are bound to produce modifications in the other two. These three elements which exist in tension with one another, have become crucial aspects of modernity and are currently undergoing profound transformations.

A basic conceptual distinction between these concepts has to be made. By 'state', taking Weber's definition, I refer to 'a human community that (successfully) claims the *monopoly of the legitimate use of physical force* within a given territory',[1] although not all states have successfully accomplished this, and some of them have not even aspired to accomplish it. By 'nation' I refer to a human group conscious of forming a community, sharing a common culture, attached to a clearly demarcated territory, having a common past and a common project for the future and claiming the right to rule itself. Thus, the 'nation' includes five dimensions: psychological (consciousness of forming a group), cultural, territorial, political and historical. By offering this definition, I distinguish the term nation from both the state and the nation-state. By 'nationalism' I mean the sentiment of belonging to a community whose members identify with a set of symbols, beliefs and ways of life, and have the will to decide upon their common political destiny.

But still another term needs to be defined and distinguished from the ones I have just mentioned, the nation-state. The nation-state is a modern institution, characterized by the formation of a kind of state which has the monopoly of what it claims to be the legitimate use of force within a demarcated territory and seeks to unite the people subjected to its rule by means of homogenization, creating a common culture, symbols, values, reviving traditions and myths of origin, and sometimes inventing them. The main differences between a nation and a nation-state, when the nation and the state do not coincide, as they hardly ever do are that, while the members of the nation are conscious of forming a community, the nation-state seeks to create a nation and develop a sense of community stemming from it. While the nation has a common culture, values and symbols, the nation-state has as an objective the creation of a common culture, symbols and values. While the members of the nation can look back to their common past, if those of the nation-state do so, they might confront either a blank picture - simply because the nation-state did not exist - or a fragmented and diversified one - since they have belonged to different ethno-nations. While the people who form a nation have a sense of fatherland and feel attached to a territory, the nation-state can be the result of a treaty, or the will of politicians who decide when to draw the line between states. One has only to look at the different maps of Europe that resulted from the Congress of Vienna in 1815, the Treaty of Versailles after the First World War and the subsequent modifications after the defeat of Hitler in 1945, and the present re-shaping of Europe after the collapse of the Soviet Union.[2]

In this chapter, I study national identity as a key feature of modern societies. In so doing, I explore the meaning of identity and consider its defining criteria and its relation with culture, offering a critical analysis of Ernest Gellner's theory of nationalism. The key questions addressed in this section refer to how is national identity created and experienced in late modernity placing a particular emphasis upon its symbolic dimension. Finally, I look at the political aspects of national identity and focus upon its link with the concept of citizenship.

On Identity

Baumeister argues that Medieval European attitudes lacked the modern emphasis on individuality since society operated on the basis of lineage, gender, social status and other attributes, all of which were fixed by birth. He points that 'only with the emergence of modern societies, and in particular, with the differentiation of the division of labour, did the separate individual become a focus of attention'.[3] By the late Middle Ages, people increasingly learned to think in individual terms and slowly solidified concepts of the single human life as an individual totality. Baumeister's analysis recalls that of Durkheim: 'the 'individual', in a certain sense, did not exist in traditional cultures, and individuality was not prized'.[4]

Thus, while the eighteenth century's rejection of the Christian models of human potentiality and fulfilment led the Romantics into a passionate search for new, secular models for human fulfilment, the rejection of the legitimacy of the traditional, stable political and social order led to a troubled recognition of the pervasive conflict between the individual and society. Yet, in the nineteenth century, the prestige of the individual self-reached an all-time high that declined in the early twentieth century when 'new social arrangements and events dramatized the relative powerlessness of the individual leading to a devaluation of the self'.[5] However, a process giving special significance to the 'uniqueness' of each individual led to a particular concern about identity reflecting the individual and collective (group) desire to be 'different'.

The key question with regard to identity is 'Who am I?'. Identity is a definition, an interpretation of the self that establishes what and where the person is in both social and psychological terms. When one has identity one is situated; that is, 'cast in the shape of a social object by the acknowledgement of his participation or membership in social relations'.[6] Identities exist only in societies, which define and organize them. As Baumeister puts it: 'the search for identity includes the question of what is the proper relationship of the individual to society as a whole'.[7] This search is also evident at the individual level through the need to belong to a community. In the current era, the nation represents one of these communities: national identity is its product.

The defining criteria of identity are: continuity over time, and differentiation from others,[8] both fundamental elements of national identity. Continuity springs from the conception of the nation as a historically rooted entity that projects into the future. Individuals perceive this continuity through a set of experiences that spread out across time and are united by a common meaning, something that only 'insiders' can grasp. Differentiation stems from the consciousness of forming a community with a shared culture, attached to a concrete territory, both elements leading to the distinction between members and 'strangers', 'the rest' and 'the different'.

Identity fulfils three major functions: it helps to make choices, makes possible relationships with others, and gives strength and resilience.[9] First, national identity to be fully expressed and developed requires that the people forming the nation enjoy the right to decide upon their common political destiny. Second, if we consider national identity at a personal level, it obviously makes relationships with others possible, since the nation appears as a common pool where individuals with common culture live and work, creating a world of meaning. Furthermore, the claim of nations to have a state, is the claim to be recognized as 'actors' within the global system of nation-states. Finally, national identity gives strength and resilience to individuals in so far as it reflects their own identification with an entity - the nation - that transcends them. Also, nationalist ideologies usually encourage the development of the nation and present it as worthwhile. Although on some occasions they focus upon a past splendour, they always promise a better future and advocate regeneration.

National Identity and Culture

But how does the individual experience his/her national identity? I suggest that community of culture and unity of meaning are the main sources that allow the construction and experience of national identity. As a collective sentiment, national identity needs to be upheld and reaffirmed at regular intervals. Ritual plays a crucial role here. As Durkheim argues in *The Elementary Forms of the Religious Life*, there is little difference between religious and civil ceremonies in their object, the results which they produce, or the processes employed to attain these results. Durkheim emphasizes the power of ritual and what he writes about religion can easily be applied to national ceremonies

Truly religious beliefs are always common to a specific group which professes to adhere to them and to practise the rites connected with them. They are not merely received individually by all members of the group; they are what give the group its unity. The individuals who compose the group feel themselves bound to each other by the very fact that they have a common faith.[10]

Individuals, through their identification with the nation, can be compared with believers. To paraphrase Durkheim, the believers who have communicated with their god are not merely people who see new truths of which the unbeliever is ignorant; they are individuals who are stronger, feel more powerful in enduring the trials of existence, or in conquering them: 'It is as though they were raised above the miseries of the world, because they are raised above their condition as mere men'.[11]

Melucci defines collective identity as 'an interactive and shared definition produced by several interacting individuals who are concerned with the orientations of their actions as well as the field of opportunities and constraints in which their action takes place'.[12] Collective identity considered as a process involves: formulating cognitive frameworks concerning the goals, means and environment of action; activating relationships among the actors, who communicate, negotiate and make decisions; and making emotional investments, which enable individuals to recognize themselves in each other.

I understand the present revival of ethnicity as a response to a need for collective as well as individual identity. Parsons suggests the term 'de-differentiation' to explain the need for collective identity among particular groups. He argues that:

> There is a growing plurality of social roles in which the individual is called upon to act. Yet none of these roles is able adequately to offer the individual a stable identity. Selective mechanisms of de-differentiation thus come into being to provide identity via a return to primary memberships. Thus ethnicity is revived as a source of identity because it responds to a collective need which assumes a particular importance in complex societies.[13]

As Melucci points out, national movements bring to light two problems central to more structurally complex societies; they raise questions about the need for new rights for all members of the community, particularly the right to be different; and they claim the right to autonomy, to control a specific living space (which in this case is also a geographic territory).[14] In terms of political action this means fighting for new channels of representation, access for excluded interests to the political system, and the reform of decision-making processes and the rules of the political game.

The current re-emergence of nationalism not only responds to the gulf between political and cultural processes, but also gains strength as other criteria of group membership (such as class) weaken or recede. National solidarity also responds to a need for identity of an eminently symbolic nature in so far as it provides roots based on culture and a common past, and offers a project for the future. As Melucci writes:

> The 'innovative' components of ethno-national movements, albeit a minority issue bound up with their struggle against discrimination and for political rights, also has a predominantly cultural character. The ethnic appeal launches its challenge to complex societies on such fundamental questions as the goals of change and the production of identity and meaning ... Difference is thereby given a voice which speaks of problems which transverse the whole of society.[15]

How is identity created? One of the main features of humans is their ability to adapt to different environments. The individual is flexible and contains many possibilities for his/her later development. The biological basis of humans allows for their extraordinary capacity for social learning and thus the richness and variety individuals are able to display through the development of a wide range of diverse cultures. Individuals with all their potential are socialized and raised within a group that is located in space and time. Values, beliefs, customs, conventions, habits and practices are transmitted to the new members who receive the culture of a particular society. The process of identification with the elements of a specific culture implies a strong emotional investment. All .cultures single out certain parts of a neutral reality and charge them with meaning. Individuals are born within cultures that determine the way in which they view and organize themselves in relation to others and to nature.

Two major implications deriving from this possess a particular significance for the analysis of nationalism. First, a common culture favours the creation of solidarity bonds among the members of a given community and allows them to imagine the community they belong to as separate and distinct from others. Solidarity is then based upon the consciousness of forming a group, outsiders being considered as strangers and potential 'enemies'. Second, individuals who enter a culture emotionally charge certain symbols, values, beliefs and customs by internalizing them and conceiving them as part of themselves. The emotional charge that individuals invest in their land, language, symbols and beliefs while building up their identity, facilitates the spread of nationalism. Thus while, other forms of ideology such as Marxism or liberalism require a careful indoctrination of their followers, nationalist leaders present nationalism as an ideology which emanates from this basic emotional attachment to one's land and culture. Social and political theory has tended to place emotions and feelings outside the sphere of its enquiry, considering the irrational inevitably inferior to the rational. My point is that the force of nationalism springs not from rational thought alone, but from the irrational power of emotions that stem from the feelings of belonging to a particular group. The double face of nationalism results from the way in which these emotions are either transformed into a peaceful and democratic movement seeking the recognition and development of one's nation, or turned into xenophobia, the will to put one's nation above others and the eradication of the different.

From a symbolic perspective, 'culture is the pattern of meanings embodied in symbolic forms, including actions, utterances and meaningful objects of various kinds, by virtue of which individuals communicate with one another and share their experiences, conceptions and beliefs'.[16] A common culture, as I have already stressed, has the capability to create a sentiment of solidarity that derives from the consciousness of forming a group. A common historical past, constructed by remembering as well as forgetting about some events in the life of the community, which includes 'having suffered, enjoyed, and hoped together', and a future common project, reinforce the links among the members of a given nation. As symbolic forms, cultural phenomena are meaningful for actors and the meaning is something that only 'insiders' know and value.

On Gellner's Theory of Nationalism

Gellner's writings probably supply the best starting point to discuss the role of culture in the creation of nationalism. Gellner's main emphasis is upon the distinctive character of nationalism as 'rooted in a *certain kind* of division of labour, one which is complex and persistently, cumulatively changing'.[17] According to him, industrial society is based upon perpetual economic growth; the need to fulfil economic necessities engenders mobility which at the same time produces egalitarianism. Industrialism involves a complex division of labour and this requires a rather different, specialized and universal educational system which provides people with the basic tools for employment, which are a standard language and literacy. To sustain an educational system whose function is the production of a 'standard culture', one needs a centralized state. Gellner points out that the state is charged with the maintenance and supervision of an enormous social infrastructure, and that a universal literacy is required of industrial society. However, I would argue that in the early stages of industrialism, which correspond to the first expressions of modern nationalism found in the late eighteenth century, literacy was only important among managers and clerks. Thus, Gellner's description of the role of the state in education would reflect the situation achieved in the mid twentieth century whilst claiming to apply to industrial societies; in other words, to late nineteenth century Europe.[18]

On the other hand, one can accept that a mass education system is a universal product of industrial societies, but as Breuilly remarks: 'Does the answer lie in the generic training such education offers?'.[19] Gellner's explanation sounds quite functionalist: education may eventually operate as Gellner envisages, but does that explain its development? Unless one specifies either a deliberate intention on the part of key groups to produce this result, or some feed-back mechanism which will 'select' generic training patterns of education against other patterns, this cannot count as an explanation. Besides, it is possible to think of other reasons: the need to train citizens or conscripts for the mass politics and mass armies of the modern age, humanitarianism, or the need to occupy children's time as soon as they began to be excluded from the labour force.

Gellner's assumptions about industrialism can also be subjected to criticism. Yet, he pays little attention to the mechanics of state-formation and deliberately turns his attention from capitalism to industrialism. One might respond by saying that nationalism exists and has existed in numerous non-industrial states. At the same time, all nationalisms claim to be historically rooted in traditions formed long before the industrial era. It seems to me that Gellner's description is useful for developing an understanding of events in Western Europe, while having less value in interpreting, for example, the Chinese experience.

Two fundamental questions still need to be posed. The first concerns the power of nationalism; the second refers to the capacity of nationalism to bind together people from very different cultural levels and social backgrounds. Liberalism and Marxism, two of the most important systems of thought from which social scientists draw, both predicted the decline of national feelings. Liberalism expected the decline of nationalism because 'trade flows across frontiers; the life of the intellect ignores frontiers; and with the progress of learning, wealth and industry, the prejudices and superstitions and fears which engender frontiers would decline'.[20] For a Marxist it appears inexplicable because only abysmal cognitive error could lead the proletariat to identify with the exploitative ruling classes of the society to which they belong against the exploited masses (and ruling classes) of another society.

Gellner, however, attempts to demonstrate that nationalism can best be understood as a necessary consequence of the very forces described by liberals and Marxists. He does so by showing how industrialism's demands for homogeneity lead to the creation of culturally unalloyed nations. To explain nationalism as a consequence of a high division of labour and a common culture seems to me an extremely simple conception when applied to a world in which globalization processes favour constant cultural inter-connections. If Gellner is right, we should be witnessing a tendency towards a single uniform world nationalism. But in fact, the effect is exactly the opposite. Old nationalisms are recovering strength and very few people wish to give up their original national identity, despite belonging to backward nations, in order to adopt a more 'successful' one. When Gellner writes referring to individuals living in industrial societies: 'For most of these men, however, the limits of their culture are the limits, not perhaps of the world, but of their own employability and hence dignity',[21] he does not take into consideration that whenever a nation is oppressed, to sustain their dignity as members of a particular culture, individuals see their chances of getting a job substantially undermined and, in some extreme cases, they even face exclusion from the labour market.[22]

Furthermore, while Gellner emphasizes how 'ardently' national identification may be felt, he does not provide a satisfactory account of how the functional imperatives he invokes can generate such powerful feelings. Seton-Watson set out to understand 'this force of nationalism which has continued to shake the world in which we have lived'.[23] Carr refers to 'the dynamite of nationalism'.[24] Dunn writes: 'no one could doubt that it has become one of the more ebullient and energizing principles'.[25] But, does Gellner's theory confer upon nationalism sufficient intellectual strength to sustain such a role? I think not. Gellner does not explain the willingness of modern populations to die in their thousands for their country (and its often repulsive rulers).

Contrary to Gellner, I argue that the power of culture lies in its capacity to create identity, something that individuals cannot live without, and that cannot easily be changed. Culture cannot be reduced to the entrance card for a concrete labour market. Culture designs the most intimate parts of humans, mediating the way in which they relate to themselves, others and the exterior world. A common culture presumes some kind of complicity that only individuals socialized within that culture can understand. Individuals do not enter a foreign culture merely by learning the language of that culture. They have the necessary tools, but it takes a long time before they are able to capture the meaning implicit in words, expressions and rituals. This 'complicity' contributes to the creation of a common consciousness and the development of links of solidarity among group members.

The attachment of individuals to their community is a constant that has adopted diverse forms through different historical periods. Loyalty has focused upon various entities: the clan, the tribe, the city, the dominion of a particular lord, the monarch, and from the eighteenth century onwards, the nation. When Gellner argues that: 'Modern man is not loyal to a monarch or a land or a faith, whatever he may say, but to a culture',[26] he fails to contemplate the role of culture in the creation of identity. This, I argue, is the main explanation for the 'loyalty' of individuals to this abstract entity that transcends their life span. In my view, the nation, personified through symbols and rituals which symbolically recreate a sense of 'people' has become the focus of a new kind of attachment. The nation represents the socio-historical context within which culture is embedded and by means of which culture is produced, transmitted and received.

Gellner is right in suggesting that: 'The state is, above all, the protector, not of a faith, but of a culture, and the maintainer of the inescapably homogeneous and standardizing educational system'.[27] However, he ignores a further dimension of this issue by failing to distinguish between what I call the 'legitimate' and the 'illegitimate' state. In the former, where nation and state are coextensive, Gellner's definition works perfectly. But in the second situation, where several nations or parts of nations are bound together under the rule of a single state, the state must decide which culture is to be given priority and how to implement a successful policy of cultural homogenization. This raises doubts about the viability of a state that compromises itself with the protection and encouragement of different cultures evolving within it. For instance, this would be the case in Spain where, as a result of the 1978 Constitution, Catalans and Basques, among other nations included in Spain, now see their cultures recognised and protected. How far can a state go in acknowledging and encouraging (financing) different cultures within its territory without threatening the cultural homogeneity that Gellner considers necessary if industrial societies wish to prosper? By neglecting this point, Gellner fails to tackle one of the major problems faced by contemporary European societies where political units are mainly characterized by the non-coextensivity of nation and state. In his latest article, Gellner acknowledges that the unevenness of economic development between different areas produces unstoppable labour migrations, so that even if a nation-state used to be coextensive, it will become ethnically plural after its industrialization.[28] This raises further questions about the will of (some) immigrants to maintain and develop their original cultures, the response of the state and the measures it will implement to homogenize the newcomers. Will they retain their original national identity or will they acquire the identity of their new homeland, and if they decide to do so, will they be accepted as full members, as equals by their by co-citizens?

To solve this question by means other than the use of force, a detailed and careful analysis of these issues is required, especially since a threat of further fragmentation is increased by the present influx of immigrants from Eastern Europe, Asia and Africa into Western Europe.

Within a given community, a hierarchical division (among its members) may be referred to as a constant. This would justify the fact that the different social classes living within the same nation still find common culture more compelling than common class. However, when the integrity of the group is in danger, the solidarity that comes from shared values, beliefs and ways of life proves that the proletarian of a particular nation feels that he/she has more in common with the exploitative ruling classes of the society he/she belongs to than with the exploited masses - and ruling classes - of another society. Dunn states that, 'certainly socialism has never looked the same since the parties of Engels and of Jaurès slunk into line and agreed to defend their fatherlands against the aggression of the largely proletarian armies of their foes'.[29] This same strong sentiment of solidarity is what makes people ready to die for their nation in their thousands. Preservation of the self and the group to which one belongs is the primary concern in time of crisis. Additional weight is added to this by the fact that our global political system is organized into nation-states, these being the major actors recognized at an international level.

The Symbolic Content of National Identity

On Symbols

Symbols and rituals are decisive factors in the creation of national identity. The nation as a form of community implies both similarity among its members and difference from outsiders. As Anthony Cohen puts it, a boundary marks the beginning and end of a community in so far as it encapsulates its identity.[30] Boundaries are called into being by the exigencies of social interaction. However, not all boundaries and not all components of any boundary are so objectively apparent. They may be thought of, rather, as existing in the minds of their beholders. Boundaries are symbolic in character and imply different meanings for different people. Yet, if we consider the boundary as the community's public face, it appears as symbolically simple, but as the object of internal discourse it is symbolically complex. 'The boundary', Cohen argues, 'symbolizes the community to its members in two different ways: it is the sense they have of its perception by people on the other side - the public face and 'typical' mode - and it is their sense of the community as refracted through all the complexities of their lives and experiences - the private face and idiosyncratic mode'.[31]

The consciousness of forming a community is created through the use of symbols and the repetition of rituals that give strength to the individual members of the nation. By favouring occasions in which they can feel united and by displaying emblems - symbols - that represent its unity, the nation establishes the boundaries that distinguish it from others. A symbol was originally an object, a sign, or a word used for mutual recognition and with an understood meaning that could only be grasped by the initiated. The meaning of a symbol cannot be deduced. Symbols only have value for those who recognize them. Thus, they provide a revealing device to distinguish between members and 'outsiders' and heighten people's awareness of, and sensitivity to, their community. The soldier, who dies for his flag, does so because he identifies the flag with his country. By means of this association he loses sight of the fact that the flag is merely a sign. As a symbol the flag is valuable: it represents the country.

All communities use symbols as markers. Symbols not only stand for, or represent something else, they also allow those who employ them to supply part of their meaning. Hence, if we consider a flag as a symbol of a particular country, its meaning cannot be restricted to the relationship flag-country. Rather it achieves a special significance for every individual since the flag - symbol - has the power to evoke particular memories, or feelings. Symbols do not represent 'other things' unambiguously. They express 'other things' in ways which allow their common form to be retained and shared among the members of a group, whilst not imposing upon them the constraints of uniform meanings. An example of the malleability of nationalist symbols is that people of radically opposed views can find their own meanings in what nevertheless remains as common symbols. The '*senyera*' - Catalan flag - for instance, although representing a country, Catalonia, holds different meanings for socialist, nationalist, republican or right wing Catalan parties, which use it in their demonstrations and other public events.

It is important to emphasize that symbols are effective because they are imprecise. They are, as Cohen states, 'ideal media through which people can speak of a 'common' language, behave in apparently similar ways, participate in the 'same' rituals ... without subordinating themselves to a tyranny of orthodoxy. Individuality and commonality are thus reconcilable'.[32] I shall argue that the nation, by using a particular set of symbols, masks the differentiation within itself, transforming the reality of difference into the appearance of similarity, thus allowing people to invest the 'community' with ideological integrity. This, in my view, explains the ability of nationalism to bind together people from different cultural levels and social backgrounds. Symbols mask the difference and highlight commonality, creating a sense of group. People construct the community in a symbolic way and transform it as a referent of their identity.

According to von Bertalanffy, symbols are signs that are freely created, represent some content, and are transmitted by tradition.[33] However, although part of the strength of symbols stems from their capacity to express continuity with the past, they need to be constantly re-interpreted, and even re-created in order to avoid the danger of becoming stereotyped, decorative or meaningless. Symbols possess an inherent non-static character, they are subject to an evolution that, as Sperber mentions, can take place not only from generation to generation, but also within one generation because the period of acquisition of symbolism is not limited to a particular chronological age.[34]

Yet if the symbols that represent the nation receive a completely fixed, restricted and confined interpretation, they will probably die and become 'empty shells of fragmentary memories'.[35] Nationalism, to retain the vitality of its symbols, must constantly re-adapt and re-interpret them within fresh contexts. Symbols have their origin in the past, but the power of nationalism lies not only in expressing this fact and linking symbols with tradition; rather, nationalism has both to re-create old symbols and create new ones to maintain and increase the cohesion of the nation.

As Durkheim argues, societies are likely to create 'gods' during periods of general enthusiasm, and he mentions the French Revolution as a period in which, 'things purely laical by nature were transformed by public opinion into sacred things: these were the Fatherland, Liberty, Reason. A religion tended to become established which had its dogmas, symbols, altars and feasts'.[36] However, it would be a mistake to think that elements once elevated to the category of symbols can remain as such forever. The celebration of the bicentennial of the French Revolution in Paris was an example of the evolution of symbols once adopted to represent the nation. Symbols have become transmuted to fulfil the task of increasing a sense of community in a radically different society from that of 1789.

On Rituals

Symbols are usually used as key elements in common rituals that hold together the members of the nation at regular intervals. In analysing the way in which national symbolism and ritual operate, Durkheim's study of religion is particularly relevant.

Nationalism began to gain strength when religion was declining in Europe, and in my view, Durkheim was fundamentally right in arguing that 'it is, indeed, a universal fact that, when a conviction of any strength is held by the same community of men, it inevitably takes on a religious character'.[37] Nationalism as religion has its rites, and these are not merely received individually. Rather, as Durkheim stresses, they are what give the group its unity: 'The individuals who compose the group feel themselves bound to each other by the very fact that they have a common faith'.[38] A common faith requires a 'church', and it could be argued that the 'nation' fulfils this role, while intellectuals could be equated with priests. As beings sharing the same totemic principle, the members of the same nation feel morally bound to one-another. But as members of the tribe, the individuals who form the nation need to renew and give strength to the community they form by periodically reviving their ideals.

Individuals who share the same culture, feel attached to a concrete land, have the experience of a common past, and a project for the future, need to create occasions in which all that unites them is emphasized. In these moments, the individual forgets about him/herself, and the *sentiment of belonging* to the group occupies the prime position. The collective life of the community stands above that of the individual. Through symbolism and ritual, individuals are able to feel an emotion of unusual intensity that springs from their identification with an entity - the nation - which transcends them, and of which they actively feel a part. On these occasions the members of the nation receive strength and resilience, and are able to engage in heroic as well as barbaric actions in order to protect the interest of their nation. As Durkheim points out, 'because he is in moral unison with his fellow men, he has more confidence, courage and boldness in action, just like the believer who thinks that he feels the regard of his god turned graciously towards him'.[39]

The creation of national identity, I argue, responds to a complex process by which individuals identify themselves with symbols that have the power to unite and stress the sense of community. This process of identification involves a continuous flow between individuals and symbols, in the sense that individuals do not merely have to accept already established symbols, but rather have constantly to recreate them and attribute to them new meaning according to the changing circumstances through which the life of the community develops. Tradition has to be re-invented and persistently actualized. Yet if, as Renan argues, the nation is the result of a daily plebiscite, the identification with its symbols also needs to be worked out constantly in order to avoid the risk of losing meaning. If this happens, the sense of community immediately weakens. All groups need symbols and rituals in order to survive, maintain cohesion and reaffirm the collective ideas which they create. Durkheim acknowledged this when he wrote: 'It is by uttering the same cry, pronouncing the same word, or performing the same gesture in regard to some object that they [individuals] become and feel themselves to be in unison'.[40]

Political Aspects of National Identity

National identity is primarily a psychological phenomenon heavily influenced by the political discourse of nationalism, and intimately connected with political concepts such as citizenship. The traditional nation-state tried to equate national identity with citizenship by either ignoring or eliminating difference within it. Cultural homogeneity became a major objective achieved with different degrees of success by Western nation-states. Thus, while France could be presented as an almost perfect example of a country in which nation and state were made to be coextensive and where French citizenship basically coincided with French national identity. Spain offers quite a contrasting picture. The weakness and ruthless of the Spanish state and the renewed strength of Catalan and Basque nationalisms from the second part of the nineteenth century onwards made it extremely difficult to equate Spanish citizenship with a Spanish national identity primarily based upon Castilian features and the imposition of the Castilian language - commonly referred to as Spanish. This exclusive construction of identity alienated many Spanish citizens who would identify themselves as Catalans, Basques or Galicians.

Today the expansion of democracy and the formal acceptance of the right of peoples to self-determination together with an increasing awareness of ethnic diversity in part propitiated by the renewed strength of some nationalist movements in nations without states, have turned impossible to sustain the equity between citizenship and national identity, if the latter is to be considered as a unique identity. At present, many Catalans and Basques define themselves as Catalan and Spanish, or Basque and Spanish at the same time, while others also add 'European' as a third source of identity. Even in contemporary France, once a practically homogeneous nation-state, some people define themselves as simultaneously French and Breton, Occitan or Basque.

The attempt to equate citizenship with a single national identity implied a unique identity usually enforced upon at least some sections of the population. Where this happens today there is a great danger of an emerging nationalism based upon exclusion, the defence of uniqueness and the superiority of one group above others. However, these are no new features in the European political arena, they have been present mainly in Nazism, Fascism and Francoism. These regimes enjoyed great power during a considerable length of time - forty years in the case of Spain! - and constructed political ideologies heavily based upon a certain conception of nationalism, one which is exclusive and seeks the eradication of difference by diverse means which range from ethnic cleansing to the socio-political repression of national minorities. A most recent example of the consequences of a violent clash of identities is the disintegration of the former Yugoslavia.

The fundamental problem of our societies is how to reconcile universal democratization with the principle of identity, or rather how to sustain a democratic society which at the same time recognizes different identities and is capable of creating certain solidarity. At the beginning of this chapter I have pointed at nationalism, the nation-state and the nation as elements of a triad which exists in tension with one another, a triad which changing nature is manifesting itself in late modernity. Numerous factors, amongst them: the intensification of globalization processes concerning communications, economic and ecological interdependence, social and political transformations provoking a profound recast of the nation-state system, the proliferation of supranational organizations, the apparently unstoppable expansion of capitalism and the deepening of uneven development, alter the relation between the triad.

In this context some major changes affecting the nation, the nation-state and nationalism can be identified. First, to consider the nation as a community sharing a common culture, attached to a demarcated territory, having a common past and project for the future, and the will to decide upon its political destiny without necessarily having a state of its own and accepting the possibility to evolve within a larger political institution which respects it, and opens channels for all its members to feel represented is an innovative concept. Second, to understand the nation-state as an institution which no longer enjoys full control of its economy, its defence, and its sovereignty as it used to do during the first half of the twentieth century implies a crucial change in the traditional definition of the state once formulated by Max Weber. Finally, to define a certain brand of nationalism as a progressive social movement based upon democracy and popular sovereignty which stands for peoples once oppressed by alien rulers, adds a further step in the transformation of the meaning and relation between the triad. In this circumstances, dialogue, respect for the different and the need to develop non-exclusive identities are the only alternatives if violence is to be avoided.

Solidarity should emerge after establishing a common model of society based upon democracy and respect. A society whose institutions truly represent the people and decide what are the minimal elements of agreement capable of orienting the pursue of a common good defined by all. Civil coherence should stem from working together in a common project of society aimed at improving conditions in the life of its members. The acceptance of a minimum set of moral values is necessary if civil coherence is to be achieved.[41] This is not an easy task, but it is clearly the only way to reconcile democracy with the principle of identity without being swamped by endless identity claims whose effect would be the fragmentation and eventual disintegration of society. People holding different identities are urged to find a manner to coexist avoiding confrontation and various forms of social exclusion depending on their culture and identity.

Notes

1   Weber, M., 'Politics as a Vocation', in H.H. Gerth and C. Wright Mills (1991), (1948) (eds.), *From Max Weber: Essays in Sociology*, London, p. 78.

2   Another example can be that of Kuwait, which borders were established in 1913 as a result of a private Turko-British agreement, being this one in many examples of borders re-drawn in imperialist map-making. See J. Jenkins, (1991), 'Shifting Sands', in *New Statesman and Society*, 8 February, p. 12.

3   Baumeister, R. (1986), *Identity: Cultural Change and the Struggle for Self*, Oxford University Press, Oxford, p. 29.

4   Giddens, A. (1991), *Modernity and Self-Identity*, Polity Press, Cambridge, p. 75.

5   Baumeister, R., *Identity*, p. 59.

6   Yardley, K and Honess, T. (1987) (ed.), *Self-Identity: Psychosocial Perspectives*, John Wiley & Sons, New York, p. 121.

7   Baumeister, R., *Identity*, p. 7.

8   Ibid., p. 18.

9   Ibid., p. 19.

10   Giddens, A. (1987), (1972), *Emile Durkheim: Selected Writings*, Cambridge University Press, Cambridge, pp. 222-3.

11   Durkheim, E. (1982), (1976), *The Elementary Forms of the Religious Life*, Allen & Unwin, London, p. 416.

12   Melucci, A. (1989), *Nomads of the Present*, Hutchinson Radius, London, p. 34.

13   Ibid., pp. 89-90.

14   Ibid., p. 91.

15   Ibid., p. 92.

16   Thompson, J.B. (1990), *Ideology and Modern Culture*, Polity Press, Cambridge, p. 132.

17   Renan, E. (1990), 'What is a Nation?', in H.K. Bhabha (ed.) *Nation and Narration*, Routledge, London, p. 19.

18   Gellner, E. (1988), (1983), *Nations and Nationalism,* Basil Blackwell, Oxford, p. 24. See also by the same author 'The Industrial Division of Labour and National Cultures', *Government and Opposition*, 17 (1982), p. 273.

19   In personal communication, professor Ernest Gellner answers to my criticism arguing that in the eighteenth century peasants began to be granted their freedom of movement, came to seek employment in towns, and therefore, aspired to become, precisely managers and clerks. Hence, their linguistic/cultural identity became important for them. However to my understanding, in *Nations and Nationalism*, he does not make this point explicit.

20   Breuilly, J. (1985), 'Reflections on Nationalism', *Philosophy of the Social Sciences*, 15, p. 68.

21   Gellner, E. (1978), (1965), *Thought and Change*, University of Chicago Press, Chicago, p. 147.

22   Gellner, E., *Nations and Nationalism*, p. 110.

23   During the Francoist regime, the Catalans who sought to defend their dignity by actively protecting their language and culture were systematically excluded from office. To make Gellner's theory plausible, they should have surrendered to the regime's pressure and subscribe to the official culture.

24   Seton-Watson, H. (1977), *Nations and States: An Inquiry into the Origins of Nations and the Politics of Nationalism*, West View, Boulder, Colorado, p. xi.

25   Carr, E.H. (1945), *Nationalism and After*, Macmillan, New York, p. 10.

26   Dunn, J. (1983), 'For the Good of the Country', *Time Literary Supplement*, 21 October, p. 1167.

27   Gellner, E., *Nations and Nationalism*, p. 36.

28   Ibid., p. 110.

29   Gellner, E. (1996), 'The Rest of History', in *Prospect*, May 1996, pp. 34-8.

30   Dunn, J. *Western Political Theory in the Face of the Future*, (Cambridge University Press, Cambridge, 1979), p. 56.

31   Cohen, A.P. *The Symbolic Construction of Community*, (Tavistock Publications, London, 1985), p. 12.

32   Ibid., p. 74.

33   Ibid., p. 21.

34   Von Berlatanffy, L. (1981), *A System View of Man*, (ed. by Paul A. La Violette), Westview Press, Boulder, Colorado, p. 1.

35   Sperber, D. (1988), (1975), *Rethinking Symbolism*, Cambridge University Press, Cambridge, p. 89.

36   Dillistone, F. W. (1986), *The Power of Symbols*, SCM Press Ltd., London, p. 213.

37   Durkheim, E. (1982), (1976), *The Elementary Forms of the Religious Life*, Allen & Unwin, London, p. 214.

38   Giddens, A. (1987), (1972), *Emile Durkheim: Selected Writings*, Cambridge University Press, Cambridge, p. 222.

39   Ibid., p. 223.

40   Ibid., p. 231.

41   Durkheim, E., *The Elementary Forms of the Religious Life*, op. cit., p. 230.

PART III
SYMBOLIZING THE NATION

5 Forging the Authentic Nation: Alpine Landscape and Swiss National Identity

OLIVER ZIMMER

Attempts to establish meaningful links between 'nature' and culture communities are not confined to the modern era. In fact, ever since Antiquity, various groups or 'peoples' have turned to 'their' natural environment as a source of inspiration and collective identification. So when Tacitus, in the first century AD, described the Germanic tribes as rude and primitive, he mentioned how closely tied they were to the Teutonic woods as evidence of his claim. Seneca, Diodorus and Plutarch wrote of the Nile, and in doing so contributed much to the creation of the myth of the fertile river.[1] Yet it is only in the sixteenth century, that is, during a period marked by both territorial consolidation and the rise of national consciousness in some parts of Europe, that we witness a fairly widespread change in perception from 'nature' as a more general idea to the more specific notion 'landscape'.[2]

More systematic efforts to illuminate the link between particular natural environments and alleged national characteristics were to follow in the eighteenth century, especially in the works of Montesquieu (1689-1755), Rousseau (1712-78), and Herder (1744-1803). In a world in which traditional forms of religious attachment and social solidarity were declining at a disquieting speed, geography and 'nature' at least seemed to offer some degree of stability, calm and purity. It was in this context that selected parts of the natural environment - landscapes - became critical as a source of social orientation and collective identity. Commenting on the rise of landscape art at the end of the eighteenth century, the German painter Philipp Otto Runge exhorted: '...we stand at the brink of all the religions which sprang up out of the Catholic one, the abstractions perish, everything is lighter and more insubstantial than before, everything presses toward landscape art, looks for something certain in this uncertainty and does not know how to begin.'[3] Furthermore, from the turn of the eighteenth century onwards, particular landscapes emerged as integral parts of many national identities.

This paper explores the role of alpine landscape in the formation and reconstruction of Swiss national identity from the late eighteenth century to the end of the Second World War. Broadly put, my argument is this: as it became apparent from the turn of the eighteenth century that the Swiss Confederation took shape as a multicultural entity, efforts to turn the Alps into a poignant mass symbol of the emerging nation state intensified. In a context in which resorting to the ethno-linguistic criterion would have been bound to cause national disintegration, landscape rather than language came to be seen as the organic principle connecting modern Switzerland with its pre-modern past, thereby endowing the Swiss state with political legitimacy and cultural authenticity.

Two historical phases, each giving rise to a distinct conceptualization of the relationship between alpine landscape and the Swiss nation, can be distinguished. The first one (prevalent from the late eighteenth century to the 1870s) - what I will call the 'nationalization of nature' - is projective and portrays the Alps as an expression of national authenticity. The second conceptualization (prevalent from the 1870s to 1945) - what I will call the 'naturalization of the nation' - is deterministic and depicts alpine landscape as the ultimate determinant of ethno-cultural homogeneity.

Landscape and National Identity

Landscape Symbolism and the Study of National Identity

Given that most modern nations attach symbolic value to selected parts of the natural environment, it is somewhat surprising that, thus far, little attention has been paid to the interplay of landscape and collective identity in the major works on nationalism and national identity.[4] On the other hand, scholars working in fields such as human geography, art history or environmental history have recently made use of existing theoretical approaches to nationalism and national identification.[5] Yet, these theories have served these researchers as signposts to be passed rather than as springboards for the construction of new theories that deal with the question of how landscapes are valued in different historical and political contexts. Lowenthal expresses this marked and apparently widespread reluctance to draw even tentative theoretical conclusions when he accuses '[t]hose predisposed toward particular explanations of landscape attachments' of misreading 'ambiguous material'.[6] Despite the absence of appropriate theoretical tools for landscape analysis, three broad positions are discernible. Adherents of a 'primordialist' perspective view people's attachments to their natural surroundings as a manifestation of basic socio-psychological needs, and as a phenomenon that is both universal and historically persistent.[7] Those taking this position are, however, at a loss to explain why people's interest in landscape can vary significantly over time. Applying an explicitly descriptive approach, a second group of researchers are concerned mainly with the way depictions of landscape are regarded as reflective of national virtues, such as freedom, liberty, independence, or honesty.[8] In contrast to the first two approaches, a third group of scholars identify the way in which the public role of landscape-symbolism is contingent on particular cultural and political contexts.[9]

Landscape and National Authenticity

Even though each of the three positions outlined above has something to recommend them, I believe that neither is satisfactory when it comes to analyzing the possible causes of the changing currency enjoyed by geographical symbolism in definitions of nationhood. In what follows I shall put forward an analytical position that places equal weight upon historical traditions and cultural structures on the one hand and on factors of a more contingent, context-bound nature on the other.

To move from description to explanation, I shall begin by defining the 'nation' as a cultural order (composed of certain idioms, symbols, values and myths).[10] Nations, thus understood, are not static entities, for, as Fernand Braudel reminded us: any nation 'can have its being only at the price of being forever in search of itself'.[11] It is thus first and foremost to this recurrent project of national reconstruction (i.e., to the process whereby nations are being fostered and redefined in the course of history) that I am referring when I make use of the term 'national identity'. The key concept with regard to national identity is authenticity.[12] That is to say, reconstructing nations over time means reconstructing them as distinctive, original and historically embedded orders. Rousseau put forward this historicist point succinctly by declaring that 'the first rule which we have to follow is that of national character: every people has, or must have, a character; if it lacks one, we must start by endowing it with one.'[13] From a formal point of view, the authentication of a national culture entails two processes: the construction of continuity with a nation's alleged ethno-historical past (historicism) on the one hand, and the creation of a sense of naturalness (naturalization) on the other. The two processes, while analytically separate, are mutually intertwined and typically reinforce each other: whereas references to significant features of the natural environment serve to bolster a cultural community's continuity-claims, the historicist curiosity for the collective past inevitably directs attention to significant features of the 'homeland'.[14] Broadly speaking, the fundamental role of both historicism and naturalization has to do, in large part, with their preventing the historical and cultural contingency of modern nations from entering into the picture.[15]

In addition, what is assumed here is that modern nations go through 'settled' and 'unsettled' periods. During settled periods, the values, symbols and myths that make up the nation as a cultural order are more or less taken for granted so that they form, as it were, a cultural tradition or common sense. During unsettled historical phases, on the other hand, national authenticity is put into question, engendering endeavours at re-defining national identity. Such efforts to reconstruct the 'nation' are both path dependent and contingent. They are contingent insofar as they present symbolic 'responses' to specific conditions and events, either domestic or international in nature. Yet at the same time, such projects of national reconstruction are path dependent. That is to say, their mostly intellectual protagonists are bound to draw - to some degree at least - upon existing cultural resources (consisting of certain national idioms, symbols, values and myths) that are deeply entrenched in a given society. The impact of such cultural resources in the process of national reconstruction is conditioning rather than determining. By furnishing the cognitive and expressive frameworks for those involved in the project of national reconstruction, these resources minimize the likelihood of pure 'invention'. And yet, it needs stressing that the situational aspect is key to any explanation of the respective outcomes of these national projects: While certain intellectuals and nationalist movements may regard it as sufficient, at one point in time, to define a particular nation by emphasizing its voluntaristic, 'civic' character, this alone may be viewed as inappropriate under altered circumstances.[16] This leads us to the Swiss example.

In Search of National Authenticity: Nationalizing Nature (until 1870)

We can envisage various ways of establishing a symbolic link between a national community and a particular landscape. As we shall see, the analogy between the Alps and Swiss nationhood thereby could take either of two forms. The first form could be called the *nationalization of nature*. What is characteristic here is that popular historical myths, memories and supposed national virtues are projected into a significant landscape in an attempt to lend more continuity and distinctiveness to Swiss national identity. In this way, an image of national authenticity is developed in which the Alps appear as the natural seat and ultimate expression of Swiss national characteristics and virtues. As a way of establishing an analogy between 'landscape' and 'nation', this first form of discourse came into use in the eighteenth century in the wake of neoclassicism and early Romanticism, and was to remain predominant in Switzerland until roughly the 1870s.

There were, to be true, ideological precedents for this pattern which go back to the Humanist interest in natural history. In 1555, the Swiss Conrad Gessner climbed Mount Pilatus and summed up his experience in emotive tones, singling out, among other things, 'the clarity of the mountain water, the fragrance of wild flowers, ... the purity of the air, the richness of the milk'.[17] Learned men like Gessner and Johannes Stumpf, along with a tiny number of mountain enthusiasts from all over Europe, no doubt set the tone for future alpine discourse.

Discovering an Alpine Republic: The Mountains as the Seat of National Virtue

Notwithstanding these precedents, the breakthrough towards 'nationalization of nature' came only in the early eighteenth century, when the mountains 'had ceased to be monstrosities and had become an integral part of varied and diversified Nature',[18] and when (towards the end of the century) a cult-like enthusiasm was forged around the Swiss Alps in particular.[19] Various scientists and poets, foreign and Swiss alike, contributed to this development. The Englishman Thomas Robinson, in his

'Natural History', for instance, described the Alps as an 'integral and necessary part of nature's harmony'. The Swiss Johann Jakob Scheuchzer, in the 1720s, after two decades of travelling the Alps, published his *Itinera Alpina,* containing a topographical description of the Alps. Also of considerable influence as well was the poem *Die Alpen* by the Bernese physician (and sometimes poet), Albrecht von Haller. His poem, first published in 1732 and subsequently translated into most European languages, became an eighteenth century best seller and an inspiration for successive generations of Alpine travellers.[20]

Thanks to the works of Johann Jakob Scheuchzer, Albrecht von Haller, and an ever-increasing body of foreign travel literature, the Alps developed into an important aspect of Swiss patriotism in the last third of the eighteenth century.[21] The intellectual focal point of this rapidly progressing movement, the Helvetic Society (founded in 1761) presented the Alps as the seat of the country's national virtues. In 1763 one of its founding fathers, Franz Urs Balthasar, expressed the significance of this connection, saying that the character of the Swiss nation found its complete expression in its untamed, Alpine landscape. In addition, the Alps were conceived of as the location where the Swiss Confederation had been founded and had experienced its golden age of the thirteenth and fourteenth centuries. The mountains of central Switzerland, especially the Gotthard, where the Habsburg army of knights had been defeated in 1315 and 1386 respectively, were portrayed as the ultimate birthplace of liberty and independence.[22]

A decisive step towards the popularization of the symbolic link between landscape and the core myths in Switzerland's history was taken with the publication of Schiller's *Wilhelm Tell* in 1804.[23] As Haller before him, Schiller presented the Alps as a natural habitat that was conducive to the emergence of a pure, simple, honest and liberty-loving character. While receiving mixed reviews when first staged in Weimar in March 1804, the play was an immense popular success. It was read and performed throughout the nineteenth century and became part of the literary canon of Swiss primary schools.[24] Although by no means single-handedly, Schiller's drama contributed much to the spread of the late medieval myths of Swiss foundation and liberation (particularly the Oath on the Rütli and the deeds of Wilhelm Tell against Gessler). Hitherto largely confined to the educated elite, the myths now reached ever-wider sections of the public.[25]

Yet it was after the founding of the modern Swiss nation state in 1848, that national identity developed conspicuously strong links with the landscape.[26] In the latter half of the nineteenth century, for example, the Alps became the most common icon on tourist souvenirs. Furthermore, alpine scenery became a prominent feature in the works of some of the most renowned Swiss painters towards the end of the nineteenth century. While Albert Anker focused on the supposedly virtuous world of the peasants residing at the foot of the great mountains, Ferdinand Hodler presented the mountains as a powerful symbol of republican will and cultural mediation. In the 1860s, the novelist Gottfried Keller, in his *Grüner Heinrich*, declared that '[w]ith the thoughtlessness of youth and childish age, I believed that the natural beauty of Switzerland was a reflection of historical and political merit and of the patriotism of the Swiss people: an equivalent of freedom itself'.[27]

The *nationalization of nature,* though crucial as a mechanism for rendering Swiss national identity authentic, was not confined to the Swiss case. We also encounter it in the English discourse on landscape which, ever since the nineteenth century (at least in its prevailing current of rural paternalism) showed a preference for the tamed over the savage lands, equating the former with stability, permanence and harmony, while associating the latter with what was seen as the anarchism epitomized in American and French republicanism.[28] In France, too, where Vidal de la Blache invented 'human geography' as a scientific discipline at the end of the nineteenth century, landscape, for a time at least, was crucial as a means of defining national identity. As in England, French geographers and historians depicted humans as having the upper-hand over nature rather than being determined by it, a theme most cogently expressed by Michelet: 'Society, freedom have mastered nature, history has rubbed out geography. In this marvellous transformation, spirit has won over matter, the general over the particular, and idea over contingencies.'[29]

Germany, to cite another prominent example, presents us with a different picture. Here, wherever since the late eighteenth century the belief in ethnic homogeneity had not been seriously questioned, the concern, at least among geographers of the late nineteenth century, was primarily with the determination of boundaries rather than with specific landscapes. After 1890, for instance, geography as a discipline became the vehicle of an attempt to elevate the 'relatively low awareness of the 'colonial question' by the public', with *Kolonialkunde* and *Meereskunde* becoming elements of the curriculum of national education.[30] At the same time, however, there had been a long-standing preoccupation in the

German case with the influence of the natural environment and of the 'soil', especially the Teutonic woods, on what contemporaries commonly called the Germanic character. Later, this notion became a centrepiece of the organicism of the Romantics, and, after that, of *völkisch* nationalism.[31]

In Search of Ethnocultural Unity: Naturalizing the Nation (1870-1945)

It has long been acknowledged by scholars of nationalism that the progression of national identities is causally related to international factors, such as geopolitics, warfare or ideological competition.[32] Nationalism established itself as the dominant cultural and political force in nineteenth century Europe, stirring competition between different conceptions of nationality and serving as a major catalyst of national self-assertion. What posed a serious challenge to the Swiss conception of nationality was the fact that of all the possible European nationalisms the 'ethno-linguistic' turned out to be the dominant version from the last third of the nineteenth century until the end of the Second World War. Particularly in Italy and Germany, this form of nationalism rapidly gained force around 1870 when it came to be seen as somewhat of a normative prerequisite of national legitimacy and served as a fertile ground for the emergence of irredentist movements in both countries. When Nazism rose to power in 1933, its *völkisch* nationalism, with its markedly racial overtones, proved tantamount to a denial of the legitimacy of Switzerland's conception of nationality.[33]

It was against this historical background that the second pattern of linking 'nature' and 'nation' (what I designate the *naturalization of the nation)* came to prevail. Resting upon a notion of geographical determinism, this notion attributed to the natural environment a role that went beyond the expression of certain presumed national virtues and characteristics. Here nature, or in the Swiss case, the Alps, was depicted as a force capable of determining national identity and giving it a compact, homogeneous, unified form. To maintain that the *naturalization of the nation* came to prevail after around 1870 is of course not to say that the break was an absolute one. Constituting a framework of perception and interpretation which was familiar to the bulk of the educated public, the 'preceding' pattern (the *nationalization of nature*) had indeed largely prepared the ground for the emergence and dissemination of its successor. Moreover, the notion of geographical determinism was not wholly irrelevant to definitions of national identity prior to the 1870s. Nevertheless, as the available evidence clearly suggests, during the 1870s, there occurred a significant change of emphasis in the prevalent pattern of linking the Alps to the nation.

The Alps as a Homogenizing Force

As early as 1884, the eminent Swiss historian Karl Dändliker warned of the challenge posed by ethnic nationalism when he declared that 'the Swiss people did not enjoy the advantage of their neighbours: Being a nation in the true and literal sense of the world, that is to say, being an entity uniform in terms of linguistic and ethnic composition'.[34] Dändliker's statement does not represent a marginal view but forms part of a concern that was apparently widespread at the time, at least among liberal intellectuals and the political establishment, the two groups that had been traditionally in charge of the definition and legitimation of Swiss nationhood. In December 1914, when German- and French-speaking Swiss had clashed over conflicting sympathies towards the parties involved in World War I, the writer Carl Spitteler, in an emphatic call for national unity, argued that in the current European climate the lack of both ethno-cultural homogeneity and a strong centralist state were 'all elements of political weakness'.[35]

Statements like the latter unmistakably testify to the significant normative force of ethno-linguistic nationalism at the time. But the ethnic option was simply not open to those willing to preserve Switzerland's polyethnic status quo. Faced with the challenge of ethnic nationalism, liberal intellectuals thus embarked on an endeavour to create a distinct national identity for Switzerland. And it was in this context that alpine landscape once more came to play a crucial part in the definition of Swiss national identity. Yet given that ethnic and *völkisch* conceptions of nationhood emphasized homogeneity in terms of its ethnic or racial composition, the *nationalization of nature* (the pattern which portrays the natural environment as an expression of the 'national character') would have been somewhat deficient as an ideological response. In view of the challenge at hand, the *naturalization of the nation,* the analogy that put the stress on external determination and can best be understood as a kind of ideological ethnogenesis, seemed to be the more appropriate response. But to arrive at a better understanding of why that particular Alpine 'response' came to predominate, let me reconstruct the overall ideological reaction in Switzerland to ethnic nationalism in its successive stages and different facets.

Some intellectuals reacted to the ideological challenge at hand by putting forward a civic brand of nationalism. At first glance, at least, the forging of a civic nationalism (the brand of nationalism that, by and large, had been dominant in Switzerland ever since the late eighteenth century) seemed to provide an appropriate antidote against the threat of ethnic nationalism. The most outspoken supporter of this kind of response in the 1870s was Carl Hilty, an academic and influential public intellectual. In 1875 he maintained that Switzerland was the perfect nation, and that it was its destiny and its secular mission to uphold a truly republican, voluntarist conception of nationality in a Europe in which the ethnic ideal was in the ascendant:

> Not race or ethnic community, nor common language and customs, nor nature and history have founded the state of the Swiss Confederation...What holds Switzerland together vis à vis her [linguistically more homogeneous] neighbours is an ideal, namely the consciousness of being part of a state that in many ways represents a more civilised community; to constitute a nationality which stands head and shoulder above mere affiliations of blood or language.[36]

But Hilty's purely civic conception of nationality (which was undoubtedly influenced by the critical school of Swiss historiography that was gaining ground at the time),[37] though widespread among liberal-minded intellectuals, did not reflect the dominant current of thought.[38] Instead, a more popular version of nationalism traced Switzerland's civic present back to its pre-modern past. This was based, on the one hand, upon the myths of liberation and foundation (in particular the legends of Wilhelm Tell and the Oath of the Rütli), and upon the memories of allegedly glorious events (especially the victorious battles against the Habsburgs in 1315 and 1386). On the other hand, it rested on the values and institutions of the modern Swiss nation state, founded in 1848. These two ideological dimensions, one inspired by legalist rationality and liberal-democratic ethics, the other by the emotive power of an ideological myth of descent, were at the heart of Swiss national identity in its most widespread form.[39] And overall, this synthesis proved to be highly effective. From the era of the Helvetic Republic (1798-1803) to at least the end of the Second World War, this was the officially propagated version of national identity, and it was popular in all parts of the country.[40]

Nonetheless, to some contemporaries, both the purely civic conception of national identity and its more popular historicist counterpart, seemed insufficient as the sole basis of Swiss nationality. Johann-Kaspar Bluntschli (1808-1881), for instance, a moderate conservative politically, and an intellectual and professional colleague of Hilty's, maintained around 1870 that, in view of current debates on nationality in Europe, and given that 'the belief in the existence of a particular [Swiss] nation vis-à-vis the German, French and Italian nationalities had recently been severely contested, it had become necessary to draw the boundaries of Switzerland's national identity more firmly. To accomplish this, Bluntschli argued, a notion of nationality that was grounded on voluntarism and the institutions of the modern state, as Hilty had proposed, would not suffice. But neither, he maintained, would the reference back to the mythical past *per se*, even if it fostered the reproduction of historical memories of wars fought for independence and liberty in the fourteenth and fifteenth centuries. Instead, to buttress the claim for a distinct national identity that could stand up to the force of ethnic nationalism, a further element was needed. It is here that Bluntschli brings the Alpine landscape into play:

> I am surprised that Hilty did not, besides referring to the influence of the political idea, seek assistance from the country's nature to make the notion of Swiss nationality acceptable. For Switzerland's landscape is indeed of a peculiar character. If the Swiss possess a particular nationality, then this feeling derives above all from the existence of their beautiful homeland.... There may well be Alps, mountains, seas and rivers outside Switzerland; and yet, the Swiss homeland constitutes such a coherent and richly structured natural whole, one that enables to evolve on its soil a peculiar feeling of a common homeland which unites its inhabitants as sons of the same fatherland, even though they live in different valleys and speak different languages.[41]

It needs underscoring that the cult of the mountains crossed linguistic divisions, just as it crossed political boundaries.[42] For example, the French-speaking intellectual Ernest Bovet, professor of French literature at the University of Zurich, in a 1909 article with the noteworthy title *Refléxions d'un Homo Alpinus,* wrote: 'Our independence was born in the mountains, and the mountains still determine our whole life, give it its particularity and unity', rejecting wholeheartedly the intellectual and moral validity of ethnic and racial conceptions of nationhood.[43] And only a few months later, in an essay entitled *Nationalité*, Bovet made the same point, linking the alpine narrative with the two other cornerstones of Swiss national identity - its historicism and its emphasis on liberty and independence (1909b, p. 441):

> A mysterious force has kept us together for 600 years and has given to us our democratic institutions. A good spirit watches our liberty. A spirit fills our souls, directs our actions and creates a hymn on the one ideal out of our different languages. It is the spirit that blows from the summits, the genius of the Alps and glaciers ... Not accidentally was the mountain the herdsmen's protective wall to keep out the knights. It was itself their place of birth; the mountain's blanc soil, its rough sky, have shaped their character, and ever since has the mountain determined our inner life.[44]

The religious socialist Leonhard Ragaz, in his popular book *Die Neue Schweiz* (published in 1918) argued in a similar vein, drawing a picture of a crisis-ridden Switzerland in need of moral regeneration. He, too, evoked alpine nature as the source the Swiss should turn to in order to find their authentic self: 'What belongs to us above all else are the mountains in their might and majesty, their tranquillity and their purity; furthermore, a certain simplicity of way of life, a certain perfume of nature and primitive force, and an air of rustic life'.[45] Some twenty years later, the geographer Charles Burky, in an immensely popular brochure that was on display at the National Exhibition of 1939, put forward the notion of geographical determinism in its purest mode: 'The physical milieu, the natural environment determines a people. This is an axiom, and apparently Switzerland cannot escape from it ... This savage and haughty nature remained untamed. Only the mountain dweller can cope with it'.[46]

Perhaps unsurprisingly, we find the most extreme forms of this geographical determinism in the 1930s. Its champions were authors who, while explicitly dealing with social-Darwinist and racial ideas, stopped short of accepting the premises of these schools of thought in the face of Swiss polyethnic reality. In his essay entitled 'The ethnic structure of Switzerland', the Zurich geographer Emil Egli puts forward a Swiss version of ideological ethnogenesis: 'For the racial scholar, Switzerland is a difficult field of study, because, for logical reasons, the racially pure must step aside in favour of the mixture'. In another paragraph of the same text, he describes how immigrants can be naturalized and thus become a part of what he conceives as the organic fabric of the Swiss nation. Becoming a Swiss national, Egli tells us, is something that is ultimately determined by the natural environment (he uses the term 'Alpinization') and is thus beyond the human will to merely assimilate.[47]

The Popularization of the Alpine Myth

The Spread of the Alpine Myth

The previous analysis has for the most part focused on intellectuals, naturally the most vocal segments within any nation's public sphere. However, the idea that the Alps formed the ultimate source of national authenticity, that they were capable of fusing different linguistic groups into a single, homogeneous nation was not confined solely to the realm of scholarly and intellectual discourse. To be sure, until the mid-nineteenth century the alpine ideal had been the special preserve of a relatively small but articulate group of intellectuals and members of the political intelligentsia. By the last quarter of the nineteenth century, however, this doctrine had gained currency among wide sections of the population, culminating in the 1930s in an almost obsessive preoccupation with the alleged national significance of the Alps.

Even though it is difficult to grasp precisely how the Alpine myth spread from its intellectual producers to ever-wider sections of the public, there are numerous examples that suggest that it had indeed become part of the national consciousness by the turn of the twentieth century if not before. This was favoured, first and foremost, by national festivals and rituals of various sorts. A great many Swiss men and women directly participated in such public national events, many of which were deliberately staged in an alpine environment. Crucial among these were historical plays, which experienced a remarkable boom after 1885.[48] Furthermore, alpine regions provided the traditional geographical setting for military training courses, which provided a fertile ground for the forging of popular patriotism; and ever since the early nineteenth century, the great majority of Switzerland's male population has had to contribute to these most prominent rituals of the modern nation state, whether they liked it or not. Of no less importance was a folk-song movement that had witnessed a rapid expansion since the latter half of the nineteenth century, thus helping to embed the Alpine myth in the hearts and minds of many Swiss.[49] Likewise, alpine symbolism played a crucial role in the ideology of *Geistige Landesverteidigung* ('spiritual defence of the country'), manifested in the National Exhibition of 1939.[50] In official pamphlets on display at the exhibition, the Gotthard was depicted as the mountain which, by fusing four different linguistic groups into a culturally and spiritually united nation, had enabled Switzerland to exist.

The ideologies of the major political movements of the time were also replete with images of the Alps. During each of the two world wars, the Liberal and Conservative parties in particular made frequent use of alpine symbolism in their definitions of the Swiss national identity.[51] So did people with direct influence on the course of national education. The school- inspector Jacob Christinger, to name but one example, in a much noticed final speech at the National Conference of Teachers in Basel in 1884, presented the argument with unmistakable clarity:

> It seems that linguistic and religious differences in particular form a barrier to the national education of the Swiss people, and some go even so far as to deny that our people possess a unified national character. We do not want to accept this delusion. We all gaze upon the same mountains, look back to the same heroic figures in our history, enjoy the same folk songs and are proud of the same rights and liberties.[52]

Moreover, recent analyses of history and text books used in secondary education in all parts of the country have revealed that the Alps served as one of the major motifs in fostering national identity within the education system.[53] Hence, in 1905, on the occasion of the 100th anniversary of Schiller's death, the *Verein für die Verbreitung guter Schriften* ('Association for the Promotion of Good Books') launched a special edition of *Wilhelm Tell,* the drama in which the Alpine landscape around the lake of Lucerne figures so prominently and which had become part of the Swiss literary canon soon after its first publication in 1804.[54]

In the field of artistic production, painting stood out in terms of the attention it devoted to the alpine theme. Already during the nineteenth century, with Alexandre Calame and François Diday, mountain painting 'had come to represent the very embodiment of national art' in Switzerland, very similar in style to the Romantic Norwegian artists J.C. Dahl and Thomas Fearnley.[55] But the peak of Swiss landscape painting was not reached until the turn of the century, in the form of the work of Ferdinand Hodler. In paintings such as *Dialogue with Nature* and *Communion with the Infinite,* Hodler revived 'the Romantic belief in the spiritual replenishment and uplifting experience to be derived from oneness with the grandeur of nature'. Hodler's naturalistic paintings, wrote the art critic Hermann Ganz, added 'an overpowering force and magnitude to the Swiss landscape, enabling Switzerland to stand out as an independent entity against the countries which surround it.'[56]

Finally, in an age of quickly expanding popular travel and mass communications, tourist propaganda and newspapers were important vehicles for the dissemination of alpine myths. In an advertisement launched by the Federal Swiss Railway Company during the inter-war period, the beauty of the country's rivers, its countryside and forests were described at length, principally to underline the outstanding significance of the Swiss mountains. For, as is pointed out in the text, it is the Alps that 'encircle the country and thus delimit its space, that defend and erect it, and that elevate it'.[57] In newspapers and pamphlets, too, the Alps figured prominently as one of the most frequently evoked symbols of national identity and unity. As a Zurich-based newspaper aimed at a lower middle-class readership put it in the 1930s:

> We understand by Swissness a certain inheritance of spiritual and physical features which we find among the people as a whole between the Alps and the Jura throughout the centuries of our history to the present day. ... We are the only typically alpine state in Europe.... The Alps are our actual strength, for it is in the alpine human being that we find our common ground.[58]

The Plausibility of the Alpine Myth

As the Swiss example shows, creating analogies linked to historically charged parts of the natural environment can be a highly effective way of reconstructing the nation as an authentic community. Because history and nature become symbiotically linked in this process, the nation is at the same time firmly located in time and space. Nature in general, and specific landscapes in particular, thus contribute greatly to buttressing the belief in the historical continuity of nations and in their being determined by external and physical rather than social factors. However, the role of landscape in the reconstruction of nations varies according to time and circumstances. In the case of Switzerland, the salience of the alpine myth was most marked between 1870 and 1945 when its polyethnic conception of nationality was severely contested by the rise of ethno-linguistic nationalism in Europe. This provoked a crisis of national identity in Switzerland which, in turn, engendered a project of national reconstruction. Unlike in France and England, where human beings were supposed to have the upper hand over their natural environment, in Switzerland, at a time of considerable social uncertainty, people sought guidance from a rugged example of nature, which they found in 'their' alpine landscape. Intellectuals and portions of the intelligentsia portrayed this landscape as a relentless force capable of determining the character of their nation and its inhabitants - an ideological pattern which I have termed the *naturalization of the nation.*

Does this mean, however, that the alpine myth became an important part of Swiss national identity during this period simply because of external challenges which, in turn, provoked a fierce national 'response' based upon public rituals and ceremonies, the education system, and the media? Much does indeed support this view. To begin with, it is surely true that 'What men see in Nature is a result of what they have been taught to see'[59] and like all sustaining national myths, the alpine narrative did not depend for its effectiveness upon its being true. For it can hardly be argued that the Alps, as the myth would have us believe, were a defensive castle, protecting the Swiss against external military threats throughout the centuries. They did not, at any rate, pose an insurmountable obstacle for the French troops when they invaded Switzerland in 1798. Nor was the military defence ring built around the Gotthard-massif in the late summer of 1940 - the *Réduit Nationale* - the main reason why Hitler's *Wehrmacht* did not invade Switzerland (a belief to which a great many Swiss growing up in the 1940s and 1950s chose to subscribe against an overwhelming amount of contradicting evidence).

Were the mountains responsible for what contemporaries called the Swiss 'national character'? Had the Alps created a people of pure and simple herdsmen, a bit rude perhaps, but otherwise proud and certainly not to be ridiculed when their independence and liberty were at stake? Again, this seems hardly plausible; especially during the time span under consideration, Switzerland, a country extremely poor in natural resources, was transformed from a rural to an industrial nation. By 1910, it was the most industrialized European country next to England, and the bulk of its population resided in towns rather than small villages, with only an insignificant number actually dwelling in mountainous regions.[60]

But why did the alpine narrative seem plausible all the same? Why, then, did so many Swiss apparently subscribe to the belief that the mountains were a vital source of Swiss national identity, that they had shaped their character, and hence that of 'their' nation? I believe that an additional argument is necessary to arrive at a fuller explanation for the important role played by the Alps in definitions of Swiss national identity. The argument asserts that the alpine myth in general (which entails both patterns: the 'nationalization of nature' *and* the 'naturalization of the nation') seemed plausible to a great many Swiss because it was grounded in certain material realities.

One such condition is plain physical topography. Topography mattered in that it formed a potentiality or 'possiblilism', as Lucien Febvre described Vidal de la Blache's conception of human geography - even if it was human actors that did the selecting of particular landscapes, and endowed them with national significance.[61] In Switzerland's case, it can hardly be neglected that of its overall territory (which is indeed small according to European standards) more than 60% is covered by mountains, many of its peaks rising above 4000 metres.[62] Furthermore, towards the end of the nineteenth century travel and tourism started to affect the masses. Consequently, many Swiss men and women became well acquainted with the mountains through lived experience. For some this was, because they took the opportunity to travel them, while for most this was because they could see them on a clear day, irrespective of whether they lived in Zurich, Bern, Geneva, Lucerne or Lugano.

The second condition of importance concerns the economic and political significance of the Alps in the evolution of the Swiss Confederation from the fourteenth century onwards. According to Perry Anderson, the mountains of central Switzerland, along with the military success of the Confederate peasant army in the battles against the Habsburgs at Morgarten (1315) and Sempach (1386), helped prevent feudalism from taking root and let the Swiss Confederation emerge as 'a unique independent republic in Europe'.[63] Moreover, gaining control over the mountain passes in order to secure the exchange of goods and capital with the prosperous Italian city-states proved vital to the economic and cultural development of the Confederate valley-communities and towns.[64] To sum it up, a specific sociopolitical context, articulate ideologies, effective means of communication, as well as the country's geographical structure and historical development were together the factors responsible for the fundamental role of alpine imagery in the reconstruction of Swiss national identity between 1870 and the end of the Second World War.

Notes

1   Schama (1995, pp. 83-4 and pp. 254-5).
2   Schama (1995, p. 10). The extent to which climatological factors might be responsible for alleged national differences preoccupied some thinkers of the Renaissance, as Hale (1994, p. 55), among others, has shown. For an excellent historical account of the relationship between nature and culture from Antiquity to the late eighteenth century, see Glacken (1967).
3   Rosen and Zerner (1984, p. 52).
4   For an exception, see Smith (1986, pp. 183-90).
5   Good recent examples are the reader *Geography and National Identity* edited by David Hooson (1994), and Daniels (1993). And there is of course Simon Schama's (1995) pathbreaking historical account.
6   Lowenthal (1994, p. 383).
7   See Hooson (1994, introduction). For a primordialist account of the connection between nature and group life that operates with the more general term 'territoriality', see Grosby (1995).
8   This approach is characteristic of most contributions in Hooson (1994).
9   A point made by both Lowenthal (1978, p. 401) and Schama (1995, p. 15).
10 This definition presupposes an analytical difference between two different conceptions of community and social organization: 'nation' and 'state'. At its most basic, it holds that the nation, as a cultural order, lends meaning and legitimacy to the state. The latter, in turn, is rooted in a set of legal, political and economic institutions. Modern nation-states can be regarded as a synthesis between these two conceptions. This distinction is spelled out in Smith (1995, chapter 4).
11 Braudel (1989, p. 23).
12 On the concept of national authenticity, see Smith (1995, pp. 65-7).
13 Quoted in Smith (1991, p. 75).
14 On the part played by 'ethnic historicism' in the emergence of nationalism, see, for example, Smith (1991, chapter 4 and 1995, chapter 3).
15 The 'naturalization of social classifications' as a measure to reduce uncertainty is discussed most illuminatingly in Douglas (1987, p. 48). Benedict Anderson, in his *Imagined Communities* (1991, p. 12), has made a related point in arguing that 'It is the magic of nationalism to turn chance into destiny'.
16 The way I conceptualize the reproduction and change of national identity draws heavily on two most illuminating theoretical essays: See Swidler (1986) and Sewell (1996).
17 Quoted in Schama (1995, p. 430).
18 Hope Nicolson (1959, p. 345).

19   This enthusiasm owed much to the early-romantic movement's turning the Alps into the ultimate symbol of wilderness and purity. On this development, see Wozniakowski (1987).

20   Bernard (1978, pp. 9-13).

21   Walter (1990, p. 57).

22   Marchal (1992, p. 45).

23   Weishaupt (1992, p. 23).

24   Bernard (1978, p. 24).

25   The Oath of the Ruetli (said to be taken in 1307 by the three valley communities Uri, Schwyz, and Unterwalden) forms the foundation myth of the Swiss Confederation; Wilhelm Tell (who according to the legend assassinated Gessler, the allegedly oppressive Habsburg bailiff) personifies its struggle for liberation. The Swiss foundation and liberation myths are discussed in Im Hof (1991, chapter 1).

26   Walter (1989, p. 287).

27   Quoted in Jost (1988, p. 19).

28   To quote Lowenthal (1994, p. 22): '... the English landscape is not natural but crafted.... Englishmen tame and adorn nature...'. For the symbolic significance of English landscape during the inter-war period, see Potts (1989).

29   Quoted in Claval (1994, p. 44). This author's translation.

30   Sandner (1994, p. 77).

31   Schama (1995, chapter 2).

32   For two recent contributions to the study of national identity that make systematic use of this assumption, see Greenfeld (1992), and Colley (1992).

33   While Bismarckian Germany rested on a statist rather than 'ethnic' conception of nationhood, it has to be borne in mind that many Germans regarded the so-called *kleindeutsche Lösung* as an incomplete nation-state. The Pan-German League certainly presented the most radical (but by no means the only) current within German ethnic nationalism prior to 1900. The *völkisch* movement that rapidly gained ground in Wilhelmine Germany and reached its peak under the Nazis could thereby capitalize on earlier ideological precedents. On German 'homeland nationalism' and its institutional manifestations, see Brubaker (1992, especially chapters 3 and 6 (1996, especially pp. 114-7). On the emergence and spread of *völkisch* nationalism in Germany, see Mosse (1964) and Greenfeld (1992, ch. 4). On European ethno-linguistic nationalism more broadly, see also Alter (1985, p. 112), Hobsbawm (1993 (2nd ed.), ch. 4), Winkler (1984, introduction), Woolf (1995, pp. 16-25). On Italy, see Alter (1985), and Schieder (1991, pp. 329-46).

34   Quoted in de Capitani (1987, p. 25).

35   Spitteler (1915, p. 5).

36   Hilty (1875, p. 29).

37   On the influence of this critical school of historians on the definition of Swiss national identity, see Kreis (1991, ch. 4) and Im Hof (1991, pp. 233-5).

38   A civic conception did come to dominate the liberal and left-of-centre discourse again during the 1930s. See Zimmer (1996).

39   The important distinction between 'ideological' and 'genealogical' myths of descent is examined in Smith (1984).

40   A view taken by both Im Hof (1991) and Marchal (1990). On Swiss nationalism during the Helvetic Republic (1798-1803), see Frei (1964). For the development of national identity in the French-speaking part of Switzerland between 1848 and 1914, see Kreis (1987). The best general work on Swiss history in the English language is Steinberg (1996).

41   Bluntschli (1875, p. 11). A second edition of Bluntschli's essay on nationality appeared in 1915, when the tensions between German- and French-speaking Swiss had reached their peak.

42   The significance of the alpine myth in French-speaking Switzerland is explored in Clavien (1993, pp. 104-18).

43   Bovet (1909a, p. 289).

44   Bovet (1909b, p. 441).

45   Ragaz (1918, p. 49).

46   Quoted in Lasserre (1992, p. 198).

47   Quoted in Kreis (1992, p. 176).

48   A very recent study of newspaper articles from August 1st (August 1st being Switzerland's national holiday since 1891) in the period from 1891 to 1935 reveals that the alpine myth - in all the dimensions discussed above - occupied a crucial place in liberal and conservative papers all over the country while the socialist press was more critical. See Merki (1995, pp. 67-71). On national festivals, see Santschi (1991). For a discussion of historical plays, see Kreis (1988).

49   Braun (1965, pp. 326-9).

50   Lasserre (1992, p. 192); Marchal (1992, pp. 49-50).

51   This is set out in Widmer (1992, pp. 619-38) and Wigger (1996, pp. 86-9).

52   Quoted in Helbling (1994, p. 160).

53   See, for instance, Helbling (1994) and Rutschmann (1994). On the significance of folk songs, see Im Hof (1991, pp. 158-9).

54   Helbling (1994, p. 173).

55   Nasgaard (1984, p. 134).

56   Quoted in Jost (1988, p. 18).

57   The advertisement was launched in 1911 and 1937 respectively. The author of the text was the Genevan poet Philippe Monnier (1864-1911). Quoted in Walter (1992, p. 14).

58   *Neue Schweiz.* October 11, 1935. Quoted in Zimmer (1996, p. 100).

59   Hope Nicolson (1959, p. 3).

60   Von Greyerz (1980, pp. 1094-5).

61   The positions of Vidal de la Blache and Lucien Febvre are discussed in Braudel (1989, pp. 263-4).

62   This is a considerably higher proportion than that of France, Italy, or Austria, the other three countries possessing major parts of the overall European Alps chain. Nevertheless, with a twelve percent share of the Alps of Europe, the percentage covered by Switzerland is lower than in Austria (twenty-eight percent), Italy (twenty-seven percent), and France (twenty-two percent). The figures are taken from Wachter (1995, p. 39).

63   Anderson (1979, p. 301).

64   Marchal (1986, pp. 152-3).

References

Alter, P. (1985), *Nationalismus*, Suhrkamp, Frankfurt am Main.

Anderson, B. (1991), *Imagined Communities. Reflections on the Origin and Spread of Nationalism*, Verso, London, New York.

Anderson, P. (1979), *Lineages of the Absolutist State*, Verso, London, New York.

Bernard, P.P. (1978), *Rush to the Alps. The Evolution of Vacationing in Switzerland*, Columbia University Press, New York.

Bluntschli, J.C. (1915), *Die Schweizerische Nationalität*, First ed. 1875, Rascher & Cie., Zurich.

Bovet, E. (1909a), 'Réflexions d'un Homo Alpinus', *Wissen und Leben*, vol. 7, April.

Bovet, E. (1909b), 'Nationalité', *Wissen und Leben*, vol. 21, August.

Braudel, F. (1989), *The Identity of France. Volume I: History and Environment*, Fontana Press, London.

Braun, R. (1965), *Sozialer und Kultureller Wandel in einem Ländlichen Industriegebiet*, Eugen Rentsch Verlag, Erlenbach, Stuttgart.

Brubaker, R. (1992), *Citizenship and Nationhood in France and Germany*, Harvard University Press, Cambridge, Massachusetts.

Brubaker, R. (1996), *Nationalism Reframed. Nationhood and the National Question in the New Europe*, Cambridge University Press, Cambridge.

Claval, P. (1994), 'From Michelet to Braudel: Personality, Identity and Organization in France', in D. Hooson (ed.), *Geography and National Identity*, Blackwell, Oxford.

Clavien, A. (1993), *Les Helvétistes. Intellectuels et Politique en Suisse Romande au Début du Siècle*, Editions d'en Bas, Lausanne.

Colley, L. (1992), *Britons. Forging the Nation 1707-1837*, Yale University Press, New Haven, London.

Daniels, S. (1993), *Fields of Vision. Landscape Imagery and National Identity in England and The United States*, Polity Press, Cambridge.

De Capitani, F. (1987), 'Die Suche nach dem Gemeinsamen Nenner - Der Beitrag der Geschichtsschreiber, in F. De Capitani et al. (eds), *Auf dem Weg zu einer Schweizerischen Identität 1848-1914. Probleme - Errungenschaften - Misserfolge*, Universitätsverlag, Freiburg.

Douglas, M. (1987), *How Institutions Think*, Routledge & Kegan Paul, London.

Frei, D. (1964), *Das Schweizerische Nationalbewusstsein. Seine Förderung nach dem Zusammenbruch der Alten Eidgenossenschaft 1798*, Juris-Verlag, Zurich.

Glacken, C.J. (1967), *Traces on the Rhodian Shore. Nature and Culture in Western Thought from Ancient Times to the End of the Eighteenth Century*, University of California Press, Berkeley, Angeles.

Greenfeld, L. (1992), *Nationalism. Five Roads to Modernity.* Harvard University Press, Cambridge, Massachusetts.

Grosby, S. (1995), 'Territoriality: The Transcendental, Primordial Feature of Modern Societies', *Nations and Nationalism*, vol. 1, no. 2, March.

Hale, J. (1994), *The Civilization of Europe in the Renaissance*, Fontana Press, London.

Helbling, B. (1994), *Eine Schweiz für die Schule. Nationale Identität und Kulturelle Vielfalt in den Schweizer Lesebüchern seit 1900*, Chronos, Zurich.

Hilty, C. (1875), 'Die Schweizerische Nationalität', in C. Hilty, *Vorlesungen über die Politik der Eidgenossenschaft*, Max Fiala's Buch- und Kunsthandlung, Bern.

Hobsbawm, E.J. (1993), *Nations and Nationalism since 1780. Programme, Myth, Reality*, 2nd ed., Cambridge University Press, Cambridge.

Hooson, D. (1994) (ed.), *Geography and National Identity*, Blackwell, Oxford.

Hope Nicolson, M. (1959), *Mountain Gloom and Mountain Glory. The Development of the Aesthetics of the Infinite*, Cornell University Press, Ithaca, New York.

Im Hof, U. (1991), *Mythos Schweiz*, Verlag Neue Zürcher Zeitung, Zurich.

Jost, H.U. (1988), 'Nation, Politics, and Art', in Swiss Institute for Art Research on behalf of the Coordinating Commission for the Presence of Switzerland abroad (ed.), *From Liotard to le Corbusier. 200 years of Swiss Painting, 1730-1930*, Zurich.

Kreis, G. (1987), 'Die besseren Patrioten. Nationale Idee und Regionale Identität in der Französischen Schweiz vor 1914', in F. De Capitani et al. (eds), *Auf dem Weg zu einer Schweizerischen Identität 1848-1914. Probleme - Errungenschaften - Misserfolge*, Universitätsverlag, Freiburg.

Kreis, G. (1991), *Der Mythos von 1291. Zur Entstehungdes Schweizerischen Nationalfeiertages*, Friedrich Reinhardt Verlag, Basle.

Kreis, G. (1992), 'Der 'Homo Alpinus Helveticus'. Zum Schweizerischen Rassendiskurs der 30er Jahre', in G.P. Marchal et al. (eds), *Erfundene Schweiz. Konstruktionen Nationaler Identität*, Chronos, Zurich.

Lasserre, A. (1992), 'Le Peuple des Bergers dans son Réduit National', in G.P. Marchal et al. (eds), *Erfundene Schweiz. Konstruktionen Nationaler Identität*, Chronos, Zurich.

Lowenthal, D. (1978), 'Finding Valued Landscapes', *Progress in Human Geography*, vol. 2, no. 3.

Lowenthal, D. (1994), 'European and English Landscapes as National Symbols', in D. Hooson (ed.), *Geography and National Identity*, Blackwell, Oxford.

Marchal, G.P. (1986), 'Die Ursprünge der Unabhängigkeit (401-1394)', in U. Imhof et al. (eds), *Geschichte der Schweiz und der Schweizer*, Helving & Lichtenhahn, Basle, Frankfurt am Main.

Marchal, G.P. (1990), 'Die 'Alten Eidgenossen' im Wandel der Zeiten. Das Bild der Frühen Eidgenossen im Traditionsbewusstsein und in der Identitätsvorstellung der Schweizer vom 15. bis ins 20. Jahrhundert', in Historischer Verein der Fünf Orte (ed.), *Innerschweiz und Frühe Eidgenossenschaft. Jubiläumsschrift 700 Jahre Eidgenossenschaft*, vol. II, Walter-Verlag, Olten.

Marchal, G.P. (1992), 'Das 'Schweizeralpenland': Eine Imagologische Bastelei', in G.P. Marchal et al. (eds), *Erfundene Schweiz. Konstruktionen Nationaler Identität*, Chronos, Zurich.

Merki, C. (1995), *Und Wieder Lodern die Höhenfeuer. Die Schweizerische Bundesfeier als Hoch-Zeit der Nationalen Ideologie*, Chronos, Zurich.

Mosse, G.L. (1964), *The Crisis of German Ideology*, Grosset & Dunlap, New York.

Nasgaard, R. (1984), *The Mystic North. Symbolist Landscape Painting in Northern Europe and North America 1890-1940*, University of Toronto Press, Toronto.

Potts, A. (1989), 'Constable Country between the Wars', in R. Samuel (ed.), *Patriotism. The Making and Unmaking of British National Identity*, Routledge, London, New York.

Ragaz, L. (1918), *Die Neue Schweiz. Ein Programm für Schweizer und solche, die es werden wollen*, 2nd ed., Verlag W. Trösch, Olten.

Rosen, C. and Zerner, H. (1984), *Romanticism and Realism. Mythology of Nineteenth Century Art*, Faber and Faber, London.

Rutschmann, V. (1994), *Fortschritt und Freiheit. Nationale Tugenden in Historischen Jugendbüchern der Schweiz seit 1880*, Chronos, Zurich.

Sandner, G. (1994), 'In Search of Identity: German Nationalism and Geography, 1871-1910', in D. Hooson (ed.), *Geography and National Identity*, Blackwell, Oxford.

Santschi, C. (1991), *Schweizer Nationalfeste im Spiegel der Geschichte*, Chronos, Zurich.

Schama, S. (1995), *Landscape and Memory*, Fontana Press, London.

Schieder, T. (1991), *Nationalismus und Nationalstaat. Studien zum Nationalen Problem im Modernen Europa*, Vandenhoeck & Ruprecht, Göttingen.

Sewell, W. H. Jr. (1996), 'Three Temporalities: Toward an Eventful Sociology', in T.J. McDonald (ed.), *The Historic Turn in the Human Sciences*, The University of Michigan Press, Ann Arbor.

Smith, A.D. (1984), 'National Identity and Myths of Ethnic Descent', *Research in Social Movements, Conflict and Change*, vol. 7, pp. 95-130.

Smith, A.D. (1986), *The Ethnic Origins of Nations*, Blackwell, Oxford.

Smith, A.D. (1991), *National Identity*, Penguin Books, Harmondsworth.

Smith, A.D. (1995), *Nations and Nationalism in a Global Era*, Polity Press, Cambridge.

Spitteler, C. (1915), *Unser Schweizer Standpunkt*, Vortrag Gehalten in der NHG, Gruppe Zürich (December 14, 1914), Verlag Rascher & Cie., Zurich.

Steinberg, J. (1996), *Why Switzerland?* 2nd ed., Cambridge University Press, Cambridge.

Swidler, A. (1986), 'Culture in Action: Symbols and Strategies', *American Sociological Review*, vol. 51, pp. 273-86.

Von Greyerz, H. (1980), 'Der Bundesstaat seit 1848', *Handbuch der Schweizer Geschichte*, Berichthaus Verlag, Zurich.

Wachter, D. (1995), *Schweiz. Eine Moderne Geographie*, Verlag Neue Zürcher Zeitung, Zurich.

Walter, F. (1989), 'Attitudes towards the Environment in Switzerland', *Journal of Historical Geography*, vol. 15, no. 3.

Walter, F. (1990), *Les Suisses et l'Environment. Une Histoire du Rapport à la Nature du 18e Siècle à nos Jours*, Editions Zoé, Genève.

Walter, F. (1992), 'Lieux, Paysages, Espaces. Les Perceptions de la Montagne Alpine du XVIIIe Siècles à nos Jours', in J.F. Bergier et al. (eds), *La Découverte des Alpes*. Actes de Colloque Latsis 1990, Schwabe & Co. AG, Basle.

Weishaupt, M. (1992), *Bauern, Hirten und 'Frume Edle Puren'. Bauern - und Bauernstaatsideologie in der Spätmittelalterlichen Eidgenossenschaft und der Nationalen Geschichtsschreibung der Schweiz*, Helbing & Lichtenhahn, Basle.

Widmer, T. (1992), *Die Schweiz in der Wachstumskrise der 1880er Jahre*, Chronos, Zurich.

Wigger, E. (1996), *Vom Burgfrieden zum Bürgerblock: Krieg und Krise in der Politischen Kommunikation 1910-1922*, Seismo, Zurich.

Winkler, H. (1984) (ed.), *Nationalismus*, Athenäum, Königstein.

Woolf, S. (1995) (ed.), *Nationalism in Europe 1815 to the Present. A reader*. Routledge, London, New York.

Wozniakowski, J. (1987), *Die Wildnis. Zur Deutungsgeschichte des Berges in der Europäischen Neuzeit*, Suhrkamp, Frankfurt am Main.

Zimmer, O. (1996), 'Die 'Volksgemeinschaft'. Entstehung und Funktion einer Nationalen Einheitssemantik in den 1930er Jahren in der Schweiz', in K. Imhof et al. (eds), *Konkordanz und Kalter Krieg. Analyse von Medienereignissen in der Schweiz der Zwischen- und Nachkriegszeit*, Seismo, Zurich.

6 Folk Culture and the Construction of European National Identities between the Eighteenth and Twentieth Centuries

ANNE-MARIE THIESSE AND CATHERINE BERTHO-LAVENIR

The study of the construction of national identities in Europe sheds light on several remarkable phenomena. First, it would seem that, in many cases, the cultural construction of nations preceded and paved the way for their political construction. As a matter of fact, the definition of nations occurred through the determination, even if imprecise for a long period, of territorial groupings quite different from those that dynastic and military history had produced: by the partition of vast empires (Austro-Hungarian, Ottoman and Russian), by the grouping together of small states (the case of Germany) or by a combination of these processes (Italy and the former Yugoslavia). The legitimation invoked for the new territorial groupings was the existence of a culture common to these spaces, the natural consequence of which would have been to operate a political division or breakdown grouping together homogeneous cultural spaces. However, this principle presupposed that such cultural homogeneity should have first been produced and made manifest, something which it was not initially clear could be achieved. In order to present the future nations as homogeneous spaces, it was necessary to transcend local and regional disparities, which were frequently pronounced: differences in matters of customs, dialects, legal regulations, social and economic statutes, etc. The shaping of national cultural identities thus made it necessary to carry out a coherent, sustained and resolute operation, in order to produce, as a first step, identity-defining frames of reference, familiarity with and acceptance of which would subsequently be spread among the populations concerned. Two aspects of this process of constructing European national identities must be highlighted, for they are *a priori* paradoxical.

Firstly, this construction process, conducted by cultured elites, was generally undertaken by reference to popular or folk culture. What in fact occurred was the creation, in the world of literature and learning, of an ideal national folk culture which enjoyed a complex relationship with actual folk practices. Secondly, this process of shaping national cultural identity on the basis of a constructed folk culture presents very striking similarities in the different regions of Europe, to such an extent that it would be permissible to speak of a transnational model for the creation of national identities.

This process breaks down into three major periods. The first is the phase of affirmation of an original and ahistorical national culture, of which contemporary folk culture may be regarded as the depositary. The second corresponds to the proliferation of representations of that national culture, and their dissemination within ever broader social groups. The third, which frequently follows upon the constitution of the nation as a political entity, is the period when representations of the nation become popularized on a massive scale and are used in order to affirm a national collective identity which transcends social differences. The dating of these different phases is not the same for Europe as a whole, since the first began much later in Southern and Eastern Europe than in the North and West. However, the 'laggards' sped through the first and second phases at an accelerating rate, with the result that by the first half of the twentieth century, and above all during the inter-war period, the third phase may be observed throughout Europe.

I. The Invention of National Cultures

As a movement, the shaping of national identities was based, by and large, on the constitution of folk culture as national heritage. The reference to folk culture was enshrined in the ambition to think through, to legitimate and to represent the social bond between individuals. Indeed, once the process of legitimation by 'imperial fiat' (individuals considered as subjects of a single sovereign) is no longer regarded as effective or acceptable, it becomes necessary to highlight an intra-community link operating independently of the vicissitudes of dynastic and military history. Above all, from the eighteenth century on, the response provided in Northern and Western Europe was dictated by a measure of materialism. The primordial, irrefutable link between individuals, making it possible to identify 'natural' groupings and to establish the nascent political nations on a sound footing, must, it was felt, be sought in the remote recesses of History and in the underlying affinities between a particular land and the people whose native soil it was. The origins of the nation were assumed to go back to the great ancestors, whose values it was seen as an urgent task to rediscover and to promote, in order thereafter to cultivate the true national virtues. Moreover, the intimate relationship which a population enjoyed with the land it occupied, and the long-term impact of climate, were assumed to have fashioned the soul, the lifestyle and the *Weltanschauung* of a people, and thereby determined its specific nature in a quasi-mimetic interaction with the natural elements. From these twin perspectives, the people, in the societal sense - but this societal aspect is in fact fictive - was seen as the most proper custodian of national values and traditions. In contradistinction to transnational and learned culture - which in eighteenth-century Europe was also dominated by France's hegemony- folk culture was supposed to have retained, since time immemorial, the values specific to the primitive community, at least in the form of vestiges and relics. Laying the foundations of the nation to be built was therefore considered to consist first of all in collecting the vestiges of tradition preserved in folk culture and in assembling them in the form of national monuments. These memorials to the past were then regarded as models and touchstones for future undertakings.

In the second half of the eighteenth century, European scholars embarked on a vast undertaking to collect folk culture and mould it into authentic national heritage. That movement began with the publication of so-called folk songs, explicitly designated as the source from which national literatures were to be forged. We find here a wilful inversion of cultural legitimacy, which located authenticity in the lower social orders, in opposition to a courtly or court culture denounced as an imitation of French culture. The movement led ultimately to the compiling of national epics supposedly transmitted down the ages and preserved intact in popular memory: the best known are undoubtedly the Highland epics attributed to the bard Ossian, which the young poet Macpherson first began to publish in the early 1760s.

Born into a peasant family, but having acquired a modest education thanks to support from members of his clan, Macpherson had been ardently encouraged by several Edinburgh literati to gather Gaelic ballads from local tellers of folk tales. On the strength of the initial results, the young man's protectors declared his collection of texts to be indisputably fragments of Celtic epics of the greatest value. The poet-collector was urged to provide a full version thereof. The Edinburgh men of letters paid his expenses for an expedition to north-west Scotland and the Hebrides and entrusted him with a clearly spelled-out mission: Macpherson was to bring back 'our epic'. This led to the successive publication of Fingal and Temora, which were instantly hailed as the Iliad and Odyssey of the North, putatively composed by a third century bard. To be sure, doubts were immediately expressed as to the authenticity of the Ossianic texts; but these forgeries rapidly came to enjoy an enormous success both in the British Isles and on the Continent. They aroused particularly keen enthusiasm, creating a positive craze for a new mood in literature, which Romanticism would make its own: a glorying in mists and storms, tormented landscapes and heroic battles, doomed romances and shy, unassailable virgins. Above all, they triggered an intense movement of emulation. There occurred a flowering of ancient national epics during the decades that followed: most notably the Kalevala, published in 1835 by the Finnish doctor Lönnrot, the Barzaz-Breiz of the Breton aristocrat La Villemarquè, the first edition of which was published in 1839, and the Kralodvorsky rukopis, 'discovered' in 1817 by the young Czech poet Hanka.

Thus the collection and publication of folk songs formed no part of any scientific project - which would indeed have been perfectly anachronistic - but rather fitted into the process of building up national literatures. In fact, such epics and anthologies of 'traditional' folk songs are certainly not rigorously assembled collections of living folk expression. It was by no means the collectors' intention to put forward popular culture in all its vitality as the true national culture, and they reformulated the original materials for consumption by a cultured elite, as part of a patriotic project.

Moreover, the European literati then engaged in shaping national identities all maintained close ties with one another: they read one another, sometimes corresponded and exchanged visits, and in any case cheerfully borrowed one another's ideas. Already in 1770, the German theologian Herder, who had just discovered the Ossianic epic, declared that the

Germans must, as a matter of urgency, imitate the English (the Scots). Some years later, he would indeed persuade the young Goethe to take up folk song collecting in Alsace. At the beginning of the nineteenth century, Scandinavian and Russian men and women of letters would seek to impress upon their compatriots the urgency of following the German example, and so it went on. Each national group marvelled at what had been 'unearthed' in the other countries, and rapidly ended up producing more or less the same thing. This activity of publishing collections of folk songs - transposed, we repeat, as required for consumption by the cultured public - was frequently attended by much pondering of the possibility of forging national languages, whose authenticity would be predicated on the reference to folk expression. On the basis of the wide range of dialects in use, languages were built which were intended to serve as media of cultural creation and national communication. Scholars who were actively committed to the task of building national cultural identities frequently took part, modelling themselves on the example of the German philologists Jakob and Wilhelm Grimm, in the compilation of dictionaries and grammars. Thus the Serb Vuk Karadzic, encouraged by the German scholars and Slavists of the Austrian Empire, produced, in addition to a collection of folks songs, a grammar and a dictionary that would provide the basis of modern Serbo-Croat. The publication of the Kalevala in Finland was followed by a considerable amount of philological work undertaken in order to create a Finnish language that would no longer be one spoken by peasants, but rather a medium of culture. The success of these undertakings is to be measured by the introduction of the new national languages into educational establishments and their adoption as the medium of speech by the social and cultural elites, who had hitherto spoken another language than that spoken by the People.

Bringing this heritage to the knowledge of the cultured public was explicitly conceived to be the patriot's first duty. When Arnim and Brentano published their volume of folk poetry, Des Knaben Wunderhorn, in 1806, the Prussian minister Stein declared that the work should spark the burst of patriotic ardour needed to resist the Napoleonic troops. Niccolo Tommaseo, who in 1842-1843 published four volumes of Italian folk songs, and who in 1848 would become a minister in the ephemeral Venetian revolutionary government, encouraged poets to draw upon such poetry, knowledge of which was claimed to be essential to the true patriotic spirit. The Bulgarian intellectuals who in the 1870s led the uprisings against the Ottoman Empire also busied themselves collecting folk songs and national epics.

It might *a priori* be supposed that this great pan-European movement aimed at building national identities by appropriating folk culture as national heritage concerned France only to a limited extent, particularly inasmuch as the movement was devised, at least initially, as a weapon in the combat against the universalistic imperialism of French culture. Nevertheless, the founding of the Celtic Academy (1805-1814) and the ministerial directives issued in the mid-nineteenth century to undertake systematic collections of French folk songs clearly demonstrate the concern of scholars not to hold aloof from the great European movement. However, the failure of these undertakings to produce results confirms the idea that the reference to folk culture did not play an essential role in shaping the French national identity. This is of course to be explained by the early development of a nation-state and of a culture having a self-appointed universalist mission. Nevertheless, it led to the construction of a 'second-order' national identity which would be used subsequently, for domestic purposes, in order to affirm a national unity that transcended social divisions. For example, the reference to folk songs and folk tales would be used in primary-school teaching in the twentieth century as the basis of a French culture aimed at the general public en masse.

II. The Profusion of Representations of National Identity

Lagging initially slightly behind literature, painting and music bolstered the movement to promote folk culture as national heritage. The collecting of folk tunes made it possible to introduce non-classical themes into the composition of symphonies and operas, and thereby to develop national styles of music that would be powerful identity-building factors. Indeed, in many cases such musical compositions made explicit reference to the legends and epics collected during the earlier period. For example, Georges Enesco's Second Romanian Rhapsody (1902) is built on a ballad theme which has its roots in the epic pages of the nation's history. Sibelius, the composer of Finlandia (1899), also wrote several symphonic poems whose inspiration is drawn from the Kalevala. Historical painting, serving to illustrate national epics and the glorious deeds of the nation's great forefathers no less than rustic scenes presenting peasants in national costume and in characteristically national settings (with an increasing focus on nationally specific fauna and flora) completed the representation of folk culture as national heritage. Thus, the Finnish artist Akseli Gallen (1865-1931), who studied painting in Paris, produced a dual body of work, devoting himself on the one hand to illustrating the Kalevala (he in fact finally adopted the pseudonym Gallen-Kalela) and, on the other, to painting 'typically' Finnish landscapes. He travelled in eastern Karelia in order to rediscover the most primitive and hence the purest forms of Finnish culture. His life's work explicitly took its cue from patriotism and the concern to show off the national heritage to maximum advantage. Lithography, and later photography, were also turned to account in order to disseminate representations of typical peasants (that is, wearing picturesque costumes designated as national) as widely as possible.

The design and production of national styles of dress, modelled on various local folk costumes worn on festive occasions and 'ennobled' through the use of costly materials, also enabled the social elites of countries which had not attained the status of nation-states to flaunt their patriotic feelings (Rattelmüller, n.d.).

Whereas those involved in the shaping of national identities had initially been scholars and men of letters (intellectuals from modest social backgrounds playing the role of privileged intermediaries between folk culture and cultured elites), the production of identity-defining representations would henceforth concern much broader communities. The development of new media of communication gave increasing weight to the cultural entrepreneurs: publishers of iconographic reproductions, organizers of shows and public events and directors of associations.

Moreover, inasmuch as the exploration, enhancement and promotion of folk culture would be extended in the nineteenth century ever more broadly to the 'physical heritage' -furniture, crafts and housing- (Bertho-Lavenir, 1995) national identities came to be placed on spectacular display in the International Exhibitions through the presentation of reconstituted domestic peasant or working-class interiors, adorned with costumed dummies. The creators of these 'domestic folk interiors', exposed to the scrutiny of exhibition visitors, borrowed the models they used for stage-setting purposes from genre painting and the conventions of Romantic scenography. At the International Exhibition held in Paris in 1878, the display of Swedish peasant costumes and furnishings met with enormous success: it provided the inspiration for the first national ethnographic museums which would be opened in the following decades. These ethnographic museums were explicitly presented as supreme expressions of national identity, and their creation was, it was pointed out, a major patriotic task.

In the great exhibitions, both national and international, entire 'national villages' were also sometimes presented; these were set up using rural buildings originating from the different regions and in some cases animated by peasants in typical costumes engaging in various domestic tasks under the visitors' gaze. Such villages were designed as emblematic, and spectacular, miniatures of the nation; however, their creation shows clearly that political issues and definitions of the nation were at the core of these representations of folk culture. The first 'ethnographic village' was built in 1867 in Moscow, on the occasion of the Pan-Slav Congress. In order to demonstrate the ethnic unity of all Slavs, it brought together representative houses of each Slav group (Slovaks, Ruthenians, Croats, Poles, etc.). At the great 1896 exhibition in Budapest, held to commemorate the Hungarian millennium, one of the major attractions was an ethnographic village made up of houses characteristic of the kingdom's different regions and ethnic groups: there were 12 Hungarian houses, and the same number of non-Hungarian houses. This reflected the concern to display Hungary's multi-ethnic character and, simultaneously, the nation's essential unity. In 1895, however, a major Czecho-Slovak exhibition was mounted (foreshadowing the future Czechoslovak Republic) at which a Slovak farm was presented that was similar to the farm which the Hungarians included the following year in their own national village.

These major exhibitions also provided an opportunity to present to both indigenous and foreign audiences the different prestige national products: those of industry, to be sure, but also handicrafts. From the second half of the nineteenth century, a fashion developed in urban environments for high-class craft goods: textiles, furniture and decorative articles which drew their inspiration from the domestic peasant output but which were adapted to a well-to-do public through the use of luxury materials and greater formal sophistication. The least industrialized countries, which could draw upon a low-cost rural work force, and which were unable to present prestige industrial goods, accordingly stepped up the production, at the instigation of the authorities, of craft work that had been 'remodelled' in accordance with the canons of the international luxury goods market. This output of so-called 'national arts and crafts' served as much as an emblem used to boost the country's sense of its identity and value as a strictly commercial resource. Thus Romanian 'national' carpets, based on peasant designs and manufactured in rural workshops but in accordance with standards laid down by intellectuals and artists, played a prominent role in the international promotion of Romania.

III. Folk Culture as a Form of Preliminary Instruction for the Masses

The invention of popular or folk culture as national heritage had initially been the work of men and women of letters whose aim it was to develop the sense of national identity among social elites. The proliferation of identity-defining representations had allowed the perception of distinctive national characteristics to be disseminated extensively, both for domestic consumption and for foreign eyes. However, recourse to folk culture served during a third stage, generally after the nation had been constituted as a political entity, to anchor the sense of national identity solidly in the population as a whole. The concern was then to popularize, for pedagogical purposes, folk culture transformed into heritage, to spread knowledge and appreciation of it among the masses and thereby to entrench a patriotic sense of identity which was national, community-based, consensual and transclassist, i.e. spanning different social classes. The political representatives at all levels and even the civil servants and state officials were parties to this process of popularization.

Thus the community festivals and ceremonies which developed in towns and cities from the early years of the twentieth century onwards drew largely upon the 'folk traditions' which brought together in colourful or spectacular settings both peasantry and working classes and the notables in order to celebrate with fervour the nation, seen as eternal in its capacity to traverse the vicissitudes of history and politics. For example, the feast of Saint Stephen, the first king of Hungary and converter of the country to Christianity, which falls on 20th of August, became, following the Treaty of Trianon, Hungary's national holiday. It drew hundreds of thousands of spectators to Budapest during the inter-war period. The procession bearing the relics of Saint Stephen was followed by young people dressed in folk costumes, escorted by dignitaries on horseback. In the Hungarian countryside, however, 20th of August was harvest thanksgiving day, celebrated by the baking of the first loaf with the new harvest, solemnly broken by the lord of the manor. In the towns, such loaves were adorned with ribbons dyed in the national colours, thus completing the syncretism of folk tradition, the great ancestor and founder of the nation and the nation itself. The Communist regime would retain the 20th of August holiday as the festival of the new constitution, discarding all reference to Saint

Stephen but intermingling with the military parades and speeches on socialism and internationalism a plethora of processions and folk dances. And the solemn ritual of breaking the harvest loaf would devolve upon the General Secretary of the party.

Since the beginning of the twentieth century, however, intensive educational campaigns have been conducted throughout Europe with the aim of reinstilling the people's traditions of which it is supposed to have been, for centuries, the faithful guardian, but which allegedly it lost, or was in danger of losing, as it entered the modern age. Whereas in the nineteenth century it was middle and upper class wives and daughters who dressed up in so-called national costumes on festive occasions, in the twentieth century it has been the young girls and women of the people whom efforts have been made to turn away from modern fashions and to persuade them to adopt their 'ancestral dress'. Such 'traditional' dress is regarded as a sort of shield of their virtue and the symbol of their attachment to national values. Generally speaking, movements that pin their revivalist ambitions to a patriotic goal, such as the Heimatschutz movements in the Germanic countries, have become even more widespread (Le Dinh, 1992).

In the modern era, youth movements and associations devoted to organizing mass leisure activities have drawn abundantly on folk or popular culture as this was modelled by the literate elite during the nineteenth century in order to provide the public at large with healthy, joyful and patriotic forms of recreation. The international congresses on leisure activities held during the inter-war period assigned considerable prominence to national folklore for communal recreation purposes. A whole repertoire of harmonized songs and 'traditional' peasant dances was thereby introduced, for many decades to come, into the educational programmes directed at European youth.

Primary schooling above all, in a deliberate, conscious promotion of patriotic values, would spread knowledge of the folk heritage. Both through their written content and their iconographic materials, school textbooks served to illustrate those essential features of national folk culture a knowledge of which had been defined as indispensable. School children were also urged to become collectors, to start museums of their own and to 'keep up the traditions' in their festivities and games. This early introduction, carried out on a massive scale, to folk customs, occurred even in those contexts where it might have been least expected, namely, in primary schooling in France under the Third Republic (Thiesse,

1997).

The Fascist and Nazi regimes would, of course, resort on a large scale to staging folk culture 'spectaculars' in order to assert their authentically national character against the so-called 'cosmopolitan' or alien culture. After the Second World War, 'patrimonialization' - the process of transforming folk culture into heritage - lost this role of consolidating national identity in Western Europe and became geared rather to certain forms of mass consumerism, in particular tourism.

However, nations whose sense of identity remained fragile continued to emphasize the links, both in official discourse and in everyday practice, between the folk or popular dimension and the national dimension. This has been particularly true of the socialist countries of Central and Eastern Europe, where the semantic ambiguity of the term 'popular' or 'people's' has made it possible to legitimize as authentically national regimes that draw their inspiration from Marxism or internationalism. In the Communist countries, so-called traditional folk, 'people's' or popular culture was used as a powerful medium or conduit for national feeling. For example, courses in folk dance and folk music formed part of the general education curriculum, and those who had received such training were strongly encouraged to become professional performers. World tours by folk song and folk dance groups were a major factor in promoting these countries and boosting their prestige. However, it has been possible to use folk culture in such countries, and in this particular instance folk culture declared to be more authentically national, as a sign or means of protest against the regime in power. In Hungary, for example, the 'dance centre' movement which developed during the 1970s served to popularize 'folk' music and dance, in particular music and dance of Transylvanian origin, the purity of which was contrasted with the 'folklorism', deemed corrupt, of the official dance companies. Following the fall of the Communist regime, the former 'no-go area' of the Budapest cemetery, which had served as a mass grave for the victims of the 1956 uprising, was covered by the people with wooden crosses carved with designs borrowed from traditional Transylvanian handicrafts and then decorated with ribbons dyed in the national colours. Indeed, it may today be observed that the disappearance of the former socialist regimes has had the surprising result of fostering the coexistence of an 'Americanized' culture and a conspicuous recourse to identity markers deriving from popular culture. For example, intellectuals in the former Communist countries today have themselves christened in accordance with Orthodox rites, dressed in 'national' costumes, and wives of nationalist party leaders make a great show of wearing such costumes at national meetings. The recent break-up of political entities in Eastern Europe has in fact led to the reactivation of the model once used to build national identities, but now applied to other territorial delimitations.

Folk culture, duly reinvented, has proved highly malleable, capable of being used as an identifying sign of affiliation to a particular community in a whole range of different contexts. None of its outward manifestations (legends, costumes, songs, dances or festivals) have any significance in themselves; but they have been successfully readapted and reused on many occasions in order to demonstrate allegiances of a highly diversified and sometimes contradictory nature. Throughout Europe, there has in fact been an ongoing production of a whole set of cultural materials, shaped in the context of an international 'highbrow' culture, whose purpose has been to make explicit and to impose the various national identities.

References

Bertho-Lavenir, C. (1995), 'Naissance et Développement de l'Idée Régionaliste. Essai de Comparaison Européenne', *Architektura and Urbanismus*, Prague, pp. 31-45.

Le Dinh, D. (1992), *Le Heimatschutz. Une Ligue pour la Beauté*, Lausanne.

Rattelmüller, P. (n.d.), *Dirndl, Janker, Lederhosen. Künstler Entdecken die Oberbayerischen Trachten*, Gräfe und Unzer, Munich.

Thiesse, A.M. (1997), *Ils Apprenaient la France. L'Exaltation des Régions dans le Discours Patriotique*, Ed. de la MSH, Paris.

7 The Shaping of a Nation: Catalan History and Historicity in Post-Franco Spain

YOLAINE CULTIAUX

Introduction

The aim of this chapter is to provide fuel for the current debate on the meaning of the concept of collective identity and, in particular, the idea of 'living together' or national identity. In order to focus our analysis, we may begin by considering that the notion of identity - collective and more particularly national identity - is a problematical one and rather ineffective as a means of explaining certain social phenomena. By adopting this stance, our position is immediately set at a remove from that of the media and the political arena, where this idea causes a great stir in that it is presented as an evidence. On the contrary, for us, the question of identity is not a starting point but something which has to be questioned. In fact, it seems more useful to deal not with identity *per se* but with the processes of identification and the construction of an identity that is attained as a result of working towards that goal. In doing so, on the scientific plane, the primordialist model is rejected and particular value is placed upon nationalism, the ideological matrix of national identity. From this point onwards, special interest is accorded to the world of ideas and the efficiency of symbolical representations of the nation.

An etymological detour will shed some light on this idea. For example, it would appear useful to recall that symbols were originally 'a single object divided in two. The holders passed each part on to their children. Joining these two parts together once again (from *sumballein*, to bring together) helped the holders to recognize each other and substantiated the relationship of hospitality contracted earlier'.[1] We grasp immediately the primary quality of the symbol, i.e., it forms a horizontal bond between contemporaries and a vertical link between generations. It is precisely this power which explains the central role of symbols in the process of construction of national identity. Attaching importance to symbols thus defined is therefore fully justified. The symbols confer substance upon abstract or absent objects by using linking signs which make the result comprehensible. This definition presupposes the intervention of different actors who, like true craftworkers, forge a national identity which may then be used as the basis for building a nation.

In order to highlight the various aspects, we shall concentrate on studying the role of one of these 'influential minorities' - to use Miroslav Hroch's expression - that of historians, in the creation of an image of contemporary Catalonia as a national collectivity.[2] We shall endeavour to underline the links - conscious or unconscious, explicit and implicit - which exist between their scientific work and the current process of national (re)construction of Catalonia[3] which, during the post-Franco era, became one of the 17 Autonomous Communities of the Spanish State. If we have paid particular attention to the role of history, this is because:

A sense of the past is something which makes us act in the present differently from the way in which we might otherwise have done. It is a device that is used against adversaries. This is an essential element in the process of individual socialisation, maintaining group solidarity and establishing or contesting social legitimacy. Above all, the significance of the past is a moral, and consequently a political, phenomenon. It is always a phenomenon of the present.[4]

First of all we shall trace the development of Catalan historiography from the perspective of historical sociology. The aim will be to bring out the close link which binds Catalan historiography to Catalan nationalism. More specifically, what we are dealing with here is the portrayal in increasingly nationalistic terms of a multi-faceted conflict which has always set Catalonia against the rest of Spain, and particularly against the political centre embodied by Castile and the capital, Madrid. We shall then stress the material conditions governing the symbolic effectiveness expected from the distribution of historical material. In this context, the institutional aspect is of fundamental importance. So, the existence of a '*meso*-government' in Catalonia which derives from the Constitution of 1978 and the development of the State of Autonomous Communities have recently given a boost to Catalan historiography. The hoped-for effect is to reinforce the legitimacy of this '*meso*-government' and the national aspirations of the Catalanists which led it since the Transition period. Following an approach which is more anthropological in nature, we shall finally describe cultural institutions and events: celebrations of Catalan historians and the new Catalan History Museum.

I. Catalan Historiography Midway between Historical Science and Political History

The distinctive feature of Catalan historiography is that it is highly politicized. It is part of a more general conflict in Spain which sets the centre against the periphery. Since the nineteenth century, historiography has been conditioned by confrontations between Spanish- and Catalan-oriented ideologies. Catalan historians still stress this dimension today: '(...) one of the clearest objectives, established long ago, is to break with the pattern of mimetical repetition of the National History model. The myths and platitudes of Spanish national historiography (mainly centred on Madrid) should find a response in a balanced historiography, half-Jacobin, based on history which is essentially Barcelona-centred.'[5] The difficulty arises precisely from the fact that Catalan historiography has tended to imitate Spanish historiography. This means that each has supported divergent political options (Spanish and Catalan nationalism), and they have therefore found it difficult to distance themselves from the 'exaltation of national power and national consciousness, which was undoubtedly the basic impetus of narrative-history and continues to be one of its main *raisons d'être*.'[6] In formal terms, they have resorted to mythical representations. 'One can never forget that myths, as explanatory stories, are also a mobilizing force. As well as contributing to the mental reconstruction of the political imaginary, they also contribute towards social restructuring.'[7] In the Catalan case, one example is that the Middle Ages are constantly referred to as the Golden Age. This refers to a period when Catalonia was not yet a part of the Spanish state, which was still embryonic. The term myth may be regarded as admissible here because this period is idealized and the existence of a Catalan nation is implied. Yet, the reality embodied in this concept today is quite different from the reality to which it would have referred in that period. This is where national genealogy, so frequently manipulated by nationalists, shows its shortcomings. Although their political aims are divergent, Spanish (mainly Castilian) and Catalan historiographies do have something in common: in its own way, each reproduces the centre-periphery model. It is only since the transition to democracy that Catalan historiography has attempted to practise scientific polycentrism in a movement similar to the one prevailing in Spain as a whole. Yet, despite endeavours to develop a 'Girona perspective',[8] for instance, the fact remains that historical output and Catalan nationalism still tend to be identified with Barcelona.

This is simply the perpetuation of a long tradition based on the model of nineteenth-century Catalan historiography. At that time, Catalan historiography helped consolidate nascent Catalan nationalism. In this respect, it is temporally, spatially and ideologically very close to others 'national biographies'[9] whose 'origins lie in the spiritualist ideal type which arose in the German domain', first with Leibniz and later with Herder. Like these biographies, it made great strides when the masses began to be integrated in political life. This kind of narrative, which rests on collective identification with an individualized national collective, is undoubtedly linked to a need for mobilization within the context of democratization. It is identified with the cultural movements of the *Renaixença* and Romanticism (in the nineteenth century), periods when the first general histories of Catalonia appeared first in Spanish and later in Catalan. Symbolically, the project of writing this history - whose aim was to appropriate both the past and the present and project them towards the future - using the term Catalonia as a frame of reference, and focus, and a popular language held in low esteem, was already the fruit of Catalan circumstances. In this regard, three great historical frescoes 'are all products of the ideological, cultural and political circumstances prevailing at the time when they were written.'[10] These are the intellectual contributions of Victor Balaguer, Antoni Bofarull i de Broca and Antoni Aulestia I Pijoan. The latter were less prone to idealization and, as a result, they were harshly criticized for the comparative absence of Catalan nationalist sentiment reflected in them. In fact, they were more moderate than the former, which may explain why they have been passed down to posterity less frequently. Works of similar ilk followed, such as the syntheses by Francesc Carreras I Candi, Francesc Valls I Taberner and Ferran Soldevila. Between the end of the First World War and the early 1960s, Catalan historiography suffered under the Franco dictatorship. The only truly outstanding figure was Jaume Vicens Vives, who is often quoted by Jordi Pujol, the president of the *Generalitat*. It was after the death of Vives in 1960, when the Franco regime was undergoing a process of relative liberalization, that contemporary Catalan historiography developed. It was profoundly marked by the 'popular front' trend, which was both Marxist and Catalan nationalist in spirit. Historical innovation was curtailed first by the need for political struggle and later by the 'strong pressure to conform'[11] i.e. to follow the path of normative nationalist historiography. After the Transition, 'a great deal of the new nationalist and regionalist historiographic output went to extremes which were just as essentialist as those of Spanish nationalism. (...) They were used to justify regional political demands when the State of Autonomous Communities was being set up'.[12] Since then historiography remains torn between scientific and political imperatives such as the need to fight against neo-Spanish nationalism, which permeates one tend of Spanish historiography. Despite the end of the Franco era and the existence of greater pluralism, Catalan historiography remains militant because it is in fact immersed in the game of political trade-offs which has characterized the political game between the centre and the periphery since the Transition. This militancy compounded with the urge to show respect for a form of 'political correctness' on the part of any intellectual who wishes to be regarded as a leading figure in Catalonia. If the territorial distribution of power in Spain has changed, the relationship between history and politics and, more specifically, between a body of clerks and hegemonic political actors remains constant. M.S. Darviche has clearly brought out the reciprocal interests which underpin this relationship: 'A national biography never becomes *the* national biography on the basis of the intrinsic strength of the ideology underpinning it, because another opposing biography based on an opposing ideology can always be set up in its place, but on the ability of that ideology to gain ground because it is a part of the rationale of state domination'.[13] In the case which concerns us here, it is the domination of a government improperly termed 'intermediate'.

II. The Material Conditions Governing Symbolic Efficacy

The Transition, which began in 1975 with the death of General Franco, has subsequently permitted a historiography which defended the idea of a 'Catalan differential fact' to be circulated throughout Catalan society. This is linked to the existence of two new factors: the reappearance of an autonomous Catalan government and the fact that since the 1980s this government has been headed by nationalists belonging to the CiU coalition (*Convergencia i Unió*) led by Jordi Pujol.

The *Generalitat* is the fundamental institution of Catalan autonomy, owing primarily to its symbolic resonance in the collective Catalan memory. The royal decree which re-established it provisionally in September 1977 summed up its historical importance as follows: 'The Generalitat of Catalonia (is) an age-old institution which, for the Catalan people, is the symbol and recognition of their historical personality within the unity of Spain'.[14] Another important dimension is the institutional reality which it represents. Article 29 of the 1979 Statute of the Catalan Autonomous Community states that the *Generalitat* 'comprises the Parliament, the President of the *Generalitat* and the Executive Council or Government'. It possesses responsibilities which are important in view of the room for manoeuvre they give to the political party in charge. Among the key areas, the following are particularly noteworthy for the politics of 'symbolic recognition' of Catalonia: the field of culture (Article 9.4); 'educational, cultural, artistic and charitable foundations and associations as well as other similar organizations whose main sphere of action is Catalonia' (Article 9.24); 'full responsibility for the regulation and administration of education in the fullest sense, at every level and degree, its methods and specialities (...)' mentioned in Article 15. The *Generalitat's* fields of action are not limited to these matters, however. Its regulatory powers (Article 1) and its executive role in the field of legislation adopted at state level (Article 11) should not be overlooked. Although they stress the limits of this statute, Arcadi Calzada and Carles Llorens recognize its potential:

> The most relevant point at this time is to establish just how useful the instruments available to us are for this task, i.e. how far it is possible to rebuild the nation within the framework drawn up by the 1978 Spanish Constitution and the 1979 Catalan Statute of Autonomy. (...) It is worth while to raise the question: just how useful is the solution designed within the legal

framework? In which areas does the Statute allow us to proceed with national reconstruction, and to what extent? In a matter as important as language, for instance, the Generalitat possesses the tools necessary to design a policy which will lead to the re-establishment of Catalan as the specific language of Catalonia. The full responsibility granted in the field of education and the exclusive responsibility in the field of culture also permit ample work to be undertaken in the task of renationalization.[15]

The second factor which may help to explain the flowering of history in Catalonia is related to a game which is more strictly political in nature. The Transition opened up a democratic space which allowed the dynamics of party politics to impose its own rules. This has led to a configuration of political subsystems characterized by competition between statewide parties and other local parties. The weight of Spanish history has determined the unique nature of the Catalan party system. The political forces have been obliged to take up double stances: on the right/left axis and on the Spanish versus Catalan nationalism axis. *Convergencia i Unió -* a coalition between the majority party of Jordi Pujol, *Convergencia Democratica de Catalunya* (CDC) and Miguel Roca's party, *Unió Democratica de Catalunya* (UDC) - got most of the votes on this checkerboard for the last 15 years, at least in the regional elections, because the behaviour of the electorate changes depending on the nature of the consultation. This has allowed CiU to hold the majority in the Catalan Parliament since the autonomous elections held in 1980. Liberal in the economic sphere, though embracing the ideas of social justice and welfare, CiU nationalists are regarded by many as the heirs to Catalan nationalism forged in the nineteenth century. Their brand of nationalism is the continuation of one of the traditional intellectual movements in Catalonia: regenerationism. When Jordi Pujol declares: 'We want to be key players in Spanish history',[16] he is expressing the desire to intervene at the central level in order to modernize the State. This political project dovetails with the desire to 'build the country', i.e. Catalonia.[17] Pujol therefore recognizes the need for actions in favour of what political scientists call 'nation-building'. Language and culture, the 'backbone'[18] of Catalan identity, are naturally the focus of particular attention. So the reinforcement of the Catalan personality - one of the priorities of the autonomous government - 'requires from us, among other things, to contemplate widespread actions in the fields of education and the media'.[19] In an internal party document, he sets out his framework for global intervention: 'Catalonia should remain a people. To achieve this, the first and main objective is to nationalize the Catalan people (i.e. to reinforce the identity, consciousness and national sentiments of the Catalan people and make them operational):

1. Strengthen the *Generalitat*, its image and the people's support for the institution.
2. Stress the policy of linguistic standardization and consolidation.
3. Strengthen all specific elements which are part of the personality of Catalonia (civil law, knowledge of history, etc.).
4. Reinforce all the factors which help to 'build the country'.
5. Direct the doctrine and actions of the government of the *Generalitat* towards Catalan integration.
6. Support all the elements which bind the country together.
7. Help create or preserve, a general climate in Catalonia which is positive in every sphere.'[20]

III. History in the Community

It is, therefore, the decision-making power of the *Generalitat*, together with the electoral platform of CiU nationalists, albeit eminently political variables, which have allowed history to expand in the bosom of present-day Catalan society. The vectors of this expansion, or 'signs and networks of symbolic organization'[21] which make up a nation are numerous. In the Catalan case, we could usefully deal with such varied topics as history teaching in Catalan schools,[22] statuary[23] and traditional holidays.[24] They all allow us to confirm the hypothesis that these elements are being used strategically for political ends. We have, however, opted to concentrate on two other symbols of Catalan national tradition which are at the same time 'instruments for moulding the tradition itself',[25] namely, commemorative celebrations and the Museum of the History of Catalonia (MHC).

Among the various events commemorating people classed as famous are those commemorating professional historians such as Ferran Soldevila (1894-1971) or 'amateur' but equally patriotic historians like Angel Guimera (1845-1924) and Felix Cucurull (1919-1996). The *Generalitat* declared 1994 'Ferran Soldevila Year' to mark the hundredth anniversary of his birth. Celebrations were held throughout the year which drew to a close with a solemn ceremony held at the University of Barcelona on 25

October 1995. Presided over by Jordi Pujol and the rector of the university, the posthumous tribute was strongly charged with symbolism on account of the place in which it was held, the auditorium - all the paintings representing outstanding events in local history and high points in Catalan resistance - the theatrical way in which the memorial service was staged; the people present - the dignitaries from the Autonomous Government and the academic institution, as well as a huge representation from the scientific community of historians, and the general public, which filled the room to overflowing. The staging of the event, the significance of the various contributions - first a speech from the authorities, then a lecture on the life and work of Ferran Soldevila, followed by a manifesto read by the historians to promote the teaching of Catalan history in schools - and the physical separation of the various categories of participants transformed the celebration in a civic rite. There was a clear demarcation between the audience and the dignitaries, similar to the set-up one might find at a Catholic religious ceremony. In what might be termed the choir, rows of professional historians sat on either side of a dais set up at the far end of the room where the political and academic authorities were seated. On the right, between the dais and these rows stood a large portrait of Soldevila, which truly inspired the gathering with its surprising presence.

Similarly, 1995 was declared 'Angel Guimera Year'[26] to commemorate the hundred and fiftieth anniversary of his birth. This also gave rise to a number of celebrations, among them an exhibition and a closing ceremony also presided over by Jordi Pujol which was held on 25 October 1995 at the Ateneu Barcelones, another historic site of Catalan resistance. This closing ceremony, imbued with the same solemnity as the one described previously, was divided into important moments: the speech of Jordi Pujol flanked by the Catalan flag and a portrait of the dead man, the speech given by the President of the Ateneu, stressing the link between past and present and the relevance for the present time of Guimerá's struggle in favour of the Catalan nation and language, the famous speech delivered by Guimerá in that same place in 1895 (which was read aloud). The ceremony was closed by Jordi Pujol, who stressed that even those observers who were alien to history would not be indifferent to the venue, so charged with historical memories.

The memorial service held on 4 February 1996 shortly after the death of the writer Felix Cucurull was similar to the above, with one outstanding feature which is worth stressing here. This time, among those attending the ceremony were representatives, and even leaders, of political parties other than CiU: ERC, representing leftist Catalan nationalism, and *IC-Els Verds*, an alliance of Catalan communists and ecology groups. One of the speeches delivered by a historian is worth singling out because, basing her arguments on the exemplary figure of the 'great man', she stressed the present need to promote a national history of Catalonia in order to fight against Spanish nationalism.

Another event worth mentioning is the exhibition and the seminar held on November 1995 and devoted to the Valencian Joan Fuster (1922-1992),[27] an initiative of the Faculty of Science and Communication Studies at the Autonomous University of Barcelona (UAB). According to the booklet published at that time, Joan Fuster was to be celebrated as 'the inspiration behind so many literary, political, social and cultural initiatives'. Still according to this document, and in line with the tenets underpinning the tribute as a whole, Joan Fuster was described as 'a vehicle of self-discovery for many of us. For that reason he was misunderstood and suffered bomb attacks, insults and aggression. The university community at the UAB has sought to recognize Joan Fuster's value as a researcher, his erudition and his socio-political significance, by opening up this exhibition to all who are curious about him'. He was also the subject of a lecture entitled 'one man, one country', which stressed his pioneering role in the definition of contemporary Valencian nationalism and his involvement in pan-Catalan nationalism - diffuse but real - centring on Catalonia. Despite the undoubted sincerity of the memorial, it is legitimate to state that it had a political dimension, all the more as Catalan nationalists are putting all their hopes for the (re)constitution of Catalonia as a nation in the University and the youth in general.

These various facts would appear to give credit to the evolution which glory has undergone throughout the course of history according to Pierre Nora. 'Christian sacrifice gave way to patriotic sacrifice; spilling the blood of the nation at war becomes self-sacrifice for the sake of the nation in times of peace: from the Middle Ages to the present day, the focus of glory has twice been displaced.'[28] It has been both secularized and democratized. As a result of a phenomenon of substitution, glory is no longer the consequence of bowing to divine will but a heroic act carried out by a nation which is accessible to everyone. The situation currently prevailing in Catalonia is similar to Jean-Claude Bonnet's description of the transformations in discourse concerning the dead in France. According to

Bonnet, in the eighteenth century: 'Everywhere a new edifying discourse was being imposed, which was targeted at a community outside the world of Letters, the community of ordinary citizens. This discourse was based on a utilitarian social ethic which replaced the old lament on the fatal outcome of all human endeavour with a new capitalizing memory'.[29] And he concludes: 'In its metamorphoses the discourse devoted to the dead is always the rite of the living'.[30]

A visit to the Museum of the History of Catalonia helps to establish a striking parallel with Thomas.W. Gaehtgens's view of the History Museum at Versailles. According to Gaehtgens,

> ...the order in which the pictures in the Gallery of Battles were arranged reveals that the basic aim is not to evoke the high points of the past but rather, at a given time, to show a certain number of past events which can justify the present political situation (...). By making the history of the country accessible to the people, Louis-Philippe aimed to put forward arguments in support of his own actions. Recalling the high points of the past should serve to unite warring parties. The programme of 'national reconciliation' exhorted citizens to put the good of the nation before their own personal interests. The political nature of the History Museum did not escape Louis-Philippe's contemporaries, giving rise to comment.[31]

If comparisons are odious because the contexts are different, a close study of the MHC can lead only to the conclusion that the museum is used in order to legitimize the ambitions, actions and accomplishments of CiU nationalists. The mission of the MHC - in the purest tradition of history as a form of public education - is to suggest which forms of behaviour are desirable and which are undesirable in this society. Moreover, when asked about the genesis and aims of the museum, the current President of the Generalitat, Jordi Pujol, did not conceal its political nature, declaring that he had 'taken up this idea after a visit to the museum of the Diaspora in Tel Aviv'. There he was inspired by 'the didactic formula used by the Israelis to transmit to the younger generations a sense of the enduring nature of the signs of identity of a people which have survived throughout its difficult history'.[32] Institutions of the same kind have therefore inspired his cultural policy. He pointed out that many countries have set up history museums, referring to the Smithsonian in Washington and history museums in Sweden: 'There is one such museum in every provincial capital in Sweden. These towns react against the ignorance of their history, because they think that it makes them vulnerable'.[33] He stated clearly: 'Why a Museum of the

History of Catalonia? Well, we hope that the people of Catalonia will know what they have been, and why, today, we are what we are and not something different'.[34] In his opinion, a museum enables us to 'understand and assimilate the idea that a country is the result of a long chain of events, both good and bad, and helps us to love it'.[35] The location of the museum, the contents of Catalan history exhibited there and the museum techniques used, all conform to this general line of action.

First of all, let us look at the location. Totalling 12,500 square metres, the museum occupies a whole wing of the *Palau de Mar*, a building which used to house old harbour stores. It is situated in the old port of Barcelona at the heart of a district which was given a new lease of life thanks to the considerable infrastructure put in place for the 1992 Olympic Games. In this regard, it symbolizes the past and what is often portrayed as Catalonia's 'Mediterranean vocation'.[36] The MHC has received considerable priority investment (4,500 million pesetas, around 35 millions of dollars) from the *Generalitat*. The whole enterprise was co-ordinated by a person who was not an historian, and who is a CiU member of the Spanish Parliament.

The nature of the history being conveyed is reflected in the names given to the various rooms which make up the permanent exhibition at the museum: 'Foundations', 'The Birth of a Nation', 'Our Sea', 'On the edge of the Empire', 'The early stages of the Industrial Revolution', 'Steam and the Nation', 'The Electric Years', 'Destruction and Reconstruction', 'Heritage and the Future'. It is a history which follows a linear chronology and, in classic manner, portrays heroes and memorable events. Among the latter are the Catalan nation's battles for emancipation from Spain which, significantly, is referred to only in terms of the State apparatus and as an economic market. Catalonia, on the other hand, is endowed with a strong personality and unity. The underlying historical model therefore favours a perennialist approach of the nation, which is described as constantly under threat of being absorbed and divided by the Spanish State. According to the works produced by professional historians both inside and outside Catalonia, it is true that the Spanish State wanted to put Catalonia in political subservience. However, since the presentation is one-dimensional, leaving no room for other complementary models and omitting certain facts, it is legitimate to see it as a partial and, consequently, incomplete history. One example is the description of Spain's colonization of America and how Catalonia was once again sidelined. As an isolated fact, this is true. However, later agreements were made with the monarchs to modify the original situation and Catalans - or at least certain specific groups of Catalans - also benefited from the overseas territories. One may also be surprised to see that the colonization of America is mainly criticized because Catalonia was marginalized in the colonial process and not from a political/moral point of view for the exploitation of other peoples. Thus, the victim-centred discourse, so frequent in Catalonia, which goes hand in hand with the defence of national minorities in the world, has to be sharply relativized.

What we have, then, is the great romance of the Catalan nation and a history which, in its capacity as an official history, is more akin to what François Furet has called 'narrative-history' rather than 'problem-history'.[37] This is a political history which has been imposed on historical science under the weight of nationalism. According to the Valencian cultural entrepreneur Eliseu Climent: 'Therefore the history propounded in this recreational -administrative atmosphere was necessarily more socially oriented than scientific or erudite in its intention'.[38] Seen from this angle, we are better able to understand the strong emphasis placed on the formal representation of history. Proud of having implemented a 'new museum concept' heavily dependent on the new technologies which thus attest to the modernity of Catalonia, the promoters of the MHC have seen their project as a way of allowing the living to experience the past. Breaking with the traditional concept of the museum as a guardian of the heritage, the MHC uses interactive techniques to fulfil its didactic mission. Once again, this leads to stress the material infrastructure itself, which is regarded as an integral part of symbolic efficacy. Among the techniques used is information technology. In every room there is a computer on which visitors can see map collections or chronologies which compare events in 'Catalonia' with the 'rest of the world'. Similarly, mention may also be made of the photographic exhibition in the entrance hall, where the map of Catalonia is made with a serie of identity snapshots of people living in the territory. However, the real innovation lies in the stimulation of the other senses and in the physical appropriation of what is depicted as the past. The visitor is invited to lift a medieval suit of armour or to sit at one of the school desks of the Republican and then of the Franco era. All this occurs in a noisy atmosphere with a sound track of speeches, war songs, etc. which creates a strange feeling which one feels until entering the room devoted to the Catalonia of tomorrow. Here, the visitor enters a kind of dark space capsule lit only by television screens where images are projected at lightning speed. A bluish light emanates from the floor and the map of Catalonia appears. Visitors are encouraged to explore it with their own two feet. This recalls the fondness for excursions which has been a part of the 'culture of Catalan nationalism since the nineteenth century',[39] because 'building the country' also involves being familiar with its topography and exploring it physically. Without wishing plead in favour of an essentially intellectual approach to history, one is entitled to question the alluring virtues of these new technologies, or at least the use to which they are put. This brings to mind a remark made by Marcel Gauchet about Augustin Thierry, the author of *Lettres sur l'Histoire de France*, who 'aimed to produce art and science at the same time'.[40] 'Let us say that the resources of art have allowed him to make good the shortcomings evident in this work of imprecise erudition.'[41]

In this regard, we shall conclude this description of the MHC with the criticisms which have been levelled against it. Although Jordi Pujol has denied it, it is the political aim of this institution which has been brought into question since its premature inauguration. It was inaugurated in a rush at the time of the last general election, when many exhibits and frescoes were either incomplete or not yet in place. Entry was also free during the election period. The Autonomous Government was then the butt of the criticisms of the political parties, which accused it of electioneering. Pilar Rahola, the ERC candidate, expressed her indignation at 'Jordi Pujol's illicit use of institutions'.[42] She declared: 'I felt I was at a CiU rally instead of the inauguration of an institution which belongs to all Catalans and which has my support, but which should have been inaugurated next week [i.e.. after the autonomous elections in Catalonia]'.[43] For his part, Narcis Serra (a member of the PSC, the Catalan branch of the Spanish Socialist Party) denounced the fact that Jordi Pujol 'appropriates the heritage of Catalonia for the benefit of his own party'.[44] Alex Vidal Quadras (the leader in Catalonia of the *Partido Popular*, the conservative party, who was replaced when this party made a pact with the CiU Catalan nationalists with a view to governing Spain) did not forgo the opportunity to point out that this inauguration 'was part of the typical nationalist strategy of reinventing history'.[45]

The press, including those journalists from openly Catalan nationalist publications, could not suppress a certain irony in their comments on what should have been perceived as a significant event for the Catalan society.

The following remarks describe the manichaean and redemptive trajectory followed by every visitor to the MHC: 'From flint tools to himself'[46] (describing Jordi Pujol) or 'from the jaw-bone of Banyoles to his proclamation as president in 1980'.[47] In a more serious vein, the opinions expressed by professional historians, though varied, are more restrained and depend on their starting-point. As citizens, they are fairly unanimous in their attachment to Catalonia and their predominantly Catalanist political position. However, they appear to be torn by their professional allegiance. Josep Benet, Director of the Centre for Contemporary History, another body attached to the *Generalitat*, declared: 'They explained the project to me two years-ago. I told them I had a different concept of what a museum of this kind should be. I was not in agreement with the project because I think this is not how things should be done in the historical field. I heard no more about it after that. It was an administrative decision'.[48] Members of the general public representing different generations and from many areas outside Barcelona expressed their great satisfaction. Grandparents and parents, visibly moved, could be seen reliving episodes of their own lives and explaining them to their children. As it is now included in the tour of educational visits, the MHC fulfils a role of secondary socialization and backs up primary socialization through the exchanges it prompts within the family circle. However, it has not been open long enough to enable us to know if the people will interiorize the image of the (re)constructed Catalan nation and the nation to be (re)constructed.

Conclusion

This study has enabled us to demonstrate the interaction between symbolic representations and collective identities. Above all, it has stressed how variable and flexible identities are, thus invalidating the essentialist thesis. As a result, it has led us to assess the contribution of the actors who forge the images creating realities, among them national realities. Did not Paul Valéry say that 'the future, by definition, has no focal point. History provides the perspective'.[49] This work prompts us to share the view of the American historian Paul J. Geary, according to whom individual, collective and historical memories (forged by professional historians) merge and reinforce one another. He states:

This dichotomy of memory/history conceals the fact that collective memory and history both have political aspects and pursue certain objectives. Historians have one aim, which is basically to forge the collective memory of professional historians and, in the final analysis, that of the society in which they live (...). All memories, whether 'individual', 'collective' or 'historical' are memories for something, and this political aim (in the broadest sense of that term)' cannot be ignored.[50]

We shall conclude along with Maurice Crubellier that:

For a group, remembering means building a heritage of remembrances, valuing, and even overvaluing, certain prominent figures and events to the exclusion of others. It involves drawing selectively on the past and on the present which is in the process of becoming the past. It is to make a treasure house of models and lessons for future actions (...). To exalt these is to exalt oneself (...). The figures and events retained by that memory must be held to be real, but they need not necessarily be real. The criteria preached by historians, although they themselves adhere to them only in part, remain alien to the groups which remember. This is because the efficacy sought in the service rendered to the present is often diametrically opposed to historical rigour. Precise knowledge might curtail the zeal of followers. The usefulness of legends is recognised. Research which is too rigorous dilutes the contagïous virtue of the model.[51]

Notes

1   According to the definition of A. Bailey quoted by Louis-Marie Morfaux, 1980, p. 352.

2   This topic has also been dealt with in a study of another group of actors, the sociolinguists. See Cultiaux, 1996a.

3   The use of parentheses is justified by the desire to distinguish our aims from those of the actors. The term 'reconstruction' presupposes support for the nationalist programme which holds that the Catalan nation once existed, was destroyed and, as a result, must now be rebuilt. This is an interpretation which may be upheld but which must not determine a scientific approach to the matter. We chose to resort to this device as a result of our awareness of the connotation attached to the use of words and their symbolic effectiveness in the scientific field and the political arena. We have thus tried to avoid the pitfall pointed out by Bernard Voutat 'because these (processes of mobilization) are underpinned by collective attempts to explain the meaning of the mobilization, historical or sociological explanations run the risk of becoming a direct extension of the militant categories of perception of the social world'. See Voutat,

1996, p. 31.

4   Wallerstein, 'La Construction des Peuples: Racisme, Nationalisme, Ethnicité' in Balibar and Wallerstein, 1986, p. 106.

5   Nadal and Farreras, 1990, pp. 5-6.

6   Furet, 1982, p. 75.

7   Girardet, 1986, p. 181.

8   To borrow the expression used by Nadal and Farreras, op. cit., p. 11. Girona is a large town in the northern part of Catalonia and the capital of one of the four provinces which make up the Autonomous Community of Catalonia. Here we might quote as an example the birth of modern Greek historiography promoted by Constantin Paparrigopoulos which has become a truly 'historiocratic' national history (p. 301). 'In the context of nineteenth century Greece, history Wawas the affirmation of an identity (...). The Hellenic context made romantic history the controversial response to various vital, and not purely intellectual, aggressions which cast doubt on the ethnic and diachronic identity of the Greek people' (p. 279). The author thus evokes 'the romantic wave' which flooded Greece from 1850 to 1880 (p. 280). See Kohler in Espagne and Werner (dir.), 1990, pp. 279-309.

9   Darviche, 1994, p. 106.

10   Sobreques I Callico, 1990, p. 19.

11   Ucelay da Cal, 1990, p. 76.

12   Riquer I Permanyer, 1990, p. 100.

13   Darviche, M.S., op. cit. p. 109.

14   Martin, 1990, p. 56.

15   Calzada and Llorens, 1985, p. 37.

16   Fauli, 1988, p. 180.

17   The following hypothesis has been put forward and checked: this ambition for national (re)construction involved not just reparation for the distant and immediate past but was also an important tool in negotiations with the central government on territorial sharing of power. For this reason, this form of Catalan nationalism has been termed 'integrative differentialism'.

18   Pujol, 1995, p. 6.

19   Fauli, op. cit., p. 87.

20   Fauli, op. cit., p. 89.

21   According to Pierre Nora's definition of a nation in his scientific project set forth in *Les Lieux de Mémoire*, it is 'not only a juridical concept or a territorial unit and a common desire to live together. It is not just the 'rich legacy of remembrances' and the 'everyday plebiscite' mentioned by Renan. It is the symbolic organization of a human group whose points of reference have to be rediscovered and their circuits lit up'. See Nora's introduction to the three volumes dealing with the nation in *Les Lieux de Mémoire. La Nation*, Gallimard, 1986.

22   Flipping through the school textbooks used for history teaching, one may be astonished to read the legend under a photograph showing a human skull from the paleolithic period, which is presented as that of one of the first 'Catalans'.

23   For information on this topic see Subirachs i Burgaya, 1989, p. 140.

24   A useful book for information on this subject is *Les Festes Populars* by Prat and Contreras, 1987, p. 167.

25   To quote Nora, 1986, vol. 1, p. XVI.

26 A Catalan political figure also involve in cultural Catalanism. Following the trend common among his generation, in the nineteenth century he set down his own interpretation of Catalan history on a number of occasions. His political speeches are eloquent on this subject.

27 A committed man of letters, Joan Fuster provided his own interpretation of Catalan history and that of the *Països Catalans* (Catalan speaking areas). Like other intellectuals who wished to participate in the political struggle, in his capacity as an amateur as opposed to a professional historian, he also wrote his own history book. This vein of historical output should not be neglected insofar as the political effects it produces are similar to those of academic historiography.

28 Nora, 1986, vol. 3, p. 9.

29 Bonnet in Nora, op. cit., p. 220.

30 Bonnet in Nora, op. cit., p. 239.

31 Gaehtgens in Nora, op. cit., pp. 160 and 165.

32 La Vanguardia, 1 March 1996, p. 40.

33 El País, Catalonia supplement, 25 October 1995, p. 11.

34 Ibid.

35 El País, Catalonia supplement, 25 October 1995, p. 13.

36 This aspect was not neglected when European construction was undertaken. In fact, there is fierce competition among the regions bordering the Mare Nostrum to present themselves in Brussels as the best interlocutor on matters concerning this area. In this regard, see Cultiaux, 1996b, pp. 39-47.

37 Furet, 1982, p.73 et seq.

38 Furet, 1982, p.73 et seq.

39 This expression is used by Marfany, 1995, p. 402.

40 Quoted by Gauchet in Nora, op. cit., p. 252.

41 Gauchet in Nora, op. cit., p. 252.

42 El País, Catalonia supplement, 20 January 1996, p. 13.

43 Ibid.

44 La Vanguardia, 1 March 1996, p. 40.

45 Ibid.

46 El País, Catalonia supplement, 1 March 1996, p. 13.

47 La Vanguardia, 1 March 1996, p. 40.

48 El País, Catalonia supplement, 29 February 1996, p. 9.

49 Quoted by Crubellier, 1991, p. 8.

50 Geary, 1996, p. 31.

51 Crubellier, op.cit., pp. 8-9.

References

Balibar, E. and Wallerstein, I. (1986), *Race, Nation, Class. Les Identités Ambiguës*, Editions La Découverte, Paris.

Calzada, A. and Llorens, C. (1985), *Reconstrucció Nacional*, Edicions Destino, Barcelona.

Crubellier, M. (1991), *La Mémoire des Français. Recherches d'Histoire Culturelle*, Kronos, Paris.

Cultiaux, Y. (1996a), 'Expertise, Politique Linguistique et Nation-Making: Les Sociolinguistes Face à la (re)Construction Nationale Catalane dans l'Espagne des Autonomies'. Paper presented to the workshop 'Public Policies and Expert Knowledge', 5th Congress of the *Association Française de Science Politique* held at the *Institut d'Etudes Politiques* en Aix-en-Provence. To be published by L'Harmattan.

Cultiaux, Y. (1996b), 'La Conférence Euroméditerranéenne et le Forum Civil Euromed: La Méditerranée et la Société Civile Vues de Madrid et de Barcelone', *Revue d'Etudes Méditerranéennes*, vol. 1, no. 2, November.

Cultiaux, Y. (1999), *Le Nationalisme comme Différentialisme Intégrateur. Le Catalanisme Face à l'Etat Espagnol et à la Construction Européenne*. Doctoral Thesis in Political Sciences, *Institut d'Etudes Politiques*, Aix-en-Provence.

Darviche, M.S. (1994), 'La Biographie Nationale ou Comment Justifier l'Ordre Collectif Moderne', *Pôle Sud*, vol. 1, no. 1, Autumn.

Espagne, M. and Werner, M. (1990), *Philologiques I. Contributions à l'Histoire des Disciplines Littéraires en France et en Allemagne au 19ème Siècle*, Editions de la Maison des Sciences de l'Homme, Paris.

Farreras, J. and Nadal, I. (1990), 'Algunes Claus de la Història Local', *Revista de Girona*, Cercle d'Estudis Historics i Socials, January-February.

Fauli, J. (1988), *El Pensament Polític de Jordi Pujol (1980-1987)*, Edicions Planeta, Barcelona.

Furet, F. (1982), *L'Atelier de l'Histoire*, Flammarion, Paris.

Geary, P.J. (1996), *La Mémoire et l'Oubli à la Fin du Premier Millénaire*, Aubier, Paris.

Girardet, R. (1986), *Mythes et Mythologies Politiques*, Editions du Seuil, Paris.

Hroch, M. (1985), *Social Preconditions of the National Revival in Europe*, University Press of Cambridge, Cambridge.

Marfany, J.L. (1995), *La Cultura del Catalanisme. El Nacionalisme Català en els Seus Inicis*, Edicions Empuries, Barcelona.

Martin, E. (1990), *La Catalogne*, La Documentation Française, Paris.

Morfaux, L.M. (1980), *Vocabulaire de la Philosophie et des Sciences Humaines*, Armand Colin, Paris.

Nora, P. (1986) (dir.), *Les Lieux de Mémoire. La Nation*, vol. 1, Gallimard, Paris.

Prat, J. and Contreras, J. (1987), *Les Festes Populars*, Els Llibres de la Frontera, Barcelona.

Pujol, J. (1995), *Qué Representa la Llengua a Catalunya?*, Edicions de la Generalitat, Barcelona.

Riquer i Permanyer, B. (1990), 'Problemes i Reptes Actuals de la Historiografia Catalana', *Revista de Girona*, Cercle d'Estudis Historics i Socials, January-February.

Sobreques i Callico, J. (1990), 'Les Històries Generals de Catalunya en el Periode Històric de la Renaixença i el Romanticisme (segle XIX)', *Revista de Girona*, vol. 1, no. 34, January-February.

Subirachs i Burgaya, J. (1989), *L'Escultura Commemorativa a Barcelona (1936-1986)*, Els Llibres de la Frontera, Barcelona.

Ucelay da Cal, E. (1990), 'La Historiografia dels Anys 60 i 70: Marxisme, Nacionalisme i Mercat Cultural Catalá', *Revista de Girona*, vol. 1, no. 34, January-February.

Voutat, B. (1996), 'Objectivation Sociale et Mobilisations Politiques. La Question Nationale dans le Jura Suisse', *Revue Française de Science Politique*, vol. 46, no. 1, February.

PART IV
TEACHING NATIONAL IDENTITY

8 Recreating the French Nation: The Teaching of History at the *École Libre des Sciences Politiques* at the end of the Nineteenth Century

CORINNE DELMAS

Love of the country does not in itself constitute patriotism. Love of our history must be included. France as a physical entity does not amount to much if our love for her is not enhanced by respect for her history. That history is our heritage as much as the land is. We must not neglect it (Fustel de Coulanges).

Introduction

In the wake of the disaster of 1870, there was a call for the re-creation of the 'French nation' ('*Nation France*'),[1] that is, a new France, able to resist foreign influences, the enemy. Emile Boutmy had a project which was in line with this ambition: to found a new school, the *École Libre des Sciences Politiques* (School of Political Sciences) whose task was to anchor democracy and reform the minds of the citizenry. His project was founded on the acceptance by democratic societies of the meritocracy movement. Boutmy was also motivated by a scientist impulse: knowledge was not merely a basis for competent judgement and social authority, it was a solvent and corrective for purging the errors of abstract theories and a stabilizer of democracy. From this view of knowledge it followed that teaching had to be reformed, and in particular, higher education. The project of organizing an *École Libre des Sciences Politiques* would be in keeping with the critique of the university system being undertaken by a group of reformers of which Boutmy was a member, alongside academics like Gabriel Monod:[2] 'At Sadowa, it was the University of Berlin that won' (E. Boutmy, 1871, pp. 5-6). Against the background of the 'German crisis of French thought' (C. Digeon, [1959], 1992), and Renan's pet theory that France needed to embark on an 'intellectual and moral reform', the reform of higher education was viewed as an imperative. Furthermore, in 1871, with the state largely paralysed, and the government not yet liberalized, it was private education that had to take the initiative.[3]

This initiative proved especially urgent in one area: the training of political and administrative personnel destined to serve the Republic. France's defeat contributed to reactivating the old debate regarding the training of civil servants and the introduction of political science and principles of administration into higher education.[4] Although in an absolute sense it was considered a 'pressing necessity' to 'recreate men, that is to instil in men the reverence for lofty concepts and a taste for arduous study', it was considered a priority in time to 'create an elite corps that would gradually impart an elevated tone to the entire nation, ... giving the people new intellectual leadership' (E. Boutmy, 1871, pp. 14-15). The training of that elite was to be based on a scientific training as construed by the scientism of the late nineteenth century. This belief can be understood within a wider opposition which developed in the course of the nineteenth century, between 'positive law' and 'moral and political philosophy'; it was the deep conviction that there must exist a social science able to adapt appropriate political solutions to a country that had arrived at a certain stage of political development. In the words of Boutmy:

> Our objective was to design a political science curriculum that was full and complete in its makeup, European or even universal in its breadth, contemporary in its choice of issues, historical-critical in methodology ... based on facts, but facts rigorously explained, commented in learned fashion ... Vague, absolute theories and rhetorical commonplaces have no place in a serious, practical discipline (E. Boutmy and E. Vinet, 1871, pp. 11-13).

Very much in the spirit of this project for national regeneration, coupled with a scientific objective, was the course in diplomatic history offered by the historian Albert Sorel (1842-1906) which he taught since the beginning of the School's existence. It is accurate to characterize this course as an amalgam of 'political realism' and patriotic optimism: realism and optimism were indeed the hallmarks of most of the school's teaching. If one does a comparative reading of the curricula and the publications of the school's faculty during the last third of the nineteenth century, there emerges in a salient fashion a recurrent, broadly-based concern to inquire into the sources of France's 'national spirit' and to lead the struggle against patriotic pessimism. This effort entailed a return to the origins of the French nation and, in line with the realistic component, a questioning of revolutionary rationalism. These writers and lecturers seem to have viewed the nation as a political entity, as much as a cultural one.

I. Political Realism and Patriotic Optimism

Most of the promoters of the *École Libre des Sciences Politiques* were convinced that they had to give back to French thought and political action some sense of reality and a clear idea of the nation's historical tradition, all the while combating any form of patriotic pessimism.

A. Political Realism

The Franco-Prussian war gave Albert Sorel an occasion to strike up a relationship with the historian Hippolyte Taine. Sorel was assigned to the city of Tours where, on the recommendation of François Guizot, he met Taine who was living there.[5] The influence of the war on Sorel and on many others, was to make it a personal duty of each French man to work at putting the country back on its feet, since Germany had shown that work by itself could lead to victory. He thought that if the new generations were gradually educated, and if, instead of dreaming up a national myth, a genuinely political creation were to be undertaken, France would bounce back. It was the ultimate plea for the restoration of discipline: Prussian primary school training had made a considerable contribution to discipline, thereby laying the foundations for Prussian superiority. France needed to restore its own spirit of discipline and counter the habits of a people who were too readily given to being revolutionaries, and were, moreover, excessively logical. The idea was to analyse the shining example of the Prussian renaissance of 1806 and restore France to health:

> The king of Prussia hesitated, and the nation forced him to act. It is the nation that set an example, whereupon all of Germany rose up. ... (Prussia) held back in order to curse, but also to contemplate. In turn, Prussia had prodigious victories. It was unable to avoid excesses and mistakes, but it knew how to wait in silence, learn from its experience and recover from its reversals. Prussia has provided a great example to us, and we should have our eyes on it constantly. The study of History would be the most frivolous and enervating of mental recreations if we were unable to draw out of its contradictions a more elevated notion of justice, a more detached view of things, a more solid self-confidence in our present behaviour, and greater confidence in future solutions (A. Sorel, 1872a, p. 65).

It is well known that Albert Sorel was an outspoken republican in 1870, and like most of his colleagues or future colleagues at the *École Libre des Sciences Politiques*, he worked on behalf of the National Defence Government. Nevertheless, he was opposed to 'All those who are convinced they possess absolute truth and imagine that men can be improved by changing their language or their clothes' (1875, p. 368).[6]

Sorel thought it necessary to channel French political thought in the direction of realism and restore a sense of France's historical tradition. Among historical figures, he showed admiration or indulgence only towards those who were pre-eminent realists: Mirabeau, Talleyrand, Frederick II, Napoleon. Regarding Danton, he observed :

> Condorcet judged Danton accurately and from high ground. This formidable demagogue was a born government administrator, and possessed the essential features of a statesman ... His proposals have nothing abstract or fanciful about them: they are entirely practical and realistic. He has no use for social theories, and has no interest in governing the ideal man. His task, as he sees it, is to lead the men around him, the people he knows and with whom he lives. For Danton, the fatherland is not the cosmopolitan city of a Utopia, but rather France, whose ground he treads and whose air he breathes (quoted by R. Doumic, 1906, p. 448).

Choosing realism entails grounding one's action in knowledge of reality. In contrast to philosophers who start with an idea and construct a system to which the facts are later fitted, Albert Sorel seeks to begin with the facts. The historian's role is to reconstruct the fabric of history by showing us the interconnection of facts; this means going back through the series of causes. Like Taine and Boutmy, Sorel's procedure is an application of the experimental - positive and comparative - method to the study of social facts. He seeks to promote a science of history, subjected like the other disciplines to scientific determinism. He subjects his own inquiry to the following rule 'Apply to the study of political and social phenomena, those works of human nature, the same methods of observation, comparison and criticism used by the sciences that study physical nature' (1901, p. 275).

This realism and promotion of the experimental method is the expression of Sorel's rejection of any sort of Utopia, and of his promotion of *homo politicus* with a pragmatic face; they are also elements in an essential philosophy of moderation in politics, the refusal of extremes. This is how Sorel put it in his course lectures (1872b, pp. 3-4):

> I do not think patriotism fades with enlightenment, that it is drained of life when it looks to history for a deeper self-understanding. As one finds the same passions, pretensions, illusions and errors in one's own history and in that of other people - cloaked in different appearances, language and customs - one's judgement of actions becomes more settled and more balanced. It becomes easier to be patient, to contain anger, to restrain personal vanity. On the other hand, such research strengthens confidence in the future. One acquires a more balanced vision of the conditions of our national life, which imparts greater certitude as to future behaviour; the mind turns from reflex to reflection, from superstition to belief, from myth to history, the mind moves toward science.

Sorel's moderation and optimism distinguish him from his master and friend, Hippolyte Taine.

B. Patriotic Optimism

Taine was one of the founders of the *École Libre des Sciences Politiques* and remained one of its directors for his entire life. Most of the School's faculty, including his disciples and friends Sorel and Boutmy, were close to Taine in their political leanings (liberal and republican), and by their conception of the profession of the historian. They were promoters of an experimental, positive approach, stressing facts - and not ideas - as a point of departure. 'Mr. Boutmy believes that the most certain way to avoid abusing someone is to stick strictly to the experimental method, to abstain from theory and generalizations at the outset, and to allow them to appear only at the end, when they emerge as consequences of the facts themselves' (*École Libre des Sciences Politiques, 1872*).[7] Although Boutmy insisted that history must begin with facts, it must not remain a mere chronicle or inventory, an 'ideograph' (P. Veyne, 1987). On the contrary, it presupposes research and depiction of the determining causes of an event using the method developed by Taine; it has been observed that Boutmy's determinism was harmonized with his liberalism through the psychological method (P. Favre, 1981, pp. 439-47).

The faculty and promoters of the new School, including Albert Sorel, stand apart from Taine by their optimism. In a letter dated 1900, Sorel wrote on his opposition to the thesis developed in Taine's *Origines de la France Contemporaine*: 'I would often say to our master, Taine' (quoted by A.-E. Sorel, 1913, p. 428), 'You look for everything that killed France, whereas I look for what gave it life. If I did otherwise I would not be - or rather ought not to be - a teacher, a guide to the young'. Accordingly, Sorel did not reject the Revolution 'as a whole', and condemned 1792, but not 1789.[8]

> In 1792, [France] declared war on kings and announced peace to the nations. It won out over kings and succumbed to the efforts of nations. The revolution stopped in France and froze, so to speak, in the form of a military despotism. And yet, working through this despotism, the revolution pursued its course throughout Europe ... however disfigured on the battlefields, the language of liberty still moved the souls deeply.

Statements like these made the revolution a fine and praiseworthy event as an expression of the aspirations to liberty it stirred in the hearts of neighbouring peoples. This Kantian notion was coupled with the affirmation of the principle of nationality and the national self-determination, principles acquired in the revolution of 1789, then denied by the politicians of 1792 and, subsequently, by the emperor:

France brought people together through military action, and by teaching them through the writings of her thinkers that nothing was finer for nations than independence, and that to obtain their freedom, the surest way was to be united. The first act of sovereign nations should thus be to set themselves free. People understood this language readily ... what they failed to understand was how France, speaking thus and having set an example, was now enslaving them and exploiting them ... they rose up against its domination (A. Sorel, [1887], 1897, pp. 4-5).[9]

Sorel took up Ernest Renan's definition of the nation,[10] and underscored its basis in human choice, declaring that the nation should be viewed as a 'daily referendum'. Like most of the faculty at the new school, Sorel thought the answer to the question of nationality was citizenship, in contrast to the German view of nationality which is based on the organic union of members in a body politic, sharing culture and blood. Again, following Renan, Sorel insisted on the importance of memory, especially the alternation between necessary forgetting of some periods of our history and the need to recall periods of grandeur. The job of the historian becomes a serious calling.

> Goethe asked himself: 'in the beginning, was it the word or action?' In the beginning of human life love came first. The same instinct that causes two beings to join together also created the bonds between children, families, and nations that are the product of such unions. It is written: 'honour your father and your mother, that you may live long'. This is the viaticum, the law of the life of nations, the entire reason for their existence and the sum of the teaching that the historian is able to draw out of those histories on behalf of his fellow citizens: remember! (A. Sorel, [1887], 1897, p. 116).

Such patriotic optimism, the struggle against the awareness of France's weakness, this Sorelian attempt to restore to the youth a feeling for the grandeur and energy of the nation, are features that stand out in all the teaching at the *École Libre des Sciences Politiques*, especially with respect to diplomatic and international history. This instruction undoubtedly echoed a broader endeavour of similar intent across academia, but it was only at the *École Libre des Sciences Politiques* that there was a course on contemporary political history as such, something relegated to the pages of newspapers up to that time, and it is in this new school that we observe a keen interest in developing the history of the revolution and especially the Empire. This movement quickly gained a wide audience in

French society. It has been suggested that this success can be explained by the desire on the part of readers to relive, at least vicariously, the periods when France was great and powerful.[11] This nostalgia for past grandeur is clear with two of the school's historians: Alfred Rambaud and Albert Vandal.[12]

As for the question of nationalities and the right of peoples to determine their own destiny, this topic would be taken up and developed by Anatole Leroy-Beaulieu in connection with the Near East. Leroy-Beaulieu came out publicly in 1896 in favour of French intervention in Armenia,[13] justifying the intervention on the grounds that the liberation of peoples was a matter of international justice. The principle of nationalities was also evoked as a counter to the German approach: although in Italy and Germany the rights of nationalities originating in France ultimately turned against France, it would be useful for French policy in the Slavic world and the Balkans as a counterveiling force to German power. For Anatole Leroy-Beaulieu, the coincidence between, on the one hand, the interests of humanity and international justice, and, on the other, the task of reconstructing France's national integrity and grandeur, was especially evident in the Armenian episode. He saw it as a particular instance of a general law according to which the national aspirations of populations - including the Turkish population - were intimately bound up with French influence. His thinking was a return to an epic, a moral conception of national grandeur in which the glory of France's past and its special vocation granted by destiny were blended in one and the same fervour. The interest in the Near East was, therefore, based on 'a certain conception of France', intensified by the notion that Slavic culture was thought to counter-balance German culture through the emergence of another great power, Russia. Anatole Leroy-Beaulieu would become a specialist of Russia, whose attraction for the nationalistic right in France was based on the idea that an alliance from the rear would enable France to encircle the German enemy. This view, in turn, helps us to understand why a liberal like Anatole Leroy-Beaulieu could succumb to the charms of an illiberal Russia, even when the picture he paints of this society is at the very least subdued. The 'Near Eastern question', an issue in 'real history' if ever there was one,[14] was the central topic of some classes at the *École Libre des Sciences Politiques*. The instructor specializing in this material was Albert Vandal, who took a position similar to that of Anatole Leroy-Beaulieu on the Armenian question[15] and on the Franco-Russian alliance.

These subjects were analysed in light of the foreign policy of Louis XV,[16] or by a study on the Napoleonic Empire and relations between Napoleon and Alexander I. (A. Vandal, 1891-1897).

The question of nationalities and the right of peoples to determine their own destiny was made all the more bitter and complex as it was turned against France itself. Underlying all these analyses was the persistent question of the restoration of the grandeur and integrity of a mutilated and humiliated France. Take for instance the matter of Alsace-Loraine, directly or indirectly a theme of instruction by most of the faculty of the *École*. The voluntarist definitions of the nation of Renan or of Fustel de Coulanges were used to justify the right of Alsatians to remain French if they chose to do so. Parallels were drawn between the oppression of certain peoples in the world and the situation of the peoples of Alsace and Lorraine. For example, Henri Gaidoz wrote of the attempt by Hungary to 'Magyarize' the Romanians: 'The Romanian people in Hungary are treated like our neighbours, the people of Alsace and Lorraine, who merely wish to preserve the memory of their French fatherland'. (H. Gaidoz, (n/d), p. 23) Anatole Leroy-Beaulieu took up the Alsace-Lorraine issue directly in his classes: 'For many years I have agonized over what our duty was with respect to the question of Alsace-Lorraine; was it our duty to debate the matter? Did we have the right to talk about it? To publish our views?' (quoted by R. Pinon, 1913, p. 89). The solution he proposed in 1911, appeared in a study entitled 'L'Autonomie de l'Alsace-Lorraine et la Lutte pour la Culture Française'; it was inspired by Kant's hope that a European federation would be established, (cf. also A. Leroy-Beaulieu, 1900) rather than in humanitarian internationalism or the pacifism of the socialists. In 1897, in the midst of the Dreyfus Affair, he wrote (1897, pp. 8-11):

> The love for one's country is a necessity. It is a duty, especially when that country is France. At the present time there are people who adopt the pose of disdaining patriotism ... which they equate with hatred of foreigners and racial pride, or they equate it with chauvinism, its gross deformation and nasty caricature ... The love of Humanity (with a capital H) as preached by the Communists strikes us as empty and disappointing to the same degree that true love of one's country is natural in well-born hearts.

In the view of Leroy-Beaulieu, what is needed is to guarantee '...the free development of every nation and each citizen. This is a lofty ideal, and is both French and universal; some will no doubt accuse it of being Utopian'

(1897, p. 11).

The nationalism Leroy-Beaulieu has in mind is not, however, of the 'open' sort - to use a term favoured by Michel Winock (1990). For instance, in his criticism of the Third Republic for allowing foreigners to play an excessive role in the management of the country's business, Leroy-Beaulieu has been accused of going along with the prejudices of his time and his political associates. (R. Rémond, 1983, p. 28) Similarly, Boutmy's critical analysis of United States policy seems like an anticipation of Ostrogorski's later critical work of democracy based on the vote, in that he brings up the need to preserve the 'homogeneous character of the people', and considers legitimate the American restrictive policy on immigration:

> The volume and quality of immigration, its objectives and motivations make it more or less able to strengthen or fragment the homogeneity of the nation ... Up to approximately the middle of the nineteenth century, American immigration reflected healthy and energetic stock, able to flourish by being grafted - Europe's gift to the New World. But later, around 1860, Europe started shedding dying and dead cells ... In this great heterogeneous mass, sloughed off by Europe, few were capable of raising their minds above sordid material gain, their meagre savings, or even their daily bread ... These were cut-rate mercenaries offering their services to the politicians, and the quality of these troops was not such as to raise and purify the manners of the political army. It would not be reasonable to expect such new-comers to have brotherly feelings for the local people or an unfaltering attachment to their new country. So it was that, between 1882 and 1885, the Congress passed laws restricting the wretched immigration by which Europe got rid of its rejects ... These repeated waves of inert and passive human substance will not change the form and character of the American population, but neither will they enrich it fundamentally, as earlier waves of immigrants did. If anything, the new addition would tend rather to impoverish and weaken the national temperament, although for a while the appearances will not reveal this subtle change (1902, pp. 64-6).

Boutmy's position appears to have lingered on in the culture of the *École Libre des Sciences Politiques*. For example, in André Siegfried's 1927 book on the United States, he spoke of a 'crisis of assimilation' due to the influx of new immigrants. (1927, p. 21)[17] He reasoned somewhat differently from Boutmy who spoke of the need for a will to live together: though Siegfried, culture had to be acquired over a long period of time, and 'roots' and 'what is permanent' were clearly given greater importance

(1927, p. 21).[18]

II. Return to the Origins of the French Nation

Imparting a sense of reality to French political thought and restoring to it a sense of its own historical tradition in the fight against patriotic pessimism presupposes a return to the historical sources of the national spirit, customs and language. This restoration was part of the effort to restore legitimacy to a 'humiliated and mutilated' French people, and also had a clearly practical goal, which was to inquire into national mores, the necessary foundation of legislation:

> Knowing the origins of a people and the country they inhabit is a significant achievement, but it is pointless if it does not show what influence these have had on the citizenry. The influence of the external world and that of the historic or religious upbringing builds into the national character. In the case of a people, politics (like business for individuals) is motivated by character as well as by self-interest (A. Leroy-Beaulieu, 1990, p. 105).

On this view, legislation cannot be decreed in the abstract: the rationalism inherited from 1789 is demolished, along with the figure of the revolutionary legislator.

A. In Search of the Origins of the National Spirit

All of the professors at the *École Libre des Sciences Politiques* based their teaching on a return to the sources of French customs, manners, and the national language. The latter is particularly emphasized as one of the major traits of the national spirit. In the words of Albert Sorel ('La Langue Française et l'Alsace', in A. Sorel, 1898, p. 111),

> In the lives of nations, everything is an expression of traditional thought and feelings. Even hope is merely the idealized reflection of memory. This constitutes the greatness and importance of language. Every sentence we speak ... expresses our national character. This character comes down to us from our predecessors, who also spoke this language, and who handed it down to us as our inheritance. As we stumble through words in earliest childhood and then eventually learn to impose order on speech, we are reliving the lives of our ancestors. Their spirits are called back to life; we

become saturated with their spirit.

For Emile Boutmy, the French language was the heritage of the ancestors and an issue in the effort to maintain a French identity in Alsace-Lorraine: 'The psychology of language expresses the psychology of the race, feature for feature' (E. Boutmy, 1899, p. 2).[19] His thinking develops that of Taine in defining a national temperament specific to each nation, and Boutmy echoes both Taine's and Gustave Le Bon in advancing the idea of a collective psychology.[20] As with Le Bon, the notion of race for Boutmy tends to get priority treatment when defining a nation, and his analysis is consistently 'racial', organic and deterministic, even though the *École's* official position was that of Renan, namely, that race was insufficient to account for the character of a nation.

Behind this last trend in thinking was the opposition to the German, romantic notion of the nation, with its basis in anthropology. Renan wrote: 'Race ... is not everything ... in addition to ethnic characteristics, there is reason, justice, the true and the beautiful, which are the same for all people' (E. Renan, [1882], 1947, t. I, p. 898). For his part, Anatole Leroy-Beaulieu denounced the confusion of nation and religion and the assimilation of nation to race; he considered such views to be backward. For him, the concept of race was outmoded since history and anthropology have shown that there is not a single pure race on the face of earth; all nations are in fact mixtures of races.[21] Henri Gaidoz, who taught geography and anthropology at the *École*, added similar challenges from his perspective:

> What are the distinguishing features of a race? Is it language? As the example of Switzerland demonstrates, various races speak different languages and yet make up indisputable distinct nationalities; the same is true of Alsace and other places. Blood does not specify race either; I am inclined to look to a community of ideas, feelings and memories (H. Gaidoz, r.a.).

What these authors do share is an insistence on the linguistic and cultural community, the ethnic group and language, as the crucial and decisive features of a nation.[22] At times the terms used are racial and essentialist, for instance, Boutmy says of England 'This country, with its mixture of so many races, where a host of lines of inheritance must create a jumble of physical and moral types, has in fact created a people whose individual members are instantly recognizable: cool, practical, businesslike' (1894, p. 274).

Regarding the English language, Boutmy notes that 'it is the preserver of the national traditions, the mirror in which the Celtic type sees his identity' (1894, p. 379). He then goes on to specify:

> There are three things that emerge together, each being the condition, the symptom, the cause and the effect of the others. They are: a national language, a national literature set within the context of a common life, a collective consciousness that stimulates them, provides them with subjects, opens up expansive new fields that are rich in far-reaching echoes ... The sign that national progress has come to fruition, with a distinct national culture standing out above blood groups, is the advent of prose literature (1894, p. 384).

Despite the emphasis on the primacy of language in the ethnic group, Boutmy warns against underestimating the depth of historical accumulation:

> Too much emphasis is placed on race as the origin of national character. It is imagined as primordial, based on unreliable, vague documentation from some poorly dated remote period of origin. This results in an unjust slighting of the importance for the natural progress of human society of the steady build-up of its intellectual, moral and material capital, its history. It also underestimates the role of chance and the conscious imitation of one's neighbours and predecessors. In short, it underestimates the wide range of complex and obvious developments of national life open to our analysis (1894, p. 380).

Henri Gaidoz concurs that it is 'difficult to find a single criterion for race; it is not blood, but more likely language, the means of communication among humans'. This he views as a criterion that is essential, yet hard to make use of. He is especially concerned to reject the racial definition of the nation in the case of the peoples of Europe, 'too mixed to allow any useful ethnographic definition of highly civilized people'. That is 'The European races are distinguished by their moral characteristics. A German acknowledges Germany as his country, whether he is native born, a Germanized Slav, or a Frenchman established in Germany in the wake of the revocation of the Edict of Nantes' (H. Gaidoz, r.a.).

At the heart of this insistence is the determination to provide a scientific grounding for the notion of 'national character'. Proceeding empirically, the historian is to uncover the distinctive traits of a collectivity and abstract their psychological features from this observation, arriving at permanent features. This procedure, with its measure of determinism, is aimed at analysing the psychic processes underlying social phenomena.[23] The focus on the 'soul of peoples' and on the motives of collective action bespeaks a desire to restore the French nation by having recourse to science. Lastly, it should be connected to the need to struggle against the reigning eighteenth-century rationalist's analytical tendency, by elevating above the individual, broader and more inclusive realities such as the family, the nation and society. The common intellectual trend at the end of the nineteenth century joined in the struggle as it feared that excessive individualism might lead to anarchy, materialism and atheism.[24]

B. Opposition to Revolutionary Rationalism

Speaking of university courses that 'touch upon ethical life most intimately', Taine remarked:

> One of the most essential [university courses], in my view, is comparative law. It is not taught in our law schools, despite the fact that everyone involved in the field of history knows that the most revealing evidence of the mores and character of a nation is its civil code, which regulates the private life of every citizen... To preserve or amend our own code, we have to know how different conditions in foreign countries produce different rules and practices (1889, p. 88).

Whence the creation at the *École Libre des Sciences Politiques* of a course in comparative law, taught from 1879 on by the jurist and historian Jacques Flach, a disciple of Taine.

According to this view, law had to be discovered through an examination of history. This was a longstanding call of the historical school of law, imported into France for the most part by one of the principal promoters of the *École Libre des Sciences Politiques*, Edouard de Laboulaye. In 1842, he wrote: 'I do not think that in all of history there is a more imposing spectacle than the gradual birth of modern civilization that we discover through Savigny'. ('Essai sur la Vie de Savigny', p. 57, quoted by P. Legendre, 1971, p. 98). Laboulaye moves quickly to what he believes to be essential, namely, the historical development of the law. Echoing Savigny's words:

> His objective was to demonstrate that law was necessarily and inevitably connected with a nation's government, customs and ideas, and that the evolution of law, government and customs was as necessary and as inevitable as the development of the nation itself; the latter development was ordained to some degree by the laws, government, customs and ideas of the preceding generation. To summarize and to limit our analysis to the immediate subject - today's law is not different from yesterday's law, rather than outgrowth of a seed contained in the preceding law (*Histoire du Droit de Propriété*, 1839, p. 33, quoted by O. Motte, 1983, p. 125).

Edouard de Laboulaye opposed the rationalism of the revolution, criticized the merging of reason and the state; and in defending the concept of national law, he questioned the view that the state stood above the governed:

> However far back we go in history, we see that the civil law of each nation has always had a specific, particular character, just as the habits, customs and constitution of each people have a particular character. Law is not an absolute rule, as in the case of ethics. Nor is law an abstract institution, without roots in the country: on the contrary, law is an outgrowth of the national spirit ... No better comparison can be suggested between its evolution and that of language development ('Essai sur la Vie de Savigny', pp. 42-3, quoted by P. Legendre, 1971, p. 98).

In opposition to the legislator's defensiveness, his rationalism and pretentiousness as a framer of laws, Laboulaye insisted that 'Law, like language, grows with the nation, suffers and prospers with it and perishes when the nation vanishes ... Law exists in a latent state in customs and in public opinion, before finding its expression in legislation. Its strength is internal ... Laws are written, they are not created' ('Essai sur la Vie de Savigny', p. 44, quoted by P. Legendre, 1971, p. 99).

It has been said that it was a vain attempt to reconcile the German notion of popular law, generated by a people's own traditions, with the French rational notion, which is destructive of custom.[25] For most of the faculty of the *École Libre des Sciences Politiques*, their mission was in fact to understand this dilemma and teach it, this is clear in reading the course lectures of Albert Sorel, Vandal, and J. Flach, and as is apparent in the ethnology course of Henri Gaidoz, geared to bring into relief the national tendencies, and bent on discovering (1) a liberal strain in the history of the institutions of the monarchy, (2) the recurring issue of the traditional organization of freedom, (3) the institution of individual and social guarantees, and (4) the establishment of a relationship whereby the state is moderated through law.

Conclusion

Although we can decipher a shared patriotism and a common liberalism in the teachings of the *École Libre des Sciences Politiques*, it is more difficult to find a clear definition of what exactly the nation is, as conceptions alternate between that of an artificial construct or a contractual arrangement, and some sort of organic notion; i.e. between the view of Renan, who stressed voluntary creation of the nation, and an organic definition, or indeed the search for the historical and cultural unity of the nation. In the final analysis, there is vacillation between a strictly political definition and a definition based on a nationalist ideology that is both rational and organic.[26] Although Anthony D. Smith is certainly right in saying that

> Conceptually, the nation has come to blend two sets of dimensions, the one civic and territorial, the other ethnic and genealogical, in varying proportions in particular cases. It is this very multidimensionality that has made national identity such a flexible and persistent force in modern life and politics, and allowed it to combine effectively with other powerful ideologies and movements, without losing its character (1991, p. 15).

Nevertheless, it is true that the thought of historians like Albert Sorel and Albert Vandal expresses the limits of an opposition between political nationalism and cultural nationalism.[27] One should remember that Renan's own definition of the nation was itself ambiguous, wavering between a clearly asserted voluntarism and a countervailing admission of the importance of the historical factor, the shared life of the community (the aspect pushed to its limits by Maurice Barrès in his theme of 'rootedness'). Another conclusion is that one can speak of is an uneasy optimism in the historians who were associated with the liberal party. The fact is there was an attempt to reconcile irreconcilables[28] at a time when the principle of nationalities favoured by France had turned against it, and when the supposedly guiding nation had become the mutilated nation, whereas the German victory appeared to bestow on that country the role of a spiritual leader. Consequently, far from promoting a universal ideal, French intellectuals tended henceforth to limit their thought to their diminished country, falling back on an idea of France perceived as a singular historic creation, mimicking the German view. Historians such as Albert Sorel, caught up in the task of national regeneration, also had to stand in opposition to the Hegelian thought of historians like, Heinrich von Treitschke and Heinrich von Sybel,[29] who had struggled for German national unity against France, thereby breaking with the idealistic teachings of Leibnitz and Kant, which were so close to French ideas.

According to historians specialized in French history, the Near East question gave the French country an opportunity to reassert its historic vocation of 'guide' to other nations. Paradoxically, these patriotic concerns may also have touched off a reaction, and a temporary or ephemeral embracing of the nationalist *Ligue de la Patrie Française* at the time of the Dreyfus Affair.[30] In the case of Albert Vandal and Albert Sorel, who joined the *Ligue*, as historians sensitive to the inheritance of the Great Nation, their minds were fixed on spreading the influence of France, and they therefore refused to take the side of justice against the army (J.-P. Rioux, 1977, p. 12).

According to Sorel:

> We must appeal to all that held our fathers together, to the patriotism that saved us a century ago. Under all our political systems, patriotism was the key element of our national life. It made our Revolution and the ensuing war against Europe the characteristically French phenomena they were. That is the tradition that I personally call upon, the still living and ever young tradition. The army has the responsibility of holding its image up to Europe, and nowadays it must be respected more than ever, since it is the very image of the united nation. France has concluded a grand alliance. It has undertaken an immense task in its colonies. Now is not the time to question what remains, alongside the liberation of our territory, the great badge of honour of our governments since 1871 (A. Sorel, A. Mézières, *Le Temps*, 1899, January 5, quoted by Rioux, J.-P., 1977, p. 13).

Those who joined the *Ligue de la Patrie Française* justified their membership by this concern, and their refusal to support what they felt was a campaign against the army. For the majority, *Ligue* membership rested on their shared patriotism, of a quite different nature than the nationalism of Barrès. There were contradictions in a position which rejected anti-Semitism and nationalism and strove to unite *the Ligue des Droits de l'Homme* and the *Ligue des Patriotes*, all the while accepting nationalists and anti-Semites as comrades.[31]

Just as we must avoid equating nationalism with anti-Dreyfusism, so we also must realize that support of Dreyfus does not inevitably lead to the defence of abstract universalism. *École* professors such as Sorel and Vandal came out against Dreyfus while remaining republican defenders of a contractual vision of the nation, whereas a republican defender of Dreyfus like Boutmy was inclined more to the organic, cultural view of the nation.

Notes

1   The non-standard expression - 'la Nation France'- is taken from: C. Beaune, 1985.

2   This group made up the Society for the Study of Issues in Higher Education, founded in 1878. Its publication, *Revue Internationale d'Enseignement Supérieur*, created in 1881, would print a number of articles on the teaching of political science by Boutmy and other faculty of his School, including Albert Sorel.

3   It should be recalled that, in 1875, Parliament passed a law authorizing the creation of 'private universities', [facultés libres], such that the foundation of the *École Libre des Sciences Politiques* was part of an emerging trend toward private institutions of higher learning or locally sponsored institutions. The trend picked up momentum subsequently: e.g. *l'École Libre d'Architecture*, where Boutmy taught, and which undoubtedly served as a model for the *École Libre des Sciences Politiques*. Other institutions to include here are the Catholic universities founded after 1875, new engineering schools like the *'École Municipale de Physique et de Chimie Industrielle de Paris* and business schools such as the *Hautes Etudes Commerciales* (1881).

4   The first essay relative to the introduction of these disciplines appeared in 1819. Regarding these debates and curriculum innovations, cf. D. Damamme, 1982, Vol. I, p. 314 et. seq.; E. Lenoël, 1865; Ch. Tranchant, 1878; G. Lame-Fleury, 1864-1865; G. Langrod, 1957, pp. 24-36.

5   Sorel was designated 'salaried attached to the political affairs directorate', by Jules Favre, Minister of Foreign Affairs, at the behest of François Guizot, and assigned to Tours. Guizot advised Albert Sorel's father, the industrialist Emile Sorel, to allow young Albert the leisure to discover his true calling. Late in 1864, Guizot advised the young law graduate to spend significant time abroad. Sorel opted for Germany, spending the year 1865 in Berlin. Upon his return, he visited Guizot, who recommended him to the Minister of Foreign Affairs. Guizot was also the one who recommended Sorel to Emile Boutmy, who had just founded the *École Libre des Sciences Politiques*. Starting with the 1872 school year, Sorel was entrusted with the course in diplomatic history: he was to teach it for more than 30 years, up to the time

of his death in 1906.

6   On Sorel's republicanism, cf. *Revue des Deux Mondes*, December 15, 1912; *Correspondance d'Albert Sorel, 1870-1871*, letter to his mother, September 24, 1870, quoted by C. Digeon, [1959], 1992, pp. 292-3.

7   On Boutmy's historical method, see P. Favre, 1989, p. 33.

8   It is well known that the year 1880 initiated a period of controversy related to the centenary celebration of the French Revolution. Acceptance or rejection of 1789 came to be the litmus test of the political left and right. It is also well known that at the time of the opportunistic Republic, and the split between moderate and radical republicans, the debate crystallized around and divided people between partisans of the champions of the Revolution (of La Fayette and Mirabeau) and partisans of the 'Revolution as a whole', in the celebrated expression of Georges Clemenceau. Cf. A. Gérard, 1970, p. 70.

9   Cf. also, p. 240 of the same work: 'The passion for unity, constantly developed under the monarchy, saved the revolution from its own excesses. It was enough for those two incurable diseases, foreign conquest and civil strife, to break out, for the French people to get a grip on themselves and come to their senses. They had not lost the soul of nations, the real principle of public safety: love of country. This was rekindled in their hearts and grew with the enthusiasm for a revolution that meant deliverance for them. These two notions were alloyed and the French people defended both their national independence and the liberty they had won'.

10   He often quotes Renan, especially in A. Sorel, [1887], 1897.

11   For that interpretation, cf. C. Digeon, [1959], 1992, pp. 294-5.

12   Cf. Rambaud's course on the Republic and the Napoleonic Empire in *Revue Bleue*, 1872, and A. Rambaud, 1873, p. 379. On Vandal, cf. *infra*.

13   In his lecture, *Les Arméniens et la Question d'Arménie*, Leroy-Beaulieu asked that Europe, with France in the lead, force the Ottoman Empire to enact reforms and grant all nationalities security guarantees, in accordance with the Treaty of Berlin.

14   On the creation of courses at the *École Libre des Sciences Politiques* in the wake of this 'irruption of real history', cf. P. Favre, 1983.

15   The subject of a controversial lecture by A. Vandal, 1897.

16   Many references could be made. Albert Sorel himself took up the Near Eastern question and the problem of the entente with Russia in ways rather similar to those of Vandal and Leroy-Beaulieu. In the same spirit, the work of other professors at the École, such as A. Rambaud and A. Viallatte was along similar lines. This Slavophilia is likely to have influenced the many studies on diplomatic history devoted to the eighteenth century and to the Napoleonic Empire.

17   Cf. also P. Birnbaum, 1993.

18   On the last point, cf. also G. Noiriel, in C.U.R.A.P.P. ed., 1994, pp. 197-205.

19   Boutmy constructs a parallel between the brisk simplicity of the English language viewed primarily as a tool by its users, and the pragmatism of the English people - 'men of action, practical, utilitarian'.

20   On Taine in that regard, see C. Haroche, in C.U.R.A.P.P. ed., 1994, pp. 17-31.

21   Cf. A. Leroy-Beaulieu, [1893], 1983, and the Preface by R. Rémond, 1983.

22   For a discussion of these criteria as innovative in the nineteenth century, cf. Th. Schieder, in H.A. Winkler, ed., 1985, p. 128. Cf. also, E. Hobsbawm, 1990, Chapter IV, on the changing face of nationalism during the last third of the nineteenth

century, the promotion of the ethnic and linguistic criteria and its political implications (the development of a language policy becoming an exercise in nation-building whose force was at least symbolic).

23   Cf. P. Favre, 1981.

24   On the 'organic' tendency in nineteenth-century thought as opposed to the analytical thought of the eighteenth century, cf. R. Nisbet, 1966; J.-P. Sartre, 1981, p. 29. On the intellectual successors of Gustave Le Bon and the increased attention given to the analysis of crowds at the end of the nineteenth century, cf. S. Barrows, 1981; J. Jaap van Ginneken, 1989, pp. 29-44.

25   For that attempt in de Laboulaye's own work, cf. P. Legendre, 1971, vol. I, p. 83-112 [esp. pp. 96-7].

26   On this distinction, cf. H. Kohn, 1967. Cf. also M. Wieviorka, 1993. L. Dumont, 1983.

27   On the limits of the opposition between political nationalism and cultural nationalism stressed by H. Kohn, cf. A. Dieckhoff, 1996. It would doubtless serve the interests of research better at this juncture to follow Dieckhoff in recalling the teachings of Louis Dumont, for whom French and German culture are subsets of a single modern ideology marked by the triumph of individualism. For Louis Dumont, 'holism' is not the negation of individualism, but something like the transfer of the principle of individualism to that of community. Cf. A. Dieckhoff, 1996, p. 45; L. Dumont, 1983, pp. 114-31.

28   Or what were considered to be irreconcilable, namely the French and German ideals: the French, rationalist ideal led to the negation of specific differences among peoples, whereas the romantic, German notion was based on the primitive, irreducible originality of the German character.

29   On German historians, cf. A. Guilland, 1899.

30   The *Ligue de la Patrie Française* is created at the end of the year 1898, within the Dreyfus Affair context, the event which divided French people. This nationalist and antidreyfusist *Ligue,* the Jules Guérin's *Ligue Antisémite* and the Déroulède's *Ligue des Patriotes,* oppos the dreyfusist *Ligue pour la Defense des Droits de l'Homme.* On these *Ligues,* see: R. Girardet, 1966; J.-P. Rioux, 1977. On the context of Dreyfus Affair, see: J. Reinach, 1903-1911; J.-D. Bredin, 1990.

31   Cf. for an example, a work that focuses on Charles Brunetière: A. Compagnon, (1997). On this contradiction, see note 30; the *Ligue des Patriotes* and the *Ligue de la Patrie Française* are very nationalist and anti-semite. However, most of the members of these anti-dreyfusist *Ligues* are involved because they are anti-dreyfusists; and they are anti-dreyfusist not out of nationalism and anti-semitism, but because of submission to Army and authority.

References

Barrows, S. (1981), *Distorting Mirrors. Visions of the Crowd in Late Nineteenth-Century France*, Yale University.

Beaune, C. (1985), *La Nation France*, Gallimard, Paris.

Birnbaum, P. (1993), *La France aux Français. Histoire des Haines Nationalistes*, Seuil,

Paris.

Boutmy, E. (1871), *Quelques Idées sur la Création d'une Faculté Libre d'Enseignement Supérieur*, Lainé, Paris

Boutmy, E. (1894), 'Les Origines de la Langue et de la Littérature Anglaises', *Revue de Paris*, November 15, pp. 374-92.

Boutmy, E. (1899), 'La Langue Anglaise et le Génie National', *Annales des Sciences Politiques*, January, vol. XIV, p. 1-19.

Boutmy, E. (1902), *Eléments d'une Psychologie Politique du Peuple Américain*, A. Colin, Paris.

Boutmy, E. and Vinet, E. (1871), *Faculté Libre des Sciences Politiques, Projet*, Archives d'Histoire Contemporaine (A.H.C.), 1 SP 14, Dr. 7.

Bredin, J.D. (1990), *L'Affaire*, Fayard, Paris.

Compagnon, A. (1997), *Connaissez-vous Brunetière? Enquête sur un Antidreyfusard et ses Amis*, Seuil, Paris.

Damamme, D. (1982), *Histoire des Sciences Morales et Politiques et de leur Enseignement, des Lumières au Scientisme. Instituer le Corps Politique, Fabriquer une 'Tête de Peuple'*. PhD thesis in Political Science, Paris I, 2 vols.

Dieckhoff, A. (1996), 'La Déconstruction d'une Illusion. L'Introuvable Opposition entre Nationalisme Politique et Nationalisme Culturel', *L'Année Sociologique, Nation, Nationalisme, Citoyenneté*, vol. 46, no. 1, pp. 43-55.

Digeon, C. (1992 [1959]), *La Crise Allemande de la Pensée Française (1870-1914)*, PUF, Paris.

Doumic, R. (1906), 'L'Oeuvre d'Albert Sorel', *Revue des Deux Mondes*, July 15, p. 446-57.

Dumont, L. (1983), *Essais sur L'individualisme. Une Perspective Anthropologique sur l'Idéologie Moderne*, Seuil, Paris.

École Libre des Sciences Politiques, *PV Conseil d'Administration, Comité de Fondation de l'École Libre des Sciences Politiques, Séance du Samedi 20 Janvier 1872*, A.H.C., 1 SP 29, Dr. 2.

Favre, P. (1981), 'Les Sciences d'Etat entre Déterminisme et Libéralisme: Emile Boutmy et la Création de l'École Libre des Sciences Politiques', *Revue Française de Sociologie*, 22 (3), pp. 429-65.

Favre, P. (1983), 'La Constitution d'une Science du Politique. Le Déplacement de ses Objets et 'l'Irruption de l'Histoire Réelle', *Revue Française de Science Politique*, 33 (2), 33 (3), pp. 181-219 and pp. 305-402.

Favre, P. (1989), *Naissances de la Science Politique en France, 1870-1914*, Fayard. Paris.

Gaidoz, H. (n.d.), *Les Roumains de Hongrie*, Paris.

Gaidoz, H. (r.a.), Lecture Notes, Unnumbered Pages, Archives d'Histoire Contemporaine, 1 SP 5, Dr. 4.

Gérard, A. (1970), *La Révolution Française, Mythes et Interprétations, 1789-1970*, Flammarion, Paris.

Girardet, R. (1966), *Le Nationalisme Français (1871-1914)*, A. Colin, Paris.

Guilland, A. (1899), *L'Allemagne Nouvelle et ses Historiens*, Alcan, Paris.

Haroche, C. (1994), 'Remarques sur la Formation des Identités Politiques dans les Ecrits de Taine', in C.U.R.A.P.P. (ed.), *L'Identité Politique*, C.U.R.A.P.P. (ed.), PUF, Paris, pp. 17-31.

Hobsbawm, E. (1990), *Nations and Nationalism since 1780. Programme, Myth, Reality*, Published by the Press Syndicate of the University of Cambridge, Cambridge

University Press, Cambridge.

Jaap van Ginneken, J. (1989), *Crowds, Psychology and Politics, 1871-1899*, Adademisch proefschrift (doctoral thesis), Amsterdam.

Kohn, H. (1967), *The Idea of Nationalism. A Study in its Origin and Background*, Collier-Macmillan, New York (2nd ed.).

Lame-Fleury, G. (1864-1865), 'De l'Enseignement Professionnel (Sciences Administratives et Politiques) et du Mode de Recrutement des Fonctionnaires Civils', *Journal des Economistes*, December, April, June, August, October, November.

Langrod, G. (1957), 'Trois Tentatives d'Introduction de la Science Politique dans l'Université Française au Cours du XIXe Siècle', *Revue Internationale d'Histoire Politique et Constitutionnelle*, no. 25/26.

Legendre, P. (1971), 'Méditations sur l'Esprit Libéral. La Leçon d'Edouard de Laboulaye, Juriste, Témoin', *Revue de Droit Public et de la Science Politique*, vol. I, p. 83-102.

Lenoël, E. (1865), *Des Sciences Politiques et Administratives et de leur Enseignement*, Durand-Dumaine, Paris.

Leroy-Beaulieu, A. (1983 [1893]), *Israël et les Nations*, Calmann-Lévy, Paris.

Leroy-Beaulieu, A. (1897), *La Patrie Française et l'Internationalisme*, Comité de Défense et de Progrès Social.

Leroy-Beaulieu, A. (1900), *Rapport Général sur les Etats-Unis d'Europe au Congrès des Sciences Politiques*, Paris.

Leroy-Beaulieu, A. (1990), *L'Empire des Tsars et les Russes*, Laffont, Collection Bouquins, Paris.

Motte, O. (1983), *Savigny et la France*, Peter Lang, Berne.

Nisbet, R. (1966), *The Sociological Tradition*, Basic Books, Inc., Publishers, New York.

Noiriel, G. (1994), 'L'Identité Nationale dans l'Historiographie Française', in C.U.R.A.P.P. (ed.), *L'Identité Politique*, PUF, Paris, pp. 197-205.

Pinon, R. (1931), 'Anatole Leroy-Beaulieu', *Revue des Deux Mondes*, November 1, pp. 74-108.

Rambaud, A. (1873), *La Domination Française en Allemagne. Les Français sur le Rhin (1792-1804)*, Didier, Paris.

Reinach, J. (1903-1911), *Histoire de l'Affaire Dreyfus*, Paris, Librairie Charpentier et Fasquelle.

Rémond, R. (1983), Preface to Leroy-Beaulieu's *Israël chez les Nations*, Calmann-Lévy, Paris.

Renan, E. (1947 [1882]), 'Qu'est-ce qu'une Nation?' in *Oeuvres Complètes*, Calmann-Lévy, Paris, vol. I, p. 887-906.

Rioux, J.P. (1977), *Nationalisme et Conservatisme. La Ligue de la Patrie Française, 1899-1904*, Beauchesne, Paris.

Sartre, J. P. (1981), *L'Imagination*, Paris, P.U.F.

See, H. (1927), *Histoire de la Ligue des Droits de l'Homme (1898-1926)*, L.D.H., Paris, 1927.

Siegfried, A. (1927), *Les Etats-Unis d'Aujourd'hui*, Armand Colin, Paris.

Smith, A.D. (1991), *National Identity*, Penguin Books, London.

Sorel, A. (1872a), 'La Prusse et les deux Empires', *Revue des Deux Mondes*, May 1, pp. 35-65.

Sorel, A. (1872b), *Le Traité de Paris du 20 novembre 1815*, (course in diplomatic history given at the *École Libre des Sciences Politiques*), Germer-Baillière, Paris.

Sorel, A. (1875), *Histoire Diplomatique de la Guerre Franco-Allemande*, Plon, Paris.

Sorel, A. (1897 [1887]), *L'Europe et la Révolution Française*, Plon, Paris.

Sorel, A. (1898), *Nouveaux Essais d'Histoire et de Critique*, Plon, Paris.

Sorel, A. (1901), *Etudes de Littérature et d'Histoire*, Plon-Nourrit et Cie., Paris.

Sorel, A.E. (1913), *Revue des Deux Mondes*, March 15, 2, pp. 403-32.

Taine, H. (1894), *Derniers Essais de Critique et d'Histoire*, Hachette, Paris.

Tranchant, Ch. (1878), *De la Préparation aux Services Publics en France*, Berger-Levrault, Paris.

Vandal, A. (1891-1897), *Napoléon et Alexandre I. L'Alliance Russe sous le Premier Empire*, [vol. I: *De Tsilsitt à Erfurt*, 1891; vol. II, Paris, *Le Second Mariage de Napoléon, Déclin de l'Alliance*, 1893; vol. III, Paris, *La Rupture*, 1897], E. Plon et Nourrit, Paris.

Vandal, A. (1897), *Les Arméniens et la Réforme en Turquie*, lecture delivered on February 2, 1897, Société de Géographie, Plon-Nourrit et Cie, Paris.

Veyne, P. (1987), 'Eloge de la Curiosité: Inventaire et Intellection en Histoire', *Philosophie et Histoire*, Centre Pompidou, Paris.

Wieviorka, M. (1993), *La Démocratie à l'Epreuve. Nationalisme, Populisme, Ethnicité*, La Découverte, Paris.

Winkler, H.A. (1985) (ed.), *Nationalismus*, Königstein im Taunus.

Winock, M. (1990), *Nationalisme, Antisémitisme et Fascisme en France*, Seuil, Paris.

9 National Identity Construction and the Teachers' Unions of the Germanys and Japan, 1945-1955

JULIAN DIERKES

This article examines the roots of post-war German and Japanese national identities. I define national identity to be the answer to the question: 'What does it mean to you to be ... (American, German, Japanese)?'. This individually perceived answer arises out of the process of a collective construction of identity. This construction is contested by (usually collective) actors and becomes institutionalized over time. In order to understand such a process of institutionalization, it is necessary to recognize the agenda of particular collective actors. The spread of compulsory education, the lengthening of time spent in school by children, and the professionalization of teaching have all contributed to the importance of education as a very important factor in the construction of national identity.

Defeat in World War II afforded collective actors an opportunity to reconstruct national identity according to their own view of such an identity. The teachers' unions in the Federal Republic of Germany (FRG), the German Democratic Republic (GDR) and Japan were among the collective actors who were most deeply involved in the reconstruction of identity. I analyse the response of the teachers' unions of three countries to a momentous event, to an exogenous shock to their social system. The complete defeat of Germany and Japan called national identity in its most basic elements into question. After a description of the institutional environment of the post-war reestablishment of teachers' unionism, I analyse statements on national identity by unions in the three countries. I situate national identity prescriptions in a multi-dimensional space delimited by three axes: cultural vs. political descriptions of national identity, internationalist descriptions vs. localism, and future-oriented forms of identity vs. backward looking ones. The statements of the Japanese union were forward-looking, politically oriented and internationalist. The West German union espoused an identity relying on achievements of the past and focusing on national cultural issues. East German union officials in turn articulated an identity that had elements of internationalism as well as localism and was forward-looking politically while remaining tradition-bound culturally. In the final section, I argue that the content of the statements on national identity varies according to the form that teachers' unionism took in the three countries.

Japan and the now-united Germany represent especially interesting cases to the student of national identities. These nations experienced a radical reconstruction in 1945 after a disastrous war by which they had caused the destruction of their and others' livelihood and the loss of countless lives. Defeat in 1945 also meant the crushing of regimes which were based to a large extent on popular nationalism, i.e., an extremely heightened and self-confident national identity. More than 'just' military defeat, defeat in World War II for Germany and Japan meant ideological defeat and proof of the blatant moral deficiencies of the reigning ideologies. This complete defeat implied a necessary and historically anomalous simultaneity in the development of cultural and political nationalism (Giesen, 1991, p. 13).

The Institutional Environment of Teachers' Unionization

In Japan as well as in Germany, education historically enjoyed high social prestige (Dore, 1984, esp. Ch. X). The totalitarian regimes of the 1930s in Germany and Japan (Thurston, 1973, Ch. II; Shillony, 1981, pp. 141-51) and the East German regime, recognized this prominence and thus paid special attention to the ideological steadfastness of teachers at all levels of state-sponsored and private education. Similarly, officers of the American occupation in West Germany emphasized the re-education of teachers (Kleßmann, 1986, p. 92). One researcher even speaks of the 'classical interdependence of compulsory education and political indoctrination' (Nishi, 1982, p. 3). Teachers as a collective actor provide an example for the claim of some scholars (Eisenstadt, 1991, p. 23) that national identity has been advanced mostly by two groups: intellectuals and politicians. It is evident that in the three countries selected for the comparison, awareness of the potential socializing power of educators was heightened due to the previous history of education under totalitarianism.

Teaching in Japan is based on a particularly long tradition of the conscious propagation of ideology and played such a role under the Tokugawa Shogunate and after the Meiji Restoration. Scholars have shown that Tokugawa schools were instrumental in the propagation of Confucian ideology and Japanese traditions (*Kokugaku*) which played such a large role in legitimizing the Shogunate and the Emperor-centred state of the 1930s (Dore, 1984; Colcutt, 1991). Under the late nineteenth century Meiji government, the 1890 Imperial Rescript on Education (*Kyoiku Chokugo*) was intended to direct schools in a similar direction and to serve the bureaucracy as a guideline in establishing educational content (Horio, 1988, pp. 65-87).

In all three cases that are to be examined, teachers were highly organized in the late 1940s, and their labour unions can be said to be representative of many of the teachers of the period. By 1949, the West German teachers' union claimed to have almost 58,000 members (Kopitzsch, 1983, p. 77). Membership in the East German union was not legally mandatory, yet in practice almost universal (Gill, 1989, p. 321). In late 1947, the Japanese Teacher's Union reported to the American military administration that its membership totalled almost 450,000 teachers or roughly 98% of all teachers (Thurston, 1973, p. 44). Apart from the collective representation of teachers, these unions played a role as significant social actors in their respective countries. However, the unions in the three countries differ as to how they related to the state. I argue that emphases by the unions in their prescriptions on national identity are related to their autonomy vis-à-vis policy-makers.

Teachers' Unionization in the GDR - Joining the State in Battle

In terms of the political environment, the GDR is perhaps easiest to describe among the three states. With few exceptions, policies were made either directly by the Stalinist government of the Soviet Union through their military commander in Eastern Germany, or by the political representatives of the Soviet government, German communist cadres who had been trained and prepared for this role during their exile in the Soviet Union (Kleßmann, 1986, Ch. VIII).

Labour unions were established in the Soviet-Occupied Zone very early on. Initially, these were genuine efforts at workers' organization, though union leadership was soon usurped by communist cadres (Gill, 1989). With the foundation of the GDR in 1949, the unions took on a character very different from unions in other countries. Since the GDR was nominally governed by the proletariat and since enterprises had been nationalized and were thus in theory governed by the proletariat as well, the opposition between labour and capitalists was no longer recognized as salient. Rather than representing workers in their struggle against capitalists, the unions now served to support the state-enterprise. Organization by firm or industry lost its relevance and teachers were thus organized as part of a single, unified union, the *Freie Deutsche Gewerkschaftsbund* (FDGB - German Free Union Federation). Although teachers were members of a subsection of the FDGB, the *Gewerkschaft Lehrer und Erzieher* (Teacher and Educator Union), all activities of the union should be seen as elements in the activities of the FDGB. The integration of teachers into the FDGB might have been aided by the lack of a politically active teachers' union in the pre-war years (see below; Kopitzsch, 1983, pp. 18-25).

Meanwhile, teaching as a profession in the GDR underwent momentous changes (Kleßmann, 1986, pp. 282-8). In line with party goals of enabling workers to occupy positions of power and influence in the state, many young farmers and workers were retrained to become schoolteachers. Apart from the ideological benefit, this also enabled schools to overcome their severe shortage of qualified personnel. Yet, such training of *Junglehrer* (young teachers) demanded considerable resources. In 1946 alone, Marshall Sukhow, the representative of the Soviet government in East Germany, ordered the education of 30,000 new teachers (*Neue Schule* 1(1), p. 14). *Neue Schule*, the newspaper of the East German teachers' union, reported that 25,000 new teachers had joined the staff of schools at all levels of education after attending training seminars for a mere eight months (ibid., 1 (6), p. 4). These numbers alone suggest the deep involvement of teachers in societal transformations in the early years of the German Democratic Republic.

The Teachers' Union in the FRG - One Among a Variety of Collective Actors and Opinions

The situation in Western Germany was much more complex. Not only was there not a single occupying army, but rather three main occupiers and a host of smaller military contingents; in addition, the three main allied countries (France, Great Britain and the United States) were divided among themselves on policy questions (Kleßmann, 1986, pp. 92-5; Kopitzsch, 1983, pp. 29-74). Teachers' unions were at first not primarily interested in educational issues; rather, attempts to organize teachers sought to secure material benefits. But even organization for such straightforward and seemingly ideologically non-threatening goals, proved difficult in varying degrees in the three sectors of Western Germany governed by the main Allies. In contrast to General MacArthur governing through a civilian Japanese government, post-war Western Germany was governed by allied military administrations (Kocka, 1992). While the British military administration allowed unionization early on, the French and US authorities were much more hesitant. With the foundation of the Federal Republic in 1949 a strong emphasis on federalism and the supreme power of the states in educational matters made the national co-ordination of union activities difficult. This emphasis was as much a function of the post-war constitution as it represented continuity from the Weimar constitution which ceded decision-making power in matters of education to the *Länder* (states) (Kopitzsch, 1983, pp. 18-25).

Historically, teachers' unions grew out of co-operative associations to ensure the financial security of teachers' dependents in case of death or accident. The repression of political unionism following the 1848 revolutions in Germany led to a general depoliticization of teachers' associations and increasing power was devolved to regional, confessional, subject-specific, as well as civil servant associations (Kopitzsch, 1983, pp. 20-2; Kocka, 1992, pp. 33-4). The same pattern persisted in the Weimar years until teachers' organizations were integrated into the Nazi dictatorship in the 1930s. Purges of teachers associated with National Socialism in Germany led to severe shortages of teaching personnel. Some areas of West Germany saw dismissals of as many as 90% of teachers and the subsequent re-hiring of teachers dismissed in 1933 or retired since then led to an unusually old faculty for most schools (Kleßmann, 1986, p. 92).

The Japanese Teachers' Union - Battling the State

Japan presents yet another set of circumstances. As was the case with the GDR, only one occupying army was involved with one, rather centralized administration. The American leadership of the occupation was very much dominated by General MacArthur, the Supreme Commander of the Allied Powers (SCAP), whose administration brought about a situation radically different from that of the German states (Nishi, 1982, p. 2, pp. 34-49). Not only was there only one occupying power, but this power presented a unified ideology and clear policies to Japan. One of these policies was to govern through the civil Japanese government rather than replacing it by a military American government (Amakawa, 1992). To enable democratic institutions that would check the power of the Japanese government internally, SCAP initially encouraged the formation of unions (Brown, 1955, p. 255). Teachers were able to organize early on, first locally then nationally. The numerous metamorphoses that the teachers' union underwent before its unification as the Japanese Teachers' Union indicate the liberty with which this organization took place. The high rate of mobilization of teachers might be taken as another indicator of the liberalism of the early post-war period (Thurston, 1973, p. 44; Marshall, 1994, p. 252).

The American occupation initiated purges of teachers in Japan as well (Brown, 1955, p. 244), though they were less extensive than in Germany by all accounts. By April 1949 only slightly more than 3,000 teachers and educational officials out of roughly one million screened had been deemed unacceptable, while 115,000 had resigned before being screened (Nishi, 1982, p. 173). Practical demands on schools also led to a relaxation of some initial 'moral demilitarization' measures. War-time textbooks were thus retained with the more offensive, i.e., ultra-nationalistic, sections deleted (ibid., pp. 180-2; Brown, 1955, p. 244).

Teachers' Unions' Newspapers

I have performed content analysis on the weekly newspapers published by the teachers' unions in the three countries from their first post-war issue through 1955 in Japan and the FRG, and through 1954 in the GDR:[1] In the case of Japan the newspaper was *Kyoiku Shinbun* (Education Newspaper, abbreviated hereafter as KS) and its predecessors,[2] for the FRG the *Allgemeine Deutsche Lehrerzeitung* (General German Teachers Newspaper, ADLZ) and for the GDR the *Neue Schule* (New School, NS).[3] These newspapers were very similar in their audience and format. I am therefore confident in claiming that the analysis of these papers represents a sound effort of comparison of functional and formal equivalents.

The research, on which this article is based, thus focuses on the first decade after the end of World War II. Since all three countries are released from military occupation and regain full sovereignty within a few months of each other, the observed period includes all of the allied occupation as well as the first years of independence. The beginning of the Cold War and the outbreak of the Korean War are also included in order to be able to examine changes in the public posture of the unions relating to the new global political situation. The year 1955 marks the beginning of economic recovery in the three countries and therefore a change of structural conditions that might well influence the stance of the unions.

In extracting data from the newspapers, I engaged in what Strauss (1987, p. 38) has termed 'theoretical sampling'. I surveyed the newspapers for the appropriate years and tried to be especially alert for keywords that suggested discussion of issues related to national identity. Some such keywords were: history, nation, national identity, ethics, school systems, foreign school systems, educational law, curriculum, teacher education, international cooperation among teachers, war/peace, the United States, the Soviet Union, democracy/democratization, textbooks. Though these keywords and the context they appeared in were readily recognisable as relevant, I did not begin my research with a categorization schema in mind. My search yielded a total of 97 articles for KS, 43 for ADLZ, and 86 for NS. I subjected these articles to closer scrutiny, searching for patterns and themes in the discussion of national identity and topics that are related to such discussions. Pattern recognition as a method was chosen for the available data in order to be able to capture the meaningfulness of terminology and the semantic symbolism inherent in the terminology employed by authors. The categories that emerged from the research captured variation along three continua: international <-> local, cultural <-> political, and forward-looking <-> tradition-bound.

Representations of National Identity in Three Nations

National Identity in the GDR: Political, Future-Oriented, and Internationalist

The *Neue Schule* clearly underwent a development in tone and content of its reporting over the time period examined; the paper became increasingly political and combative. Whereas many of the earlier issues (1946 to approximately 1948) focused on very pragmatic problems of how to set up new schools in Eastern Germany, many later issues spoke of the necessity for vigilance against attacks from imperialist sympathizers. Not only did the focus of the paper change, but in the later years articles and especially editorials became increasingly formulaic. The words '*Heimatkunde*' and 'democratic' provide good examples of these developments.

The debate surrounding the issue of the inclusion of *Heimatkunde* in the official curriculum exemplifies many of the currents represented in the *Neue Schule*. *Heimatkunde* is first and foremost simply the study of the *Heimat*, the region of origin of the student, the homeland. It is usually a form of local history education that is combined with visits to local historical sites and includes the study of plant and animal varieties. Even though one might refer to a nation as one's *Heimat*, the term carries a more local connotation and *Heimatkunde* is usually strictly focused on a region or locality. Since *Heimatkunde* is usually aimed at elementary school children, it represents the most basic form of historical education in the school.

The debate over *Heimatkunde* in the *Neue Schule* was centred on the question whether knowledge of one's region is conducive to the goal of a socialist and universal identity. In 1949, an article was entitled 'What does *Heimatkunde* consist of?' (NS 4 (7), pp. 220-2) and described in detail what content and methods might be appropriate for the teaching of *Heimatkunde*.[4] Whereas *Heimatkunde* was thus advocated early on and the spirit of patriotism that is invoked in the later years was very similar to lessons learned in *Heimatkunde*, the word itself disappeared entirely from the discourse by 1952. Since *Heimatkunde* is aimed at elementary school students, the following 1953 statement might serve as a good comparison to the earlier endorsement of *Heimatkunde*: 'Students should leave elementary school with a patriotic self-awareness and pride in the progressive cultural achievements of the German people.' (NS 8 (1), pp. 4-

6). The discussion here was focused on the creation of patriotic self-awareness, but *Heimatkunde* was not mentioned as a vehicle for the promotion of such an awareness. Rather, 'humanist patriotism' was meant to infuse all teaching.

Whereas the adjective 'democratic' referred to a system of government in which ultimate power rests with the people of the nation until about 1949, 'democratic' later on merely became a generic part of the name of the East German nation and thus took on the meaning of 'East German' especially in combination with 'German'. For example, in an article on the important role of teachers in the 'National Front', an author entitled his report: 'The National Front and Teachers in the German Democratic School' (NS 5 (8), pp. 244-5). Clearly, 'German democratic' in this case meant the school as it existed in the German Democratic Republic and this usage does not imply a school controlled by the rule of the people. By joining 'German' and 'democratic', national identity was redefined in terms of the nation as a political entity, rather than in terms of cultural, historical or linguistic unity.

Not surprisingly for an organ of state-propaganda, much of the content of the *Neue Schule* was framed in terms of Marxist 'science'. However, such 'scientific' approaches were interwoven with articles that seem to appeal to a sentimental side of socialist patriotism. Many of these discussions seem to follow the tradition of German identity-construction as being focused on culture, especially during the Romantic era (Greenfeld, 1992, pp. 322-52; Giesen, Junge, Kritschgau, 1994). The best example for this romantic appeal came in 1953 with a two-sided pictorial of scenes of 'Germany, dear Fatherland' (NS 8 (17), unnumbered). On these pages, black and white photographs portrayed such popular tourist spots as fortresses and scenes of natural beauty. Although the majority of the twelve pictures consisted of scenes in East Germany, the pictorial was obviously meant to instil a romantic affection for all German spots of beauty. The article accompanying the photographs extolled the beauty of Germany in flowery prose, reflecting articles of a similar orientation that seemed to multiply in 1952. An article in the same year specified what the intent of such appeals to romantic patriotism might be by describing the content of patriotic education as consisting in, 'youth's education in patriotic thinking, feeling and action, which manifest themselves in a deep love for one's people and for the peace-loving, democratic German fatherland, in pride in the progressive traditions and historical accomplishments of one's people and its leaders, and in the willingness to participate actively in the solution of national and social problems facing the German people' (NS 8 (34), pp. 6-10).

The *Neue Schule* frequently reassured readers that the patriotism that was being instilled in children is utterly different from the pre-war chauvinism or the patriotism that capitalists exploit to further their imperialist goals. As an example of such differentiation, a *Neue Schule* columnist wrote that, 'There is no hate between peoples, except for artificial, blind hate, incited by imperialists to pit people against each other in order to benefit imperialism' (NS 9 (6), p. 3). Presumably, 'true patriotism' differed from pre-war chauvinism in that it incorporated internationalism and friendship between peoples. But as the discussion of other peoples shows (cf. discussion of foreign models of education below), friendship was only offered to other progressive peoples.

The discourse surrounding the 'struggle for peace' represents another seeming paradox. Readers were exhorted to participate in this struggle as 'active fighters for peace'. This fight mainly seemed to involve vigilance against attempts by the West to undermine the construction of a socialist state in East Germany. As years of a policy of nuclear deterrence by both parties in the Cold War have shown, a position that one must fight for peace or at least be armed and prepared to fight for peace, is not an oxymoron to all. It is striking to what extent the *Neue Schule* adopted a militarist vocabulary in describing the relations between so-called 'progressives' and 'militarist reactionaries'. Examples, such as 'conscious hate is an element of love', 'war criminals are to be hated, not loved', and 'How can you love humanity without hating its enemies?' (NS 9 (6), p. 3) abound in articles throughout the time period. Articles referring to the remilitarization of West Germany under Adenauer (a decision that was highly controversial in West Germany as well, if largely ignored by the GEW), were especially powerful in this regard (see for example the letter penned by educators and students at the Winckelmann school, NS 9(6), p. 3).

Although one might expect class-identity to play a very prominent role in the propaganda of the teachers' union, this role was not as readily observable as the creation of a new national identity. Rather, class-identity was subsumed under national identity. Even discussions of World War II referred surprisingly little to class-conflict. Instead, the conflict was framed as one between opposing political factions, militarists, imperialists, and fascists against progressives and democrats. Although the political factions might be assumed to include the same individuals that a class-oriented analysis of the war might point to as those guilty of furthering the war, this connection was rarely made. Opposition to the West German 'Adenauer-Clique' was also not phrased in terms of a class struggle, but rather as opposition against imperialism and especially American imperialism.

Friendship with the Soviet Union and East German membership in the emerging Communist Block played a dominating role in the articulation of national identity in the *Neue Schule*. Calls for patriotism were coupled with appeals for friendship with other socialist peoples. Such appeals went beyond the relativization of the focus on the German nation mentioned above. Friendship with other socialist nations was a goal in itself and an integral part of the national identity that was to be instilled in readers as well as in the students of such readers. As early as the seventh issue of the newspaper an author extolled readers that, the 'great achievements of the German people are only great, because they benefit not only the German people but all humanity' (NS 1 (7), p. 247).

Much attention was paid to the educational system of the Soviet Union in the pages of the *Neue Schule*. Although this attention also increased over the observed time-period and became increasingly focused on ideological issues (cf. Kleßmann, 1986, p. 96, pp. 282-8), reports of the state of education in the Soviet Union were flattering throughout. In the early years (1946-49), the Soviet Union was often impersonated by various officials sent to East German conferences as representatives of the Soviet Military Administration (e.g., NS 1(8), p. 297). Later, news about the Soviet Union were often relayed by officials of the teachers' union or of the Ministry of People's Education travelling to the Soviet Union and reporting on their voyages (e.g., NS 4(4), pp. 105-6). However, the general impression of education in state-socialist countries had led me to expect a much greater emphasis on the Soviet Union in the East German discourse. Surely, Soviet education was admired as a model, but it was not invoked as frequently as might have been expected. Patriotism, for example, was often discussed in the context of 'Soviet patriotism' which was equated with true, socialist patriotism (see above) yet, these discussions rarely went beyond the use of the Soviet Union as a somewhat distant model.

The national identity that was showcased in the *Neue Schule* was thus culturally backward looking and politically future-oriented, while it purported to be international in orientation. German culture and cultural history were drawn on to illustrate what it means to be German, while political and ideological statements made clear what the German of the future shall feel and identify with as part of an international advance toward socialism. The forward-looking emphasis on a political identity brought with it the frequent attempts to separate an East German identity from an all-German one.

National Identity in Japan: Forward-Looking, Political and Internationalist

After being published under a variety of different names, the Nikkyoso (JTU)[5] finally settled on the name *Kyoikushinbun* (Education Newspaper) for their publication. From its very beginning in May 1946, KS took an aggressive stance supportive of the general democratization of education. In contrast to the East German discussion, democratization in the Japanese context was associated with very specific policy implications. Democratization to the JTU meant local control over teaching and the adoption of teaching methods that focused on the fostering of individualism and democracy in students.

The discussion of 'progressivism' in the JTU was at times surprisingly similar to that of the *Neue Schule*. Whereas the East German paper emphasized the struggle of an entire nation for peace and against the forces of the imperialist reaction, KS cast the JTU as '50,000 educational labourers who love peace and establish democracy' and as struggling against 'domestic reactionaries' (7 (147), p.1). Although KS used this term much more rarely than the *Neue Schule*, it also spoke of a *heiwa no senso* (KS 7 (150), p.1) which seems as self-contradictory as the East German 'fight for peace'. However, it should be noted that the JTU was directly engaged in a struggle against the politically reactionary Ministry of Education (*Monbusho*), whereas it is much less clear how the East German union was involved in a specific struggle.

Much emphasis was placed by almost all articles of the period surveyed on the 'democratization of education'. With this call for an educational policy that meets the needs of the populace rather than one that is decided upon by the state, the JTU set itself in opposition to the Ministry of Education almost from the outset. The very claim to a popularly determined educational policy contradicted the conservative claim that education is politically neutral (Thurston, 1973, p. 94). But the JTU not only demanded the democratization of the policy-making process, but the democratization of education itself on the smallest level. The democratization envisioned was symbolized by local control over education versus the centralist control of the Ministry of Education. This issue of local autonomy in educational policy was discussed throughout the entire time that was surveyed and these discussions showed little variance. KS called for local autonomy repeatedly (KS 3 (90), p. 1; 3 (120), p. 1; 4 (5), p. 1) and used the example of the US to justify such a call (KS 1 (13), p. 1; 1 (15), p. 3).

When Prime Minister Yoshida called for 'education to patriotism (*aikokushin*)' in 1951 (reported in KS (6 (103), p. 2), the reaction to this announcement by the opposition was fierce (Dore, 1952; Brown, 1955, pp. 264-5). Within the JTU a discussion about what position to take vis-à-vis conservative demands to reestablish an ethics curriculum (reminiscent of the pre-war ethics classes, yet changed in style and content) ensued. The JTU likened such proposals directly to pre-war practice and voiced its opposition especially to the implied central control over the content of education. Articles on the difference between the pre-war ethics curriculum and the 'new education' advocated by the JTU point to individualism as the post-war basis of ethics and the fostering of individualism in children to instil ethical beliefs (Brown, 1955, pp. 264-5). Opposition to the Ministry of Education in terms of ethical beliefs that underlie political convictions shows the political focus that was evident in the statements on national identity by the JTU.

In specifying the content of democratized education, the JTU advocated the creation of the *atarashii kokumin* (new people) as well as of *shinkyoiku* (new education) (Thurston, 1973, p. 98). Education of the new person would be based on the realization of a person's position in Japanese society and scientific understanding of that society. This process of consciousness-building would be supported by advocacy of more interactive teaching methods than had been practised under pre-war education. From their revered position as lecturing teachers, post-war teachers would change to provide guidance to students (Thurston, 1973, p. 99).

In addition to democratization, calls for the education of Japanese youngsters to be peace-loving dominated the articulation of national identity in KS. The formulaic headline on almost every other title page was a call for the defence of peace (*'heiwawo mamore'* (Let's defend peace!) or *'sensowa iyada'* (We hate war!)). The JTU called for the education of students in terms of peace as a higher goal. Concretely, this involved the fore-swearing of war as an element of state policy as specified by the constitution, opposition to the recreation of a Japanese army, and defence of the so-called 'peace-constitution' (Thurston, 1973, p. 107). In May 1952, KS reported from the 11th Meeting of Japanese Educators, claiming that the most basic motivating principle for Japanese teachers was the hope for a future in which people are taught to love peace (KS 7 (166), p. 1). Peace was not desirable for the Japanese people only, but rather for the world and the JTU called for children to be educated in this spirit. Although this connection might seem obvious now, these discussions were never linked to Japan's role as an aggressor in World War II.

The emphasis in the discussion of identity was almost exclusively on the newness of educational content. References to cultural continuity or Japanese history were virtually non-existent in the late 1940s and early 1950s. Discussion of identity was thus entirely forward-looking. Pictorial representations of Japanese history or cultural artefacts were extremely rare in the paper. Great writers or great artists were not discussed and neither was the potential importance of cultural artefacts in the education of children. The national identity that authors in KS were trying to establish emphasized democratization and education for peace over any traits rooted in Japanese cultural history. This new identity had political as well as personal implications. Politically, the authors presented positions advanced by the Nikkyoso such as local control over educational matters including curricula and textbook approval. The emphasis on democratization also implied a teaching style radically different from the pre-war emphasis on memorization and recital of classic texts.

National Identity in the FRG: Cultural, Historical and Localist

In the *Allgemeine Deutsche Lehrerzeitung* (ADLZ) there was very little of the ideological saber-rattling that distinguished the other two papers. The catch phrases and references to peace and democratization that are shared by the Japanese and East German paper only made rare appearances in the ADLZ. That is not to say, however, that a national identity was not promoted by the teachers' union and its publication. Instead of the radical reconstruction demanded by its counterparts, the union sought to reform.

Although some elements of German tradition were rejected, large parts of the historical and literary heritage of the nation were emphasized.

The data reflected many of the tensions that influenced the West German situation. On the whole, there was little advocacy of a national identity in terms of something to be fostered or reconstructed actively by teachers. If such attempts at conscious socialization of children are visible at all, they were connected to an effort to instil democratic virtues in children. Especially in the latter volumes, there was a tendency to proclaim that democracy could not be taught other than through lived experience. One article, for example, points out that democracy can not be taught by lecturing, but that students should be educated to hold democratic attitudes of their own (ADLZ 6 (21), p. 307).

Even if a German national identity per se was not mentioned, there were references to elements of purportedly German culture. From a contemporary point of view it was indeed surprising how often topics were discussed with reference to their German-ness or in terms of a German cultural heritage. One author thus worried whether his 'grandchildren will be speaking German' and described German as a '*Kultursprache* (language of culture) that grew over millennia' (ADLZ 6 (12), pp. 156-9). German classicism and romanticism were emphasized in the discussion of German cultural heritage and authors invariably pointed to the particularly German character of such literary eras.

This tendency to discuss Germany in cultural terms is demonstrated by remarks on formerly German territories in Poland. Where today this would be a taboo for teachers and certainly for teachers' union, there were a number of articles discussing the importance of this issue in teaching. A decision by the Bavarian state parliament in 1953 to include lessons on the areas of origin of German refugees in the East (i.e., formerly German territories in Poland and the Soviet Union) in curricula, was welcomed by an editorial and seen as a means to broaden the political and cultural horizons of students (ADLZ 5 (2), p. 26). An article that appeared in the same year emphasized that all references to the German *Heimat* (homeland) should include the former territories in the East as well as East Germany, lest students might come to see those as separate from Germany (ADLZ 5 (8), p. 101). Use of the term *Heimat* reflects an emphasis on localism and a regional identity as it did in the East German discussion of *Heimatkunde*.

In contrast to the *Neue Schule*, the ADLZ did not proclaim a distinctively West German identity. By emphasizing the virtues of the Western, and especially the American model of education and democracy and by the occasional demonizing use of the Soviet Union as an anti-model, it was made clear that West Germany's future was in 'the West'. Historians have argued that the increasing integration of the Federal Republic into the West (especially, close ties with the US and France) was not a conscious choice for West Germans, but occurred largely by default (Mommsen, 1983). Yet, Germany's future was envisioned as one encompassing all of Germany, including the East, and even including some of the former territories. The frequent use of the terms *Ostzone* (Eastern Zone) or *Sowjetisch Besetzte Zone* (Soviet-Occupied Zone) reflected West German attempts to insist on the unity of the German state despite the existence of two political entities as proscribed by the (West) German constitution.

The discussion in the West German ADLZ reflected international political situation to a great extent. East Germany and descriptions of educational reform in the East played a prominent role in the newspaper. An article in 1949 thus described the basis of schooling in East Germany as largely political. Prominent elements were the orientation towards Soviet pedagogy, historical materialism, and teachers as political beings and as party members (ADLZ 1 (14), p. 140). Another article in the same volume pointed to a 'cultural tragedy' in the making in East Germany due to the careless, rapid and politically-oriented education of teachers in the East (ADLZ 1 (18), p. 193). However, these discussions of events in East Germany were largely limited to the early volumes of the ADLZ, i.e., the time around the foundation of the two German states and the official acknowledgement of the division of Germany.

Discussions of history, historiography and the role of history in teaching students played a very prominent role in the ADLZ. Whereas early issues referred to the importance of history in the abstract, later on the discussion was more concrete and focused on the recent German history. Debates over the prominence that should be given to German acts of resistance to the Nazis in historical narratives provided the impetus for reflection on the horrifying elements of recent German history. An article in 1949 stated that 'the recent historical catastrophe had the effect of eroding traditional values and making the establishment of new values a necessity' (ADLZ 1 (14), p. 138). This sentiment was reiterated by an article in 1951 (ADLZ 3 (3), p. 137) though there were no references to potential sources of such alternative values. In reaction to a dismissive treatment of the attempt on Hitler's life in July 1944 an author wrote of the necessity to overcome the mistakes and sins of the past to create something new (ADLZ 5 (14), pp. 184-5). Another author expressed his surprise at the lack of a public discussion of the events of July 1944 in particular and of recent German history in general. He contrasted this with the great national elation at the victory of the German soccer team at the 1954 World Cup (ADLZ 6 (14), p. 175).[6] Most explicitly, a lead editorial in May 1955 used the anniversary of German capitulation to address the topic of the role of recent history. The editorial described attempts to ignore an entire political era as 'unnatural' and called for an honest appraisal of the Third Reich specifically by Germans rather than foreigners. The editorial criticized attempts by an unnamed journal to point out to Germans that the ten post-war years had been spent 'denying German achievements, law, abilities, and normal national identity'. Instead the editorial demanded of educators to point to forces 'that are superior to violence, stronger than the law, and greater than power' as a way for Germans to repent and to develop into an internationally acceptable nation (ADLZ 7 (10), p. 188). The same issue spoke of the responsibility of teachers as the 'social consciousness of the nation' (ADLZ 7 (10), p. 190).

In sum, the ADLZ articulated a national identity through discussions of history. Such discussions were using the past as guidance for the identity of the future. Cultural elements of identity were privileged over political elements. Thus, the division of Germany was ignored and cultural unity emphasized. Democracy was espoused as a goal, but it was not discussed as an element of a new identity. With the emphasis on German cultural heritage and relatively little discussion of political ideals, the ADLZ focused on local issues and a local identity rather than international ones.

The Conditions of Reconstruction of Identity Compared

My analysis has pointed out a number of significant differences between the three cases. The unions differ first in the degree to which they attempt to effect a reconstruction of identity, and second in the content of the new identity. Are there specific historical or institutional circumstances that favoured one course of action for a union over another? How did the institutional environment influence the unions' advocacy of a particular identity?

The three cases have one element in common, namely that anyone keen on the reconstruction of national identity must have found the immediate post-war years to be an ideal moment for such attempts. The break that defeat in World War II afforded such actors cannot be underestimated in terms of the opportunities it presented. The post-war situation not only offered new institutional arrangements that were in many ways more favourable to the participation of organized interests in policy-making, but the discrediting of the extreme nationalism preached and practised under the Nazi and militarist dictatorships, presented post-war ideologues with a *tabula rasa*.

It is noticeable that the discussion in the Japanese paper is entirely focused on post-war events and on future international developments. In contrast, both the East German as well as the West German papers used references from German history as elements of their identity construction. Cultural references came in many forms, as references to literary and intellectual figures, as graphic representations of important events or locations, in discussions of the curricula of German classes in schools. However, the German cases differ by the degree to which they mixed forward-looking elements and historical references as well as an internationalist perspective. Although writers for the East German papers frequently mentioned historical roots, they also emphasized the future of German identity embedded in the socialism that was being built up in the country. West German articles very rarely mentioned any elements of identity that might be called forward-looking. Instead, such authors focused on the historical, cultural achievements of Germans. They also frequently discussed the importance of historiography itself in the reconstruction of a national identity.

The discourse in the three cases differs greatly as to the extent to which cultural issues of identity were privileged over political concerns. The Japanese national identity presented by authors in KS focused on changes of political attitudes and practices. Democracy as a goal was argued for on the basis of its universal superiority in Japan, while East German authors referred to the tradition of progressivism in Germany from the nineteenth century on. Democratization of educational practice was emphasized only in East Germany and Japan. After some initial discussions of proposed changes of the West German educational system, authors in the ADLZ did not devote a lot of attention to such questions of pedagogy.

References to culture were much more frequent in the German discussions. Education was often claimed to be rooted in German cultural traditions of humanism. References to (culturally) great Germans occurred often and in contexts of awe and emphasis on the continuity of German education. Even the East German authors who emphasized their opposition to reactionary West German policies voiced their approval of knowledge of German literary classics.

The three unions differ in the extent to which they espoused an international orientation. The JTU coupled its calls for 'democracy with a concern for world peace that made an international orientation of national identity necessary. This orientation is also evidenced by the use of foreign educational systems as models for the restructuring of the Japanese system. Since peace was defined as the absence of inter-state warfare, more than just domestic peace was at stake. East Germany's ties to the international movement of socialism predisposed its teachers' union to emphasize internationalism in identity-construction. Internationalism was viewed as an antidote to chauvinist tendencies in the self-confident identity that socialism was intended to foster in its beneficiaries. In West Germany the international context was only discussed as it pertained to the Allies and the FRG's ties to the 'West'. Internationalism played almost no role in identity-construction and the frequent use of cultural traditions reinforced this political localism.

The JTU was established as a unitary body representing Japanese teachers vis-à-vis the Ministry of Education. It presented itself to and was accepted by the occupation authorities as the legitimate representative of teachers. The attention paid to matters of education by these authorities not only legitimated the debates invoked by the union, but also strengthened its commitment to the achievement of a new era in Japanese education. The unions' roots in political action and in structural change of education were mirrored in the exclusive attention to political elements of national identity.

The initial impetus for a political focus was reinforced by the activism of progressive educators. These educators were able to seize a leadership role in the union based on their opposition to 1930s militarism. Ideologically, the political impetus was thus channelled into cooperation with the Japanese Socialist Party (JSP). However, socialists, including progressive educators, had not reached a point before the war at which they were able to institutionalize their proposed redesign of education. In their discussion educators therefore focused on the promise of the future, rather than using historical examples of their project. The role of the JSP in the early political history of post-war Japan and the radicalism of Japanese intellectuals in turn legitimated this focus. The political orientation of the union also dictated a commitment to internationalism and a disavowal of Japanese cultural particularism. With the advent of the Cold War, the focus on peace and education of peaceful democrats remained legitimate and was bolstered by opposition to attempts by the Ministry of Education to regain control over policy-making decision regarding education. References by conservatives in government to a more cultural orientation of national identity served to increase the union's concentration on political issues.

In East Germany ideological legitimacy was not established in opposition to domestic political actors. The enforced absence of such actors under the Stalinist regime that emerged in the GDR allowed the union and teachers to incorporate cultural claims to legitimacy in their construction of an East German identity. Cultural legitimacy needed to be established vis-à-vis the public and parents to forestall opposition to political and structural changes of education that formed a major part of the project of state socialism. References to German humanism and to cultural achievements in the past were able to provide this legitimacy. The foundation of the GDR and the arrival of international political opposition redirected the discourse in a more political way and added elements distinguishing an East German identity from a unified German identity politically. Not only the Cold War, but also East Germany's staunch political support of socialism, predisposed its leaders to emphasize some elements of internationalism.

The domestic political situation in the Federal Republic and the onset of the Cold War prevented the West German union from playing an active role in encouraging discussion of issues of identity. Not only was it difficult for the union to organize in light of diverging policies of the occupying powers, but the federalism inherent in the occupation by three major powers, as well as a history of federalism regarding educational policy, led to the decentralization of decision-making on questions of school curricula. Lacking influence over the policy-making process, the teachers' union espoused cultural achievements and educational traditions as elements of a new national identity and formed a largely backward-looking sense of its mission. Although a discussion of structural changes flourished briefly after the war, democratic pluralism allowed for opposition to such reform-proposals from other political actors. The federalist structure of education encouraged a concentration on local issues for union leaders as well as a focus on the historical roots of teaching.

Many of the debates surrounding the 50th anniversaries of the German and Japanese capitulation suggest that popular attitudes towards recent history differ greatly in Japan and now-united Germany. Whereas today it is a journalistic truism that Germany (esp., West Germany) has at least attempted to deal with its history (*Vergangenheitsbewältigung*), the Japanese, and especially their elected representatives, are still seen as insensitive to the legacy of the Japanese past in World War II. A deeper understanding of the reconstruction of national identity as begun by this paper will serve to answer some of the questions posed by the contemporary contrast of Japan and Germany.

Notes

1　In 1954 the *Neue Schule* is reborn as the *Deutsche Lehrerzeitung* (German Teachers' Newspaper) with an altered format and slightly varying content so that I chose to include the East German material only as far as the format remained the same. An editorial in the final issue of the *Neue Schule* hints that the *Neue Schule* was discontinued due to criticism of its inability to educate teachers to be functionaries of the state. The new publication was designed accordingly to remedy this shortcoming (NS 9 (13), pp. 4-5).

2　The union paper is first published under the name *Nippon Kyoiku Shinbun* (Japanese Education Newspaper) on May 3rd 1946 for one issue. Then there were 12 issues under the name of *Kyoiku Rodo* (Education Labour). From August 1946 until March 1949, the paper was called *Shukan Kyoiku Shinbun* (Weekly Education Newspaper), until it reverted back to *Kyoikushinbun* on April 11th, 1949.

3　I cite from the papers in the following format (volume (number), page number). All translations from German and Japanese are mine.

4　One might notice with some amusement that it is probably only in Germany that '*Heimatbewanderung*' (hiking through the homeland) would be discussed as a teaching method.

5　Just like the KS, the JTU underwent a number of organizational changes and mergers in the immediate post-war period. Most of the separate organizations involved infighting between union organizers committed to the Japanese Communist Party and the Japan Socialist Party. These metamorphoses are well-documented elsewhere (Thurston, 1973, p. 61).

6   Though not discussed in the academic literature, this victory in the World Cup obviously played a large role in the reestablishment of Germans' identity (Bernhard Giesen, personal communication). For an extensive treatment of the relationship between sport and nationalism see John (1976).

References

Amakawa, A. (1992), 'Besatzung und Bürokratie in Japan', in D. Petzina and R. Ruprecht (eds), *Wendepunkt 1945?*, Universitätsverlag Dr. Brockmeyer, Bochum.

Brown, D.M. (1955), *Nationalism in Japan*, University of California Press, Berkeley.

Colcutt, M. (1991), 'The Legacy of Confucianism in Japan' in G. Rozman (ed.), *The East Asian Region*, Princeton University Press, Princeton.

Dore, R.P. (1952), 'The Ethics of the New Japan', *Pacific Affairs*, vol. 25.

Dore, R.P. (1984), *Education in Tokugawa Japan*, Athlone Press, Ann Arbor.

Eisenstadt, S.N. (1991), 'Die Konstruktion Nationaler Identitäten in Vergleichender Perspektive', in B. Giesen (ed.), *Nationale und Kulturelle Identität*, Suhrkamp Verlag, Frankfurt am Main.

Giesen, B. (1991), 'Einführung', in B. Giesen (ed.), *Nationale und Kulturelle Identität*, Suhrkamp Verlag, Frankfurt am Main.

Giesen, B., Junge, K., and Kritschgau, C. (1994), 'Vom Patriotismus zum Völkischen Denken: Intellektuelle als Konstrukteure der Deutschen Identität', in H. Berding (ed.), *Nationales Bewußtsein und Kollektive Identität*, Suhrkamp Verlag, Frankfurt am Main.

Gill, U. (1989), *Der Freie Deutsche Gewerkschaftsbund (FDGB)*, Leske+Buderich, Opladen.

Greenfeld, L. (1992), *Nationalism - Five Roads to Modernity*, Harvard University Press, Cambridge.

Horio, T. (1988), *Educational Thought and Ideology in Modern Japan*, S. Platzer (tr.), Tokyo University Press, Tokyo.

John, H.G. (1976), *Politik und Turnen*, Verlag Ingrid Czwalina, Ahrensgburg.

Kleßmann, C. (1986), *Die Doppelte Staatsgründung*, Bundeszentrale für Politische Bildung, Bonn.

Kocka, J. (1992), 'Kontinuität und Wandlungen', in D. Petzina and R. Ruprecht, (eds), *Wendepunkt 1945?*, Universitätsverlag Dr. Brockmeyer, Bochum.

Kopitzsch, W. (1983), *Gewerkschaft Erziehung und Wissenschaft (GEW) 1947-1975*, Carl Winter Universitätsverlag, Heidelberg.

Marshall, B.K. (1994), *Learning to be Modern: Japanese Political Discourse on Education*, Westview Press, Boulder.

Mommsen, W.J. (1983), 'Wandlungen der Nationalen Identität', in W. Weidenfeld (ed.), *Die Identität der Deutschen*, Hanser Verlag, Munich.

Nishi, T. (1982), *Unconditional Surrender*, Hoover Institution Press, Stanford.

Shillony, B.A. (1981), *Wartime Japan*, Clarendon Press, Oxford.

Strauss, A. (1987), *Qualitative Analysis for Social Scientists*, Cambridge University Press, New York.

Thurston, D.R. (1973), *Teachers and Politics in Japan*, Princeton University Press, Princeton.

10 Hindu Nationalism and the Social Welfare Strategy[1]

CHRISTOPHE JAFFRELOT

The rise of Hindu nationalism has been one of the most significant developments in Indian politics over the last ten years. It is a recent phenomenon in terms of election results: the most representative party of this political trend, the Bharatiya Janata Party (BJP - Party of the Indian People) increased its number of seats from two out of 542 in the general elections of 1984 to eighty-five in 1989, 120 in 1991, 160 in 1996, 178 in 1998 and 183 in 1999. But the ideology on which this movement is based is an old one and may even be said to constitute a structural feature of the Indian political scene.

Since the late 1980s, the movement largely owes its success, to its ability to alternatively mobilize support in the streets on ethno-religious issues and to make alliances with regional partners, but also to earlier grassroots work by its activists. These on-the-ground activities are mainly centred on a strategy of social welfare to which few observers have paid attention, doubtless because such a technique is unexpected on the part of a movement dominated by a high-caste elite.

'Hindu, Hindi, Hindustan'

Though some seeds of Hindu nationalism were sown by socio-religious reform movements in the nineteenth century, Hindu nationalist ideology was first thoroughly codified in 1923 by Vinayak Damodar Savarkar (1883-1966) in *Hindutva, who is a Hindu?* In this work, Hinduness (*Hindutva*) is considered as membership of an ethnic community possessing its own territory and sharing the same racial characteristics:[2] for Savarkar, a Hindu is primarily someone who lives in the land beyond the Indus, between the Himalayas and the Indian Ocean, an area 'so strongly

196

retrenched that no other country in the world is so clearly designated by the finger of nature as a geographical unit'.[3] This is why the first Aryans, in Vedic times, developed there 'a sense of their nationality'.[4] Here we have an ethnic rationale in the sense that the enclosed character of what Savarkar calls 'Hindustan', the land of the Hindus, is described as a factor conducive to unity of the population through intermarriage: 'All Hindus claim to have in their veins the blood of the mighty race descended from the Vedic fathers...'.[5] Focusing on the racial criterion, postulating the existence of an invisible yet potent bond, that of blood, is a way of de-emphasizing the internal divisions in Hindu society.

Though the pillars of Hinduness are, according to Savarkar, geographical and ethnic unity, *Hindutva* also allegedly meets all the criteria of national unity - cultural, religious and linguistic unity (the latter because Sanskrit is set up as the referent of all Indian languages) - that Savarkar had read about in the European authors on whom he had been nurtured.[6] Thereafter, every political programme based on the Hindu nationalist ideology would call for recognition of Sanskrit or Hindi - the vernacular language closest to Sanskrit - as the national language.

The tenets of Hindu nationalist ideology were subsequently revised by the Rashtriya Swayamsevak Sangh (RSS - Association of National Volunteers), which was founded in 1925 by an admirer of Savarkar, Keshav Baliram Hedgewar (1889-1940). The RSS soon became the leading organization in the Hindutva movement.

Golwalkar, who succeeded Hedgewar as chief of the RSS in 1940, gave the movement its ideological charter in 1938 with his book *We, or Our Nationhood Defined* where religious minorities were called upon to pledge allegiance to Hindu symbols of identity as the embodiment of the Indian nation. Hindu culture being the essence of Indian identity, religious minorities were requested to limit expressions of community distinctiveness to the private sphere.

The concept of 'Chiti' or 'Race-spirit' in the writings of Savarkar and later of Golwalkar conveys the idea of the soul of the nation rather than biological conceptions.[7] This is doubtless the aspect of German-style ethnic nationalism - in which the 'nation-spirit' idea is central - which was most attractive to the ideologues of Hindu nationalism. This conception allows - in fact insists upon - integration of minorities by means of acculturation and at a subordinate level, whereas the tenets of biological racism, reasoning in eugenic terms, would have incorporated an idea of total exclusion. This difference reflects the importance of social categories in Hinduism, a civilization which has always been characterized by an ability and a determination to assimilate the Other at a subordinate level as part of the organicist, hierarchical rationale of a caste-based society.[8] Golwalkar considered as *mlecchas* (barbarians) foreigners 'who do not subscribe to the social laws dictated by the Hindu religion and culture',[9] a definition which closely coincides with the traditional usage of this term. In ancient India, a *mleccha* was someone on the fringe of the orthopraxy specific to the caste society dominated by Brahminical values.[10] Gyanendra Pandey has described Hindu nationalism as 'upper caste racism',[11] and this neatly sums up the ambivalence of this ideology.

Hindu nationalism clearly grew up as a form of ethnic nationalism based on social organicism. It owes its relative distinctiveness to the influence of the caste system, which accentuates its hierarchical aspect (minorities only being allowed to exist at a subordinate level) but - in theory - steers it clear of eugenics. These tenets continue to form the basis of the Hindu nationalist movement.

The Hindu nationalist network first spread among the high castes of northern India and is still largely confined to this area. This geographical situation can be explained in two ways. Firstly, the Sanskrit Great Tradition on which their ideology is based is closely related to the Hindi-speaking north; secondly, this is a region inhabited by a large proportion of high-caste Indians who are attracted by Hindu nationalism because of its affinities with their own ethos and because the movement seems well equipped to protect them from the rising power of the low castes.

However, the Hindu nationalist movement, especially the RSS has always regarded itself as destined to encompass the whole of India.[12] First, it developed a network of *shakhas* (local branches), which organized daily physical training and Hindu nationalist propaganda sessions in urban neighbourhoods and villages. The RSS's ultimate ambition was to reach all the cities and villages of India in this way. Its membership rose from 10,000 in 1932 to 600,000 in 1951 and today stands at around 2 millions, divided among 25,000 branches (*shakhas*) and 31,000 sub-branches (*upshakhas*) (the *upshakhas* are the RSS's real basic units since the number of *shakhas* simply indicates the places where the movement is present: a town may contain several sub-branches).

To take roots at the grassroots level, the RSS exploited the readiness of the local notables to support its activities. Its organization chart provides striking proof of this: at the local and regional levels the *pracharaks* (propagandists) in charge of an area work under the patronage of a leading citizen known as a *sanghchalak* (director) who provides guidance. Many *sanghchalaks* are merchants or industrialists who happened to be also very useful for the RSS's welfarist strategy.

From Working on Society to Working 'for Society'

Social welfare work for Hindus is one of the main activities of the RSS. Its first action of this type, in 1926, was to provide essential supplies (especially drinking water) for the devout in the Nagpur region who were taking part in the festival marking the birth of Ram and were being exploited by priests.[13] It later often intervened in this way when natural or political disasters occurred. To take one example, it set up a Hindu Sahayata Samiti (a Hindu mutual aid society) in Delhi in 1947 to house, clothe and even find work for the millions of refugees who were fleeing West Pakistan.[14] Similar efforts were deployed on behalf of Hindu refugees from Kashmir who were housed in camps under canvas at Jammu and Delhi. In a different context but along the same lines, RSS volunteers invariably distinguish themselves by aiding victims of floods and earthquakes.[15] This social welfare strategy has, however, been implemented more systematically since 1989 when the RSS set up a new affiliate known as Seva Bharti (Service of India).

This movement's founder, Vishnu Kumar, is a former RSS *pracharak* whose brother became a *sadhu* (an ascetic), something that his colleagues make much of because *pracharaks* are often equated with *sadhus* and for this reason receive gifts more easily, such gifts being associated with moral virtue like those made to religious figures. The other Seva Bharti officials are *jivan vratti* (literally, those who have made a vow to dedicate their lives), i.e. *swayamsevak* who have reached the age of retirement and who serve the organization on a full-time basis.[16]

The official objectives of Seva Bharti, whose motto is 'social welfare is my duty', are:

1) to eradicate untouchability, 2) to imbue people with the spirit of service and unity [social and national], 3) to promote and perform literary, cultural,

social and charitable activities among the poor and our underprivileged brothers who live in rundown districts, and 4) to serve the economically needy and socially backward sectors by contributing to their physical, educational, social, moral and economic development without distinction of caste, language or region, so that they gain self-confidence and are integrated into society.[17]

Seva Bharti's ideological purpose is, clearly, to assimilate marginal populations which are naturally appreciative of charitable work, into a Hindu nation, the model and spearhead of which is the RSS. This scheme has proved particularly worthwhile for the Hindu nationalists since these social groups have been growing rapidly and neither the RSS nor its affiliates had ever succeeded in putting down roots within them. It was difficult for a movement dominated by high castes to reach this working-class population set apart by many socio-cultural features (caste awareness and social habitus, such as language since low caste people sometimes speak a dialectical version of Hindi, for instance).

For the moment Seva Bharti is concentrating its activities in northern India. In Delhi it has opened twelve dispensaries and runs an ambulance service in twenty-odd slum areas, providing virtually free medical assistance. Strong emphasis is placed on all forms of education. A van with video equipment visits needy neighbourhoods and slums to promote 'moral and cultural education'. 'Education does not end with the eradication of illiteracy' explains the secretary of Seva Bharti when talking about these video films. 'We want to instil in slum-dwellers national awareness and a sense of hygiene, to teach them what is good, what is good for society and how they can be useful to society'.[18] Among the films shown we find the *Ramayana* and *Mahabharata* epics which were tremendously popular when broadcasted on nationwide television. Significantly, the van used is referred to as Samskar Rath. *Rath* is the word used to designate the vehicles which transport divinities in processions; the use of the word *Samskar* conveys a cluster of far richer meanings.

'*Samskar*' designates a rite of passage but also, more generally, everything that shapes the personality of the individual from childhood on.[19] In Hindu tradition, 'to have good *samskar*' usually means having no vices (not smoking or drinking alcohol, for example), having very polished manners, even following a vegetarian diet, in short, imitating Brahmins. It refers to the Sanskritization process.[20]

The RSS's uses of the term *samskar* reflects its aspiration to reform mentalities in line with the high Hindu tradition and, more specifically, to infuse Hindu awareness and national discipline. It reinterprets the concept of *samskar*, which it adapts to its own needs, presenting it as a vector of Sanskritization for the low castes. Many untouchables enter *shakhas* to learn how to live a disciplined life, in which they recognize good *samskars*.

In keeping with the RSS's approach, Seva Bharti's concentrates on low caste children, to which they offer the free education for which their parents are longing. In the early 1990s there were fifteen Sanskrit Kendra (Sanskrit learning centres) and 129 Bal and Balika Samskar Kendras (*samskar* learning centres for boys or girls) attended by 19,304 children supervised by 352 teachers, many of whom are voluntary workers connected with the RSS. The organization emphasizes that in these centres 'children learn not only to read the alphabet and books but also receive *samskars* (moral education)'.[21] Seva Bharti has set up twenty-six tutorial centres for students from needy families and three electricity and electronics apprenticeship courses for adolescents who have dropped out of the school system. A reported 2,550 girls were attending sixty-three dressmaking centres with the goal of making their families 'economically self-sufficient'. Brochures published by Seva Bharti add that its activists 'regularly visit them to instil in them a spirit of devotion and love of the motherland'.

All these activities are made possible by gifts, either in rupees or in kind (one donor has given the organization a large area of land south of Delhi for an orphanage others gave sewing machines). Benefactors, as the Secretary General of Seva Bharti admits, are mainly recruited from the merchant castes, in keeping with their tradition of patronage of charitable works with religious overtones. 'Gifts from merchants cover around half our expenses. We go to see traders in the bazaars. We talk to them about our work, they come and see our centers and show their approval. They make gifts. These gifts are the foundation of all our work'.[22]

The fact that a substantial proportion of Seva Bharti's resources comes from these philanthropic practices is essential to the effectiveness of its social welfare strategy in terms of instilling and diffusing Hindu nationalist ideology. However, this effectiveness, of which the figures published by the organization are not a reliable indicator, also needs to be tested on the ground.

Ideology in Schools for the Poor

Motia Khan is a slum squashed between the approaches to Connaught Place (which opens on to New Delhi) and the Jhandewalan neighbourhood (built after Partition to house refugees from West Punjab). It comprises some 600 Jhuggi Jhonpri (rundown dwellings) housing 3,000 or so people mainly from Bikaner district in Rajasthan. Most of these people are Sassi (untouchables) the first of whom settled there in the early 1980s and were afterwards joined by other caste members. They often have no permanent employment but do odd jobs which are sometimes remunerative, like selling maps of India to tourists. Some households have a television which works using current taken from a line along the main road - the slum area is not hooked up to the electrical grid. Some inhabitants of Motia Khan get by fairly well, but because of the high cost of building land in Delhi they are not able to live anywhere else. They are frequently threatened with 'expropriation' by the municipality to which the land belongs,[23] and in addition they can never escape their condition as untouchables. They complain of the humiliating treatment meted out to them by the teachers in the state schools where they have tried to enrol, and of their failure to keep up with lessons.

Thanks to its social welfare strategy the RSS has managed to put down roots in this slum area by responding to the demand for education on the part of the Sassis. The RSS's second Headquarters - the main one being in Nagpur - is at nearby Jhandewalan and one of the *pracharaks* who live there permanently got into the habit of paying regular visits to Motia Khan. This man, Virendra Bhatnagar, who comes from an upper caste family, *Kayasth*, from Uttar Pradesh, joined the RSS at the age of eight at his schoolteacher's instigation and decided at a very early age to become a *pracharak*; he left school in order to start out on this 'career' and was posted by the leadership of the movement - keen to make the best possible use of its cadres' skills - to the RSS's trade union, the Bharatiya Mazdoor Sangh. From 1963 to 1986, he worked for this organization as a local then a regional secretary in Uttar Pradesh and finally in Delhi. This unbroken commitment was a reflection of his 'deep-rooted choice', his liking for 'the service of the underprivileged'.[24]

In 1989, on the occasion of the centenary of the birth of Hedgewar, its founder, the RSS launched a far-reaching programme called Naran Seva (For the service of man). Virendra Bhatnagar was chosen to co-ordinate its activities in Delhi. He immediately gave priority to the development of schools and personally took charge of the school at Motia Khan which he named Vivekananda Shishu Mandir, Temple of the pupils of Vivekananda, from the name of one of the late nineteenth century precursors of militant Hinduism in Bengal. The school, which opened in July 1991, soon had 120 pupils aged from four to twenty divided into three classes, all at elementary level, not even basic education being available in the slum.

In August 1992, a year after its foundation, women teachers at the school claimed that it comprised three classes of sixty pupils, including adult women. In fact there has probably been a downturn in numbers since UNICEF set up a rival school in the same slum area with more substantial resources. The RSS is clearly focusing on the same populations as this international organization[25] but for imbuing them with its ideology.

A little textbook distributed to pupils includes many patriotic poems, starting with the RSS prayer which includes the statement that the national flag is none other than the flag of the organization which is saffron, the colour of Hinduism. Another song, entitled 'Our dear country', ends with this couplet: 'Once it was happy and prosperous, today it is shattered into a thousand pieces and unhappy/ But look, now it is reborn, our dear country'.

A song entitled 'We must have pride' is more insidious as it is implicitly directed against minorities. It goes as follows:

Every inhabitant of this country must have pride.
Bande Mataram [*Salute to the Mother*, the first, Hindu-oriented anthem of the independence movement] should be sung every day.
The country is not made of earth but of feelings.
If it breaks, we must take stock of the break. [...]
The tie of blood must be recognised.
The enemy has infiltrated his way among us and is fomenting a plot.
Now we must be heedful of the fear that possesses households.
Fearful is he who pretends to ignore the problem.
We must be on the watch for the smoke that comes before fire. [...]
How much longer shall we go on doing nothing?
We must launch a campaign from a high platform.
Our sole desire is to bear the country to the pinnacle of greatness...[26]

The enemy mentioned can only be the Muslims - 12 per cent of the Indian population - regarded by Hindu nationalists as a fifth column linked to an Islamic International of which Pakistan is the main component. The image of the smoldering fire probably refers to the communal riots that sporadically erupt throughout northern India and for which the Hindu nationalists recommend people to be ready.

It is hard to assess the impact of such propaganda on the school's pupils. One might simply suppose that if they are faced with it over a long period their outlook is bound to change. The teaching is not restricted to this kind of indoctrination, however. Seva Bharti tries to dilute ideology by giving prominence to noble and virtuous themes which are easily incorporated into ideology while flattering youthful idealism, a feeling particularly strong among the low castes seeking respectability. The women teachers insist that their main concern is to instil into children born into a dirty, rough and violent world habits of basic hygiene, better manners and respect for their elders and for society.[27] The nationalist, hierarchic and even organicist connotations of this socialization are found in the cult of Saraswati, the goddess of learning. Each lesson begins and ends with a Sanskrit prayer to Saraswati, with a strong ideological content:

> Oh she whose vehicle is the wild duck
> Oh knowledge bearer [*gyandayini*]
> Oh mother, give us a pure thought [*amba vimal*]
> Let us make India the diadem of the world
> Give us this heroic strength, give us a pure thought,
> Fill our hearts with courage and virtue,
> Make our lives full of renunciation and asceticism,
> Grant us temperance, truth and love,
> Fill us with pride.

This prayer explicitly combines emphasis on *samskars,* whose appeal is of a type to encourage children to attend school, with overt nationalism. The children recite the prayer - clumsily, because of the difficulty of the language - facing the image of the goddess and with their hands clasped together. When Virendra Bhatnagar and the schoolmistress talk to the pupils they make it a point of honour to bring in the few words of Sanskrit the pupils know, doubtless because the pupils consider this a mark of prestige.

The school owes some of its appeal to the fact that it is an instrument of Sanskritization. But other factors are also involved. Schooling is free and the modest equipment the pupils need (textbook, pencils, exercise books and slate) is provided by the organization. The schoolmistresses are unpaid volunteers; they give two hours a day to the organization, a service they present as the highest form of sacrifice (a cardinal notion in Hinduism, together with renunciation). One teacher, a Brahmin, is the wife of a singer who is popular for his renderings of religious texts, and is an active RSS member; the other is the wife of the head of a local RSS *shakha*, who is a member of a merchant caste. Another of the school's strong points is that the teachers have been specially trained not to humiliate the children. Last but not least, the school offers vocational training for girls via dressmaking classes. Seventeen girls assiduously follow this course for which the school possesses seven sewing machines. Those who complete the course receive a certificate of qualification. A competitive mood was created when the first shirt made by a pupil was sold, for twenty-five rupees. The same shirt, bought from a tailor, would have cost at least forty rupees.[28]

Study of the Motia Khan school leads to the conclusion that the social welfare strategy really does provide the RSS with new outlets for its ideas. Indeed, Virendra Bhatnagar also points out that though there is still no *shakha* in Motia Khan, a few boys attend the *shakha* at the Jhandewalan headquarters. I saw the same mechanisms at work in a rural environment in the village of Piparsod in central India (Madhya Pradesh) near the town of Shivpuri.[29]

Ideology in the Village, via the School

Shivpuri is a district capital with some 100,000 inhabitants located 120 km south of Gwalior on the Delhi-Bombay road. Its literacy rate is 47.84 per cent compared to 16.48 per cent for the district as a whole. These figures were linked to the percentage of Scheduled castes (untouchables) in the town, 15.6 per cent, which is comparable to the national average, but which is exceeded in 667 of the district's 1,300 villages.[30]

In this district, the main RSS affiliate which seeks to meet local educational needs is not Seva Bharti but Vidya Bharti (Indian knowledge). This is an organization which was founded in 1977 to co-ordinate the network of some 700 Saraswati Shishu Mandir schools (Temples of Saraswati' Children) which the RSS has been developing since the 1950s.[31] Fifteen years or so later, Vidya Bharti had 40,000 teachers and 1.2 million pupils in 5,000 schools (including 1,325 in Uttar Pradesh and approximately a thousand in Madhya Pradesh), more than a third of them providing education up to higher secondary level.[32]

At Shivpuri are one of the 5,000 Saraswati Shishu Mandirs and one of the 40 Vidya Bharti boarding schools. Vidya Bharti defines its goal as training 'children full of self-confidence, proud of their religion and showing respect and love for the glorious past [of their nation]...'[33] This ideological slant is apparent in the timetable of the 130 boarders: from 5:30 to 8 a.m., they pray together, then they do yoga exercises and recite the *Bhagavad Gita*, which the Hindu nationalists are attempting to set up as the Book of Hinduism. A leaflet describing the boarding school presents it as a modern form of the ancient *gurukuls* (traditional teaching places centred on a *guru* where young Brahmins learned the *Vedas* - literally 'Knowledge').[34]

The school thus claims a place within the Great Hindu Tradition. At first sight, it does not fit readily into the rationale of a social welfare strategy: the annual fees for a boarder are 8,000 rupees, plus the cost of two uniforms, one for winter, one for summer. Nevertheless, in line with current trends, a kindergarten has been opened there which is free for untouchables from the mainly low-caste neighbourhood where the school is located. Despite the high standard of the state school in the sector - which is recognized by those responsible for the boarding school - forty young untouchables come to the Ambedkar Saraswati Shishu Mandir to learn 'the *samskars,* how to behave, etc.'[35] It was opened in July 1991 in the aftermath of the celebration of the centenary of Ambedkar, the untouchable leader, when there was strong collective mobilization on the part of the lower castes.

This social welfare strategy and the very existence of the boarding school are the result of philanthropic initiatives, since the enrolment fees are not sufficient to cover maintenance costs (especially since the school has carried out building work costing 30 million rupees, including a theatre and a swimming pool). While the principal is an RSS cadre, the school is supported by leading local citizens sympathetic to the RSS, a landlord and the head of a small carrier firm with two trucks. The Shivpuri population, from whom gifts were solicited, had an obvious interest in the development of the school in their town since 200 day-pupils attend it in addition to the 130 boarders and the education has a high reputation. Brochures about the school emphasize its discipline, the teaching of English, which the Hindu nationalists regretfully accept as indispensable, and selection on the basis of merit. Shivpuri's upper middle class has thus helped to finance the school, with its own young people in mind. However the principal explains the amount of funds collected (several hundred thousand rupees) in terms of the socio-ritual implications of gift-making rather than in terms of this less praiseworthy transactional motivation: 'People give to build a temple, people give to build a school'.[36]

In a similar type of philanthropic gesture the Angre family, which owns considerable property (land and buildings) made available to the school the spacious nineteenth-century buildings, plus some 8.5 hectares of grounds. The family descends from the first *jagirdar*, landed noble, of the former princely State of Gwalior, one of the biggest in northern India in colonial times. Until independence, Shivpuri (located on a plateau with a more temperate climate) was the summer capital of the reigning dynasty, the Scindias. The court, of which the *jagirdar* were leading members, travelled to Shivpuri and had its summer quarters there. The Angre family's gift, a sort of ideological-religious act of charity, is replicated on a more lavish scale by the Scindia.

Patronage of religious foundations and festivals (e.g. the Kumbh Mela at Ujjain, one of the seven holy cities of Hinduism) formed part of the Scindia dynasty's traditional attributions and duties. In the 1950s, a son of the Angre family became the private secretary of the deposed Maharajah and, more importantly, of his wife, whose political career he furthered. Her affinities with the Hindu nationalists led the Rajmata Scindia to join the Jana Sangh and then the BJP and to actively support the RSS to which she has given part of her palace at Gwalior. It is as if she had simply shifted her religious patronage to a more ideological ground.

These acts of generosity go hand in hand with a skill in managing the family fortune which has made it possible for the Rajmata and her secretary Angre to invest in merchant shipping and the popular press. The Rajmata Scindia officially presents herself as an 'industrialist'.[37]

Patronage of a 'religious charity', which generally involves philanthropy designed to win merit, also exists at village level where any attempts by the RSS to establish *shakhas* are usually hampered by a number of factors that are less marked in the urban environment. Firstly, the farmers do not have enough free time to assemble each day for physical exercise or for an ideology session. Secondly, they are too divided to envisage collective activity of this kind. At Piparsod (a village seventeen kilometers from Shivpuri), the Brahmins and the *kirar* (a farmer caste dominant in the region)[38] compete for pre-eminence.[39] RSS *pracharaks* have tried to develop a *shakha* in the village from their base at Shivpuri but have always given up after a few weeks' effort. During the summer of 1991, the new *pracharak* tried a new tactic and opened a Saraswati Shishu Mandir.

This was an extremely astute move because, despite its 2,500 inhabitants, Piparsod had no school, though it is becoming increasingly clear to everyone that studying is the only way to rise in the world. The result is a real 'hunger for education'. (The only school to open there was sabotaged by the Brahmins who were loath to see the low castes getting an education).[40] Furthermore, the Shishu Mandir was able to charge affordable registration fees - thirty rupees per pupil per month - because the two teachers accepted low pay (600 rupees per year) saying they were motivated by a spirit of devotion. Both were Brahmins, graduates from Shivpuri with an RSS background.

Apart from teaching arithmetic and spelling, these teachers seemed very keen to get the children to recite the *Gayatri Mantra*. This is a Sanskrit prayer which is in theory a high caste prerogative but the Shishu Mandir are open to all and are an instrument of Sanskritization for the low castes. The father of one girl pupil from the very impure barber caste emphasized that the children learn good manners there, implying these are Brahmin manners.[41]

So this Shishu Mandir - whose single class contains some forty pupils aged around six - owes its success to the appeal of Sanskritization and inexpensive education. Here too, the social welfare strategy is made possible by resources obtained via an important aspect of the Hindu economic ethos: religious gifts. The school's main asset is the building it occupies, one of the village's few two-storey houses, which was given to the Shishu Mandir by a Gwalior doctor who was born in Piparsod.[42]

This man, a Brahmin, had always wanted the building to be used for a holy purpose. After his death, Vidya Bharti officials from Shivpuri plus village notables such as members of the *panchayat* (village council) and the founder of a local co-operative, went to see his widow. She agreed to let them have the building for what she considered to be a worthy cause. She came to Piparsod to preside over the inauguration ceremony which included worship of Saraswati (*Saraswati puja*), without which the gift would have lost much of its value. In the same spirit, the village notables founded an association bearing her husband's name in order to perpetuate his memory and to run the school.[43]

A few months after its opening, the school was being used in the evening for a new RSS *shakha*: one of the two teachers, Madan Lal Pandey, was assembling twenty-odd villagers there for a physical and ideological training session. He complained that these new *swayamsevaks* did not 'have much in their heads [*dimag*]' and was trying to teach them basic discipline (standing in line, sitting down and standing up) using orders given in Sanskrit, a language none of them knows, but which has prestige because, according to M.L. Pandey, it is the oldest language and therefore the mother of all the others. Pandey had also invented games to teach the villagers the names and deeds of historical heroes of the Hindu nation in order to fill his pupils with noble sentiments.[44]

Conclusion

The Hindu nationalist movement obviously owes its recent successes not only to the radical and populist mobilization strategies it has deployed, but also to its excellent local roots linked to its network of activists and its social welfare strategy, regarding schooling especially. This strategy exploits the philanthropy of patrons wishing to gain merit by their gifts. In other words, a modern ideology draws advantage from a tradition-bound ethos.

In spite of certain limitations, this strategy seems to be sound for two reasons. Firstly, it facilitates an approach to families whose political culture is not Hindu nationalist. When the organizations concerned are distinctively not the RSS, the BJP or any other well identified offshoots of the RSS, the project's affiliations are concealed, prominence being given to its right-thinking Hindu aspect alone, notably via emphasis on *samskar*. In answer to one of my questions, the Piparsod barber mentioned above stressed that the Shishu Mandir is separate from the BJP for which, as a Congress voter, he had no respect. In other words this method of proceeding allays the ideological susceptibilities of parents in order to better shape the political culture of their children.

The second asset of the Hindu nationalist social welfare strategy lays in the goodwill shown it by some official bodies. The public authorities, under pressure because of the budget deficit (7% of the GDP), are cutting investment in the social sphere and are very willing to pass on their responsibilities to private organizations. This is happening particularly quickly in the States where the BJP came to power in the 1990s (Madhya Pradesh, Rajasthan, Himachal Pradesh, Uttar Pradesh, Delhi, Gujarat and Maharashtra) whose governments clearly supported RSS projects;[45] but this encouragement - sometimes associated with financial aid - was already perceptible within central government dependent bodies before the BJP came to power in 1998. In 1991, the government awarded Seva Bharti the 'Certificate of Merit' and a 50,000-rupee reward. The Minister of Health and the Family pays Seva Bharti an annual subsidy of 6,000 rupees and the Delhi Development Authority has provided them with eight offices in the capital even before the BJP took over in Delhi in 1993.[46]

This official patronage is explained by the budget belt-tightening which compels the State to find channels for its action, via Seva Bharti or via a recognized NGO. This evolution may reduce the RSS's dependence on philanthropists. The main handicap the RSS social welfare strategy will have to overcome, is connected with the social categories it targets, the most underprivileged strata. In India these are the low castes whose culture is often far removed from the Great Tradition which the RSS seeks to instil in them. The cleavage can be perceived in the language - often a dialect - used by these strata of society, and in their clothes and dietary habits, in short their life style. It is true that their desire for Sanskritization is conducive to the diffusion of RSS ideology, but militant associations of untouchables and the Bahujan Samaj Party (the party of the majority of society) are actively engaged in a counter-political conscientization programme. According to their logic, the untouchables need not imitate the Brahmins but stand on their own and eradicate the caste system. In the long run, this egalitarian agenda is more likely to make inroads among the Dalits (the broken men), to use these activists' terminology .

Notes

1   A shorter version of this chapter has been published in French: 'Oeuvres Pies et Rationalité Économique en Inde', in J.F. Bayart, (1994) (dir.), *La Réinvention du Capitalisme*, Paris, Karthala, pp. 145-74.
2   Savarkar, V.D. (1969), *Hindutva; Who is a Hindu?*, S.S. Savarkar, Bombay, p. 32.
3   Ibid., p. 82.
4   Ibid., p. 5.
5   Ibid., p. 85.

6   He was thoroughly acquainted with the writings of J.S. Mill, Spencer, Darwin, Tyndals, E. Haeckel, T.H. Huxley, Carlyle and Emerson (Savarkar, V.D. (1984), *My Transportation for Life,*Veer Savarkar Prakashan, Bombay, pp. 269-70).

7   For more details on this point, see Jaffrelot, C. (1995), 'The Idea of the Hindu Race in the Writings of Hindu Ideologues in the 1920s and 1930s: A Concept between Two Cultures', in P. Robb (ed.), *The Concept of Race in South Asia,* Oxford University Press, Delhi.

8   Hindu nationalist cadres often describe Muslims as 'salt in the earth': they make no harm so long they remain in a minority and a subordinated position.

9   Golwalkar, M.S. (1939), *We, or Our Nationhood Defined,* Bharat Prakashan, Nagpur, p. 62.

10   Romila Thapar explains that this exclusion is not based on a racial criterion; it is social and ritual and hence can be overcome via acculturation and recognition of the superiority of the Brahmin (Thapar, R. (1978), *Ancient Indian History,* Orient Longman, New Delhi, pp. 165, 169 and 179). Even today, the common assumption among the Hindu nationalists is that the brahminical values are superior, including that of repression that is equated with *samyan* (self-control). They would disapprove of the low castes' spontaneity. (I am grateful to Jayati Chaturvedi for this piece of information).

11   Pandey, G. (1993), 'Which of us are Hindus?' in G. Pandey (ed.), *Hindus and Others - The Question of Identity in India Today,* Viking, New Delhi, p. 252.

12   See Jaffrelot, C. (1996), *The Hindu Nationalist Movement and Indian Politics, 1925 to the 1990s, Strategies of Identity-Building, Implantation and Mobilisation,* Columbia University Press, New York, ch. 1.

13   Andersen, W. and Damle, S. (1987), *The Brotherhood in Saffron. The Rashtriya Swayamsevak Sangh and Hindu Revivalism,* Vistaar, New Delhi, p. 34.

14   This organization was under the patronage of the *sanghchalak* of Delhi, Hans. Raj Gupta (*Organiser*, 21 August 1947, p. 16).

15   After an earthquake that claimed some 3,000 victims in northern India, the RSS sent 500 volunteers to the scene and distributed clothing and medicine valued at 400,000 and 250,000 rupees (*Organiser*, 8 December 1991).

16   Interview with Vishwamitra Pushkarma, Vice President of Seva Bharti and himself a *jivan vratti*, on 12 August 1992 in New Delhi. The status of *jivan vratti* is equated with that of *vanaprastha*, i.e. the penultimate stage of life, before renunciation, in the Brahmanic tradition. The RSS newspaper, *Organiser*, carries advertizing fliers calling on retired persons interested in social service to be 'initiated *vanaprasthis'* of Seva Bharti (24 November 1991).

17   A tract entitled *Seva Bharti*, New Delhi, [undated].

18   Ibid.

19   L. Kapani, *La Notion de Samskara*, Paris, Collège de France - De Boccard, 1992, p. 43.

20   This concept was introduced by M.N. Srinivas to designate all the practices used by low castes to improve their social status, which consist of copying certain distinctive traits of the Brahmins (Srinivas, M.N. (1965), *Religion and Society among the Coorgs of South India*, Oxford University Press, London, New York, pp. 214-5).

21   Duplicated document entitled *Introduction-Seva Bharti: Delhi* obtained from the movement's headquarters, p. 2.

22   Interview with R. Atri.

23   Times of India, 10 October 1992, p. 4.

24   Interview with Virendra Bhatnagar, 7 October 1991 at Jhandewalan.

25   Seva Bharti states in its typewritten newsletters that it wishes to be associated with UNICEF programmes in order to benefit from foreign funding. This goes counter to the RSS claim to indigenous self-sufficiency, the notion of *svâvalmban* (self-dependency).

26   Duplicated Hindi textbook giving no details of publisher, place or date.

27   Interview with Sadhana Ojha and Gita Goyal on 14 August 1992 at Motia Khan.

28   The sewing machines are an instance of a classic ploy in the Hindu nationalist social welfare strategy. The way in which they are acquired illustrates an important aspect of the Hindu economic ethos, the making of gifts with religious overtones. The machines are supplied by merchants or bought by private individuals and then given to the school during a ceremony, which invests the gift with its full significance. At the Jhandewalan headquarters, panels of photos illustrating RSS activities (rather like those used in catechism groups) are displayed: there are photos of gleaming new Singer sewing machines covered with *mala* (garlands of flowers, often saffron yellow French marigolds). Another important factor is the presence of a local religious figure, the head of the Udaisin ashram (a sect mainly found in the Punjab and relatively open to the low castes). This holy man, Swami Raghavanand, performs for Seva Bharti the rites that consecrate the gift, especially *havan* (Vedic sacrifices). He is even willing to teach the low castes the technique involved in doing the *havan*, and also Sanskrit - indispensable for uttering the sacred formulas. He explains that Westernized politicians are destroying Hindu traditions and that it is therefore essential to go out of the ashrams and regenerate society on its most ancient foundations. Swami Raghavanand and Virendra Bhatnagar, the *pracharak*, represent two variants of the same ideological project. Their strength lies in their ability to expound this project in terms of the protection of Hinduism, thereby attracting to themselves a flow of gifts.

29   I am grateful to Jean-Luc Chambard for inviting me just at the time when the social welfare strategy was starting to be in evidence there and for helping me to carry out my survey.

30   *Census of India 1981 - Series II - Madhya Pradesh District Census Handbook Part XIII-B - Shivpuri District*, Bhopal, State Government Publications, [undated], pp. 15-22.

31   *Organiser,* 19 November 1978, p. 1. This network was particularly dense in Uttar Pradesh where the first Saraswati Shishu Mandir was founded at Gorakhpur in 1952. In 1972, 5,000 children attended these schools in forty-three districts of Uttar Pradesh (Ibid. 25 March 1972, p. 15).

32   Khanna, N. (1991), 'Education: the RSS Way', *Sunday,* 1 December 1991, pp. 22-3.

33   *Saraswati Vidhyapith Avasiya Vidhyalaya-Vivarnika,* 1985 [brochure without indication of place] (Hindi).

34   *Saraswati Vidhyapith Avasiya Vidhyalaya - Shivpuri* [undated].

35   Interview with Ram Hari Pandey, secretary of the boarding school, 18 August 1992, at Shivpuri.

36   Interview with Kamal Kumar Pandey, 16 August 1992, at Shivpuri.

37   This is the profession she gives in the biographical notices published by the secretariat of the Lok Sabha (the Lower House, to which she has been a candidate since 1957,

except in 1977).

38   The dominant caste - another concept we owe to Srinivas - is that which, locally, is most numerous and owns most land. The village leaders traditionally come from its ranks.

39   For a detailed analysis of this phenomenon, see Chambard, J.-L. (1980), *Atlas d'un Village Indien*, EHESS, Paris.

40   I am grateful to Jean-Luc Chambard, the instigator of this initiative, for this piece of information.

41   Interview with Sarvan on 27 October 1991 at Piparsod, carried out in collaboration with Jean-Luc Chambard.

42   Chambard, J.-L. (1994), 'Les Violences d'un Village Hindou. Suicide de Femme chez les Barbiers et 'Violences Légitimes' des Dominants en Inde Centrale', in D. Vidal, G. Tarabout and E. Meyer (dirs.), *Violences et Non-Violences en Inde, Purusharta*, EHESS, Paris, pp. 61-80.

43   Interview with H.S. Sharma, 17 August 1992, at Piparsod.

44   Interview with M.L. Pandey, 17 August 1992, at Piparsod.

45   In Madhya Pradesh, 200 5,000-square-metre plots, total value 100 million rupees, have been turned over to Vidya Bharti schools for a trifling sum (*India Today* 31 October 1992, p. 43).

46   Ghinurie, Y. (1992), 'Altruistic expansion' *India Today*, 31 July 1992, p. 27.

PART V
DISRUPTED NATIONAL IDENTITIES

11 Nationalism and the Politics of National Identities in Latin America: Gender, Power and Racism

SALLIE WESTWOOD

..To think in terms of Latin American women's gender identity it also means turning to the paths of conquest, of colonisation; to how peasant women have been forced into submission; to the slavery of black women; to the historically rooted isolation of middle class women; and other crises in women's lives;... (Vargas 1990, p. 10).

The writing of Virginia Vargas with whom I begin my paper foregrounds the complexity of gendered identities in Latin America and insists that our theorization address diversity and historical specificity. There is no longer the certainty of an essentialist position in relation to 'woman' or class, or nation. We have instead, to find a route through the fissures and fractures which contribute towards a politics of identities which is articulated with a growing number of 'sites' in which the politics is discursively created. My concern in this paper is to elaborate some of the ways in which it is possible to analyze and understand a current politics while that politics is being made and re-visioned most especially within the context of the nation-state of Ecuador. However, while Ecuador is the main focus of the paper it is important to draw upon this context while understanding and elaborating the specifities of Ecuadorean national identity. As will become clear the understanding of Ecuadorean national identity discussed in this paper is premised upon the disjuncture between a codified national project and its complex construction by the diverse citizens who lay claim to Ecuadorean national identity. But more simply, despite the national project which seeks constantly to centre Ecuadorean national identity it is constantly decentred and disrupted by counter-claims that relate to racialized, regional, ethnic, class and gender identities.

In part the discussion in this paper relates to what has been called the 'new social movements' a term much debated but, nevertheless, used to signal the ways in which political action has been generated by collectivities of women and men creating new collective identities and political subjects in Latin America. The term Latin America is itself problematic in so far as it has been homogenized and trivialized within a Eurocentric construction which seeks to domesticate this 'outsized reality' as Gabriel García Márquez calls the diversity of peoples, terrain, histories and current political forms that are part of America. I use the term by convention. It is an imagined reality in part, constructed and framed by a colonial encounter that was marked by brutality, genocide and exploitation and which produced discourses of 'Otherization' with which we live today. The colonial encounter also produced resistance and rebellion which continues to the present time and was generated within specific histories, and spaces. It is this complex temporal and spatial politics that is overridden within the account of 'Latin America'.

The universalizing tendencies of subject disciplines within social sciences have had a major impact on the construction both of 'Latin America' and on conceptions of 'new social movements'. Generated within the Enlightenment view of rationality and science for progress the social sciences are the products of modernity and within this seek ways of ordering the world and providing classificatory models as a basis for explanation. This tendency has been evident in the literature on the new social movements - a sociologizing which offers categories of movements, systems for progression, and roles for 'actors'. One of the most important of these within the feminist literature has been Maxine Molyneux's distinction between practical and strategic interests which suggest a move from the everyday world of material struggles for the sustenance of life to that of a wider systematic set of political demands. This opposition in part reproduces the notions of the public and the private and by setting up such oppositions reproduces a hierarchical notion of the value of different forms of politics (Radcliffe and Westwood, 1993). It reproduces the 'grand narrative' of the Enlightenment project predicated upon a rational move towards progress and wider goals and thereby detextures the world of political concerns (Boyne and Rattansi, 1990). It is an issue raised in the recent volume by Escobar and Álvarez (1992) in which they turn attention to the construction of identities and collective subjects in formation using, in part, a theorization from Laclau and Mouffle (1985), but one that has also been mindful of the major contribution made by Alberto Melucci (1989). In their overview of recent approaches to the theorization of social movements Calderon, Piscitelli and Reyna (1992) emphasize an important eclecticism which is related to the ways in which, in Latin America, there has always been a highly creative transformation of the categories and theories generated at the center' (p. 35). They are aware of the creative tension that exists also between an account of politics in terms of collective subjects and the economic conditions within which collective subjects are generated and sustained, most recently in Latin America the impact of structural adjustment programmes within the states re-emerging as democratic on the model of representative democracy. It is a fragile coalescence of economic imperatives from without and the re-visioning of civil society from within.

The new social movements are bound up with the historical development of populism in Latin America and the ways in which populism has been articulated with the consolidation of the nation-state across Latin America (Rowe and Schelling, 1992). It is part of the way in which national stories generated within the diverse nation-states have constructed conceptions of 'the people' in ways which draw diverse sections of the populations into the hegemonic relations that are essential to the production and reproduction of national identities. The 'national story' has been produced in opposition to the conquest story and more recent forms of cultural and economic imperialism. But, rather like the way in which capitalism both seduces and generates an internal critique, so too, national stories have produced a terrain of inclusion and exclusion via a series of discourses and practices organized around constructions of 'fictive ethnicities' and imagined communities.

Ethnicity as a mobilizing factor is increasingly privileged in Latin America generally and more specifically in Ecuador. This does not mean that class and gender are written out or put on hold. It is clear that ethnicities are both classed and gendered, subject to regional variations and in constant process of being re-worked within a developing political contestation. It is a politics of the nineties, in part, a development of the struggles around democracy in Latin America. The arrival of the new era of democratization, however fragile, has opened up an arena of collective claims in relation to both the definition of the nation and the powers of the state, enabling a politics of national identities to take shape as part of the reconstitution of civil society and the relations between civil society and state.

Historically, colonial domination and its neoliberal variant in Ecuador, like other parts of Latin America, was secured via the hegemony of Hispanic colonial conquest with the assistance of other Europeans. In Ecuador, for example, British adventurers who fought with Bolívar stayed on to become major players in the economic development of the country while contributing towards the consolidation of the nation-state. Later, they were to be joined by the Lebanese traders who prospered and settled. It was a descendant of these early migrants to Ecuador, Abdalá Bucaram, who became the infamous president, 'el loco'. Thus, while it is possible to concur with Raymond William's (1983) view of the nation-state as a project by and for the bourgeoisie in the interests of capital accumulation via orderly markets, it is only one (rather economistic) part of a complex story. The fractionalization of the bourgeoisie is not only economic but also ethnic (in which gender plays a major part). Thus, the consolidation of the bourgeoisie is organized around the nation and the primacy of a 'fictive ethnicity' which weaves together class interests with ethnic diversity as in Ecuador.

The historical background to the construction of the nation in Ecuador is not only concerned with the creation of a 'fictive ethnicity' as a powerful symbol of unity across class, gender and ethnic divisions. Like other Latin American states ethnicity and the processes of racialization are core organizing principles for economic development. The plunder of indigenous land and resources was achieved not only within the context of superior fire power but within the context of racialization which fashioned within the colonial imagination the indigenous population as 'the Other' and thereby superexploitable and worse as the genocidal objects of the Latin American 'adventure'. Similarly, the enslaved African was brought to Ecuador as to other parts of the continent, as chattel and again for the proceeds of his or her labour. But, the processes at work were complex not simply layered but articulated, for example. As Taussig (1987) shows the nineteenth century rubber (robber) baron used indigenous labour but enacted murderous regimes upon this labour to the point where economic considerations were demoted in the pursuit of barbaric practices that turned workers into corpses. At the same time imported African labour was used to control the indigenous labour, setting in place a series of contradictions which survive today in the *haciendas* of the Ecuadorean Sierra where owners employ black African descent Ecuadoreans as private security forces. Thus, it is possible, as more recent history shows, that certain ethnicities can be simultaneously racialized and co-opted.

As Benedict Anderson's analysis makes clear 'the nation' is an 'imagined community' but no less powerful for being so. In part, this is due to the structure and practices which organize the nation-state via the legal apparatuses of citizen and alien and the geopolitics of nation-states which has been so important in the Latin American context (Hepple, 1992). These apparatuses are articulated with legal and official discourses to generate a 'national story' alive with the drama of heroes, battles and the literary and artistic canon. But, as Rowe and Schelling (1992) have so engagingly elaborated there is within the Latin American context a powerful popular/oral tradition currently in the process of being re-invented and revisioned by the growing power of both the indigenous and African movements throughout the continent.

One major part of this all too brief excursion into Ecuadorean history is the issue of racism and racialization. This too, requires an historical background which cannot be fully developed here. Briefly, European racisms are marked by similarity and diversity expressed in the Spanish and Portuguese legacy in a history of the contestations between Christianity, Judaism and Islam and the presence of settled and large populations of black African and Jewish peoples. Spanish and Portuguese imperialism reinforced a sense of the specificities of European identities, however fictitious, and amplified the process of Otherization in relation to the indigenous populations and those enslaved and transported to South America. The point as Stuart Hall writes:

> The story of European identity is often told as if it had no exterior. But this tells us more about how cultural identities are constructed as 'imagined communities', through the marking of difference with others than it does about the actual relations of unequal exchange and uneven development through which a common European identity was forged (Hall, 1987, p. 18).

Such a process has had a profound impact on the cultural development of Latin America not least upon the ways in which gender identities and relations are forged by racisms in Latin American societites, whether in the form of the hegemonic gendering of the Hispanic *marianismo* figure, or the subaltern masculinities and femininities associated with subordinate groups. Gender cannot be separated from nor lived outside racisms and the processes of racialization in Latin America. In Brazil the women's movement is crosscut by racism as well as class. Thus, opportunities for women in the modernizing period from the 1960s onwards were opportunities for 'whiter', urban women. By contrast for most working women concentrated in domestic service, who tend to be of African descent, these opportunities remain remote (Sarti, 1989, p. 77).

Constructing 'the Other' has, in part, been about the ways in which the diversity of colonial peoples has been re-presented in relation to racial categorizations. In Latin American states, especially Brazil, this has been organized around an ideological configuration known as 'racial democracy', which is, in effect, the process of 'whitening' through miscegenation. Thus the figure of the mulatto woman becomes crucial both as a sign of transgression and of the coincidence of gendered and racialized identities. Peter Wade concludes his discussion of Colombia:

> The emergence of a large mixed intermediate group...has established the myth of a Latin American 'racial democracy' based on the predominance of the *mestizo* and the mulatto and in which racial marks are no barriers to marriage and social mobility. It is important to recognize, however, that the mechanisms of racial and social vertical mobility that exist in Latin American societies draw their dynamic from an attempt to escape blackness that has been and continues to be negatively evaluated, and thus to whiten oneself and eventually the population as a whole (Wade, 1986, p. 16).

Such a view is the base from which General Lara could claim via the production and reproduction of *mestizaje* identities that 'everyone is an Ecuadorean now'. It provides a crucial link between 'whitening' and national identity to which I shall return. For the black population the 'escape' from blackness is marked by violence, a violence of distance and disavowal. It is not surprising, therefore, if leading Black intellectuals like Nascimento from Brazil attack the notion of 'racial democracy' and seek to provide a new narrative which offers a central place to those of African descent. He writes:

> The attempt was to silence millions of Brazilians of African origin with the illusion that, by solving the dichotomy between rich and poor or between worker and employer, all racial problems would be automatically resolved. This position of the white Eurocentric ruling élite was taken to the extreme of

elaborating an ideology called 'racial democracy' whose goal was to proclaim the virtues of Brazilian race relations, presenting them as an example to be followed by the rest of the world (Nascimento, 1989).

Slavery was not abolished in Brazil until 1880 but as Nascimento comments (ibid., p. 42) 'The enslaved African became a 'citizen' as stated under the law, but he also became a 'nigger', cornered from all sides'. The contradictions posed by this statement foreground the chasm between the rhetoric of citizenship and the reality of racism in the African diaspora. Nascimento's revised version of Brazilian history places African Brazilians at the centre of a history of displacement in which the white migrations from Europe marginalized the black population thereby reinforcing white racisms and a Eurocentric account of Brazil.

Nascimento's account highlights the complexities of racisms in Latin America. He writes as an African-Brazilian, as a black man from within the experience of racism, a racism which is organized around the signifier of skin colour and has been elaborated in relation to complex Western fantasies around black sexualities, male and female (Gilman, 1985) and which the cultural heritage of the African diaspora is denied. It is a form of racism which has been globalized but which finds its expression in the everyday. One example will suffice. Norma Rodríguez, who is president of the African-Ecuadorean Association in Ecuador, was in downtown Guayaquil when a white man stepped on her foot, she turned to him and as she did he said: 'What do you want, get back where you belong, the kitchen or the whorehouse'. It is also clear from this incident that racialized identities, like ethnic and class identities are always constructed and refracted through gendered identities.

Blackness is not alone in signifying a racialized identity, racism is itself unstable and multiple as the histories of the indigenous peoples of South America clearly show. Leaders of indigenous peoples across the Americas are in the process of forging a collective subject from great diversity - a diversity which has been ignored in the very language that has been used to describe indigenous peoples. Some leaders have coined the term 'forth world' for the fate of their peoples. The language of '*Indios*' is a pejorative term used to denote backwardness and thereby marginalization which is currently contested. These connotations are part of a form of racism which denied diversity and specificity and re-cast cultural attributes as negative, a form of cultural racism which fixes on difference and thereby constructs members of the indigenous peoples as 'Others', par excellence. This was made apparent in the ways in which ethnic identities were subsumed, and still are, within and between economic identities, *campesino/a*, a political-economic class identity with the ethnic referent made invisible. Peoples designated by their labour-power both within discourses of the right and the left. However, such designations could be reappropriated and used to define a politics of collective subjects in relation to resources, land, capital and workers rights.

The symbolic use of 'peasants' and 'workers' is also part of public language in relation to the construction of the nations of South America. Nationalist discourses are generally organized around very specific ethnicities which privilege a Eurocentric account of the nation against the indigenous voices that have to fight for a place in the nation. The terrain on which they choose to fight is ethnically defined while it recognizes the economic importance of land and labour. Neither should this be understood as an already forged identity complete and unitary. The situation in Ecuador, one small part of the whole, expresses the complexities of ethnic identities and claims to authenticity.

My discussion so far suggests a need to consider the plurality of racisms in play in any specific time/space frame. Racisms have histories and are embedded within the processes of racialization which organize racisms around specific signifiers most especially, colour and physiogamy and culture. Racisms, like sexisms are in Foucault's language, 'regimes of power' organized via institutional frameworks especially within the state as part of the disciplinary power of state agencies like the police, but which is subject to ongoing contestations. Foucault makes a vital point in this respect in relation to visibility and its importance in disciplinary modes - racialized populations are always highly visible, marked out within the public sphere and within the discourses that construct the state and the nation. It is to the complex of state/nation articulations that I now turn.

Nations and States

To invoke nations is to foreground not the commonly assumed geographical inertia of state boundaries, but the terrain of national identities and the struggles around these which are ongoing throughout South America. In the case of Ecuador, of course, even the inertia of geographical boundaries remains under contestation. Gramsci's now familiar analysis of ideological hegemony is crucial to our understanding of the ways in which the nation is constructed through a consensus around 'the people'. The ideological construction of the nation is organized around specific ethnicities and constructs 'fictive ethnicities' and national identities as part of a national story. Thus in Argentina the 'Indian' presence was both forced from the land and made invisible in terms of the national consciousness (in ways similar to the exclusion of both indigenous and African Brazilians in Brazil) through a series of discourses that wove together the history of Argentina in such a way that the ethnic diversities of the nation were written out. What is especially interesting about this is the presence in the Argentinian history of a well-articulated socialist and anarchist politics organized through the labour movement. Thus, it was citizens and workers who sought political and economic rights and who were the collective subjects of politics.

In the recent history of Latin American states, nationalism and nationhood were key rationales for the interventions by the military during the 1970s. These interventions defined the state and its power as the nation and the national interest, at the same time as 'the people' were defined as dangerous. Although in Peru the military interventions did have a more progressive character, military interventions generally, especially in the Southern Cone, were tied to levels of state repression that remain firmly entrenched in the popular imagination as the key indicator of politics in the region. This is, in part, because the symbols of nationhood were militaristic, redolent with masculinity. The generals justified seizure of power on the basis of their privileged position to push through 'national development'. However, despite the creation of regimes of terror and of increasing wealth for upper and middle class groups, the nation was not secure; fractions, coups, splits within the bourgeoisie were one problem, the other was organized resistance from diverse sections of the population: workers, peasants, intellectuals, indigenous peoples, the urban poor, and women with diverse backgrounds. Citizenship and civil society were in this period repressed by the state and the organs of civil society tried to survive at a subterranean level - they went underground and people went into exile.

A more subtle version of authoritarian models of nationalism was to be found in authoritarian populism, the most famous example being Peronism in Argentina, which sought to forge national identity by welding certain sections of the population into 'the people' who were identified via the leader Peron with the national interest, national culture and nationhood. Trade unionists (of the official kind), socialists, women's organizations, peasant organizations and ethnic identities were perceived by the national project to be outside the nation, sources of danger because they had an alternative class-gender-ethnic perspective from which to generate their own version of populism and thereby a degree of autonomy from the view on offer. Thus, authoritarian populism ties a specific class interest (or section of the bourgeoisie) to the national interest; for it to succeed ideologically its class interest is, therefore, submerged in the political discourse, and ethnicity, nation and gender are far more likely to be privileged in the construction of nationalism. Historically, in Latin America, men and masculinity are tied to the defence of the nation and the protection of family, home and the people, while women are cast as reproducers of the nation as wives and mothers, much as it is throughout the globe (see Yuval-Davis and Anthias, 1989).

The authoritarian populism of Peronism in Argentina and Vargas in Brazil gave way to new settlements in the 1970s and 1980s that Guillermo O'Donnell has characterized as Bureaucratic Authoritarian (BA) regimes. This suggests that following the economic crisis the military was given a new role in economic development but this view fails to take account of the legitimation crises suffered by the military regimes and the impact of resistance from wide sections of the population explored in relation to feminisms and women's organizing by Jaquette (1989).

Undoubtably the state is a powerful player in the politics of the region but it is too easy to slip into an undertheorized account of the state which presents the state as a collective social actor or as having functions in relation to the reproduction of capitalism, or as a sort of referee in relation to competing interests. There is some suggestion of the reproductive model in Sonia Alvarez's path-breaking study of the state in Brazil (Alvarez, 1990). Instead, I want to posit a disaggregated state, a state as contested terrain in which power blocks seek to impose an agenda for development and control in the social formation, the outcomes of which within any specific social formation are variable. As an arena of contestation this also offers spaces for counter-hegemonic politics especially in relation to the national story. The state articulates the exclusivity of the nation via the legal requirements surrounding citizenship and thereby it interpellates 'citizens', but may also find that those not included contest their exclusion, or those subjected to state abuses answer the state from within the state's own rhetoric about the protection of nationals and the rights of citizens. This is, of course, precisely what women across Latin America did in relation to the repression of the 1970s and early 1980s. The new period of democratization fuels these contestations by offering a revival of civil society and a new emphasis upon citizenship and democratic rights. But what is also very clear is that the frame within which these contestations are taking place from Brazil to Ecuador is one in which ethnicities and racisms are foregrounded which highlights once again the national question.

Making and Remaking the Nation in Ecuador

I want now to turn to the specificities of Ecuador in relation to the issues outlined above. As General Lara's famous comment '*Todos nos hacemos blancos cuando aceptamos los retos de la cultura nacional*' suggests national identity in Ecuador is organized around the familiar notion of *mestizo/a* and this is built into the legal apparatuses of the state in relation to citizenship. The Ecuadorean census, like many others in South America, does not include an ethnic classification and the ethnic breakdown of the population (of eleven million) is based on estimates offering a majority *mestizo* population with an estimated forty per cent indigenous and five per cent of Ecuadoreans of African descent. These figures are both official and part of the common sense within the country. They do not go uncontested. African-Ecuadoreans claim that they constitute fifteen per cent of the population which is much more likely and equally, it is suggested that the indigenous population is about twenty-five per cent. Thus, the proportion of non-*mestizo* population remains very similar. The fusion of Ecuadorean with *mestizos* also hides, of course, the importance of the white elite who exercises a powerful cultural and economic hegemony in the country. But, they do not have it all their own way. To complicate the ethnic contestations there are powerful regional loyalties and an economic rivalry between the *Costa* and the *Sierra*. The shifting power relations of these two regions are also racialized with Guayaquil, home to powerful Lebanese financiers and politicians and to many black people while the *Sierra* and Quito is home of the state bureaucracies and the intellectual life of the country. The cultures of the two regions are enormously different - one new money, active, life affirming, all salsa and good times in the popular imagination while the other cooler like the climate, low key and contemplative. Ecuadoreans understand these differences well and have regional loyalties further divided by town and country and within this localities within the city - Quiteaneans from the north of the city despair of the south and so on.

Ecuador is now a predominantly urban society and within this national identity as Ecuadorean is part of the popular consciousness to the extent that migration to the city means a change in self-designation and complementary designations from others, that is, indigenous people become *mestizo/a* in the urban world. Thus, we have a nation-state in which 'the people' are organized around a *mestizo/a* identity but who are often represented by the symbol of an indigenous person and in which Ecuador announces itself as 'País Amazónica' below the Quitanean coat of arms. As Crain (1990) has shown the ways in which indigenous culture has been incorporated into a construction of the nation in Ecuador has shifted over time, from an initial position in which indigenous culture was used as the binary which helped to construct Ecuadorean culture against this, to the incorporation and re-framing of indigenous culture as uniquely Ecuadorean. Ecuador is named after the Equator which is now a major tourist attraction with an ethnographic museum showing the great diversity of peoples that live in the country, from the Marimba dancers of *Esmeraldas* to *Oriente* and body painting. This form of 'multi-culturalism' is dutifully recorded by the school children who crowd the exhibits. Culture as exhibit is one of the problems of this approach, static and with its elaboration of difference in signifiers of colour and dress as privileged markers of 'culture'.

One key to national identities in Ecuador is the role of the military who are everywhere in evidence as military personnel but also as entrepreneurs and bankers. It is the military football team that uses the name *Nacional* and includes five and sometimes six African Ecuadorean players. This is not surprising in view of the clearly articulated strategy to involve all sections of Ecuadorean society but most especially those citizens of African and indigenous descent. Thus, many rural areas have a military school which provides military and technical training and a route upwards. The complex ideologies which fuel this cannot be understood simply as the incorporation of potentially dissident groups, rather, the military articulate a modernizing ideology which includes a consensus notion of the nation and citizenship evidenced most recently by the announcement that military personnel will receive 'human rights training'. The nation building role of the military in Ecuador cannot be underestimated. It is the military that maps the terrain of Ecuador from the *Instituto de Geografía Militar* set on a hill above Quito with its panoptic gaze across the country, producing detailed maps of every valley and river, *casa* and *hacienda*. The military define the spatial relations of the nation and in order to effect this have successfully constructed Peru as 'the Other' of Ecuadorean national identity which is defended in the ongoing border dispute which periodically erupts into declarations of war and the exchange of fire power between the two nation-states.

Men are drafted into military service or 'national service' for a period of two years. Women have been offered an opportunity to serve at times of crisis - often connected to the border dispute with Peru. But, the masculinist symbols of the military from the Ruminahui bank to the football team provide a vision of the nation that is highly gendered. The militarized nationalism is reproduced in the schooling system where children, on transfer from primary to secondary school, swear allegiance to the flag and the nation. All schoolbooks have the national anthem printed on the back cover, a celebration of the national story - the defence of the nation against the Spanish and a celebration of liberty and loyalty. The use of Ruminahui also, of course, draws on an indigenized past and a symbol of resistance of colonial oppression. This, clearly, is the public face of the military. As is well known the infamous General Pinochet came to Ecuador to advise on strategy and modernization and, in the last instance, of course, the military controls the means of violence. But, as people in Ecuador say, this is Ecuador a nation-state where politicians and financiers have their phone number in the phone book. It speaks of a sense of security and openness unknown in most parts of the world.

And yet, nothing is settled in Ecuador and nationhood and citizenship are contested most especially now with the growing confidence of the indigenous movement. Indigenous people in the Amazon have filed a class action against Texaco for the destructive basis of oil development in the region. It is an action by 'the people' of Amazonia against the power of the multi-national corporation. This action comes against a backdrop of organization and protest by the diverse indigenous groups in Ecuador which has gained in strength over the last twenty years and which culminated in the 1990 Uprising, *Levantamiento*, which brought thousands of self-identified indigenous people on to the streets of Quito and localities throughout Ecuador in support for a wide range of demands articulated by CONAIE, the federation of indigenous organizations and groups. Although the issue of land was high on the agenda, the basis of the demands was much broader including the call for designated territories for diverse groups and changes in the constitution to support a 'plurinational' state. Issues of discrimination and 'Otherization' were put into circulation and with this the processes of exclusion and inclusion in relation to the nation. Equally, the call for a trans-national understanding of indigenous identities has grown throughout the region supported by an organizational base which is cross-national.

CONAIE was recognized by the Borja government as the legal representative of indigenous peoples and bi-lingual education programmes emphasizing Quichua were instituted including a bilingual education project central office in Quito, which has since closed, along with other initiatives which the now ousted President Bucaram (1997) refused to acknowledge. As Selverston (1992, pp. 8-9) comments, 'although an Office of Indigenous Affairs came into being it had no links with the grassroots organizations'. CONAIE in a situation of greater openness to diversity and the recognition of democratic rights had seized a moment in which they presented a collective and disobedient subject to the state, the indigenous peoples who are an immensely diverse people (for whom Quichua is one of the languages but not the only one). The importance of the resource politics cannot be underestimated in relation to land claims and against the multi-national/state oil interventions in Amazonia. They form part of the language of rights in relation to a citizenship which was to be re-visioned within an understanding of difference.

In relations to the 'imagined community' of the nation the Uprising raised a series of pressing issues that states and nations across the globe are currently in process of addressing. Although, in parts of Europe the talking and the state have dissolved into genocidal violence in the name of ethnicity and nation, the debates in Ecuador have a very different mode of address. Thus, Hendricks (1991) writing of the Shuar Federation, formed in 1964 by the Shuar of Amazonia, an organization which negotiates with the state and generated a counter-hegemonic rhetoric based as much in claims to land and a degree of autonomy as in an understanding of reflexivity which is contrasted with that of the 'white man' who is seen to be a person who does not speak 'with a good heart'. This is based on a mode of address which emphasizes the Shuar language and cultural identity and which regards the white man's language and mode of address as 'uncivilized'. The Shuar are respected as warriors and as enterprising, forward looking people who are important to the Ecuadorean state because their lands are on the disputed Peruvian border. But, from within, the Shuar see their negotiations and resistance to the Ecuadorean state as opposing the colonization of the Shuar which has gathered pace during the last fifty years. As Hendricks (1991, p. 68) concludes: 'The interface between the Ecuadorean state and the Shuar is being formed, not solely by the impact of nationalist/capitalist penetration of the indigenous culture, but also by the creative response of that culture in applying its own cultural meanings to the current situation in order to counteract the perceived dangers'.

The Shuar Federation was an important forerunner to the CONAIE and Shuar members hold important leadership positions in the current federation of indigenous peoples. A consideration of the demands and negotiations of the Shuar Federation help us to better understand the calls from CONAIE for territorial rights and plurinationalism, securing the relationship between land and nation, space and history. In part this is the language of an anti-colonial struggle and anti-colonial struggles throughout the world have used a counter-hegemonic nationalism to promote resistance but often as a way of promoting unity among diverse groups and generating a collective identity in opposition to the colonizing power. In Ecuador currently the call is a more complex one which offers a collective subject who 'represents' diverse interests and peoples in ways that acknowledge diversity and the multiplicity of claims that cannot be unified in one collective but, on the contrary, demand that the state systematize multiplicity. There is also in play a racialized language in terms of the category of 'white' which implies power and a specific colonial heritage but in speaking of and for themselves the Shuar and CONAIE do not position themselves within a binary opposition, rather cultural diversity is foregrounded. It cannot be otherwise due to the cultural, linguistic and economic differences between the indigenous peoples who are defined in opposition as one voice, but a voice of plurality. Thus, the demand for a plurination is one that recognizes Ecuadorean identity is 'fictitious' but relates to a history and geographical space organized by the state. Against this homogenizing identity are a set of claims to place and specific cultural identities that cannot be, and will not be, incorporated. This is not a simple matter of old traditions against the modernizing national project which defines the opposition as backward; rather than forward-looking.

The wealth-creating prowess of the Otavaleneans, for example, is well known but their distinctive dress is also a symbol of cultural difference, a claim to authenticity and a resource in relation to economic integration. Thus, the integrationist (colonial) project of the state is met with a counter that produces a series of multiple identities. Thus, the notion that the urban world and integration as workers or entrepreneurs into the capitalist system generates a *mestizo/a* identity is forestalled. Instead, for some sections of the Ecuadorean nation pluri-identities will define a sense of location and a place in the nation - Shuar-Ecuadorean, a hyphenated sense of belonging in which an ethnic identity is co-joined but simultaneously separated from a national identity. This has major implications for citizenship, the processes whereby within democratic systems (however flawed) an abstracted citizen is offered certain rights in return for an acknowledgement of the power of the state. The CONAIE demands break open the abstracted notion of the citizen and place the notion that citizenship is colour-coded, is culturally and ethnically specific, is regionally specific and is gendered, at the centre of discussions around democracy and citizenship. In so doing, the margins come to the centre to disrupt and redefine. In part, this brings the discussion back to new social movements and the ways in which the major task for such movements is to shift the agenda and make symbolic claims (Melucci, 1989).

The promotion of an indigenous account of Ecuador and Ecuadorean national identity has further prompted a reaffirmation of African-Ecuadorean identity with the hyphenated designation already in place. But, it would be a mistake to believe that this identity is any more homogenous than that of the multiplicities of indigenous identities. There are a series of discourses in play that provide resistance to racism and discrimination within in Ecuador. While one narrative, importantly, places African-Ecuadorean within the African diaspora and weaves a story of African roots and culture displaced and remade this co-exists with an American story which draws upon the popular culture of black America from New York to Los Angeles and is clearly evidenced in the youth styles of Guayaquil and *Esmeraldas*. In the *Esmeraldas* the African-Ecuadorean population have an autonomous and powerful past and one which importantly criss-crosses national boundaries between Ecuador and Colombia. Thus, the black population, like the indigenous population, generates a community of resistance across national borders which is very much in evidence and has been recognized by the Ecuadorean state in the recent amnesty for illegal entrants from the black Colombian population of the Northern Pacific coast. This suggests most powerfully the limits of the national story and returns us to shared histories and cultural forms as a basis for identities rather than identities constructed as a response to white racism.

Clearly, the trajectories for the indigenous movement and the African-Ecuadorean population are allied and separated. In both cases the terrain of national identity is a crucial field of vision and debate into which new agendas are being inserted. The multiplicities of this are being worked out in ways that will have profound effects on Ecuador in the decades to come. But, so far, I have given little attention to the ways in which these processes, demands and strategies are gendered. I want to close my paper by returning to Virginia Vargas, with whom I began, and her concern with the importance of histories, communities and difference in relation to a progressive politics of gender.

En-Gendered Power

The elaborated concerns of this paper have powerful 'genderic' elements. It is clear that racisms operate and are lived through gendered identities which are also sexualized, producing the vision of exotica or the 'Other' and using the signifiers of skin colours and of cultural difference. Thus, racism is unstable and cannot be understood as a fixed unity except in the sense that 'races' are ideologically constructed as 'imagined communities'. It is also clear that nations too, are powerful 'imagined communities' that exact, like 'races', loyalties alongside hostilities and that nations and nationalism can be articulated from diverse perspectives and constructed within a variety of discourses. Consequently the national identity articulated in Ecuador within the modernizing process is an 'official' identity contested by popular nationalisms in counter-hegemonic ways. But there are interesting contradictions evidenced if we foreground gender. The contestations over the nation are taking place within a social formation organized on democratic principles which themselves invite contestation. While this is not a participatory but a representative democracy in which all those eligible are bound to vote, the rhetoric of democracy is bound to conceptions of collectivities in competition for power, represented by individual and collective subjects. It is also clear that women are not slow to exercise democratic rights and have been in the forefront of securing the return of democratic institutions and civil society. But, within Ecuador, as in many parts of the world, citizenship is 'colour coded', that is, it is racialized through an ideology of 'whitening' which incorporates both colour and culture and is expressed in the notion of *mestizo/a*.

These categories of *mestizo/a* are tied to the urban world, to the centre rather than the margins or hinterland of rurality. Because they are given an urban location they are also articulated with the sale of labour power and the notion of the 'worker', the modern worker. While women workers are a crucial part of the labour force they are often invisible in relation to formal sector employment. Thus, citizenship is constructed as an economic category which is highly gendered. In addition, the constructions made by language distinguish women and workers, peasants and workers. But, there is an important twist to the story of the urban setting of citizenship and this relates to the development of the 'nationalism of the neighbourhood', the relationship between locale and the construction of an imagined community at the local level. Cohen (1988) has used this notion in relation to white working class masculinities in Britain, highlighting the ways in which in marking their own territory young men mark it against the 'alien' and the 'Other' which fuels the racism of working class urban life and can lead to physical aggression between groups over the defence of the neighbourhood. While one can see this in action in the cities of Ecuador, both in Quito and Guayaquil, the notion could equally well be explored in relation to femininity and women's politics in the cities. This suggests an alternative understanding of the 'nationalism of the neighbourhood' which, while it promotes a sense of belonging and exclusivity, does so on the basis of a more progressive politics which seeks to mobilize women, especially in pursuit of resources for the *barrio*, while offering a sense of identity tied to locale which can generate a community of resistance with an emancipatory agenda.

At the nation-state level, as many others and I have suggested, Latin American military/state relations and politicians evidence a masculinist style of politics. In the case of Ecuador the important role of the military in nation-building through the military-economic complex and in relation to popular culture through football suggests a national identity that is again tied to masculinity. It is not that women are absent it is rather, that the ideological constructions of femininity offer women different subject positions in relation to the nation. It is within the family that women are positioned and in relation to reproduction as mothers of the nation (although some women did volunteer for armed service in relation to the ongoing border dispute with Peru). The newspapers in Ecuador celebrate family and motherhood but this is racialized and classed creating important divisions between women, some who work for others as *empleadas* in domestic service which has brought women from the countryside into the town. These definitions are reinforced among a strongly Catholic population where definitions of femininity are offered in terms of motherhood. This is not, I must underline, to reproduce a simple view of the complexity that comes with a Catholic identification. Catholicism is many discourses all of which are in operation in Latin America. It figures, for example, as a backdrop to the popular *telenovela* Guadalupe watched by millions in Ecuador where the central character, Guadalupe goes from crisis to crisis including divorce and projected single motherhood.

Popular nationalisms expressed within indigenous peoples movements and the African-Ecuadorean organizations have involved many women in their struggles. In CONAIE, however, the major figures in the public eye are men but, more importantly, the forms of cultural nationalism elaborated offer subject positions to women as keepers of culture and reproducers of the nation through motherhood, positions for which there is considerable support among women themselves. For many African-Ecuadorean women the position is similar. These discourses privilege heterosexuality and offer no subject positions to lesbian women or gay men.

These similarities may suggest a consistency between the official nationalism of the Ecuadorean state and the popular nationalisms of the indigenous and African peoples of Ecuador. This is, however, a superficial view which needs to be set within the contexts of racisms and marginalization that have generated communities of resistance in which women's reproductive powers come to assume a powerful symbol of autonomy and emancipation. But this, too, reproduces the notion of woman as symbol of the nation and in relation to reproductive rights for black and indigenous women these are often constructed within a nationalist discourse that, given the extent of racism, puts women in the frontline of national survival. Discourses around reproductive rights in relation to national survival emphasize the embodied quality of power and resistance so clearly displayed by women in Latin America from the *Madres* of Argentina to the freedom fighters of Guatemala and Salvador. And as one

Salvadorean woman Malena made clear, 'The Salvadorean movement cannot coexist with *machismo*. We can only survive with *compañerismo*, a consciousness which requires the full integration of men into childrearing and into all family tasks' (A Dreams Compels Us: Voices of Salvadorean Women, 1988).

Current debates and political action in relation to the remaking of the nation and national identities place ethnicities and racisms at the forefront of the struggles but these sites of struggle are also gendered and part of a re-visioned identity politics. The debates on the nation, exclusion and inclusion, offer place and ethnicity as signifiers of belonging but they seem to leave women in place where they have previously been, as daughters, wives, mothers within the family which is tied to the nation as the primary unit within a discourse organized around culture. Thus Gilroy (1993, p. 63) comments: 'The term culture has expanded to displace any overt references to 'race' in the older biological sense of the term. Culture is reductively conceived and always primarily and 'naturally' reproduced in families, the nation is, in turn, conceived as a neat symmetrical accumulation of family units'. This official version of the nation and national identities is recognizable in relation to Ecuador, but also within the counter-hegemony of popular nationalism. This is what Gilroy (ibid.) calls 'the narrow practice of cultural nationalism'. Instead, he wants to celebrate the African diaspora and a black Atlantic culture which has become a resource for peoples around the world and is much in evidence within youth cultures. He wants to move away from a narrow definition of blackness and recognize the complex exchanges and inter-relationships that have produced the multiple selves of both black and white people in Britain and the States. Nowhere is this more resonant than within the states of Latin America and it is regrettable that Gilroy ignores this.

Thus, we return to the ways in which the national story in Ecuador divides women through the processes of racialization and by the boundaries of the 'imagined community' but also, as I suggested, in relation to class and the power relations of women's lives. Upper class 'white' women are bought into the national story through the family and their reproductive powers but not African Ecuadorean or Indigenous women who are constructed as on the periphery of the nation, marginal to the fictive ethnicity which makes them invisible. The struggles around national identities are, therefore, of prime importance for women 'at the margins' and one way in which the centre can become de-centred and a plurality of national stories be honoured. To rephrase this, the counter-claims by the indigenous movement and the African Ecuadorean group promise the end of the grand narrative of Ecuadorean national identity. But, the counterclaims do not seek to reconstruct the space of women within the communities of resistance, this too, has to generate a pluri-view of woman acknowledged as a sign of multiplicity, as de-centred as the counter-hegemonic national identity that is proposed. Only in this way is it possible to offer alternative subject positions to 'women of colour' because as Iragaray (1985) suggests 'the subject is always, already masculine' but this is not the whole story because the subject is simultaneously, 'always, already white' and heterosexual as well.

In part this returns us to the issues of multiple selves, of histories, cultures and the narratives within which these are constructed and the ways in which these are discursively produced. Thus, '...the limited evidence available suggests that the lived experience of being Ecuadorean is highly differentiated and separated from the representation of Ecuadorean nationhood in public discourses (Whitten, 1981; Radcliffe and Westwood, 1993, 1996). This paper has been an attempt to explore these disjunctures and to examine the ways in which new collective subjects seek to intervene in the making and remaking of the nation in Ecuador.

Acknowledgements

I owe very special thanks to Gabriela Castellanos and Miryan Zuñiga E. for their invitation to participate in the Cali, Columbia, seminar. My warmest thanks also to Vera Bakker, Monique van't Hek and her team who worked so hard to make the seminars so successful and to all the wonderful participants. Thanks also to the editors for their comments and Robert Ash for his work on the text.

Glossary

CONAIE - *Confederación de Nacionalidades Indígenas de Ecuador*
FCUNE - *Fundación para la Cultura Negra Ecuatoriana*

References

Álvarez, S.E. (1990), *Engendering Democracy in Brazil*, Princeton University Press, Princeton.

Anderson, B. (1983), *Imagined Communities: Reflections on the Origin and Spread of Nationalism*, Verso, London.

Boyne, R. and Rattansi, A. (1990) (eds), *Postmodernism and Society*, Sage, London.

Calderon, F., Piscitelli, A. and Reyna, J.L. (1992), 'Social Movements: Actors, Theories, Expectations' in E. Escobar and S.E. Álvarez (eds), *The Making of Social Movements in Latin America*, Westview Press, Colorado.

Cohen, P. (1988), 'The Perversions of Inheritance: Studies in the Making of Multi-Racist Britain', in P. Cohen and H. Bains (eds), *Multi-Racist Britain,* Macmillan, London.

Crain, M. (1990), 'The Social Construction of National Identity in Highland Ecuador', *Anthropological Quarterly*, 15 (3), pp. 43-55.

Escobar, E. and Álvarez, S.E. (eds) (1992), *The Making of Social Movements in Latin America*, Westview Press, Colorado.

Foucault, M. (1979), *Discipline and Punish*, Penguin, Harmondsworth.

Gilman, S. (1985), *Difference and Pathology: Stereotypes of Sexuality, Race and Madness*, Cornell University Press, Ithaca.

Gilroy, P. (1993), 'Nationalism, History and Ethnic Absolutism' in P. Gilroy, *Small Acts: Thoughts on the Politics of Black Culture*, Serpent's Tail, London.

Hall, S. (1987), 'Minimal Selves', *I.C.A. Document 6*, Institute of Contemporary Arts, London.

Hendricks, J. (1991), 'Symbolic Counterhegemony among the Ecuadorean Shuar' in J. Urban and J. Sherzer (eds), *Nation-States and Indians in Latin America*, University of Texas Press, Texas.

Hepple, L.W. (1992), 'Metaphor, Geopolitics and the Military in South America' in T.J. Barnes and J.S. Duncan (eds), *Writing Worlds: Discourse, Text and Metaphor in the Representation of Landscape*, Routledge, London.

Iragaray, L. (1985), *The Sex which is not One*, C. Porter and C. Burke (trs.), University of Columbia Press, Ithaca, New York.

Jacquette, J. (1989) (ed.), *The Women's Movements in Latin America: Feminism and the Transition to Democracy*, Unwin Hyman, London.

Laclau, E. and Mouffe, C. (1985), *Hegemony and Socialist Strategy: Towards a Radical Democratic Polites*, Verso, London.

Melucci, A. (1989), *Nomads of the Present: Social Movements and Individual Needs in Contemporary Society*, Temple University Press, Philadelphia.

Molyneux, M. (1985), 'Mobilisation without Emanicipation? Women's Interests, the State and Revolution in Nicaragua', *Feminist Studies* 11 (2), pp. 227-54.

Nascimento, do A. (1989), *Brazil: Mixture or Massacre: Essays in the Genocide of Black People*, Majority Press, Dover.

O'Donnell, G. (1973), *Modernisation and Bureaucratic Authoritarianism: Studies in South American Politics*, University of California Press, Berkeley.

Radcliffe, S. and Westwood, S. (eds) (1993), *'Viva': Women and Popular Protest in Latin America*, Routledge, London.

Radcliffe, S. and Westwood, S. (1996), *Remaking the Nation: Place, Identity and Politics in Latin America*, Routledge, London.

Rowe, W. and Schelling, V. (1992), *Memory and Modernity: Popular Culture in Latin America*, Verso, London.

Sarti, C. (1989), 'The Panorama of Feminism in Brazil', *New Left Review,* 173, pp. 75-92.

Selverston, M. (1992), 'Politicized Ethnicity and the Nation-State in Ecuador', unpublished paper given at the Latin American Studies Association, Los Angeles, USA.

Taussig, M. (1987), *Shamanism, Colonialism and the Wild Man: A Study in Terror and Healing*, University of Chicago Press, Chicago.

Vargas, V. (1990), *The Women's Movement in Peru: Rebellion into Action*, Institute of Social Studies, The Hague.

Wade, P. (1986), 'Patterns of Race in Colombia', *Bulletin of Latin American Research,* 5 (2), pp. 1-19.

Whitten, N. (1981), *Cultural Transformation and Ethnicity in Modern Ecuador*, University of Illinois Press, Chicago.

Williams, R. (1983), *Towards 2000*, Chatto and Windus, London.

Yuval-Davis, N. and Anthias, F. (1989) (eds), *Woman-Nation-State*, Macmillan, London.

12 The Difficult Stabilization of Turkish National Identity

GÉRARD GROC

Introduction

Just when it seemed that the Turkish nation was united in a modernist, secular outlook and of one mind about its own economic development and international recognition, centrifugal tendencies are emerging within it as various groups try to differentiate themselves from the national whole, deriving their criteria of identity from various sources. This is revealing an unexpected crack in a system renowned for hammering home, if need be by authoritarian means, its nationalist credo.

At the moment, dissidence centres on the Kurds (15 to 20% of the population) and their rejection of Turkish assimilation; on religious movements (accounting for 20% of votes hitherto cast in elections) and their rejection of secularism; and on an ill-defined Alevi group (12 to 15% of the population) and their awakening to a new sense of identity.[1] The first two of these are old-established movements which, despite its achievements, the republic has never managed to curtail,[2] and which call in question the effectiveness of Turkish nationalism and, more generally, the advent of a Turkish nation. As to the third case, the wide-ranging and effective formulation of an Alevi identity, backed by many historical, sociological and even religious arguments,[3] appears to be the expression of a new desire for individuality which would use political and social readjustments, internal and external, to reject an over-restrictive national framework.

This is not to say that nation and nationalism are losing their power to mobilize support.[4] In addition to its positive connotations[5] and long record of victorious partisan activism, mobilization around these concepts occurs as a natural, mass reaction to any turn of events considered detrimental to the country's interests, such as the Cyprus question, the Luxembourg decision to reject Turkey's bid for European Union membership (December 1997) and the more recent Italian refusal to extradite the leader of the Kurdish Workers' Party (PKK), Abdullah Öcalan. On such occasions, the expressions of indignation, such as demonstrations, petitions and boycotts, are largely spontaneous, showing that nationalism still has a substantial reservoir of active support.

What, then, do these developments mean?

Has the idea of a national community, as set forth by the Kemalist regime, been rendered obsolete by the opening up of the economic market, the phenomenon of one-way migration to Europe or the free flow of communications, to which the Turks are particularly sensitive? Will the 'obsolescence' of the nation then push certain social groups, aware that an inevitable transition is under way, to reformulate the basis of their identity? Or, on the contrary, is it a case of the inadequate national integration of social groups which are having to cope with sweeping change, expressed in an exponential growth of urbanization, increasingly insecure living conditions and the bulldozing of traditional social and cultural landmarks? If so, people will, in their frustration, opt for divergent expressions of identity which provide more immediate solidarity, backed if need be by political movements. For that matter, the two hypothesis can be combined: Islamists and Kurds, while often calling for greater integration, are also capable today of developing strategies that go beyond the national framework (the Kurdish diaspora in Europe, Islamic business leaders' command of the international trade circuits). Or - third hypothesis - is it a more traditional political crisis, whereby the State, faced with the drive to democracy, is coming increasingly under fire for its incompetence in resolving such basic issues as the economic crisis, the Kurdish question, the issue of civil liberties, or illegal involvement - or indeed involvement by organized crime - in the political system? If so, then it is rejection of the State's central role that would present a challenge to its very foundations, foremost among which is nationalism; but it must also be emphasized that the previously mentioned rampant urbanization goes together with a conquest of the political centre by the periphery, releasing the divergent identity-based processes needed for effective political competition.

The problem is further complicated by the fact that there are several levels, all linked to the Kemalist experience, at which Turkish nationalism can be understood but also contested: national independence, nation-building and national unity. Another factor is that the current centrifugal tendencies are themselves tinged with nationalism,[6] including nationalism with a republican slant, as demonstrated by the support given by the religious leader Necmettin Erbakan to the 'national interest' during his time in power. As to the Alevis, they also provide the bedrock of support for the parties on the republican, Kemalist, secular left. Hence, we must examine carefully both the existence of a gap between political practice and expressions of protest, and the discrepancy between official nationalism and marginal forms of nationalism, tinged in some cases with communalism. In a political history where the State came before the Nation, in a country where the State is held to be so entirely Kemalist, is it not possible to imagine a national option opposed to the State, or even outside the State whereby the nation would become the social basis of political protest, as is the case of the present-day religious party *Fazilet Partisi*, which is looking afresh at the concept of '*millet*'?

The Modern Nation, A Difficult Equation

Kemalism has been a foundation-laying experience in terms of nation and nationalism, not because it was the first to take an inquiring look at those concepts[7] but because it made them central to its undertaking to recover independence and restore sovereignty, on which basis it has constructed a long-term political project in a republican framework. The idea, developed by Bernard Lewis, of the invention of a fatherland seems fairly accurate,[8] since it was proceeding from a particular set of circumstances - territorial, social and political redefinition - that Mustafa Kemal gave an inspirational lead to a pragmatic movement of nation-building wherein the idea of the Turkish Nation stemmed first from the affirmation thereof; anything that had even the slightest federating effect was subsequently added on in order to create a national awareness[9] on the basis of a shared existence. However, the Kemalist revolution also introduced certain complications: on the one hand, several disparate, even fragmentary 'national' or 'nationalist' aspects came together within the various phases of its concentrated development; on the other hand, the revolution both positioned itself in a historical continuity (with the themes of safeguard and restoration) and presented itself as a break with history (themes of revolution and modernity), making the 'national' project's linkage with the past[10] and at the same time the future quite complex.

Hence, and this is our hypothesis, the Turkish Nation has been traversed by contradictory currents that were to be accentuated by the vagaries of political and social evolution, but the need to assert nationhood led the regime, in a shift towards authoritarianism, to focus on building State power: it then made nationalism an ideological touchstone, the metaphor of national unity. Kemalism, which subsequently became the touchstone of political legitimacy, the nationalist project that formed its backbone, ideologically as well, became the primary concern of all political regimes, whoever was in power.

(a) The Keys of National Destiny

In 1923, under the new republican regime, the Kemalist movement possessed, in the service of the Turkish Nation, several solid assets:

1. An unprecedented mobilization of the people had created a rallying point for different social strata and corporate bodies, and for specific regional, linguistic and even ethnic elements (women and men being mobilized in equal measure), and came as the first demonstration of resistance and collective cohesion in the service of a common goal: national combat (*millî mücadele*) and liberation of the national territory from the presence of foreign troops;
2. Victory and independence constituted a firm basis for the construction of a 'national' future;[11] the nation had in addition a national leader who was a victor and liberator;
3. The regime controlled a territory, centred on the Anatolian plateau, that had, from that time on, an almost definitive configuration, the border with Iraq being established in 1925 and that with Syria in 1939;
4. The Lausanne international conference and Treaty (24 July 1923) sanctioning the Kemalist victory were an endorsement of the restoration of Turkish sovereignty and of the introduction of the new State into the international community;
5. Emerging at a very early stage, representative democratic institutions adumbrated the new political structure of the country, helped in establishing the credibility that the Kemalist rebellion rapidly enjoyed, and introduced a mode of political legitimization: the Grand

National Assembly gave the Turkish Nation a concrete existence and a voice, placed at the service of the popular will.[12]

(b) Diversity of National Referents

Nevertheless, the territorial configuration that the nation ended up with bore no directly historical character; it was initially a territory defined by default,[13] the fortuitous outcome of an unfavourable armistice. Its 'Anatolian' character was problematical because for nomadic Turks originating from eastern Asia, for whom land only has value when it has been conquered, it was not a territory of 'origin'. Anatolia was, at the very most, only a recent historical heritage, essentially Ottoman, and as late as 1920 its ownership was still highly debatable (Greek, Armenian and Kurdish demands were endorsed by the Treaty of Sèvres, August 1920).[14] It implied absolutely no linguistic, religious or, in a general sense, cultural exclusivity. Greater consistency nevertheless emerged gradually on two points at least, Turkishness and Islam (albeit it is difficult to distinguish between them), since it was gradually relieved of the problem of managing the Christian and even Arab communities, while the long decline of the Empire led to a continuous influx from the lost lands of Turkish or Muslim populations who rejected any other national identity. During the Kemalist episode, this represented an undeniable bastion of resistance which, from East to West, with many local uprisings[15] acted as a solid base for the 'national' uprising (National Pact of April 1920).

Nor was the Turkish language, which was subsequently to become so important, an obvious vector of nationhood. Although, like many other languages, it had withstood the penetration of Islam, it was not officially invested with religious or cultural legitimacy (the language of government, for instance, was peppered with Persian loan-words), and its transcription in Arabic characters was a source of confusion (Lewis, 1998). There also existed a demotic language (a further dimension of the 'Anatolian' phenomenon) out of range of foreign influences and the pretensions of the Ottoman court; it was intimately linked to popular resistance movements going back to the thirteenth century and bore the imprint of the popular Islam of the brotherhoods.

The Nation was itself a tangled web of references. To begin with, nationalism was synonymous with the gradual split-up of the Empire, which was receiving a battering from non-Muslim 'nationalities' confident in their territories, languages and cultural identities. An initial riposte was primarily 'Ottoman', intended as much to come to terms, as was necessary, with modernity as to define a specific imperial identity capable of adjusting to changing times. In fact, the 'Ottoman' nation emerged as 'Islamic', an outcome emphasized, with defeat in the Russo-Turkish War of 1876-1878, by the refocusing of Ottoman power towards the Middle East - which enabled Abdül Hamid II to develop his pan-Islamism, but also ran up against the prevailing tendency to lay blame on Islam as a generic factor in Oriental decline. Although nineteenth-century European historians such as Léon Cahun and Vambery drew attention to the existence of an ancient, victorious Turkish civilization with a written language (the Orkhon inscriptions), it was only in the early twentieth century that a 'Turkist' version, based on ethnicity and religion, emerged in Russia in resistance to Tsarist designs, reached Turkey and took hold at a time when the Empire, was looking on powerless as its own Muslim possessions seceded. Turkism therefore emerggd, between an equally suspect East and West, as a new synthesis capable of assimilating both modernity and Islam,[16] and of leading on to the Nation-State, a prospect that was gradually gaining ground in people's minds. According to Ziya Gökalp, a Kurd from Diyarbakir and a leading ideologist of Turkish nationalism, it involved modernization through a social revolution which, on the basis of certain values, was to produce a new national awareness, an idea that Mustafa Kemal would pick up at a later date.

(c) Contradictory Processes

While the reality of this national sovereignty posed no problem, there remained the question of its content. We know that the essence of the Kemalist project was to set in motion a process of modernization such as would guarantee the country's definitive independence, building upon the changes to create a leading structure. Did it create a new nation *ex nihilo*, or did it safeguard certain older values, translated into the terms of a generic national discourse?[17]

It is first of all difficult to distinguish between the logic of restoring a former condition and that of breaking with it. At the national mobilization stage, Mustafa Kemal advocated the re-establishment of sovereignty in terms of authority freed from foreign interference and reinstated in all its attributes, in this case dynastic and religious. When he called upon the people to unite against the foreign enemy, he was appealing to individual or collective interests and values rooted deeply enough in them for them to rise up; in that respect, the present came to the aid of an endangered past. However, his determination to break with the past also implied the birth of a new State, cut off from its historic base (thus, the writing system was reformed in 1928) to construct something new that would no longer have the weaknesses inherent in the old political organization. The national synthesis had to be 'balanced' but able to provide itself with new foundations, and the introduction of the 'Turkish' reference was part of that newness.

The difficulty of defining a nation also stems from the fact that the modernizing process dissociates the present from the future, in as much as the justification for present policy hinges on a change whose constituent parts are neither known nor accepted, except in the discourse of modernizers themselves. Such hypothetical legitimization apart, this also means that traditional social determinants, such as ways of life or cultural references, are judged to be insufficiently relevant and inherently weak, and need to be abandoned. Individuals are asked to give up their current values and social practices, having paid that price they will be worthy of becoming the future citizens of the emergent 'nation'. But how was the 'popular' dimension of the national will to be articulated in the absence of genuine Turkish or Anatolian ethnic and cultural considerations? Modernization entails a denigration of social continuity - whereas social continuity is central to the popular dimension - and it builds a future 'nation' that no longer has anything to do with the present nation.

Another source of discontinuity was the fact that the criterion for modernization was the West, but the West was also the source of the Ottoman decline, the barometer of its backwardness and the cause of its loss of identity; more specifically, it was behind the partition which was decided by the Treaty of Sèvres and which gave rise to the national Kemalist mobilization. There is, then, an ambiguity in seeing the same concept signifying, in practical terms, the loss of independence, and at the same time the prior condition for the recovery of independence through the acquisition of a culture of progress and a resultant return to parity with strong countries. It was therefore necessary to manage, simultaneously, the opening of one chapter and the closing of another, and also to explain to the ignorant masses what was going on. Furthermore, the West mobilized another dimension of nationalism, the relationship between 'us' and 'the other'; but in a climate of change 'our' side finds itself without values with which to counter 'the other'.

(d) The Three Faces of Kemalist Nationalism

The three components of the Kemalist experience, national independence, nation-building and then national unity, confirming the legitimacy of the State, condense certain contradictory ideas whilst declaring them cumulatively legitimate, all in a very brief period of time.

From 1919 to 1923, when 'the people' was in fact the only tangible national reality, the independence movement surged ahead on the basis of a form of popular mobilization that was without any restrictive ethnic, linguistic or local criteria (something later held against Kemalism by the Kurds), that encompassed the broadest social plurality, recognized all the elements making up its diversity, excluding none, and accepted *a priori* the values and traditions in the name of which the people was ready to rise up (as witness the many appeals of the Kemalist rebellion to the safeguarding of Islam). It was the genius of Mustafa Kemal to bestow the name of 'national interest' on the sum of all the individual interests, and give them, through the creation of a rebel National Assembly in 1920, a central representative body, entrusted with expressing the popular will and making it the national will, thus enabling it to obtain exclusive representation at the Lausanne talks.

From 1923 to 1930, nation building proceeded differently: with modernization as its determining factor, it aimed to shift the points of reference towards the acquisition of more modern determinants, with a greater potential for independence. Within the idea of a new cohesion, however, this phenomenon still takes the social body into account since, even while undergoing change, it remains the ultimate intended beneficiary of modernization and hence of the potential for autonomy.[18] It should nevertheless be noted that this experiment in nation building was disrupted by the Kurdish revolt of 1925, which represented popular resistance on two levels, ethnic and religious, and that even then the regime's response to this danger was coercion, in the form of martial law. Even so, the need for partnership between modernization and social evolution nonetheless remained evident, and presided over the relaunching of the democratic process and the recognition of an opposition political party in 1930.[19]

However, the failure that put an end to this second attempt - the new party falling hostage to a religious protest which could not be contained - brought nationalism to a turning point and faced it with a choice between respecting social values and saving the modernization project. Thereafter, the political process was tightened up, the social body, wherein the seeds of resistance were to be found, was marginalized (thus halting the mechanism of representativity) and established political control was put in place at every level (single-party rule, primacy of the party over governmental action, party networks set up alongside the institutions of local government). The 'emergent nation' was soon reduced to the State and to those *milieux* (urban elites, civil servants and the military) that gravitated around it. From then on, nationalism, as an ideological discourse, was aimed at consolidating national unity,[20] for which purpose all the symbols were now needed: anthems, flag, parades, watchwords and slogans, the most famous of which being *ne mutlu türküm diyene*, 'Happy is he who can say: I am a Turk!', and which definitely effaced particularisms and specificities. That led to some oddities such as the *Theses of History* (1930) and the theory of the *Sun Language* (1936),[21] which claimed a prehistoric ancestry for the Turkish language and civilization which, through certain migrations, were supposed to have given birth to most of the world's civilizations and left their mark upon their languages. Thus, the Anatolian civilizations were found to have had Turk ancestors. That way, national unity meant enlisting support from a past that was not recent but 'anterior'.

The Nation, An Affair of State

The 'nationalist' mix described above remained controllable as long as it was in the hands of a single political authority capable of keeping it on course. In the democratic process inaugurated by the introduction of multiparty politics in 1946, however, it resulted in the adoption of competing standpoints which, though they still claimed to be nationalist and were consequently 'legitimate', albeit in a sense that could be adapted to individual interests, in fact diverged from one another as to the conception of the nation. The apologists of official Kemalist nationalism, for instance, were increasingly obliged to dissociate themselves from a nationalism that might appear racist, aggressive, totalitarian-fascist, chauvinist or theocratic (Feyzioglu, 1987, p. 44).

Inevitably, a latent but major conflict arose between the diversification of political competition, a move that was proclaimed to be irreversible, and the idea of national unity. If political life tends to be based on social pluralism, this leaves open the risk of a break-up of the national community, fatal in the event of attack.[22] It places the division and opposition of interests above national union. In this respect, Nation and Kemalism are so closely identified that the 1961 Constitution, followed by that of 1982, declared certain of the major Kemalist reforms of the 1920s and 1930s unrepealable.

The system seems to have settled into alternating phases where, on the one hand, political competition releases centrifugal tendencies that, on the other hand, national 'concern' takes it upon itself to bring back into line, willingly or by force (the successive military coups of 1960, 1971 and 1980, and the milder version of 1997), in a mobilization of support for the great national causes or at the instigation of an overtly nationalist political line. Tension in the system increases all the more since political diversification always runs up against the power of a State that acts on the pretext of safeguarding the nation.

In fact, antagonism in relation to the Nation had three main aspects: firstly, the promotion of Kemalism with the status of an ideology, as an instrument of the State bureaucracy, then as a factor generating a supra-political authority responsible for controlling the political system by referring back to the 'sources' of the national experience; growing political competition, due both to the 'supply' of multiparty politics that was made available, and to the diversification of a demand that was encouraged by the redistribution resulting from the economic progress occurring throughout this period; lastly, resulting from this antagonism, the challenging of the idea of the State as the central embodiment of a nation that does not necessarily want to define itself in such terms.

(a) The Test: The Alternation of the Parties in Power, 1950-1960

The establishment of multiparty politics meant that the era of the single party system was called into question and its achievements subjected to criticism. The struggle for power that was now institutionalized was based on a new type of mobilization of the electorate and on a platform of freedoms recovered. In order to win power in 1950, the Democratic Party in fact took the idea of national unity apart, demonstrating that a section of society had been marginalized by the Kemalist regime for having opinions judged not to be in conformity with modernization, and that the regime itself was selective. To recruit an electorate, it of course paid lip service to all the themes of political resistance, foremost among them the return to religion and traditional ways of life, but also economic liberalism. Now, a party-based nation found itself facing a society-based nation with known characteristics (Adnan Menderes' slogan was '*Artik, yeter, söz milletindir!*', or 'Enough, now let the Nation speak!', and it is often used today, by the present religious party among others). In fact, the success of the 'democratic' challenge was even more impressive because it was late in materializing (1946, proclamation of multiparty politics, May 1950, election of the Democrats to power) and had plenty of time to develop its campaign themes.

It would be misleading to say that the Democratic regime took the opposite tack to Kemalist modernization, since it was during this period that the actual process of attaching the country firmly to the West began, through the Marshall Plan (1948), the Atlantic Alliance (1952) and the first contacts with the European Economic Community (1958), which changed daily life in the country - giving a boost to the economy (agricultural mechanization, industrialization), and leading to the growth of an urban bourgeoisie, and to new cultural and intellectual references - and paved the way for capitalism and the foreign presence in the country while also beginning a process of distributing the benefits of this economic effort. It was not so much the political category (republican regime, political rationality and secularization) that posed a problem for the old elites who were removed from power, as the fact that the very foundations of political legitimacy were changing profoundly and were linked with a social transformation that they no longer controlled and which was foreign to their authoritarian and Statist outlook.

That is why the political response of 1960 - a military coup followed by an overhaul of the Constitution - which signalled the return of the sections of society (the armed forces, civil servants and teachers) formerly cosseted by Kemalism presented itself as coming to the rescue of national unity,[23] defined by reference to the original Kemalist republican master plan.

(b) Political Participation, 1960-1980

The period starting with the '1960 revolution' is special in two respects. First, it meant an increase in the power exercized by the State in the name of the nation and it established greater institutional control over the regime's main ideological options (the management of religious affairs, for instance, was integrated into public administration in 1965). Of the six principles of Kemalism written into the Constitution in 1937, the new text retained two, nationalism and secularism, and set itself the task of strengthening their impact (Hirsch, 1966). At the same time, the revolution proceeded to mobilize the 'modernist' elites (autonomy for the universities and for radio and television, rapid development of trade unions) in order to control a political force already suspected of deviancy and hence of abandoning the national perspective. Two conflicting processes were therefore set in motion: firstly, the referents of the national dimension were clearly circumscribed in order to be submitted to a single decision-making process; secondly, political participation was extended so as to obtain the broadest possible support for the said national dimension. In other words, new tutelary authorities and the energies of the nation were mobilized together, through institutional provisions, to back up the political authorities.

The two processes soon began to function in opposition, all the sooner because the increase in political 'supply' was inversely proportional to the restriction of the legal framework within which it could be expressed. The period was marked by an increase in, and greater diversification of, the parties. With the post-coup 1965 elections a political repositioning occurred, the first surprise being the return to power of the heirs of Menderes, the very person who had provoked the intervention of 27 May 1960. First there appeared a centre-right majority tendency which was thus not directly Kemalist (Süleyman Demirel, now President of the Republic). At the same time there was a repositioning of the Kemalist Turkish 'left of centre' left (emergence of Bülent Ecevit, now Prime Minister) with the eviction of the Kemalist old guard (Ismet Inönü). New currents representing new demands also emerged, such as the Marxist-inspired Workers' Party of Turkey (*Türkiye Isci Partisi*), acting directly under the banner of class division; such as the Kurdish movements whose demands were couched in cultural terms and who also used Marxist-linked arguments;[24] and as the Anatolian challenge to Kemalist modernization, which advanced the viewpoint of the provincial petit bourgeoisie (*esnaf*, shopkeepers and artisans) and shifted in a religious direction under the leadership of N. Erbakan (only recently - June 1996 to 1997, Prime Minster, stripped of his political rights in January 1998).[25] We must include in this picture the emergence of a specifically 'nationalist' trend,[26] half-way between pan-Turkism and national exclusivity, which was not averse to draping itself, if need be, in the colours of Islam (rise to prominence of Alparslan Türkes, who died in March 1997, and whose party made a breakthrough in the elections of April 1999).

From the 1960s onwards, there was very strong political competition which, owing to the narrow limits of the 'legal' political arena, rapidly spilled over into a radicalism fed by the anti-imperialist and anti-American feeling that was fairly common at the time.[27]

A further political response to this 'drift' was the coup of March 1971, which put civilian politics on hold until the end of 1973, and whose main chosen line of action was to restrict the liberal provisions of the 1960 Constitution while inserting a reference to 'safeguarding the integrity of the State with its territory and its nation'. Generally speaking, the 1970s were marked by a profound crisis, that of distrust between the two major partners, State and society. From 1973, the State, through its governmental components, was manifestly unable to ensure a minimum of political stability for its actions, and wasted its energy in unviable coalitions. These structural uncertainties affected every level, right up to the Presidency. Very onerous political choices, such as the two Turkish military operations in Cyprus in the summer of 1974, meanwhile precipitated total diplomatic, political and strategic isolation. The combined effects of the oil crisis and the suspension of economic aid from the country's traditional partners, in particular the EU, coming on top of these developments, brought the Turkish economy to the verge of bankruptcy. In a state of disorientation, society's reactions increasingly ignored the framework of the law and were soon caught up in a spiral of terrorism. From the end of 1978 - the time of the Kahramanmaras massacre of Alevi by militant nationalists - terrorism became a lasting feature of the political landscape, scarcely counter-balanced by the declaration of martial law (1979) that neither the government, nor parliament nor the army itself had the means of enforcing. Blind terror turned what had been differences of opinion into irreversible and implacable antagonisms. The 'national' community came apart under the pressure of ethnic, religious, economic, social and political resentment.

(c) The Democratization Process after 1980

The gravity of the crisis, or at least the way it was perceived by the authorities responsible for the *coup d'état* of September 1980, is reflected in the preamble to the 1982 Constitution, which refers to 'a time when the approach of a ... bloody civil war unprecedented in the Republican era threatened the integrity of the eternal Turkish Nation and Motherland ...'. At the time of the *coup d'état*, it was not only repression that was on the agenda; the armed forces wanted to re-establish as fast as possible, in a context of economic, political and institutional bankruptcy, a minimal social and political consensus, whilst re-examining the weak points of the political system and its ideological underpinning, Kemalist nationalism.[28] How had 'imported' ideologies managed to supplant a nationalist credo that had been powerfully inculcated, and to divide a society in which all State institutions had always denied the existence of economic, ethnic and cultural divisions?

With the 1980 coup, there began a process of the confiscation of politics by a military authority which had become the last bastion of the national reference[29] and which in order to save it, stifled - by an intervention that was, despite everything, popular - all forms of political expression: parliament, political parties and trade unions alike.

In 1983, on the forcible return to a civilian regime, an interesting relationship was henceforth established between the 'political' domain set aside for the armed forces whereby, in a much-vaunted 'Turko-Islamic synthesis', precedence was given to the ideological restoration of national cohesion (which now entailed the incorporation of religion into republican values[30] and to a freedom of 'economic' initiative, left to the new civilian government of Turgut Özal, on condition that it mobilize national capacities in a manner that was not susceptible of being politicized. Even more interesting are the consequences of this division of tasks: it firstly accelerated the process of opening up the Turkish economy to the world market, encouraging it not only to dismantle the last bastions of Kemalist statism and to transcend 'national' borders, but also to become in itself a political point of reference of a new type. It also accelerated a social change that would soon affect every section of society, precipitate the exodus from the countryside to the outskirts of the cities, and lead to a remarkable redistribution of the electorate according to social difficulties; lastly, and most unexpectedly, it set off a 'civilian' reversal of the ban on politics, firstly by way of the search for a new political actor to set against the power of the State (i.e. the social body), and then by the beginnings of a democratization process.

Since then there have been two factors determining politics in Turkey: on the one side is a 'higher' political will responsible for the national destiny, fundamentally statist, distrustful of democratic representation and civilian governments and justifying control over political life by various means, including a National Security Council (what Islamists today call the 'deep State' - *derin devlet*). This increasingly ideological dimension clings to Kemalist principles as to a means of safeguard; it operates from the position of the 'State in danger', for which purpose it mobilizes - overstepping legal rules if necessary - all the means needed to ensure its 'security'. The difficult handling of the Kurdish question has given it redoubled power; in addition, it is the focus for increasingly numerous social demands, as was reflected in the recent elections (April 1999) when a much younger electorate voted for the 'national winners', first of all Bülent Ecevit who, having been behind the Turkish landing in Cyprus in 1974, also had Abdullah Öcalan arrested and then the National Movement Party, a major plank in whose platform related to the severity of the punishment to be inflicted to Öcalan.

On the other side is a new political approach, couched in terms of human rights, freedoms, democracy and civil society, that is trying to impose new criteria. As in the previous case, the State is central to its concerns, but the State viewed from a critical angle, critical of its inability to manage the natural plurality of Turkish society and to cope with the dividing lines between ethnic groups, beliefs and levels of development; a State which, while tending to produce uniformity and simplification, also produces marginalization and violence, lawlessness and terrorism, a State whose unavoidable centrality exacerbates the politicization of social conflict, that transforms any social demand into a political struggle 'verticalized' by the attempt to get the backing of the State. The seminal idea that then emerges is that of basing the political system on a re-established equilibrium where, with the introduction of the social body as the new fully-fledged political actor, the State would no longer play the lead role in the political process, but would see its decision-making overseen by means of the active participation of citizens in political choices (decision-making and implementation), the implication being that the expression of plurality becomes a basis of political coherence and stability.[31] It should be noted that this critique of the State implies a challenge to the formal democracy that has been a feature of the Turkish republican regime since its beginnings, but which has led all too often to a 'delegation' of power rather than to 'representation'.

Thus, there is latent confrontation over the question of the State, a question kept on the agenda of each of the camps - albeit with differing interpretations - by the crisis in the political system, the impossibility of basing a government on a stable majority, the involvement by organized crime in State action, and above all the deterioration of the Kurdish question since 1984; but that confrontation never manages to express itself since the political parties, which are still the main sensors of political demand, in fact end up aligning themselves with the yardstick of State centralism from which they then derive their authority.

The Turkish Nation, with its obviously plural composition, is stuck between its traditional style of political culture and the need to put its trust in democracy in order to expand the framework of its political evolution - with the attendant risk, for many people and above all for the establishment, of damage to or even dismantling of the complex framework of its 'national' ideological dimension. Conversely, in a political competition of increasingly uncertain outcome (in 1995 the winning party obtained 21.7% of the votes, and in 1999 Ecevit's party won control of the government with 23% of the vote), political demand, inclined towards diversifying, can exploit the claims of reconstituted nationalisms, which it then sets up, with its arguments, in opposition to the power of the State.

Conclusion

Turkish nationalism, with its complex superimposition of ancient strata, is a phenomenon so closely linked to the political formation of the Turkish State that it seems to be its protective matrix, from which it is impossible to extricate oneself, and which it is unthinkable, for anyone who would lay claim to a public role, to renounce. It is in any case expressing a positive value to declare oneself 'nationalist'. At the same time, like a political evolution that takes on global dimensions, the permanence of an authoritarian political regime appears at times to be unbearable, and nationalism, which provide its ongoing justification, suffers from the calling into question of the political system, or indeed the realization of its inadequacies.

Paradoxically, it is thus indirectly, more through its employment as an ideology and a discourse than for what it represents directly, that nationalism is today the subject of criticism.

Notes

1 Gökalp, A. (1994), 'Les Alevî', in S. Yerasimos, *Les Turcs*, Autrement, Paris.
2 Recurrence of Kurdish revolts against the republican regime since 1920 and considerable Islamic resistance to each advance of Kemalist secularization since 1923.
3 Vorhoff, K. (1995), *Zwischen Glaube, Nation und Neuer Gemeinschaft, Alevitische Identität in der Türkei der Gegenwart*, K. Schwarz Verlag, Berlin, p. 158 *et seq.*
4 At the elections on 18 April 1999, the nationalist party unexpectedly came second with 18% of the vote; one of its campaigning planks was to demand the death sentence for Abdullah Öcalan, leader of the Kurdish Workers' Party (PKK).
5 Feyzioglu, T. (1987), *Atatürk ve Milliyetçilik*, TTK, Ankara, p. 8.
6 Bozarslan, H. (1997), *La Question Kurde*, Presse de Sciences Po, Paris, p. 97.
7 Berkes, N. (1994), *The Development of Secularism in Turkey*, McGill University, Montreal, p. 313 *et seq.*
8 Lewis, B. (1998), *Islam et Laïcité*, Fayard, Paris, p. 308.
9 A national framework is defined more from a community of destiny (*Schicksalgemeinschaft*) captured in a specific moment than through a bundle of historical logic. See Hirsch, E. (1966), *Die Verfassung der Türkischen Republik*, A. Metzener Verlag, Frankfurt, p. 81.
10 See Hobsbawm, E. (1992), *Nations and Nationalism since 1780*, Cambridge University Press.
11 Article I of the Constitutional Law of 1921 (revised in 1923): Sovereignty belongs without reserve or condition to the Nation. Its government is a republic. The administration of the State rests on the principle that the people takes in hand and guides its destiny itself.
12 1924 Constitution, Article 4: the Great Assembly of Turkey alone genuinely represents the Nation and in its name holds the right of sovereignty.
13 'All the parts of the Turkish territory included within the frontier drawn up by the armistice signed on 30 October 1334 (1918) between the Turkish Government and the Allies and inhabited by an overwhelmingly Turkish population form an indivisible whole. All the Muslim elements living in the aforementioned territories are full of mutual feelings of respect and devotion and form a veritable fraternity', Article 1 of the decisions of the Congress of Siva (first congress of the 'nationalist' rebellion, September 1919) in Georges-Gaulis, B. (1931), *La Question Turque*, Berger-Levrault, Paris, p. 15.
14 Yerasimos, S. (1991) 'Les Kurdes et le Partage du Moyen-Orient, 1918-1926', in E. Picard (dir.), *La Question Kurde*, Ed. Complexe, Paris, pp. 19-36.
15 Oran, B. (1997), *Atatürk Milliyetçiligi*, Bilgi Yay, Istanbul, 4th ed., pp. 71-2.

16   Georgeon, F. (1980), *Aux Origines du Nationalisme Turc*, Ed. ADPF, Paris.

17   'But our enemies believed that, with the Ottoman Empire, the Turkish Nation had been destroyed. Well, they were fundamentally wrong about that. The Turkish Nation that had founded many States before the Ottoman State, could not be destroyed (...). Therefore as of now our nation has entered a genuinely national era', Mustafa Kemal quoted by Eyüboglu, Ercan, 'Discours inaugural de Mustafa Kemal au 'Congrès Économique de Turquie', Izmir, 1923: Justesse et/ou Justification d'un Choix', *Anatolia Moderna* (5), Maisonneuve, Paris.

18   It is under this heading that we place the major innovations introduced by the Kemalist regime in terms of citizenship, law, civil status (complete overhaul of the civil and penal codes in 1926), the practice of electoral suffrage including its extension to women in 1930, education, social secularization (laws on clothes, European time, patronymics, weekly rest, declaration of secularism as constitutional in 1937) and also the renewed will to create currents of opinion and autonomous initiatives (Economic Congress of Izmir in 1923, existence of the Progressive Republican Party in 1924 and launch of the Liberal Party in 1930, to which we will return). Cf.: Groc, G. (1997), 'La Laïcité Turque' in A. Mahiou, *L'Etat de Droit dans le Monde Arabe*, CNRS Editions, Paris, pp. 175-203.

19   Weiker, W. (1973), *Political Tutelage and Democracy in Turkey*, Brill, Leiden.

20   1937 revision of Article 2 of the 1924 Constitution: The Turkish State is republican, nationalist, populist, statist, secular and revolutionary (/reformist).

21   Copeaux, E. (1997), *Espace et Temps de la Nation Turque*, CNRS Editions, Paris, p. 58 *et seq.*

22   'Most conspicuous among those who deny that Kemalism is an ideology are those who would like to create an ideological vacuum in Turkish society, which they would then fill with various out-of-date, alien and despotic totalitarian ideologies of right or left', Giritili, I. (1984), 'Kemalism as an Ideology of Modernisation', *Atatürk and Modern Turkey*, Landau, Jacob ed. Leiden, Brill, p. 252.

23   'The Turkish Nation carried out its revolution on 27 May 1960 by exercizing its right to oppose an authority that had lost its legitimacy by its conduct and its unlawful and unconstitutional actions; moved and inspired by the Turkish nationalism that unites all individuals joined in their fate, their joy and their pain around the national awareness and national ideal in an indivisible whole having the constant aim of raising our nation in a spirit of national unity as an honourable and equal member of the world family nations ...' (Preamble to the 1961 Constitution).

24   Bozarslan, H. (1986), *Le Problème National Kurde en Turquie Kémaliste*, EHESS These.

25   Agaogullari, M.A. (1982), *L'Islam dans la Vie Politique Turque*, Pub. Sciences Politiques, Ankara.

26   Landau, J. (1981), *Pan-Turkism in Turkey, a Study of Irredentism*, Hurst, London.

27   Oehring, O. (1984), *Die Türkei im Spannungsfeld extremer Ideologien (1973-1980)*, K. Schwarz Verlag, Berlin.

28   W. Hale, Military rule and political change in Turkey 1980-1984 in A. Gökalp, (1986), *La Turquie en Transition*, Maisonneuve, Paris, pp. 156-76.

29   Heper, M. (1985), *The State Tradition in Turkey*, Eothen Press, Beverly, see the chapter 'Resurrection of a Partially Transcendental State', p. 124 *et seq.*

30   In this set-up, Islam acquires the value of being an element in the recomposition of the
      sociological landscape with, in replacement of the urban elites, too often the cause of
      political explosions, the rehabilitation of conservative forces which have remained
      loyal to a traditional way of life, with the idea of making them the new actors in a
      calmer political development.
31   Groc, G. (1998), 'La Société Civile Turque entre Politique et Individu', *Cemoti* (26),
      pp. 43-74.

13 Between Mimesis and Rebellion: The Vicissitudes of Romanian Nationalism

CATHERINE DURANDIN

Introduction

Romania is a young nation-state which has been independent since 1878. But its national political culture took shape before that date, taking its bearings from the Enlightenment in the Habsburg empire during the eighteenth century and from contacts with the Romantic movement in the West in the years before the popular uprisings of spring 1848. This was the backcloth against which the national identity was forged. Groups who relayed the message of this identity wove the Romanian national dynamic into the vast and changing tapestry of central Europe. The issues revolve around the question of origins, and bring into play concepts such as people/ethnic group, territory and language. The process of constructing a national memory involved anxious questionings about discontinuity in the history of the State, a young modern State whose genesis, since the achievement of independence in 1878, successive political regimes have sought to locate in a very distant past, the Dacian era. In the absence of a memory of past glories, the same process made much of victimization as part of the country's destiny. In the case of Romania the national question is based on a quest for normality, i.e. sovereignty and synchronization of development with the model, a Western model compounded of fiction and stereotype. Nationalism oscillates between singularity and similarity, it is a quest for alterity in conformity.

259

Each democratic nation is distinctive. But characteristic of all nations is a tension between a quest for a formal, abstract rationale of citizenship, which is of a legal and political order, and every society's need to establish a social bond between citizens which is perforce of a 'community' or 'ethnic' type, in other words direct and emotional (Schnapper, 1996, p. 316).

Nationalist Tensions in Romania

On the basis of a straightforward chronological account of the history of Romanian political thinking, one might jump to the conclusion that nationalism in Romania has been a continuous phenomenon. The propagators of nationalism have differed, interests and causes have evolved, but there has been little change in the overall content of the message. In schematic terms it would be possible to chart a course that is Herderian, Romantic, ethnicist, Orthodox, national communist and post-communist nationalist. Herderian, Romantic nationalism coincided with the Nation-State's accession to independence and sovereignty between 1848 and 1878; ethnicist, Orthodox nationalism encouraged the self-assertiveness of this small nation whose development lagged behind that of the West, which was perceived as hegemonic in the inter-war period; national communism encouraged the integration of the masses into the Party-State, and post-communist nationalism seems to wish to express and safeguard distinctiveness in a world threatened by standardizing globalization originating from faraway in the West. It would be easy to define a relatively stable corpus of significant themes and a historical and geographical area regarded as the sacred home of Romanity: any amputation of this area tears apart and supposedly inflicts suffering on the national community. This is a comfortable approach and reasons can be adduced to support it, but it leaves in abeyance a central question: the reasons for the upsurges of nationalism giving rise to cultural commitments and political choices; the reasons why today in 1997, for example, there should be a sudden relaxation of tensions and crises hitherto regarded as insoluble and based on a kind of historical inevitability. Within a matter of months, between September 1996 and May 1997, Bucharest signed two treaties to improve neighbourly relations, one with Hungary, the other with Ukraine. These are regarded by some people as a repudiation of the national cause and by others as a restatement of it. Has there really been a sudden breakthrough into a post-national era, and if so why? What factors make it possible to understand the superseding or at least soft-pedalling of national causes and the consequent historicizing of the national idea? Our approach is historical and endeavours to understand the function of Nationality during the long process which saw the emergence of the sovereign State and the independent Nation. What collective passions has the national idea served and nurtured? How is the self-image of present-day Romania being reshaped now that communism is a thing of the past and the country has decided to seek recognition of its rights to Euro-Atlantic integration?

Imported Nationalism and Distorted Identity

When it first emerged as a politico-cultural programme, modern Romanian nationalism was a product of avowedly Westernized elites. The Romantic generation broke with the past and rebelled against its fathers, their oriental life-styles and their provincial mentalities. The Balkans opened up to a form of Westernization which brought with it a new vision of time, an idea of the march of progress, questions about status, an anxious concern for memory and a determination to use memory to shape a coherent picture of the future (Durandin, 1994 and Hitchins, 1985). In Romania the generation of 1848 was imbued with French Romantic culture, the late Romanticism of the 1840s which blended the legacy of 1789 and an interpretation of Herder's work *Outlines of a Philosophy of the History of Man*, which Edgar Quinet had translated and prefaced in 1827. This culture was acquired in France through direct contact with intellectual leaders such as Jules Michelet and Edgar Quinet and in the Paris salons open to Polish exiles and the Russian opponents of Tsar Nicolas II. It developed alongside European - especially Polish and Italian - nationalist movements. This was a heady time, for these travellers felt a sense of glory acquired in the rebellion against oriental despotism, whether Russian or Ottoman; it was also an anxious time, for the police of the Second Empire were soon exercising close surveillance. The Romanian activists were strongly drawn to Poland as the torchbearer of a shared anti-Russianism and to Italy as a Latin sister with whom they could look back to a shared Roman antiquity. The nation which emerged from this process, in the publications, reviews, and political projects of the 1840s, was Daco-Roman in origin, and in the sense that it was a nation of peasants and warriors it was close to the

French patriotic ideal of Michelet. Daco-Romanism first emerged from investigations by the Transylvanian School supported by the Vienna court in the second half of the eighteenth century, which protected the high dignitaries of the Uniate church. The nation was also regarded as a victim. The theme of the wretchedness of nations rediscovering themselves but deprived of statehood is a recurrent one among the peoples which experienced Ottoman and Habsburg domination. It was conducive to an idealization of the people and a misappreciation of politics, which in the long run was to be a handicap. So history passed Romania by, it was 'forgotten' and repressed for centuries by imperial domination. Misfortune came from the East: it was the result of the Ottoman conquest and the consequent vassalization of the Principalities, and was inseparable from Russian despotism, whose shadow fell heavily on the Principalities. The nation was victimized and treated unjustly. The idea of a wrong inflicted on the Romanians by history is a factor in the construction of modern Romanian nationalism - an active wrong perpetrated by empires. In the twentieth century, the offenders have been the Great Powers, the United States and the USSR. The West Europeans in Paris and London who failed to look to the eastern confines of Europe and did not register how far their own salvation might have depended on the Romanians' anti-Ottoman crusade were guilty of a sin of omission. The correspondence between Jules Michelet and one of his pupils, Dumitru Bratianu, sheds much light on the recrimination and reproach directed at France. The future lay in the conquest of independence, with elites looking towards the people, a people of idealized peasants, and a restoration of the Westerness which is the essence of Romanity and which derives its justification from the significance attached to the Latin origin of the Romanians. The relevance of this national theme is grounded in a demonstration of the continuity of Romanian occupation of the territory that was once Dacia. This need for an ancestral territory and for a long-term attachment to the soil influenced identification of the enemy as the Hungarian who contests the continuity of Romanian occupation of Dacia (Durandin, 1995). At the outset of Romania's quest for identity, there was thus an enemy, soon to become hereditary - the Hungarian - and a geopolitical threat - that of the empire, of Russian power.

These themes were used to support the arguments of the men who made Greater Romania in 1919 and the exponents of nationalism in the inter-war period. Emil Cioran's book, *The Transfiguration of Romania*, first published in 1936 (Cioran, 1993) is emblematic of the violence engendered in a competitive relationship by a combination of self-hatred and hatred of the Other. The first chapter of the book is entitled 'the tragedy of small cultures'. The same sense of threat recurred in the final speeches of the Romanian Head of State, at bay in December 1989, when he denounced those who had triggered the Timisoara rising of 17 December. Faithful to this obsessional view of an encircled Romania, Ceausescu was here returning to the theme of a plot jointly hatched in West and East.

These ideas inspired the political action of the men of 1848 who launched an abortive attempt at revolution, first in Moldavia, then in Wallachia. This revolution was crushed by the Russian and Ottoman armies and did not gain a footing in Transylvania because an agreement was not made until the last minute between Hungarian Jacobin revolutionaries and Romanian insurgents. The nation proclaimed in 1848 was patriotic, democratic and resolutely modern, i.e. in line with models developed in France during the 1848 revolution. The Romanian students' club in Paris enjoyed the patronage of Lamartine, minister of Foreign Affairs in the provisional government. The model was definitely imported, and there was awareness of this fact, i.e. of the difficulty of getting the peasants to conform to the identity and role earmarked for them by the militants. The peasant, who is associated with the idea of durability, is a good subject for History but a handicap in political terms. In other words the committed intellectuals of 1848 lacked a public and an audience on the spot, and argued their case for independence before foreign Powers. This displacement of the struggle was of supreme importance and introduced a habit of appeal and interference, an oscillation between demand and rejection in the process of identity formation. This was the point at which there emerged a direct and enduring awareness of the discrepancy between a national ideal whereby each nation is a subject of History on equal terms and a premise of feasibility which accepts that the Nation needs to have recourse to foreigners. This being the case, it is imperative to adapt to the interplay between the Great Powers and their prospects in the European balance of power. Importing a model, places the importers in a position of weakness - they are imitators, creating a history which merely mirrors the main course of history. All the same, these importers have the means to use blackmail. If they present themselves as pupils or disciples, help is due to them. This tense dynamic has recurred throughout the long course of

Romanian relations with the outside world. Likewise, dislocations of identity have occurred because of the need to please external centres of power in order to win their support and avoid their condemnation. The pupils of Jules Michelet had read and assimilated his work 'The People', which appeared in 1846. This relationship conferred a responsibility on the Teacher (Durandin, 1995, p. 89). That part of the local identity which did not fit in with the great power vision began to be repressed, left unsaid and sidelined. The men of 1848 did not present themselves as Orthodox. They effaced this decisive ingredient of identity in the Principalities because it did not fit into the categories of European modernity. Many of them were freemasons, or close to French Masonry; it was not natural to them to bring Orthodoxy into play. Furthermore, the Orthodoxy of the great majority of Romanians tied Romania to a Byzantine Orient which conflicted with a Roman affiliation. Even today Orthodoxy - a source of pride and a burden - still influences Romania's relations with the West, and some politicians wonder whether Euro-Atlantic integration via NATO enlargement will stop at the frontiers of the Christian East. Bucharest therefore moved closer to Athens in 1997 in order to show that Orthodoxy is no hindrance to democracy. The arguments put forward by Samuel Huntington (Huntington, 1993) are very hard on the self-image of the Romanians, who refuse to accept the permanence of the boundary between underdeveloped Eastern Europe and development-oriented Central and Western Europe. The problem remains of this 'residual factor' which does not fit in with the reflection seen from outside, and brings us to the link between specificity and affiliation with the West. The fact of Orthodoxy creates another area of solidarity with Constantinople or Moscow which is not to the liking of the Westernizers.

A distortion of the central core of identity lies at the very root of Romanian independence as if after a botched process of decolonization: the men of 1848 who spoke the same anti-Russian language as the French Romantics decided in 1877 to join the great Russian cause against the Turks at a time when Russian Panslavism was going through an explosive phase. This extraordinary distortion of the rationale of the 1848 discourse and the assertion of a desire for independence set the very birth of independent Romania on an unsound basis. The desire for Westernization was checked by the alliance with Russia, and the method of organization of the Berlin Congress gave the lie to assertions of sovereignty: the Romanians were only listened to as suppliants and complainants; they played no part in the debates and negotiations, and the decisions of the Great Powers were handed down to them in the form of dictates. We have shown elsewhere how this troubling inconsistency and this recognition of the reality of dependence at the very time when the Principalities were being freed from Ottoman sovereignty came to engender a culture of resentment incorporating ideas of insular self-defence and self-sublimation. An ultra-national tradition in poetry came into being with the work of Mihai Eminescu in 1878. The process of withdrawal into an acute sense of victimization was intensified.

The nationalism which took shape with the construction of the sovereign State was incapable of standing up to the external enemy, and found an outlet by targeting itself on the internal enemy, the Other who received outside support, namely the Jew (Iancu, 1978; Moscovici, 1997; Volovici, 1995). The ingredient of exclusion was now added to those of an imported model, a cause it was inexpedient to speak of, and an impotent nationalism. Exclusion reflects a longing for an unattainable wholeness which would at the same time bring total freedom. National Romania, shackled by judgements and decisions from outside, refused to allow scrutiny by the Other. The quest for power, which could not take place at the European level, took place in a process of internal elimination. The nationalism of nascent modern Romania was thus particularly violent because it was subject to control and constraint. At the Congress of Berlin in 1878 the Great Powers, influenced by Bismarck, compelled Bucharest to modify the constitution of 1866 and confer on the Jewish population the full citizenship denied them in the 1866 document in which they were regarded as foreigners. This pressure was rejected and finally obviated: Bucharest paid in economic terms for the right not to obey Berlin's injunctions fully. Jews could be naturalized, but their applications for naturalization would have to be made on an individual basis. Between 1878 and 1919, a very small minority became Romanian citizens. Meanwhile, the Romanian government was forced to buy a bankrupt railway company and save the interests of Prussian investors. It is worth noting that where the exclusion of the Jews was concerned, the Liberals, those veterans of 1848, found themselves on the side of the most conservative elements, notably in Moldavia. An insistence on regarding the People as a People/ethnic group extraneous to the political contract set in, revealing the paradox of repressive action, which is normally carried out from a position of strength, being taken by a State weakened by its lack of representativity.

At the time of the formation of Greater Romania in 1919 the components of modern nationalism reappeared in an amplified form (Spector, 1995). In 1877 Romania did not decide to wage 'its own' war but joined the anti-Ottoman crusade of the Russians, who were intent on avenging their defeat in the Crimean War. In 1914 too, Romania did not take a decision. It entered the war on the side of the Entente in August 1916 after protracted negotiations and hesitations: where did the national interest lie? With hindsight, nationalist historiography regarded the choice of alliance with the Entente as inevitable, but in fact there was a debate and other choices were possible between 1914 and 1916 - neither an alliance with the Central Powers or neutrality - and were opted for by certain politicians and intellectuals. Finally, was the formation of Greater Romania in 1919 a response to an aspiration towards an ideal? In other words what satisfactions and frustrations were involved? The Romanian delegation was not satisfied with the frontiers drawn up by specialists and by the great powers: haggling took place. The historical-ethnic idea of the frontier took precedence. More importantly, Bucharest, which feared Hungarian revisionism on one side was confronted on the other with the most serious of threats, namely non-recognition of the Russo-Romanian frontier and of the annexation of Bessarabia to the old kingdom. Bolshevik expansionism fuelled Romanian fears of a Russo-Soviet threat. The 1919 period again showed Bucharest's failure to adjust to a new European and international order, which was absolutely rejected. The order was rejected because it was imposed from above: it was the French and American Presidents who laid down the law and decided in its name. The negotiating positions of Wilson and Clemenceau were profoundly different and the trade-off of American and French interests undermined the legitimacy and credibility of the new order from its very inception (Durandin, 1994). The Europeanized elites felt they were being used like pawns on a chessboard over which they had no control. The law was perceived as an instrument of interference or as an alibi for manipulation from outside. The fact that Romania was on the victorious side did not prevent the country from feeling sidelined and insignificant. There was a sense of latent defeat that was nurtured by dissatisfaction and bred sentiments of victimization. The malaise was particularly profound because the knowledge and resources of the Romanian politicians and elites put them on a par as negotiators with their Western opposite numbers. The underlying problem lay within

Romanity and its terrible anxiety about 'how to be Romanian'. Inter-war political circles, Westernized intellectuals whose horizon was limited to that of a European 'province' which they found unsatisfactory constantly spoke, in increasingly strong terms, of withdrawal from the order desired by the victors in 1919: the Western liberal democrats were forced onto the defensive. The whole process of nation-building was based on the traditional confrontations with the Hungarians (revisionists), the Russians (expansionist Bolsheviks) and the Jews (associated with the Red Hungarians of 1918-1919, with the Bolsheviks or with Western capitalists). At this point in the process Emile Cioran's anger and distress at being a mere Romanian rings in one's ears. The works of the philosophers Nichifor Crainic and Nae Ionescu sowed the seeds of the extreme right-wing movements and the youth legions. They suggested a new basis for identity distinct from the Liberal/Western thinking inspired by the 1848 Romantic movement, proclaimed the right not to be Western, and argued for a return to the People, its ethnic roots and its Orthodox spiritual setting. The disaster of 1940, the amputation of Romanian territory under Hungarian and Soviet pressure, seemed the outcome of a situation perceived as disastrous. Afraid that they would be crushed, the Romanians did not offer resistance in the summer of 1940; they looked on as their fears were realized. A desire for revenge lay behind the policy of Marshal Antonescu and the accompanying discourse glorifying the alliance with Hitler's Germany and brotherhood in arms in the war against the Soviet Union. The desire to avenge the humiliation of 1940 existed but does not entirely explain Romania's conduct between 1940 and 1944. As an ally of the Reich, the country was deprived of full autonomy to make decisions: the war of June 1941 was desired by Berlin, Bucharest followed. Meanwhile, in the choice between Romania and Hungary, Berlin came down on the side of the latter, and northern Transylvania went to Hungary. If Antonescu's Romania did not feel humiliated by the Reich, it was because the Conducator and his followers fully shared and supported the German approach to the construction of the new Europe. In other words, Antonescu was not primarily a patriot and for this reason was faithfully bound to Hitler. His patriotism led him to imagine something beyond traditional national sentimentalism, transnational modernity that would integrate Romania into the new Europe and finally do away with the heritage of the Enlightenment and 1789. According to Antonescu's own statements, Romania would enter the front rank of history by espousing a cause and making it her own, in a satisfying relationship of ideological partnership. Analysis of the support given to the Hitlerian anti-Bolshevik and anti-Semitic model by some members of the Romanian political and intellectual elites shows the transnational nature of national discourse. This discourse is a demand for status: in the anti-Soviet war, Romania raised itself to the level of Germany. In 1878, Romania had not been able to rise to the level of Russia engaged in an anti-Ottoman crusade because its own cause was extraneous to the crusade and to pan-Slavism. Romania's war-aim was independence. There were no joint convictions, simply a tactical alliance between the Principalities and a great empire, an alliance that Bucharest lacked the resources to orchestrate alone. The 1941-1944 fraternity with Germany was based on joint convictions.

Obsession with Status: The Nationalist Communist Version

The fact that small power nationalism is a quest for status and the recognition of this status within a field of identity defined by attachment to a common model helps to identify the dynamics of national communism. National communism functioned as part of a competition with Moscow within a framework of shared values. It was part of a rationale of partnership, not dissidence. Through lack of vision or, more ingeniously, in an attempt to convince themselves or Moscow of the flaws in its system of domination and the limits of its grip on the popular democracies, Westerners, especially the Americans and the French, made much of Romanian dissidence. It should not be forgotten that in 1965 Nicolae Ceausescu coolly inherited the post of Secretary General of the communist party from a Stalinist, Gheorghiu Dej, that he energetically promoted Soviet-style collectivization of the countryside in 1949 and that in December 1989 he died singing the Internationale, after demanding from the court the right to address representatives of the working-class avant-garde.

The first frictions, tensions and negotiations between the Romanian party and Moscow date from the late 1950s and bear eloquent witness to the nationalism at the heart of Romanian communism. The issue that brought about this confrontation is well known: Moscow wanted a certain division of labour within Comecon and tried to direct the Romanian economy towards agricultural production. This plan was unacceptable to the Romanian party, which saw itself as a Stalinist party and was convinced of the need to advance along the path of Promethean industrialization and the promotion of the working class. National communism owed its extraordinary success to the fact that the public, outraged by the heavy-handed Russian occupation, seemed to welcome this Soviet-Romanian tension. The State/Party/Nation discourse was familiar to people still imbued with the anti-Russian, anti-Bolshevik framework of modern Romanian nationalism and this enabled the authorities to open up a dialogue between rulers and ruled. The ruled seized with both hands an instrument of survival which offered the dual satisfaction of a return to a familiar traditional culture and prestige in relation to their powerful neighbour. Without going back over the chequered history of national communism, which has been exhaustively studied (Verdery, 1991; Trond, 1990) let us simply note here that the climax of this extraordinary confusion of representation systems, which never quite coincide, came in August 1968 when Ceausescu came out against the Soviet decision to use Warsaw Pact troops to stamp out the Czech communist reform movement. He did so in the name of a different interpretation of the Czech reforms and a better way of promoting socialism, to which Czech reformism, according to the Romanian head of state, was not a threat. Ceausescu doubtless aspired to be an ideologist, and ran the risk of a debate and a confrontation with Moscow. The population misunderstood what the Romanian head of State was saying on that occasion: he did not leave the beaten track of socialism, nor did he opt for a kind of humanistic third way. He set himself up as a guarantor of Socialist values and simply considered that Dubcek's reformism was in no way inimical to the construction of socialism. What was at stake was not independence or dissidence but the promotion of Bucharest in the sphere of ideology. In 1968, the Romanian communist party was twenty years old and had attained maturity. In the party ranks veteran militants trained in Moscow during the war rubbed shoulders with newcomers aspiring to a career and political-social advancement via the communist youth movement and study in party schools. These new elites were confident of their status and this social standing gave them the right to a hearing and to confront Moscow.

From Competition to Exclusion

This rationale of a quest for and a right to status led to two reactions in the last two decades of the regime. One was the blind persistence of anti-Western feeling when in the early 1970s stagnant production and popular disillusion became fully apparent. This was the reaction of a potential loser opting out of the competition. The other reaction was to produce an ideology based on the anteriority of all Romanian creative output, whether artistic, conceptual, or cultural. Time was regarded vertically, in Romano-Romanian terms, thus disposing of any anxiety about being out of step with neighbouring European countries. At the heart of the reasoning behind Ceausescu's excesses was a rejection of measure. This 'protochronistic' school was active in the fields of literature, linguistics and history and was associated with increasing insularity. An ideal of insularity coexisted, in practice, with the control and confinement of the population. Romania rejected and left the field of competition and became an island unto itself, the rhythm of its existence being punctuated by celebrations of the Nation, the Party and the Party Secretary. The 'Cântarea României' festivals organized in schools throughout the country formed part of these celebrations: teachers, parents and pupils were mobilized to write poetry and to organize dancing to perpetuate folk traditions and celebrate the glorious history of the Nation, its 'Conducator' and his wife Elena Ceausescu, duly promoted Mother of the People. In the political field, however, the real extent of this confinement should not be overestimated: Bucharest turned away from the West but maintained close relations with representatives of revolution like Arafat and Gaddafi (Pacepa, 1987). A generally uncompromising outlook was adopted. Bucharest rejected Gorbachev's socialist humanism and was condemned in international human rights bodies in Vienna and Geneva.

The real break/confrontation with Moscow was ideological: it occurred when Mikhail Gorbachev launched the new programme of perestroika and glasnost and proposed a new conception of international relations. The Romanian leadership rejected this revision of the founding dogmas. Ceausescu's client nomenclatures were afraid of being criticized by the new generation of communist cadres, who were weary of failure: there was no longer any sharing of values with the Soviet Union. For Bucharest, Moscow was at fault. Convinced of the existence of a Soviet plot, Ceausescu reasserted his freedom, and at the 14th Party Congress in

November 1989 dared to criticize the consequences of the Molotov-Ribbentrop pact, which had led to the loss of north Bukovina and Bessarabia. At that time, dissidence was defined as a break in the ideological partnership. The Romanian party still tried to save the good aspects of the heritage: in November 1989, the president's brother, Ilie Ceausescu, called for the strengthening of the Warsaw Pact.

For this small power which owed its independence to the advance of the Russian empire in the Balkans and the Ottoman retreat, the driving force behind nationalism is essentially a quest for recognition of status, a demand to be accepted on the same terms as the representatives of the developed, dominant Europe which determines the criteria of normality. Any hint of non-recognition leads to the exaggeration of differences: frontiers are drawn, firstly in the name of Orthodoxy, then of communism, then of Ceausescu's communism in the late 1980s. This hyper-sensitivity to potential humiliation is exacerbated when Romania is unable to handle crises triggered by discontinuity and adaptation, and explains the spiralling development of hatred against the Jewish and Hungarian communities whose presence and prosperity pose a challenge and a threat. One long-term component of contemporary anti-Semitism which is found all across the spectrum, from extremist rightwing movements to the populist left, is the hatred aroused by the rise of an enlightened Jewish bourgeoisie. The populist C. Constantin Stere explained at length in his articles which reached a wide audience at the beginning of the twentieth century in the review *Viata Româneasca* ('Romanian Life') that the Jewish bourgeoisie was an obstacle to and a brake on the rise of the Romanian bourgeoisie. Furthermore, the Jew was feared because he received support from abroad and was accepted as an equal partner by a Paris or a Berlin Jew. Interventions to protect Jewish nationals by the Universal Israelite Alliance in 1867 at the time of the formation of the modern principalities caused exasperation, as did campaigns by the French left, and by Bernard Lazare in 1902, and the solidarity in the 1930s of European left-wing anti-fascist movements with a Jewish communist activist arrested in Romania, Ana Pauker. The other foreigner, the Hungarian, reacted to the Romanian peasant ideal by assuming the identity of a conqueror, a warrior and an aristocrat and was rejected in a similarly competitive process and atmosphere. National communism destroyed the arrogance of the Hungarian urban elites by peopling Transylvanian cities like Cluj with Romanian peasant/workers (Durandin, 1990).

From Competition to Integration

This process of national construction poised between mimesis and rebellion led to some surprising recent events. Are we witnessing a change in Romanian identity and a new-found support for nationhood based on citizenship?

After Bucharest had been engaged in desultory negotiations with Budapest and Kiev for over four years, two treaties were recently signed. The Romano-Hungarian treaty has been ratified by the Bucharest and Budapest parliaments. This ratification is the outcome of political determination on the part of the government, though the treaty has not to date come up against any major opposition. The prime reason for this widespread aquiescence, notwithstanding a few extremist remarks and some violent emotional reactions by members of the present majority and a number of major figures in exile, is the political change which occurred in November 1996 in Bucharest. The legislative and presidential elections in that month saw the victory of the Democratic Convention and President Emil Constantinescu. The new leadership is democratic and profoundly Western-looking and has obtained the support of the party representing the Hungarian minority (UDMR/Hungarian Democratic Union of Romania). The political project is based on a desire to make Romania a 'normal' country (Manulescu, 1991), in other words, a liberal democratic country which asserts and comes to terms with its largely Orthodox identity and at the same time accepts religious and cultural pluralism. The current team does not regard itself as a dutiful pupil or an obedient client of the West but as a partner. Some recent developments - Romanian military participation in the European Alba operation in Albania, the argument of Foreign Affairs Minister Adrian Severin that Bucharest is signing the treaty with Kiev not to meet Western constraints but to stabilize an eastern area - illustrate this desire to demonstrate partnership. Certain political declarations illustrate the same trend, e.g. Defence Minister Victor Babiuc's statement at NATO Headquarters that Romania now came with proposals, not demands. By reversing the traditional discourse, the leaders are setting themselves up as partners.

In 1997 Romania had a project which mobilized opinion around the hope of achieving a modern identity, namely integration into NATO alongside Poland, Hungary and the Czech Republic at the July 1997 Madrid Summit. Here it was in competition with Central Europe and ran the risk of being rebuffed. The rejection of its application for NATO membership is regarded as further proof that the Balkans are being kept on the sidelines of central Europe, a confirmation of the inevitability of their affiliation to the backward east. The desire to play a role and to put forward a new vision for the area led Bucharest to define and present itself as the southern flank of NATO in the east, balancing the Polish northern flank. Bucharest argues on the basis of strategic normality/rationality.

Many surveys show that over 90% of the population and the army favour NATO membership and that they understand this means that problems with neighbours should be settled first. Public opinion is being reasonable - passions are now focused on joining - and accepts the agreements made by the government in the bilateral negotiations with Hungary and Ukraine. Each side recognizes the principle of the inviolability of frontiers and respect for the rights of minorities in pursuance of resolution 1201 of the Council of Europe. The reasoning behind this acceptance is unclear. Either it is the result of a pragmatic appraisal of the price to be paid for joining; in case of refusal, the price will be considered unwarrantably high. Or it may reflect a profound determination to change the landmarks of identity and the priority accorded to them. For the democrats, rationality means analysing the present situation and looking beyond it. The historical-ethnicist vision of the Nation is being discarded in favour of support for a Nation based on citizenship. The democratic political actors skilfully play on the links between memory, emotion and citizenship: on the one hand there are emotionally charged memories such as the loss of Bessarabia and Bukovina, and in the treaty with Kiev, Bucharest obtained protection for the rights of the Romanian minority in Bukovina. On the other, there is the memory of a shared experience of communist oppression. In June 1997, the government organized a joint Romano-Hungarian tribute to the Hungarian Imre Nagy, who was detained by the Gheorghiu Dej regime in Snagov after the repression of the Budapest revolution of 1956. A new democratic fellowship is being organized. It is astute to encourage respect for all memories, and not a selective memory only responsive to the sanctity of the national territory and historic law. In line with the same rationale, Bucharest is arguing for the organization of a Romano-Ukrainian Euro-region, which is a new way of perceiving the frontier. Whether a cautious tactic is adopted - negotiating to obtain more with integration into NATO - or a Westernist philosophical-political vision of Law and the

Nation, a profound change is observable: the full right to Kantian Western universalism is today a factor in Romanian political discourse.

This balance is complex and precarious. It combines the conviction of some, and the tactical support or mistrust of others who are ready to return to a reaction of humiliation. The country has experienced three failures: the 1920s experiment in mimetic democracy; the Fascist rebellions and the Communist revolution; and the confusion of the Iliescu years (1989-1996) when the aim was to enjoy the benefits of Euro-Atlantic integration whilst preserving the achievements of communism (Durandin, 1997). The national/Westernizing framework has survived and is developing by the organization of a significant liberation movement. Westernism is neither in the West nor in the East, it is inherent in those who believe in its values and freedoms. Romania's new opportunity in the late 1990s lies in this sense of freedom which is no longer mimetic but a sovereign choice. The risk of a confrontation with the West is a handicap that still exists. Romania is in a position of economic dependence and realizes it: hard work is needed to keep economic factors separate from politics, to adapt to and at the same time to accept a painful transition to a new form of economy; to adopt IMF programmes and at the same time to think of oneself as free. The intellectual and ideological liberation of a sector of public opinion which no longer feels threatened by the hereditary enemy or the eastern neighbour does not coincide with economic liberation and it hurts to belong to this other, poorer Europe. Hopefully the current economic situation will be seen as short-term and not as inequitable. A revival or recrudescence of nationalism would be indicative of the defensive disarray of a poor country. The growth of nationalistic tension would be indicative of a new humiliation and a resurgence of resentment.

Romanian nationalism is, paradoxically, a product of Western culture and was shaped at a time when the elites were being absorbed into the dynamics and avant-garde mentalities of the nineteenth century. It is a factor of identification with and differentiation from the West. The process of identity-building oscillates between mimesis and rebellion. Some thinkers, attached to a complex, plural heritage, have looked beyond the inevitability of these swings and opted for a post-national type citizenship. But it is difficult to be part of contemporary transnational humanism and yet to live and survive in a needy land. As the philosopher Andrei Plesu declared some three years after the fall of the Communist regime 'Why are we poor and ill-placed?'

References

Cioran, E. (1993), *Schimbarea la Fata a României*, Humanitas, Bucharest.

Durandin, C. (1990) (ed.), 'A Propos du Conflit Roumano-Hongrois', *Les Temps Modernes*, January, Paris, pp. 96-126.

Durandin, C. (1994a), *Histoire de la Nation Roumaine*, Complexe, Brussels.

Durandin, C. (1994b), *La France Contre l'Amérique*, PUF, Paris.

Durandin, C. (1995), *Histoire des Roumains*, Fayard, Paris.

Durandin, C. (1997), 'Roumanie, la Fin de l'Ère Iliescu', *Relations Internationales et Stratégiques*, no. 26, Summer, pp. 109-14.

Hitchins, K. (1985), *The Idea of Nation, the Romanians of Transylvania 1691-1849*, Editura Stiintifica si Enciclopedica, Bucharest.

Huntington, S. (1993), 'If not Civilizations, What? Paradigms of the Post-Cold War World', *Foreign Affairs*, November-December, pp. 186-94.

Iancu, C. (1978), *Les Juifs en Roumanie (1866-1919). De l'Exclusion à l'Émancipation*, Editions de l'Université de Provence, Aix-en-Provence.

Moscovici, S. (1997), *Chronique des Années Égarées*, Stock, Paris.

Pacepa, I. (1987), *Red Horizons, Chronicles of a Communist Spy Chief*, Regnery Gateway, Washington.

Schnapper, D. (1996), 'Suite', *Commentaire*, Summer, pp. 316-20.

Spector, S. (1995), *Romania at the Paris Peace Conference*, The Romanian Cultural Foundation, Iasi.

Trond, G. (1990), *Nationalism and Communism in Romania, The Rise and Fall of Ceausescu's Personal Dictatorship*, Westview Press, Boulder.

Verdery, K. (1991), *National Ideology under Socialism. Identity and Cultural Politics in Ceausescu's Romania*, University of California Press, Berkeley, Los Angeles.

Volovici, L. (1995), *Ideologia Nationalista si Problema Evreiasca în România Anilor '30*, Humanitas, Bucharest.

PART VI
CONCLUSION

14 Culture and National Identity

ALAIN DIECKHOFF

In the different articles assembled in this volume, culture - understood in a broad sense as a coherent system of meanings that members of a group know and use in their interactions - is a determinant factor in the shaping of national identities. This is hardly surprising if one admits with Anthony Smith that 'nationalism is primarily a cultural doctrine or, more accurately, a political ideology with a cultural doctrine at its center' (Smith, 1991, p. 74). How does culture foster the preservation or valorization of the specificity to which nationalism aspires?[1]

The Uses of Culture

First, it should be underlined that we consider that cultures are not entities endowed with a timeless and permanent substance. They do not constitute organic totalities with impermeable frontiers but are constantly wrought, shaped, and recomposed by a constant process of borrowing and exchange. Yet even though each culture undergoes continual transformations, it possesses its own configuration that allows it to be identified and distinguished from others. Without this minimum of internal coherence, cultural diversity would be unthinkable.

Nevertheless, the diversity of cultures that has accompanied humanity's progression since its origins became a political and social issue only after the appearance of two major phenomena - the emergence of the individual as an autonomous subject and the advent of the nation as a collective subject. This did not come about until the second half of the eighteenth century. The concept of culture imposes itself as synonymous with education when societies experience a radical transformation in the manner in which they are organized: a hierarchical order of social groups is replaced by a collection of individuals who share equality, in the eyes of the law, within a national community. This Copernican revolution radically modified the place of culture, as Gellner has shown with talent. In agrarian societies, only the leadership class, itself divided into different strata (warriors, bureaucrats, and especially priests) possessed high culture. The majority of peasants, locked in rural communities that are themselves isolated, not only do not participate in high culture in any way, they do not even share a common popular culture given their major internal differences. Each individual is assigned a precise position within the social structure as a member of a given group. The industrial revolution radically disrupted this order of things. The division of labour in effect requires increased social mobility that occurs through standardized instruction, and therefore through the diffusion of a common culture, particularly through a spoken and written language (Gellner, 1989). The function of culture changes in meaning. While in pre-modern society it served to mark the differences of status, culture now underlines the closeness of people and serves to consolidate a new form of community: the nation. Culture also displaces the line of differentiation. While in traditional society culture reiterated the rigid *social* demarcation between the ruling stratum and the peasant masses according to a horizontal stratification, it now establishes the lines of *national* separation between modern societies in a vertical fashion.

This culture, called upon to play an essential role in the national structuring of society, also has a polysemous characteristic since it covers customs, habits, memory, beliefs, *weltanschauung*, that make it particularly attractive to nationalistic actors whose strategies can in effect solicit highly diversified levels depending on the moment. Thus the creation of Belgium in 1830 was the result of a political rupture with the Netherlands that coincided with a 200-year old religious rupture, with the Catholic south opposing the Calvinist north. Catholicism was a central element in the formation of the Belgian identity, to such an extent that even the emergence of a powerful secular movement can be understood only as a reaction to the weight of an omnipresent Catholicism since the Counter Reformation in the sixteenth century in what was then the Spanish Netherlands. Nevertheless, this religious factor progressively lost its relevance, and the linguistic division between Francophones and Dutch speakers, which at the beginning was only secondary, became increasingly important as a result of nationalist actions, to the point of awakening in some a separatist temptation. Today, language has overtaken religion as a source of identity.

Let us add that the same resource can be used, depending on the actors' intentions, to totally opposite ends. This is the case of language in former Yugoslavia. In the nineteenth century, linguistic reformers deliberately forged a common language for the Croatians and the Serbs from a central dialect in order to emphasize the 'Illyrian identity' of the southern Slavs, an identity that was precisely supposed to transcend religious differences and go beyond divergent historical trajectories. With the dismemberment of the Yugoslav federation, the Croatian authorities began a campaign against 'Serbian expressions' trying to replace them with 'purely Croatian' words. Linguistic dissociation is thereby encouraged in order to reinforce the political separation with their Serbian neighbours. We can see how culture's elasticity makes it particularly conducive to a wide variety of strategic uses. This culture does not need to be high culture at the start, served by men of letters, or even a popular culture in search of recognition. It can be a culture in a limited sense, such as that of the Northern League in Italy that fights against Rome's centralism in the name of a business culture, of the Christian democratic zones of the Northeast and the work ethic of the small businessmen and artisans who live there (Diamanti, 1993).

Culture's remarkable malleability makes it a political resource to which all nationalisms, whether 'Western' or 'Eastern', have resorted. This geographic metaphor was introduced by the American political scientist of German stock, Hans Kohn, to distinguish between the civic, rational, voluntary and universal nationalism of 'the West' and the cultural, mystic, organic and particularistic nationalism of 'the East'. Since Kohn contributed to the popularization of this dichotomy, it is worth quoting him at some length.

> In the Western world, in England and in France, in the Netherlands and in Switzerland, in the United States and in the British dominions, the rise of nationalism was a predominantly political occurrence; it was preceded by the formation of the future national state, or, as in the case of the United States, coincided with it. Outside the Western world, in Central and Eastern Europe and in Asia, nationalism arose not only later, but also generally at a more backward stage of social and political development... this rising nationalism found its first expression in the cultural field (Kohn, 1946, p. 330).

Various versions of this binary typology can be found among a certain number of scholars today. The political nationalism born in the wake of the

French Revolution around a long-established and powerful State, is said to contrast with a cultural nationalism nourished by the language and history that has prospered in countries devoid of a State such as Italy, Poland, and throughout the Third World in general (Kamenka, 1976, pp. 3-20). This distinction should nevertheless be nuanced if only because, far from being the prerogative of 'Eastern' nationalisms, culture has been just as often invoked 'the the West' (Dieckhoff, 1996, pp. 43-55). Here, too, the sedimentation of national identities occurred through an intense mobilization of culture. The various national affirmation movements probably differ in their varying uses of culture, but one cannot irreducibly oppose two types of nationalism - one entirely political, the other cultural - that are historically incarnated in distinct national models (Great Britain, France, the United States, versus Germany, Eastern Europe, the Third World). An effort at clarification is imperative.

Culture, The Emblem of National Identity

Using the distinctions introduced by Andréas Kappeler, culture has been invoked with even more insistence when it has had to compensate for a strong 'national deficiency'. This was particularly true for the 'small nations' of Eastern Europe that suffered from a maximum deficit: a deficit at once political - a lack of political unity - social - a lack of local leadership elites - and cultural - a lack of high culture (Kappeler, 1992, p. 1). The case of the Slovaks illustrates well this triple deficit. Integrated into the kingdom of Hungary, dominated politically by the Hungarian nobility, deprived of an entrepreneurial class that was German and Jewish, they could not even take pride in an ancient literary tradition. In this devastated landscape, the creation of a national culture constituted the easiest task, and in any case an essential prerequisite to the creation of their own political and economic elites and the achievement of political independence. Nevertheless, even if the 'small countries' over-invested in culture - those that had never been endowed with their own political entity (Estonians, Latvians), or who were deprived of it due to a secular oppression (Bulgaria, Lithuania) - because it was the only exploitable resource with which they could affirm a collective identity, it was never their exclusive prerogative. If we limit ourselves to nineteenth-century Europe, cultural nationalism was a reality in all the cases studied by

Andréas Kappeler. It was true also for countries that suffered from more limited 'structural deficits' than those of the 'peoples without history'. Let us take two examples. Nineteenth-century Hungary suffered from a dual frustration. Contrary to the peasant nations of Eastern Europe, Hungary appeared as a complete society, from the rural masses at the base to the nobility at the summit and including the clergy, the gentry, and an emerging bourgeois class. Social completeness, then, but one that was fettered by the country's political submission to Habsburg Austria and by the cultural pre-eminence of Latin (as well as, to a lesser extent, German) that hindered the emergence of a national literature in Hungarian until the end of the eighteenth century. This literature was inaugurated by a group of poets (Kazinczy, Vitez) who gave Hungarian letters the brilliant lustre that allowed them to enter the pantheon of great European literatures (Sugar, Hanak and Frank, 1990). Germany is another example, but of a different nature. At the end of the eighteenth century, its major deficiency was of a strictly political nature. The Holy Roman Empire of the German nation was only an extremely loose association of more than 300 virtually independent territories and 1,500 imperial dominions. In this case as well, culture had a decisive role in giving birth to the sentiment among Germans that they shared a common identity beyond political divisions. Nevertheless, contrary to the 'small nations', cultural entrepreneurs in late eighteenth century Germany had a high culture immediately available to them and with two principal assets - a national language and national myth. When Luther translated the Bible into German, he gave the language of the people an extraordinary legitimacy and, thus, a decisive momentum to the development of a national literature. At the same time, the rediscovery of the Germania of Tacitus enabled humanist historians to trace a filiation between the Germanic tribes and the Germans of the late Middle Ages. Arminius, the chief of the Cherusci tribe that fought against Roman domination, was to have his name germanized to Hermann and became the central figure of the German national myth as well as the incarnation of Germany's superiority despite its chronic political weakness (Werner, 1994, pp. 43-61). This national conscience in gestation received a decisive impetus with Herder, the poets of Sturm und Drang and later the romantics that made culture the receptacle of the people's national genius. Schiller had sensed just how much this hypertrophy of the cultural possessed compensatory virtues in the face of the political anemia in exclaiming: 'while the political Empire totters, the intellectual Empire has constantly reinforced and perfected itself'. This effervescence in all artistic domains (literature, theatre, music, painting), gave birth, in the heart of the elites, to the sentiment of a shared cultural community that would prove to be highly precious in the subsequent phase of political mobilization, when it became a question of establishing a unified German state.

Recourse to culture was nevertheless not limited to territorialized nations that were deprived of political sovereignty to different degrees. It is also apparent among the national minorities, that is to say among the ethnic groups living in a given State while at the same time belonging culturally to a neighbouring country. This was the case until 1945 of a multitude of groups able to invoke the protection of a 'mother country' - Hungarians, Germans, Ruthenians. Emphasis on culture played a determinant role among these minorities because it facilitated the preservation of the group's collective identity as well as its transnational character. Finally, given its interest in weaving a link of solidarity beyond established frontiers, culture has been constantly promoted as a unifying cement for different diasporas. The publication of newspapers and books in Hebrew and Yiddish reinforced the conscience of unity within the dispersed Jewish world (Dieckhoff, 1993, pp. 123-53; Baumgarten, 1994, pp. 405-29). The accumulation of titles published in Greek across Europe, from Venice to Saint Petersburg and Vienna, as well as in the Eastern Mediterranean, from Jerusalem to Istanbul to Aleppo, was a stimulating factor for Greek identity from the eighteenth century onward.

In all of these cases culture was precious because it was a means of highlighting particularisms. The cultural systematization undertaken by cultural entrepreneurs ('language builders', folklorists, historians) was intended to serve a dual strategy. First, culture served as testimony to the existence of the people on which is conferred a semblance of 'primordial' unity. Thus, despite its political subjugation, the people was endowed with its own specificity. Culture can also provide a means to challenge the political order to which the people was subjected. It serves as 'the ideal basis for any tribunicial endeavor'. (Badie, 1992, p. 212), because it stands in opposition to the universal pretensions of Empires or States in the name of claimed particularisms. Recourse to culture should in time facilitate the rejection of political subordination. By insisting on cultural particularisms (even if this frequently means accentuating them), nationalist entrepreneurs seek above all else to distinguish their people as much as possible from the others so as to give full legitimacy to their inclination for political independence. As such, promoting Ukrainian, Bulgarian, or Latvian culture fits into a rationale of forging an identity and protesting against the imperial order of the Habsburgs, the Osmanlis, and the Romanovs. In the same manner, the exaltation by Third World national liberation movements of the Black, Arab or Hindu cultures aimed to renew with a past frequently denigrated by colonialism while at the same time distancing themselves from the West, a process essential to their political success. Frantz Fanon emphasized just how much the reappropriation of an 'indigenous' culture was indispensable to the success of the anti-colonial struggle. 'The passionate search for a national culture preceding the colonial era acquires its legitimacy from the desire shared by colonized intellectuals to distance themselves from the Western culture into which they might otherwise become mired' (Fanon, 1981, p. 144). The unconditional affirmation of the dominated culture is therefore the driving force in the strategy of denouncing the West and becoming unalienated from it. Let us, however, not mistake the reasons for the success encountered by the invocation of 'national culture'. This success is not due to the fact that the standard-bearers of nationalism have rediscovered some sort of original, intact and virgin identity, even if this is what they claim. Their aspiration to restore lost purity is in fact largely illusory, given that cultures are always forged through borrowing from other cultures, cross-breeding, and infinite recompositions. Even so, despite its chimerical nature, the return to the 'culture of origin' indeed fosters a multifaceted identity-based mobilization because it encourages a break from the dominant culture and restores dignity to the dominated. In order words, the invocation of a so-called natural culture is likely rooted in myth, but this in no way detracts from its unquestionable social effectiveness.

The Intelligentsia, Organic Agent of Nationalism

Culture could not have fulfilled its dual strategic role of affirmation and opposition if it had not been vigorously upheld by a particular social category concerned with its promotion, that is to say, the intelligentsia. Most studies devoted to the expansion of nationalism in the nineteenth century show how much culture has been the driving force behind nationalistic demands. The intelligentsia owed this vital conscious-raising function to its nature as an intermediary. The product of a more open educational system, it appeared during a phase of social transition, the moment of passage from an agrarian and feudal society to one that is industrial and national. The intelligentsia found itself in a situation of double alienation, with relation to the society as a whole in which it evolved and also in relation to the traditional elites of the group to which it belonged. Therefore, it was the ideal agent for *translating modernity* into the popular language. This modernity, previously transmitted by a transnational language of culture (such as French during the eighteenth century), is now transmitted through the language of the people - codified and standardized. This language had even greater value given that it was supposed to be the repository of an unadulterated authenticity exalted by romanticism. Nationalism is closely linked to the emergence of a modern society that accelerates contact, through increased exchanges and migrations, between worlds that until then ignored each other. This leads to new levels of conscience. Thus industrialization in central Europe during the nineteenth century led to the migration of a fraction of peasants (Slavs) toward the great urban centres of German culture. At the same time, social ascension for their small elites meant their incorporation in the German-speaking universities. This cultural integration was successful to a degree but it also sustained a sense of uneasiness, even resentment, among a fraction of the educated class, fed by the contempt in which their original culture was held. Some members of the intelligentsia were simply not prepared to pay the price of their social ascension by supplanting, even extinguishing, their cultural universe. This led to a reaction by a group of folklore specialists, historians, musicians, and writers that valorized the rejected culture. Such a defense of culture is incontestably a disinterested enterprise to a certain extent, motivated by a thirst for dignity, and Ernest Gellner is right to insist on the ardour and generosity that animated the nationalistic intellectuals. Nevertheless, such 'pure' intentions do not rule out individual, strategic motives.

Though it is better to avoid a reductive materialistic explanation, it is also a mistake to disregard it. When the social ascension of educated individuals is paid at a heavy social and symbolic price (uprooting to cities far from the native soil, abandonment of the mother tongue) and when they must also deal with strong competition from other national groups, it is often in the interest of the intelligentsia to create a specific national space where, as master of its own culture, it will be able to eliminate or at least reduce the influence of rival groups. The destiny of the Austrian-

Hungarian Empire fully verifies this hypothesis. The creation of independent states on the ruins of Kakania opened immediate opportunities for the Slavic intelligentsia in its own bureaucracies while, until then, competition was fierce in a state apparatus dominated by German speakers. On the contrary, if social mobility is favoured by the central power and it offers real economic and social advantages, the intelligentsia only has a residual interest in employing a strategy of dissociation even if social promotion is paid by total deculturation. The failure of Occitanism is clearly explained at least in part by the success of the strategy of co-optation of the southern elites by the Parisian political centre. The former supplied the Third Republic, especially in the Southwest - long a bastion of radicalism - with many of the leaders that the new regime needed, thus making any inclination toward independence less than appealing. Félibrige, a literary movement promoting the renaissance of the Occitan language, could not hope to attract the lawyers and professors that saw themselves massively integrated in Republican institutions. Only those nostalgic of the old order, the downgraded nobility and the bourgeois clerics were enthralled by a discourse defending the cultural specificity of the Occitan community, linked to a backward-looking exaltation of rural life.

The role of organic agent of nationalism played by the intelligentsia is hardly a thing of the past. The intelligentsia continues, on the contrary, to assume it fully because they control a culture they have an objective interest in defending, even in making prosper. Nationalism probably does not have the same appeal for all intellectuals. Some resolutely take the opposite road of post-nationalism, striving to go beyond the nation. Nevertheless, it would be pointless to hide the fact that the cohort of organic intellectuals of nationalism remains impressive. In 1992, in a nationalist manifesto proclaiming the sovereign right of Catalonia to self-determination, one could find the same battalion of writers, artists and professors that a century earlier signed the Bases of Manresa, a political programme in which the demand for Catalonian autonomy was explicitly formulated for the first time.

Just as the intelligentsia's engagement in the nationalist combat can be explained at least in part by materialistic motives, these also play an important role in the progressive diffusion of nationalistic ideology among the masses. In this case, the powerful attraction of the cultural reference is essentially explained not by its power to create a national myth, but by its profound social resonance and its political implications. Social and political demands are in effect expressed through cultural demands. The example of Belgium will serve to illustrate our point. The independence of that country in 1830 through the joint action of the liberal middle class allied with the landed aristocracy and the Catholic clergy led to the establishment of a constitutional monarchy guaranteeing fundamental political rights within the framework of a nation-state, as in France (Mabille, 1986; Bitsch, 1992). This State was nevertheless principally associated from the beginning with one culture, the French culture. French became the dominant language of the political authorities, even though almost 60 percent of the citizens of the kingdom spoke Flemish dialects. If, despite Belgium's linguistic heterogeneity, French benefited from a monopoly from the start, it was due to the fact that it was the language of the voting bourgeoisie that lead the new country in French-speaking Belgium as well as in Flanders, where the elites had been profoundly Frenchified. In the northern part of the country only the lower social classes (peasants, workers, the lower middle class) remained loyal to Flemish. Because this linguistic division covered a social demarcation and an asymmetry in the access to the political centre, the cultural battle for the defense of Flemish could only be a combat for social and political equality as well. This link was not immediately perceived by the first Flemish nationalists (Hendrik Conscience, Jan Baptist David) who confined themselves to a literary celebration of the popular language (Deprez and Vos, 1998, pp. 83-138), but it was very quickly underlined by their successors.[2] The growing Frenchification of the civil service in Flanders due to the nomination of Walloon bureaucrats with whom the popular classes could not communicate fostered a growing social frustration on which the Flemish movement capitalized in the 1860s. To halt the Frenchification of Flemish society, the government resorted to two measures. The first was parliamentary. By cultivating a certain influence among liberal and Catholic deputies, the Flemish nationalist movement succeeded in 1873 in having a series of linguistic laws passed that officialized the use of Dutch in the public administration of Flanders. This incomplete legislative device only moderately slowed the process of Frenchification. The Flemish movement then undertook a much more ambitious project - Dutch-only schooling in Flanders. This goal, which was progressively attained between 1883 and 1932, was only marginally cultural. In reality, imposing one language from primary school to university fulfilled a double objective - brushing aside the Frenchified elites and allowing the social rise of the Dutch-speaking popular classes. In other words, it was a matter of "nationalizing" the Flemish within their own cultural space where they no longer had anything to fear from the competition of French-speakers who had until then benefited from the privileged status of the French language to occupy, in Flanders, numerous posts in the bureaucracy as well as in private companies.

The Flemish case may be particularly topical but it is not unique. In Quebec as well, the linguistic cleavage had very obvious social implications, to the point that one can say a cultural division of labour existed until the 1950s. The English-speaking bourgeoisie, concentrated in the western neighbourhoods of Montreal, controlled the economy of the province while the Francophones were concentrated in the working and peasant classes. By encouraging the use of the French language in shops and businesses through legislation, the successive Quebec governments increased employment opportunities for French speakers beginning in the 1960s, thereby favouring their social ascension. This voluntaristic policy allowed Francophones to work in their own language and led to the creation of a business middle class that partially replaced English-speaking businessmen. These two examples verify Ernest Gellner's hypothesis linking the emergence of nationalism and the inadequacy of the communications system. When a language functions as a communication barrier that prevents, or at least hampers, the social advancement of a group sharing certain cultural traits, the latter is incited to build a 'protective niche' where its members will be assured social mobility by embarking down the road of cultural nationalism and then political nationalism (Gellner, 1989, pp. 90-6). It appears clearly that the invocation of culture is only rarely an end in itself. It almost always leads to political mobilization, as Miroslav Hroch has shown in his meticulous analysis of the development of nationalism among the 'small nations' of Eastern Europe (Hroch, 1985). Nevertheless, we need to go further.

It would in effect be a mistake to think of culture as only a force of protest in the name of which nationalists rise up against the established State in order to demand self-determination for the group they represent. John Breuilly argues that nationalism is a political force that pretends, in the name of a cultural nation, to rise against the established State in order to abolish the separation between the public sphere and civil society (Breuilly, 1982, p. 374). To reduce nationalism to a form of opposition to the State is purely and simply to disregard the capacity of governments to mobilize people on nationalistic grounds. In fact, the State is a particularly zealous creator of nationalism. Its elites (political, social, cultural) work, through the school system, the army, and literature, not only to reinforce national cohesion in order to develop the adhesion to the State, but frequently also to exalt the specificity, originality, and glory of the nation, even to underline its superiority in relation to its neighbours. The role of the State as an agent to instil nationalism likely varies depending on the type of State (republican, liberal, authoritarian) as well as the period, but it is very real indeed. And when the State upholds, stimulates, and encourages nationalism, it also resorts to culture as a particularly useful resource.

The Consolidation of National Identities by the State

The Belgian example previously discussed highlighted an essential phenomenon. The slow but real success of the nationalist movement to defend the Flemish culture is explained by the social impact of the language issue. If language was able to become a stake in the power struggle, it was simply because the central State, far from being neutral on the cultural level, was itself the protector of another culture, French, that it planned to diffuse and impose on all its citizens, particularly through the educational system. Up until the 1870s, the dominant bourgeois class obstinately attempted to rely on the central government, which it controlled, in order to Frenchify the entire society. Though this endeavour was gradually abandoned, it was not due to a lack of political will but to the weakness of the State, torn between Catholics and liberals, as well as to the early resistance of the Flemish movement. How can one interpret the government's plan to standardize culture? One can see in it, as Gellner does, a structural necessity of industrial society that requires standardized training and therefore the creation of a State-controlled educational system that diffuses the same culture all over the national territory. Without denying that the imperative of exosocialization is a functional need of modern society, the will of the State to instil a common culture (particularly a standard language), constitutes a fundamental political objective that existed frequently before industrialization and is, on the one hand, intrinsically linked to how the State is structured, and on the other, to the bestowing of sovereignty to the nation.

The appearance of the first modern nations (France, Spain, England) in the fourteenth and fifteenth centuries is in effect marked by a double phenomenon. First, the king reinforced his power over his lords as well as the Church, affirmed his prerogatives in the military, judicial and fiscal domains, and progressively set up a bureaucracy. Second, this consolidation of the political foundation went hand in hand with the beginning of a cultural integration made up of two components: linguistic and religious. In Spain, this process appeared with particular force in 1492. That year in fact marked the ultimate unification of the kingdom with the taking of Grenada - the last episode of the Reconquest -, the expulsion of the Jews (followed later by that of the Moors), and the publication by Antonio de Nebrija of his Castilian grammar. Political and cultural unity were for the Catholic Kings two sides of the same coin.

Britain and France are not exempt from this political entwining of the political and the cultural even if the process was extended over a longer period of time. In Britain, the unification of the State was difficult, with the king forced to compromise with the barons and the burghers. From the beginning of the fourteenth century, however, the English language, to which Chaucer had given considerable luster with his Canterbury Tales, was the ferment of specificity for a budding national conscience. The kingdom's authorities devoted themselves to spreading the use of the vernacular language in administrative acts. This linguistic zeal had an indisputable strategic objective, 'to assert through language the English identity with regard to that of the French' (Schulze, 1996, p. 139). The translations of the Bible into English, that of John Wycliff and then of William Tyndale, which would serve as the basis for the King James Bible, equally favoured the formation of an autonomous cultural environment that reinforced the geographic insularity of the British Isles. Finally, the religious schism under Henry VIII, with the establishment of Anglicanism as the state religion, marked the final stage of England's 'cultural nationalization'.

In France, too, the progressive affirmation of royal authority went together with the will to make the French language the sole vector of State communication. In the Villers-Cotterêts ordinance of 1539, François I prescribed the use of French for judicial decisions and legislative acts at the same time that Pierre de Ronsard, Joachim du Bellay, Henri Estienne and others praised the eminence of the French language. State defense of the language continued throughout the Classic period, with the creation of the French Academy (1634) and the compilation of the dictionary (1694). At the same time, although Henry IV demonstrated a spirit of tolerance unique in Europe by granting Protestants religious freedom, its grandson Louis XIV consolidated royal absolutism. In this perspective, the revocation of the Edict of Nantes was an attempt to make State unity coincide with unity of faith. The extension of State political control always went along with an aspiration to achieve cultural unity. Nevertheless, there was one limit. The objective of the Bourbons was to promote French as the language of the State as well as that of high culture without seeking to standardize the country in an authoritative manner. Whether the peasants of Anjou or Burgundy continued to speak patois or that the people of the Roussillon or Navarre spoke Catalan or Basque posed no threat to a power in which the rural masses and the plebeians of the cities had no vocation to participate. This indifference with regard to France's linguistic plurality disappeared with the French Revolution. As sovereignty was supposed to be incarnated in an indivisible nation, only the political body of citizens had a legitimacy in the public sphere and it was imperative that it should not be divided by social, regional and linguistic cleavages. It should reflect the Republic - one and indivisible. The Abbot Gregoire conducted a study in 1792 the title of which was a policy in and of itself: 'Report on the need to annihilate the *patois* and to universalize the use of the French language'. Barère, who presided the Convention during the King's trial, having exalted French as the 'most beautiful language of Europe, whose role it is to transmit to the world the most subtle thoughts on liberty', also declared a relentless war against local languages in the name of consolidating national unity. The concern with wholesale Frenchification totally satisfied the frenetic need for uniformity, induced by revolutionary egalitarianism, that Benjamin Constant revealed in such appropriate terms 'the same code, the same measures, the same rules, and if possible to achieve gradually, the same language, this is what one proclaims to be the perfection of all social organization' (Constant, 1980, p. 146).

The spread of the French language and the confinement of regional tongues to an increasingly narrow circle of speakers met a dual objective. One was functional. If all citizens could speak and read French, they would be directly affected by the revolutionary ideology emanating from Paris. The second objective was purely political. Namely, to create among the French the sentiment of belonging to the same symbolic community: the

French nation. Reading the same newspaper from Paris should serve, as Benedict Anderson has brilliantly shown, to instil in each reader a sense of communion with dozens of thousands of people absorbed at the same moment in the deciphering of the same lines (Anderson, 1983). Caught up by more urgent tasks, the revolutionaries did not have the time to impose the French language in Corsica or the Basque region. The Third Republic proved to be more effective in this matter.

By the time the Republican regime arrived, France was still a country of a thousand different facets, with highly varied customs, traditions and languages. This extreme diversity was a flagrant contradiction of the credo of republican unity, making it imperative to turn the credo into social reality. It is therefore hardly surprising that the arrival to power of republican opportunists in 1879 was immediately accompanied, under the aegis of Jules Ferry, by the implementation of an extremely ambitious educational policy. While they were consolidating the political institutions, the new elites established the foundations of a national education that was to educate the people. It could now be won over to republican ideas and partake in the same culture, the French culture. For the peasants that made up the overwhelming majority of the French population, the nation as a collection of citizens remained an abstraction, a meaningless slogan that it was imperative to turn a living reality, a community. More than a daily plebiscite, the nation was to become an everyday experience. Cultural standardization (especially linguistic) was therefore indispensable so that each person could directly experience the intimate sentiment of belonging to the same national entity. This nationalization of the mind could only come through a formidable effort of inculcation carried out through its educational system by the State, zealous propagator of the 'right culture' and tireless dispenser of the 'beautiful language' (Weber E., 1976, pp. 303-38). It was impossible for the founders of the Third Republic to admit that one could be a French citizen while maintaining a 'primary culture' - Basque, Breton, or Catalan. Local particularisms were denigrated as archaic regionalisms. There were thus combated and relegated unhesitatingly to the private sphere, which eventually could only lead to their slow extinction. Without a reliable means of conveyance (schools, newspapers, social institutions), those cultures were condemned, if not to disappear, at least to become folklorized and increasingly marginalized. It would be without doubt abusive, as Jean-François Chanet points out in a beautiful book, to speak of 'cultural genocide' regarding the Third

Republic's educational policy (Chanet, 1996, pp. 203-83). Teachers showed that they could - at times through pragmatism, at times as a result of attachment - show a certain tolerance towards the patois and the regional languages. But the fact is that they were caught up in a system where everything was done for the promotion of the French language through the official monopoly of French in the schools and the devaluation of regional languages that were associated with clericalism and anti-modernism. Evidently certain social processes, such as the development of internal migrations such as those of the Auvergnats and the Bretons, were a powerful vector of Frenchification. In the provinces, however, the linguistic loss would have been much more limited if the Republic had not put into place a linguistic nationalism in which the 'nationalization' of the Bretons, Alsatians, or Provencals involved a veritable enterprise of deculturalization.[3] Once again the contrast between the French conception of the nation, essentially political, and the German conception, which is seen as cultural, clearly shows its limits, with the Republic consolidating its political power through a vast enterprise of cultural normalization. While of a fundamentally ideological nature, the republican project could not neglect instituting the nation through an intense cultural project so as to create a basic solidarity among citizens. In the neighbouring monarchies such as Belgium and Spain, things were not much different, frequently as a result of copying France, which under absolutism had rationalized the functioning of the State even before inventing the modern nation-state.

Whether they succeeded or failed, the policies of cultural assimilation carried out by the different nation-states proved one thing. In order to bind people into one national community, the associative relationship (*Vergesellschaftung*) woven by citizens' allegiance always seems insufficient. The political link which, under law, alone defines membership in a nation had to be reiterated, in reality, by a social link established on a common culture whose epicentre was a national language. Putting it in Weberian terms, membership in the same nation cannot be based only on rational interests. It requires a communal relationship (*Vergemeinschaftung*), that is to say the appearance of a subjective sentiment of belonging to a national community sharing the same identity (M. Weber, 1968, pp. 40-3).

France's recent evolution shows that this concern for creating a community has not disappeared. A great deal of flexibility may have been introduced, with concessions accorded by the central government in the areas of national education for immigrants (courses taught in their original language and culture) as well as towards the regions. As a result, a series of legislative measures introduced during the past half-century have allowed the optional teaching of regional languages (Breton, Basque, Catalan, Corsican, Occitan) in schools in those regions where they are practised. Teacher training in regional languages has also been facilitated.[4] Yet these advances are cautious ones, and the financial means made available by the State for these programmes remain limited. More significantly, the State has always refused to give real legal guarantees to protect these languages, which are in fact clearly penalized by a recent constitutional provision. In June 1992, a new paragraph making French the language of the Republic was added to the Constitution during the debate on the Maastricht Treaty. The stated objective for this addition was to prevent any unwanted Anglicization of public life in the context of an increasingly integrated Europe. Nevertheless, it also prevents regional languages from being officially recognized. The two highest judicial authorities, the Council of State and the Constitutional Council, have ruled that the amendment to the Constitution prevents France from ratifying the European Charter on Regional and Minority Languages adopted by the Council of Europe in 1992. The Charter asks the member States to adopt a series of measures designed to facilitate and encourage the oral and written use of regional languages in the school system, the media, and the cultural area as well as in judicial proceedings and in communications with administrative authorities and the public services. The solemn and exclusive reaffirmation of French as the language of State authority clearly underlines that far from being confined to virtuous impartiality, the Republic clearly shows a cultural commitment consonant with the unifying ideology on which it was founded. The much-vaunted 'French exception' is therefore not reduced to the invention of an entirely political nation. Rather, the exception resides in the fact that in order for this nation, which is legally founded solely on the tie of citizenship, to become a reality, the State, and only the State, used the entire array of resources at its disposal, not only social and economic, but also cultural resources. A formidable protecting power, the State in France had a role in creating the nation that was probably unequalled in other latitudes, particularly by its voluntaristic action in the shaping of a national culture. At the end of the collective reflection on the French nation Pierre Nora concludes: 'No state has established as close a correspondence between the national State, its economy, its culture, its language and its society' (Nora, 1986, p. 654). In the same manner as the economy and the society, culture was also at the heart of the republican political project. The ultimate proof, if there is still need for one, is that there has never been a national political project that was not also a national cultural project, with nationalism aiming to achieve 'the fusion of culture and political society' (Gellner, 1989, p. 28 and pp. 57-61).

Notes

1   For a global reflection on the links between culture, nationalist movements and states, see Dieckhoff (2000).
2   The Flemish example confirms fully the validity of Miroslav Hroch's thesis on the pre-eminence of the cultural aspect in the emerging phase of nationalist movements among the 'small nations' of Europe (Hroch, 1985).
3   Numerous accounts evoke the determinant role of teachers in the process of Frenchification. See, for example, Pierre Jakez Hélias (1975, p. 229): 'Teachers speak only French even though most of them spoke Breton when they were our age and continue to speak it at home. According to my parents, they have orders to do this. Orders from whom? From 'the guys from the government.' Who are they? The ones who run the Republic. Therefore, is it the Republic that does not want Breton spoken? It does not want it for our own good.'
4   The situation in the school system as well as the evolution of the legislation and the regulations are detailed in Bernard Poignant's report for the Prime Minister (Poignant, 1998).

References

Anderson, B. (1983), *Imagined Communities: Reflections on the Origin and Spread of Nationalism*, Verso, London.
Badie, B. (1992), *L'Etat Importé. L'Occidentalisation de l'Ordre Politique*, Fayard, Paris.
Baumgarten, J. (1994), 'La Définition Nationale de la Langue et de la Culture Yiddish chez les Savants de la Wissenschaft des Judentums', in M. Espagne and M. Werner, *Philologiques III*, Ed. de la Maison des Sciences de l'Homme, Paris.
Bitsch, M.T. (1992), *Histoire de la Belgique*, Hatier, coll. Nations d'Europe, Paris.
Breuilly, J. (1982), *Nationalism and the State*, Manchester University Press.
Chanet, J.F. (1996), *L'Ecole Républicaine et les Petites Patries*, Aubier, Paris.
Constant, B. (1980), *De la Liberté chez les Modernes*, Le Livre de Poche, coll. Pluriel, Paris.
Deprez, K. and Vos, L. (1998), *Nationalism in Belgium. Shifting Identities, 1780-1995*, Macmillan and St. Martin's Press, London, New York.

Diamanti, I. (1993), *La Lega. Geografia, Storia e Sociologia di un Nuovo Soggetto Politico*, Donzelli, Rome.

Dieckhoff, A. (1993), *L'Invention d'une Nation. Israël et la Modernité Politique*, Gallimard, Paris.

Dieckhoff, A. (1996), 'La Déconstruction d'une Illusion. L'Introuvable Opposition entre Nationalisme Politique et Nationalisme Culturel', *L'Année Sociologique*, vol. 46, no. 1.

Dieckhoff, A. (2000), *La Nation dans tous ses Etats. Les Identités Nationales en Mouvement*, Flammarion, Paris.

Fanon, F. (1981), *Les Damnés de la Terre*, Maspéro, Paris.

Gellner, E. (1989), *Nations et Nationalisme*, Payot, Paris.

Hélias, P.J. (1975), *Le Cheval d'Orgueil*, Plon, coll. Terre Humanie, Paris.

Hroch, M. (1985), *Social Preconditions of National Revival in Europe: A Comparative Analysis of the Social Composition of Patriotic Groups among the Smaller European Nations*, University Press, Cambridge, Cambridge.

Kamenka, E. (1976), 'Political Nationalism. The Evolution of the Idea', in E. Kamenka, *Nationalism. The Nature and Evolution of an Idea*, Edward Arnold, London.

Kappeler, A. (1992), *The Formation of National Elites*, New York University Press and Hants, New York, Dartmouth.

Kohn, H. (1946), *The Idea of Nationalism. A Study in its Origins and Background*, Macmillan, New York.

Mabille, X. (1986), *Histoire Politique de la Belgique. Facteurs et Acteurs du Changement*, CRISP, Brussels.

Nora, P. (1986), 'La Nation-Mémoire', in *Les Lieux de Mémoire*, II-La Nation, vol. 3, Gallimard, Paris.

Poignant, B. (1998), *Langues et Cultures Régionales*, La Documentation Française, Paris.

Schulze, H. (1996), *Etat et Nation dans l'Histoire de l'Europe,* Seuil, Paris.

Smith, A.D. (1991), *National Identity*, Penguin, London.

Sugar P., Hanak P. and Frank T. (1990), *A History of Hungary*, Indiana University Press.

Weber, E. (1976), *Peasants into Frenchmen: The Modernization of Rural France, 1870-1914*, Stanford University Press.

Weber, M. (1968), *Economy and Society. An Outline of Interpretative Sociology*, Bedminster Press, New York, vol. 1.

Werner, M. (1994), 'La Germanie de Tacite et l'Originalité Allemande', *Le Débat*, no. 78, January-February.